Marketplace for Telecommunications

COMMUNICATIONS

George Gerbner and Marsha Siefert, Editors
The Annenberg School of Communications
University of Pennsylvania, Philadelphia

Marketplace for Telecommunications

REGULATION AND DEREGULATION IN INDUSTRIALIZED DEMOCRACIES

Marcellus S. Snow
University of Hawaii at Manoa

Longman
New York & London

For my wife
Jo
and for our children
David, Jonathan, and Matthew

Executive Editor: Gordon T. R. Anderson
Production Editor: Ronni Strell
Cover Design: Steven August Krastin
Text Art: J & R Services, Inc.
Production Supervisor: Eduardo Castillo
Compositor: Graphicraft Typesetters Ltd.
Printer and Binder: The Alpine Press, Inc.

Marketplace for Telecommunications:
Regulation and Deregulation in Industrialized Democracies

Longman Inc., 95 Church Street, White Plains, N.Y. 10601

Associated companies: Longman Group Ltd., London; Longman Cheshire Pty., Melbourne; Longman Paul Pty., Auckland; Copp Clark Pitman, Toronto; Pitman Publishing Inc., Boston

Library of Congress Cataloging-in-Publication Data

Snow, Marcellus S.
Marketplace for telecommunications.

Papers from a conference held at the Washington Center of the Annenberg School of Communications, Apr. 30–May 2, 1984.
Bibliography: p.
Includes index.
1. Telecommunication policy—Congresses. I. Title.
HE7645.S57 1985 384′.068 85-23900
ISBN 0-582-28600-X

86 87 88 89 9 8 7 6 5 4 3 2 1

Contents

About the Contributors

Alan Baughcum holds a Ph.D. in economics from the University of North Carolina. He is at present Manager of Telecommunications for R. W. Beck and Associates, Engineers and Consultants, in Washington, D.C. Before joining that firm, he was affiliated with Charles River Associates of Boston as Director of Telecommunications Research. He has also had teaching positions at the University of North Carolina and at North Carolina State, and worked for 3 years as an economist for the U.S. Department of Justice. Dr. Baughcum is co-author of *The Economics of Competition in the Telecommunications Industry*, which deals with economic issues affecting telecommunications in the United States. He has contributed to numerous professional publications, including *Public Utilities Fortnightly* and *Antitrust Law and Economics Review*. Among other professional organizations, he belongs to the American Economic Association, the Southern Economic Association, and the Society of Government Economists.

Youichi Ito is a communications scientist with a B.A. in economics from Keio University. He pursued a doctoral course with a communications science major at the same institution. Study in the United States brought him a B.S. from Boston University's School of Public Communication and an M.A. from the Fletcher School of Law and Diplomacy at Tufts University. Dr. Ito is at present Associate Professor at the Institute for Communications Research for Keio University; he also serves as Vice Director of that institute. Previous positions have been as a Fellow at the East-West Center, Honolulu, and as an adjunct lecturer at Waseda and Tokai universities. He has researched and written widely on communications policy in Japan and Western countries, including the "information society" school in Japan. His publications have appeared in *Keio Communication Review*, the *Mass Communication Review Yearbook*, and as articles and book chapters in both English- and Japanese-language publications in Japan. He is a member of the International Communication Association, the Japan Society for Studies in Journalism and Mass Communication, and the Japanese Society of International Politics. He has served as a member of numerous government and professional planning and advisory committees, and is chief editor of *Keio Communication Review*.

Charles Jonscher holds a first class honors degree in engineering from Cambridge University and both an M.A. and a Ph.D. in economics from Harvard University. At present he is lecturer and Associate Director in the Research Program on Communications Policy at Massachusetts Institute of Technology, and a Director of CSP International, an international consulting firm specializing in economic and business studies in the communications sector. He has previously been executive engineer with the British Post Office, a lecturer and tutor in economics at Harvard, and a tutor in engineering at Cambridge. He has published and conducted research on economic and information policy aspects of communication. His articles have appeared in edited collections as well as in publications such as *Information Economics and Policy* and in workshop proceedings volumes. He has received the Kennedy Fellowship for graduate studies at Harvard and the Senior Scholarship at Trinity College, Cambridge. He is currently a member of the editorial board of *Information Economics and Policy*.

Gordon E. Kaiser holds a B.A. in economics from the University of Toronto, an M.A. in economics from Queen's University, and an LL.B. from Queen's University. He is currently a partner with Gowling & Henderson, Barristers & Solicitors, in Toronto, having previously been affiliated with the firm's Ottawa office. He is a Special Lecturer in law at both Queen's University and the University of Toronto, and was formerly a partner with the law firm of Lang, Michener, Cranston, Farquharson & Wright in Toronto. He has published widely on legal aspects of regulation and antitrust relating to telecommunications. His articles have appeared in the *University of Ottawa Law Journal*, *Canadian Business Law Journal*, *Queen's Law Journal*, and as chapters in compendium volumes and conference proceedings. He is a member of numerous law and economic professional organizations, including the Canadian Bar Association, the American Association of Trial Lawyers, the American Economic Association, and the International Bar Association. He has appeared before numerous regulatory boards in Canada, including the National Energy Board, the Ontario Energy Board, the Canadian Radio-Television and Telecommunications Commission, and the public utilities commissions of several provinces.

Don M. Lamberton is Professor and former Chairman at the Department of Economics at the University of Queensland, where he is currently affiliated with the Information Economics Unit. He holds a B.Ec. from the University of Sydney and a D.Phil. in economics from Oxford University.

Previous teaching appointments have been at Case Western Reserve University and at the University of New South Wales. He has had visiting appointments at Stanford University, the University of Pittsburgh, Oxford University, the East-West Center's Communication Institute, and the Technical Change Centre in London. Professor Lamberton has published widely on economic aspects of information and technological change. He is the author of *The Information Revolution* and co-author of *Communication and Economic Development*. His articles have appeared in *The Information Society*, *Annual Review of Information Science and Technology*, and in numerous collected volumes and conference proceedings. He is Chairman of the Pacific Science Association Scientific Committee for Economics, a member of the International Social Sciences Council, and several Australian government committees. He has consulted for many clients, including the Organisation for Economic Cooperation and Development, Telecom Australia, Stanford Research Institute, and the Public Service Satellite Consortium.

Karl-Heinz Neumann holds a doctorate in economics from the University of Bonn, where he served as Wissenschaftlicher Assistent while earning his degree. He is currently Director of the Deutsche Bundespost's research center for economic aspects of communications, the Wissenschaftliches Institut für Telekommunikationsdienste der Deutschen Bundespost. This newly created institute has published a number of studies regarding telecommunications regulatory trends in West Germany and elsewhere. Two lengthy studies, of deregulation in Great Britain and of the AT&T divestiture in the United States, have also appeared. Dr. Neumann is co-author of "Welfare Analysis of Telecommunications Tariffs in Germany," a comparison of the present structure and a hypothetical regime of Ramsey (inverse elasticity) prices in West German telecommunications tariffs. He is also author of the recently published general treatment, *Gebührenpolitik im Telekommunikationsbereich* (Tariff policy in the telecommunications sector). He has participated widely in conferences devoted to economic aspects of telecommunications regulation, has published in professional journals, and belongs to several professional organizations.

Eli M. Noam holds an LL.B. from Harvard University as well as a Ph.D. in economics from that institution. At present he serves as Associate Professor and Director of the Research Program on Telecommunications and Information Policy at the Graduate School of Business of Columbia University. Previously he was Visiting Assistant Professor at the Woodrow Wilson School of Princeton University. In his current capacity he has organized numerous symposia and research efforts that have concentrated on business and economic aspects of telecommunications policy in the United States and particularly in Western Europe. Much of this work has been funded by grants from organizations such as the Friedrich Naumann

Foundation, France Telecom, Home Box Office, Merril Lynch, and the National Science Foundation. He has published numerous articles and has edited *Telecommunications Regulation Today and Tomorrow*, which was selected as a "Book of the Month" by *Communications Booknotes*. He is a member of the American Economic Association and other professional organizations.

Roger G. Noll holds M.A. and Ph.D. degrees in economics from Harvard University. Recently he became Professor of Economics at Stanford University. Previously he was at California Institute of Technology, where he served as Institute Professor of Social Sciences and Chairman of the Division of the Humanities and Social Sciences. He has also been Professor at Stanford's Graduate School of Business and a Senior Fellow and Co-Director at the Brookings Institution. He has researched and published widely in regulatory policy, cable television, political foundations of economic policy, and telecommunications. He is co-author of *The Political Economy of Deregulation*, co-editor of *Regulatory Policy and the Social Sciences*, and co-author of *Economic Aspects of Television Regulation*. He has published widely in the *American Economic Review* and other scholarly journals. He is on the board of editors of the *Journal of Economic Literature* and *Information Economics and Policy*. He has been a member and chairman of numerous advisory panels of the federal government, including those of the National Science Foundation, NASA, and the Office of Technology Assessment. He has been a Fellow of the Guggenheim Foundation and of the Center for Advanced Study in the Behavioral Sciences. He has consulted for numerous governmental and private organizations, including CBS, the RAND Corporation, the Federal Communications Commission, the Environmental Protection Agency, and the Aspen Institute.

Marcellus S. Snow is Associate Professor of Economics at the University of Hawaii at Manoa. He has an M.S. from Massachusetts Institute of Technology; an M.A. (in international relations) from the School of Advanced International Studies of Johns Hopkins University; and a Ph.D. (in economics) from the University of California at Berkeley. He is author of *International Commercial Satellite Communications*; co-editor of *Economic and Policy Problems in Satellite Communications*; and has published in numerous scholarly journals, including the *Bell Journal of Economics*, *Journal of Communication*, *Journal of Information Science*, and *Economic Modelling*. His areas of interest include regulatory theory and policy, satellite communications, and econometric testing methodology. For 2 years he was a financial and political analyst for the Communications Satellite Corporation in Washington, D.C., and Geneva, Switzerland. Since joining the faculty at Hawaii, he has been awarded a Fulbright research professorship at the Universität Bonn and spent a summer as a Visiting Scholar at Stanford University. He has consulted for numerous firms and government agencies, including NASA, INTELSAT, the U.S. Department of Commerce, and ITT. He has been awarded research grants by the Institute for Public Utilities and the National Science Foundation. He is a member of the American Economic Association, the Econometric Society, the Pacific Telecommunications Council, the Society for Satellite Professionals, and other professional organizations.

Jean-Paul Voge holds a baccalaureate degree in mathematics and philosophy and has engineering degrees from the Ecole Polytechnique and the Ecole Nationale Supérieure des Télécommunications. At present he is Deputy Director and Special Adviser in the Direction des Affaires Industrielles et Internationales of the French Ministry of Posts and Telecommunications. He serves as Chairman of the research institute IDATE in Montpellier and as Professor at various universities. Previously he represented the French government in INTELSAT. He has written widely on a variety of topics, including information and economic aspects of organizational complexity, information and business cycles, space telecommunications, and the role of communications in society. He has published in journals such as *Information Economics and Policy*, *Les Cahiers Français*, *Technological Forecasting and Social Change*, and *Revue Française des Télécommunications*. He has served on numerous national and international professional bodies, including as President of the International Union of Radio Science; as Chairman of the French Section of the Institute of Electrical and Electronic Engineers (IEEE); and as a member of the board of the Ecole Polytechnique. Among his many honorary positions are those as a Commander of the Legion of Honor; a Fellow of the Institution of Electrical Engineers (IEE); and an Officer of the Order of Leopold (Belgium). He is listed in *Who's Who* for France, Europe, and the world.

Carl Christian von Weizsäcker has attended the Universities of Zürich, Göttingen, Hamburg, and Freiburg, and received his doctorate from the University of Basel. He has been on the economics faculties of the Universities of Heidelberg, Bielefeld, and Bonn. At the latter institution he was head of the Economics Department of the Institute for Social and Economic Sciences. Since 1982, he has been Professor of Economics at the University of Bern. His research interests are in the areas of capital theory and theory of competition as applied to the telecommunications sector. He is the author of *Steady State Capital Theory*, *Zur ökonomischen Theorie des technischen Fortschritts*, and *Barriers to Entry*; and co-author of *Die Rolle des Wettbewerbs im Fernmeldebereich*. In addition, he has published in numerous scholarly journals, including the *Bell Journal of Economics*, *Information Economics and Policy*, *Journal of Economic Theory*, *Kyklos*, *Zeitschrift für die gesamte Staatswissenschaft*, and *Zeitschrift für Nationalökonomie*. He is a Fellow of the Econometric Society as well as a member of the American Academy of Arts and Sciences.

Acknowledgments

I wish to thank a number of individuals and institutions who helped bring this book to fruition and who stimulated my efforts in carrying out the research, grant proposal, funding, and workshop on which it is based.

The idea for comparative research on telecommunications regulation formed the basis of my sabbatical leave during 1980–1981 at the Universität Bonn, where I was a Fulbright research professor. I am indebted to my academic host during that year, Professor Carl Christian von Weizsäcker, who at the time was head of the Wirtschaftspolitische Abteilung of the Institut für Gesellschafts- und Wirtschaftswissenschaften at Bonn and is now at the Universität Bern. Because of rewarding discussions at Bonn and elsewhere in Germany with him and with other colleagues—Jörg Finsinger, Hans Mathias Keplinger, Günter Knieps, Jürgen Müller, Karl-Heinz Neumann and Ingo Vogelsang—I became so interested in telecommunications policy in West Germany that my original plans for cross-country research were postponed.

After returning to the University of Hawaii and continuing my research and writing on West Germany for about a year, I again felt ready to examine telecommunications regulation in a number of other countries. With the patient help of Roger Noll of Stanford University (whose valuable suggestions on editing this volume I also very much appreciate), I explored the possibility of a research workshop funded by the U.S. National Science Foundation that would bring economists and others together from several industrialized countries to present papers on regulatory topics in telecommunications, broadcasting, and information and draw up an agenda for future research.

The exacting process of composing a grant proposal to the NSF was aided by a stay at Stanford University during the summer of 1983. As a Visiting Scholar at the Hoover Institution, I had access to individuals there and throughout the Stanford campus who were of great help in focusing and refining my ideas. I wish especially to thank Dennis Bark and Tom Moore of the Hoover Institution and James Rosse of the Department of Economics for their valuable comments and perspectives.

Logistics for the workshop—held at the NSF's behest in Washington, D.C.—were facilitated by the kind offer of meeting rooms at the recently established Washington Center of the Annenberg School of Communications. I am grateful to the Center's director, Maurice Mitchell, and deputy director, Barry Cole, for their collegial hospitality at this handsome new facility. During the workshop itself, held April 30–May 2, 1984, Diana Murrell provided expert and efficient help as the workshop assistant and rapporteur and has the thanks of all the participants.

My deepest appreciation is reserved for the conference participants and contributors to this book. It is they who took an idea on paper and brought it to life; the contents of this volume testify to their success in doing so. Thank you, collectively and individually, for your written contributions and your stimulating discussions at the workshop.

My home institution, the University of Hawaii at Manoa, generously provided me with a 2-year, half-time appointment as an Associate Researcher with the Social Science Research Institute from 1982 to 1984 that gave me the time to perfect my grant proposal, organize and conduct the workshop, and prepare this book. I would like to thank Donald Topping, the SSRI director; also Sady Sakai of SSRI was extremely helpful in aiding me with the fiscal and administrative details of the grant. Freda Hellinger and Karen Ah Mai provided able assistance in manuscript preparation. My colleague Moheb Ghali, director of the Office of Research Administration, stood by me on the university's behalf with the grant proposal.

Many other colleagues, at the University of Hawaii and elsewhere, have provided advice, insights, suggestions, and critiques over the years and have honed and greatly improved my thinking and writing, both regarding this project and my research generally. For this encouragement I am indebted to Norman Abramson, Richard Barber, Henry Breitrose, George Codding, Wilson Dizard, Herb Dordick, Oswald Ganley, Heather Hudson, Jane Hurd, Meheroo Jussawalla, Kas Kalba, Sumner La Croix, Kenneth Leeson, Harvey Levin, Joseph Pelton, the late Ithiel Pool, Delbert Smith, Christopher Sterling, Nozomu Takasaki, Majid Tehranian, Jeremy Tunstall, and many others.

For their decision to publish this volume in the Annenberg/Longman Communication Books series, as well as their thoughtful suggestions for its improvement and technical assistance in the editing process, I wish to thank George Gerbner and Marsha Siefert of the Annenberg School of Communications at the University of Pennsylvania, who co-edit the series; and Gordon T. R. Anderson and Ronni Strell, editors at Longman Inc.

Finally, I wish to thank the Division of Information Science and Technology and the Division of Policy Research and Analysis of the National Science Foundation for funding Grant No. IST-8320473, on which the research workshop was based. Charles Brownstein of the NSF began providing generous advice and suggestions well before the grant proposal was submitted and followed through with useful guidance after the grant had been approved. I appreciate his help at all stages.

Although some chapters of this book are critical of certain aspects of the public sector, I hope that the volume as a whole, funded as it was by the taxpayers of the United States, argues convincingly for the continuing importance of governmentally supported research, particularly that of an international collaborative nature.

My wife Jo has been supportive throughout. This book is dedicated to her and to our children.

Marcellus S. Snow

PART 1

Introduction and Analytical Tools from Economics and Political Science

One

Communications Policy in Seven Developed Countries: Introduction, Background, and Conclusions

Marcellus S. Snow

The purpose of this book is to summarize and compare how seven industrialized countries—Australia, Canada, France, West Germany, Japan, the United Kingdom, and the United States—regulate their telecommunications, broadcasting, and new electronic media in the mid-1980s. A secondary purpose is to interpret these regulatory trends from the viewpoint of an increasingly interdependent world economy, one in which the advanced Western democracies are seeking policies and political consensus to accommodate the transition of their industrial base from manufacturing to information. This metamorphosis, comparable in scope and impact to the Industrial Revolution, is arguably the major long-term global economic trend of the late twentieth century and will continue well into the twenty-first century.

Eleven economists and communications scientists from these seven countries have contributed to this volume. Chapters 2 and 3 present important conceptual background material in the economic and political spheres, respectively, that will be helpful to nonspecialists in using the balance of the book. Each of Chapters 4 through 10 contains a description and analysis of regulatory trends in one of the countries covered. Chapter 11 attempts a comparative treatment of regulatory policy in a transatlantic setting. Chapter 12 summarizes and draws conclusions based on the foregoing contributions. In addition, it contains an agenda for future research in telecommunications regulatory policy arrived at by the authors.

Most of the contributors participated in a research workshop held in Washington, D.C., in mid-1984 that was sponsored by the U.S. National Science Foundation (NSF).[1] Research time furnished by the Social Science

Research Institute at the University of Hawaii at Manoa enabled me to compose the grant application on which the workshop was based and to serve as the grant's principal investigator.

Although written contributions to the workshop have formed the core of this book, they have been updated and otherwise edited to suit its needs. In addition, a certain degree of homogeneity and uniformity of coverage across countries was enforced. Each author, however, was given ample editorial freedom to explore and examine the unique characteristics of regulatory policy in his own country, using the outline and modes of analysis best suited to do so.

The aim of Chapter 1 is twofold: (1) to present a descriptive and conceptual background against which readers can feel some sense of cohesiveness and familiarity in exploring the contributions of the individual chapter authors; and (2) by references to insights of the contributors, to convey an idea of what the book contains. The following section discusses the technological backdrop of telecommunications regulation, distinguishing the engineer's perspective and concerns from those of the economist, the communications theorist, and the political scientist. In addition, it asks why there is such a current interest in the conduct, performance, and regulation of the telecommunications sector, and along what dimensions that sector tends to be regulated. The concluding section makes a number of broad observations, draws several conclusions, and in doing so highlights the content of the chapters that follow.

WHY AND HOW TELECOMMUNICATIONS IS REGULATED: A PRELIMINARY DISCUSSION

The Technological Backdrop

If a prime mover is sought in the telecommunications revolution that began in the 1960s, it can be found in the technology itself. Even the conventional categories of classification—transmission, switching, and terminal equipment—have become somewhat outmoded, since technological advance has successively merged these functions. A glance at the progress achieved in these areas should suggest that the overused word *revolution* is for once appropriate. New transmission processes include communications satellites, optical fibers, and various signal compression techniques such as polarization and speech interpolation. Foremost among switching innovations are packet switching—allowing computerized determination of optimal transmission paths via switching centers—and electronic switching itself, made possible by recent discoveries in microelectronics. Finally, terminal equipment has undergone steady improvement in quantity, and particularly in quality and variety of services and hardware, encompassing developments such as private switchboards, intelligent terminals, call forwarding, and various data applications. Overarching the entire technology of telecommunications is digitalization, which may lead from the present proliferation of services and systems to the new harmony and order of the ISDN (integrated switched digital network) currently being discussed and designed in a number of countries. All these trends, in turn, have been both causes and consequences of the inexorable merger of telecommunications and data processing technologies during the past several years.

Conceptualizing technological progress is a good deal simpler for an economist than for an engineer. Where the engineer sees a vast assemblage of novel and qualitatively different processes and components, the economist conveniently puts these inside a black box and simply asks how output costs are affected by new technologies. If, other things being equal, the same output can now be obtained at a lower cost, or—equivalently—a higher output can be obtained at the same cost, then "dynamic" technological progress is said to have occurred. This is to be distinguished from the "static" benefits of a given technology, usually identified with economies of scale, where costs per unit of output decrease as the level of output increases. The distinction is one between a downward shift of the entire cost curve and a descent along a given average cost curve as the scale of output increases.

This strategic agnosticism of the economist on the matter of the black box makes for easy conceptualization and mathematical tractability, but it flies in the face of some of the subtler aspects of technological change. Two of these aspects—one quantitative and one qualitative—bear mention at this point. Quantitatively, the working assumption has traditionally been that there is just a single output resulting from any given production process. Only since the mid-1970s has a serious effort been made to allow for multiple outputs—in sustainability of monopoly and contestability of market structure theory.[2] These developments, while extremely valuable, have dealt more with the industrial organization aspects of production than with the technology of production itself. Nonetheless, the relaxation of the single-output assumption has led to new insights of a qualitatively different nature that are hinted at from time to time in this volume but are in general outside its scope. The primary qualitative drawback of the conventional economic analysis of technological change has been to ignore the emergence of wholly new products and services, while focusing on more efficient methods of producing existing ones. Ways of explaining uniqueness, novelty, and diversity of product mix as a result of technological change—an obviously crucial task, given the wide variety of new technical advances—have thus met with less success in economic theory than has the multiproduct setting in general.

In summation at this point, it can be asserted that the telecommunications and information revolution of the past two decades has drawn principally for its sustaining power on the emergence of (1) cheaper ways of producing existing goods and services; (2) wholly new goods and services, the production of which has also generally entailed exponentially falling costs; and (3) the vital synergism afforded by the ongoing convergence of telecommunications and data processing.

A final observation on technological developments in telecommunications is that different countries, administrations, and operating entities are able to select from a very wide range of available products, processes, and services, and thus choose only a proper subset of what is technologically, operationally, and commercially available. The ways in which this selection takes place depend on a combination of economic, political, and perhaps sociological factors. From the neoclassical economist's standpoint, the choice is made within a framework of optimization (typically cost minimization or welfare maximization) subject to constraints imposed by the technology, resource scarcities, market imperfections, and institutional factors. Carl Christian von Weizsäcker sets forth and derives some of the economic considerations affecting telecommunications pricing in Chapter 2. His focus is on the distinction between value-based and cost-based pricing. He sees value-based pricing in a context of monopoly provision of several services given economies of scale and scope. Cost-based pricing, by contrast, emerges as a logical alternative with the introduction of competition, especially when technological innovation and diversity of services are important to the user community. For a communications scientist, as Youichi Ito describes in Chapter 9, the choice is dictated by a different set of considerations, having to do primarily with shared social values; if anything is maximized here, it is perhaps the flow of various kinds of useful information. In a political framework, still other factors assume the upper hand in selecting the technology, such as the way in which members of the national parliament are elected or the relative power of special interest groups. These important considerations, generally ignored in the context of telecommunications, are examined from a theoretical perspective by Roger Noll in Chapter 3. Eli Noam pursues these political ramifications in the more concrete setting of transatlantic telecommunications in Chapter 11. Naturally, these different conceptual models of economics, communications theory, and political science apply to the choice of form of regulation as well as to the choice of technology. In general, the contributors to this book examine the choice of regulatory methods more thoroughly than the choice of technology, although technology figures prominently in the papers of Charles Jonscher (Chapter 7, United Kingdom) and Don Lamberton (Chapter 10, Australia).

Why Regulate Telecommunications?

The regulatory literature contains many points of departure as to why regulation has assumed its present and historical forms (see Joskow and

Noll 1981; Peltzman 1976; Stigler 1971). The "public interest" school held that regulation was a public trust to keep monopolistically structured industries from earning supranormal profits by contriving a scarcity and charging high prices. The "capture" school sees regulators as manipulated by their client industries, and political economy approaches (see Noll 1983; Noll and Owen 1983) attribute present regulatory forms to structural and institutional issues such as the composition of national parliaments and the pervasiveness of special interest groups in a given country.

These perspectives, as valuable as they are, seldom address the question of why a *particular* industry has the form of regulation that it does. Since telecommunications is so unique and important, it is worth some thoughts on the matter.

Historically, communications—the term *telecommunications* was not coined until the 1930s—has been of strategic importance for national survival, whether for internal administration (as in the Roman Empire) or defense against external military threat. Later, with the evolution of international banking, modern accounting techniques, and state trading companies, communications was as important as transportation to emerging national governments, and it became even more firmly entrenched in the strategic arsenal of statecraft. The evolution of early forms of electronic communications in the nineteenth century both supplemented traditional communications (post, semaphores) and substituted for and facilitated many kinds of transportation (railroads, ocean travel). It was only natural that telecommunications emerged by and large within the public sphere and under its regulation, again with the exception of the United States, for which special historical factors have been adduced (Brock 1981).

Aside from strategic factors and the inertia of habit applied in a historical perspective, many arguments for regulating telecommunications are drawn from very current considerations. Jean-Paul Voge puts forth some of them in the French context in Chapter 5. Given the particularly rapid and spectacular developments in recent telecommunications technology, one finds the usual "creative destruction" of Schumpeter's (1975) capitalism upstaged by something that many orderly souls find more akin to disarray or anarchy. Certainly the effects of the AT&T divestiture in the United States, while disruptive domestically, appeared downright chaotic to observers across the Atlantic, as Eli Noam chronicles in Chapter 11. Although there is risk in appealing to a sociologically based theory of regulation, it seems clear that many people welcome regulation in a rapidly changing environment because it normalizes expectations, retards change, and tidies up the landscape. Don Lamberton considers this in the Australian context in Chapter 10.

Finally, the strategic arguments have resurfaced in a contemporary guise. Telecommunications and information technologies are seen as catalysts of an ongoing transformation of the economy at large, as Porat's (1977) "information economy" insights suggest; or even of society itself, as in the perspective of the Japanese "information society" studies that began to emerge in the late 1960s.[3] More specifically, developed nations see themselves in vicious economic competition to stay at the cutting edge of new technological developments so as not to lose both their domestic markets and their export markets (generally in developing countries) to foreign rivals. Rightly or wrongly, until recently only the United States has felt confident enough in the relatively unregulated marketplace to entrust this transformation to private enterprise. Ad hoc government interventions of quite recent vintage have been the rule, whether in the guise of trade barriers masquerading as privacy protection in transborder data flow (Cheah 1984) or in the more open but equally interventionist efforts of countries such as Brazil to develop domestic microcomputer industries by effectively prohibiting imports in strategic industries.

What Is Being Regulated?

A final task before suggesting conclusions based on this volume's contents is to elaborate the dimensions along which the regulation of telecommunications generally takes place.

Perhaps the least regulated aspect is the technology itself, unless government subsidies and other incentives are considered as "positive" regulation. In addition, restrictions are often imposed on the conduct and diffusion of research and development for purposes of national security. Finally, the patent system places certain constraints on the spread of scientific and technological discoveries in order to preserve economic incentives for inventors and researchers to pursue their activities. These interactions of law and regulation with the production of technology itself, at least in the area of telecommunications, are relatively uncontroversial and will not concern us further here.

The most immediate dimension of governmental intervention is naturally whether the state owns and operates the telecommunications system. Ownership and operation generally come in tandem, although exceptions—perhaps state operation of privately owned facilities during periods of war or disaster—may exist. Privatization of telecommunications facilities previously owned by the state is, as this volume indicates, one of the principal aspects of deregulation currently in progress. Charles Jonscher's account of the public sale of stock in British Telecom and the establishment of Mercury, a competing carrier, is particularly enlightening in this regard. Japan's overseas carrier, KDD, has been owned privately for some time, and Youichi Ito describes the recent privatization and demonopolization of NTT, the domestic carrier. At the advent of the satellite age, indeed, a powerful faction in the U.S. Congress favored government ownership of what was to become the privately held Communications Satellite Corporation.[4] In most cases, the regulatory arrangements for state-owned telecommunications facilities are disarmingly simple, as Chapters 5 and 6 make clear with respect to France and West Germany. Day-to-day policy is determined at the ministerial level, and government white papers air views relative to longer-range concerns.

More generally, regulation in the usual sense of the word refers to governmental policy toward the economic activities of certain industries in the private sector. Price, rate of return, and market entry are the most common policy levers chosen by regulatory authorities, and each has received extensive attention in the literature. For telecommunications, other dimensions of regulation are also important, such as terms and conditions of service (including the obligation of universal service) and requirements for implicit or explicit cross-subsidization using tariff structures. These different kinds of economic regulation emerge in the rest of this book. Chapter 2, for example, reviews pricing and entry issues in telecommunications and gives some new perspectives as well.

CROSS-COUNTRY COMPARISONS AND CONCLUSIONS

The following are broad observations and conclusions in a number of areas. They draw on the succeeding chapters of this book, as well as on the authors' verbal interaction at the NSF workshop and on my own ideas and research. More specific conclusions, usually pointing toward the compilation of an agenda for future research in comparative telecommunications regulation, are set forth in Chapter 12.

Technology as the Major Force

Technology is the pervasive driving force in the global trend toward telecommunications deregulation. Alan Baughcum reaches this conclusion in surveying the U.S. experience. Carl Christian von Weizsäcker lists technological innovation as one of the major reasons for a transition from value-based pricing to cost-based pricing, and from monopoly to competition. Youichi Ito observes that technology provides more resources, leading to less regulation. Gordon Kaiser, more metaphorically, says that, like water, technology can flow around any institutional barrier. Ito, furthermore, is accurate in saying that the pace of technological change has outstripped the ability of regulatory arrangements to accommodate it. One particularly important aspect of this is the ongoing merger of telecommunications and data processing technology, which is a critical factor in Charles Jonscher's distinction between horizontal and vertical competition.

It is certainly correct to want to "endogenize" the regulatory framework in the model linking technology, regulation, institutional factors, and performance. Roger Noll, for example, has suggested that regulatory policies toward cable television in the United States have to some extent affected the development of cable television technology. Yet it is clear that, more often than not, institutional and regulatory changes have been reactions to advances in telecommunications technology, rather than the converse.

Demand-side Pressure

Pressure for change in regulation—typically, for deregulation—has come by and large from the user community, especially from large multinational business users. This demand-side pressure is the cutting edge of the technological changes already mentioned. Suppliers, by contrast, usually perceive themselves as having more to lose than to gain by aggressively accommodating new technologies and services and making them available at cost-based prices to users. This dynamic emerges with particular force in Eli Noam's chapter; it is also evident in the chapters by Youichi Ito and Don Lamberton.

The United States as an Example for Other Countries

Although the United States has served as a model for other countries by establishing the first and most conspicuous telecommunications deregulation, its example has by no means been uniformly positive, nor has there been slavish or uncritical imitation on the part of others. Alan Baughcum emphasizes this point in the conclusion of his chapter, citing in particular regulatory delays, uncertainties, and possibly inefficient court-mandated divestitures of various parts of large telecommunications concerns as negative aspects of the American experience. Karl-Heinz Neumann and Youichi Ito indicate that American-style regulation of certain aspects of telecommunications and broadcasting in their two countries, introduced shortly after World War II, did not succeed.

One might extend this line of thought by analogy with the experience of Great Britain as the first country to undergo the Industrial Revolution. In doing so it suffered as well as prospered, and countries experiencing later industrialization were able to avoid some of its more unfortunate distributional and social consequences as a result. The socially and technologically progressive policy of the otherwise conservative Prussian state comes to mind.

There are certainly some negative aspects to the rapid and widespread telecommunications deregulation in the United States today, although most economists—and most of the contributors to this book—probably feel that social welfare has on the whole been increased. Examples of this discomfort include the access-charge controversy that erupted between the Federal Communications Commission (FCC) and the U.S. Congress in the wake of the AT&T divestiture, which is detailed in Alan Baughcum's chapter. When long-standing patterns of subsidy become transparent or disappear as deregulation allows or forces prices to be aligned with costs, distributional politics then becomes sharpened, often as a counterweight to deregulation. Another macroeconomic concern in the wake of deregulation in the United States involves the changes in employment structure and educational requirements that will be entailed as liberalization stimulates certain kinds of industries and discourages others. Certainly there are lessons in these potentially negative aspects of deregulation as well as in the overall positive assessment of liberalized telecommunications in the United States.

Quantity and Quality

There is an important qualitative aspect to technological progress and deregulation in telecommunications that is difficult to capture in theoretical models. Alan Baughcum touches on it when he cites "costs of foregone diversity" that must be borne by countries choosing not to deregulate telecommunications. The economist's black box, noted above, is as yet unable fully to incorporate this important dynamic aspect of the production process over time. The final section of Chapter 12, however, discusses recent theoretical advances in industrial organization theory in which the quantitative assumption of more than one output has yielded insights of a qualitatively different nature from those offered by the conventional single-output model. Two such insights are the concepts of economies of scope and sustainability of natural monopoly. These are referred to elsewhere in this volume as well, in particular by Carl Christian von Weizsäcker.

The Interaction of Theory and Experience

Economic and communications theory has expanded admirably to accommodate new developments in technology and in regulatory style. Roger Noll reviews four separate political theories that, while not new, have been extended to account for telecommunications regulatory phenomena. He finds the institutionalist approach particularly amenable to his new "political economy of deregulation" analysis (Noll and Owen 1983). Similarly, existing neoclassical welfare theory, as Karl-Heinz Neumann's research with colleagues has indicated, can be used to illuminate welfare losses resulting from nonoptimal telecommunications pricing regimes (Neumann, Schweizer, and von Weizsäcker 1983). Youichi Ito uses communications theory to account for a jurisdictional battle between two ministries of the Japanese government and describes the ascent of the important "information society" paradigm in that country in the late 1960s. Finally, the "information economy" approach introduced by Marc Porat in the mid-1970s was a conceptual breakthrough that came about for the specific purpose of accounting for recent developments in the role of information activities in the macroeconomy.

It might not be far off the mark to speak of the endogenization of theory with the phenomena for which theory is supposed to account. To be sure, some concepts—complex number theory or perhaps game theory, for example—arose well in advance of empirical needs to which they could be applied. Many of the models used to account for recent telecommunications technologies and their economic regulation, by contrast, seem to have been driven and to some extent hastened and anticipated by the events to which they have subsequently been applied.

The Case against Deregulation

Complementing the arguments above regarding the probable inappropriateness of the American deregulatory model for other nations without thoughtful modifications, we now summarize a number of general reservations about deregulation mentioned by some of the contributors and refer the reader to the chapters in question for more detail.[5]

Economies of scope and scale are certainly two mainstays of the natural monopoly argument traditionally used to justify monopolies in communications and other sectors. Jean-Paul Voge mentions the smaller scale of European PTTs (Postal, Telegraph, and Telephone ministries), implying that such economies may be less likely to have been exhausted there than in the United States. Economists consulting for the West German Monopoly Commission (Knieps, Müller, and von Weizsäcker 1981) voiced similar reservations in the context of that country.

Voge also proposes decentralization as a substitute for, or at least as a complement to, deregulation. He is referring, however, primarily to the special historical context of the traditionally overcentralized French state. In addition, he lists cooperation as an alternative to the competition presumably introduced by liberalization or privatization in the telecommunications sector.

Don Lamberton touches on price stability and slowing the rate of change as possible motives of unions and civil servant groups in combating deregulation in Australia. Eli Noam identifies an extremely broad and heterogeneous coalition of social, economic, and political forces in the "postal–industrial complex" that joins the PTTs in opposing deregulation in continental Europe.

In the international arena, finally, American deregulation can lead to actions that seem arbitrary and unilateral when viewed from overseas.

Voge mentions the violation of "unwritten rules" by the FCC in introducing certain value-added and other services between the United States and Europe, and both he and Lamberton state their countries' opposition to private, commercial transatlantic facilities as disruptive of current institutional arrangements (see Snow 1984b).

Ideologies and Deregulation

Charles Jonscher, while outlining a number of technical arguments for deregulation in the British context, notes that the motivations of the Thatcher government in privatizing British Telecom and introducing Mercury as a competitor derive primarily from straightforward considerations of political ideology, namely less government ownership and more competition as matters of principle. Jean-Paul Voge indicates that the prevailing political point of view in France is in the opposite direction. Don Lamberton, quoting at length from the information policy plank of the Australian Labor Party platform, indicates a host of ideological concerns generally unsupportive of telecommunications deregulation.

Although ideology certainly has played a role in the U.S. experience as well, support for deregulation has been by and large bipartisan. Trucking and airline deregulation, for example, began in earnest under the Carter administration. In retrospect it seems fair to argue that considerations of economic efficiency, drawn from the patient advocacy of neoclassical welfare economists and others, have been more important in the American deregulatory experience than have ideological concerns per se. Canada, as Gordon Kaiser demonstrates, has followed the American deregulatory timetable quite closely with a few years' lag, and can also be presumed to be acting according to welfare and efficiency arguments similar to those in the United States. Nonetheless, he detects a degree of "religious fervor" in the American conviction that telecommunications is no longer a natural monopoly. The work of Karl-Heinz Neumann and his colleagues using neoclassical welfare theory, as well as the arguments of German Monopoly Commission consulting economists with a similar conceptual focus—including economies of scope and sustainability of monopoly—indicate that a more "technical," less ideological framework has received a hearing in West Germany, although there are clear ideological differences between the two largest parties in that country. The advent of the Christian Democrat–Liberal coalition in 1983 makes adoption of a faster pace of telecommunications liberalization there ultimately more likely, although there is little evidence of it to date.

Broadcasting

Alan Baughcum points out that broadcasting is also being deregulated in the United States, although at a slower pace than the balance of the telecommunications sector. This he attributes, among other things, to political considerations.

Such constraints are much more strongly operative in other countries. Youichi Ito indicates the general consensus in Japan that the public presence in broadcasting policy has assured a certain overall quality level that would not otherwise prevail. Karl-Heinz Neumann notes that German radio and television, which are still predominantly noncommercial despite the recent licensing of a few private stations, are foreseen by broadcasting law and practice to serve as an engine of pluralism and a counterpoise to the highly concentrated private print media in that country. Canada and the United Kingdom have a hybrid public–private broadcasting structure not unlike that of Japan, and even the United States has popular but chronically underfunded public radio and TV networks.

Deregulation in the context of broadcasting means most importantly the licensing of commercial, privately owned radio and TV stations. By that criterion, all the countries examined in this book are either at least partly deregulated or about to become so. It is nonetheless clear that a powerful consensus remains as to the desirability of a public presence in broadcasting in those countries that have one now—and all appear to, to one degree or another.

The most probable conduit by which commercial television will be introduced into the European context is not domestic but transnational: commercial, privately owned direct broadcast satellites financed and launched by countries such as Luxembourg. Great political strain has accompanied the discussion of financing and operating such satellites from the geosynchronous orbit. Controversy centers on the possible diversion of revenue and viewers to such satellites from the public networks, particularly on the more ideological concerns of those who regard broadcasting primarily as an aesthetic, cultural, educational, and political organ rather than as a source of mass entertainment.

We cannot pursue such concerns of content, since they are outside the scope of this book. Yet it is clear, to borrow a phrase from Marshall McLuhan, that the medium of telecommunications affects the message it carries. We turn to such interrelationships in our next cross-country conclusion.

Telecommunications in the Broader Matrix of Information and the Electronic Media

The research proposal on which this book is based embodied the ambitious notion of relating telecommunications to the information and media activities of the countries under examination, and comparing these links internationally. Since time and other resources were not equal to the task, however, it might be well at this point to elaborate my original idea, even though it could not be brought to fruition in the scope of the present investigation.

The nexus between telecommunications, on the one hand, and the information and media sectors, on the other, is a good deal more transparent in countries other than the United States. This is so primarily because these activities are conducted by largely separate, though sometimes financially overlapping, private concerns in the United States. Elsewhere, by contrast, the usual PTT ownership and operation pattern places the timing of new telecommunications links at the discretion of government planners rather than market-oriented entrepreneurs. The electronic media and data processing industries in such countries are thus directly affected by the extent to which transmission and distribution bottlenecks arise. There are secondary effects on the print media, which often face markets saturated with print journalism and are anxious to expand into the new electronic media, such as satellite television by direct broadcast, where the returns are more promising. Here, a German example comes to mind: the offer by the German Newspaper Publishers' Organization to Radio Luxembourg for equity financing of a commercial direct broadcast satellite (Snow 1982). The basic point is that if the government—albeit through different agencies or ministries—provides both the physical channels of telecommunications and the broadcast programming and other services that are transmitted over those channels, then a tight bond can be said to exist between telecommunications and the media. The link with other information activities and services is more diffuse, but depends similarly on the government ownership, operation, and policy direction of telecommunications facilities in most developed countries other than the United States.

It seems fair to assert that most of the advances in regulatory economics in the neoclassical framework have been developed by American economists to describe conditions observed in the United States. There is surely nothing surprising or objectionable in this, but problems arise when conceptual paradigms tailored to uniquely American conditions—private, commercialized ownership of the telecommunications, broadcasting, and information sectors—are extended to explain regulation of those sectors in other countries, where altogether different conditions usually prevail. An indirect example of this trend can be found in the observations of Eli Noam in Chapter 11 and in the conclusions of Chapter 12, to the effect that there seems to be very little scholarly discussion of telecommunications policy in Europe, and relatively little academic discussion of broadcasting in the United States.

Planning for and Managing Deregulation

Deregulation need not be the random, chaotic, or uncontrollable force characterized by its detractors. At least two countries, West Germany and

Japan, provide evidence that telecommunications can be gradually liberalized in a planned, principled, and beneficial way.

We have noted the careful welfare-theoretic and industrial organization studies that have been conducted regarding the possible effects of deregulation in West Germany.[6] Although the issue of deregulation is politically sensitive in that country, there is a gradually emerging consciousness of the need for an orderly progression toward greater reliance on market forces, if for no other reason than to make the West German information sector more competitive domestically and internationally. Karl-Heinz Neumann's chapter bears this out. Moreover, it seems clear that the measure of deregulation toward which the West German political consensus is steering will involve an accommodation within the current monopoly position of the Bundespost, rather than its privatization or loss of telecommunications "sovereignty" as has been the case in the United Kingdom or Japan.

Japan in particular has shown that telecommunications deregulation can be part of a successful "industrial policy" in a particular sector. Youichi Ito suggests reasons why this approach has succeeded in Japan (in the telecommunications sector) and failed in the United States (in efforts to revive declining industries). Eli Noam's observations suggest that an "industrial policy" of maintaining regulated monopoly in telecommunications and actively opposing deregulation has failed in the case of European PTTs; the example of France, however, described by Jean-Paul Voge, shows some successes that might qualify Noam's overall assessment. In addition, Karl-Heinz Neumann describes efforts in West Germany to use a measure of deregulation to make the telecommunications equipment industry there more competitive domestically and abroad.

In any event, while U.S. deregulation has involved something of a leap of faith on the part of a national economic and political consensus, this volume contains ample evidence that deregulation in the telecommunications sectors of other countries can be introduced and managed in a way more consonant with specific planning goals for both the macroeconomy and particular industries. Carl Christian von Weizsäcker, for example, makes a specific proposal for the gradual and politically acceptable introduction of more competition into the telecommunications sector. In the section in Chapter 2 on institutional implications he suggests the admission of competing suppliers by requiring them to pay an access fee for connection with the PTT network, adjusted so as to stabilize the overall market share of competitors at a predetermined level.

The Lack of Dependable Cost and Demand Data

Many of the arguments of economic theory regarding the possible effects of deregulation require the use of cost data and the estimation of cost functions. Particular concepts include subadditivity of the cost function, economies of scale and scope, and sustainability of natural monopoly.

For a number of reasons, it is difficult to obtain accurate, complete, and dependable cost data in the telecommunications sector. Two of the main causes bear mention here. First, theoretical problems in cost accounting and allocation have yet to be resolved—for example, the allocation of common costs. Second, and perhaps more important, individual PTT ministries or other telecommunications providers generally have economic incentives to engage in strategic obfuscation of costs to prevent the scrutiny of regulatory authorities, the press, and the public. Naturally, the quality of conclusions regarding, say, the extent of natural monopoly depends on the reliability of the cost and other data used, as well as on the model selected and the methodology employed to apply it to the data.

The relative lack of success to date in obtaining better cost data might suggest that deregulation has been decided on (or rejected) for reasons other than the technical arguments of economics, engineering, or law. Charles Jonscher is explicit about this point in discussing deregulation in Great Britain, which he attributes to the political philosophy of the Thatcher government. Gordon Kaiser, as noted, detects a "religious zeal" in the United States regarding the proposition that monopoly no longer exists in telecommunications markets, implying that this notion is beyond the pale of reason or theory.

Finally, a similar data problem, though not equally serious, exists with respect to obtaining price elasticities of demand for different categories of telecommunications service. Once again, the data are incomplete and unreliable, although the problems involved in their measurement and collection are more practical than theoretical. These elasticities are vital in estimating welfare-maximizing optimal tariff structures such as Ramsey prices, as well as welfare losses implicit in nonoptimal tariffs. The 1983 study by Neumann, Schweizer, and von Weizsäcker is instructive in its approach to calculating welfare losses when cost and elasticity data are less reliable than one would wish.

NOTES

1. For a brief summary of the workshop's papers and conclusions, see Snow (1984a); for a lengthier summary, see Snow (1984c).

2. The most complete single compilation of sustainability and contestability theory is Baumol, Panzar, and Willig (1982). A more accessible introduction is Sharkey (1982). Bailey and Friedlaender (1982) provide a bibliographic essay. Baumol (1982) is a useful summary and recapitulation. Coursey, Isaac, and Smith (1984) furnish experimental results regarding natural monopoly and contested markets, whereas Shepherd (1984) is a critical assessment of contestability theory.

Bailey and Baumol (1984) is an application to deregulatory issues, including telecommunications, in the United States.

3. See Youichi Ito's coverage of this topic in Chapter 9.

4. For a description, see Kinsley (1976) or Snow (1976).

5. For a summary of arguments for and against deregulation, see Snow (1984b) and Snow (1985).

6. See Snow (1982, 1983) for general treatments of telecommunications policy in West Germany.

REFERENCES

Bailey, Elizabeth E., and William J. Baumol. "Deregulation and the Theory of Contestable Markets." *Yale Journal on Regulation* 1 (1984): 111–138.

Bailey, Elizabeth E., and Ann Friedlaender. "Market Structure and Multiproduct Industries." *Journal of Economic Literature* 20 (1982): 1024–1048.

Baumol, William J. "Contestable Markets: An Uprising in the Theory of Industry Structure." *American Economic Review* 72 (1982): 1–15.

Baumol, William J., John C. Panzar, and Robert D. Willig. *Contestable Markets and the Theory of Industry Structure.* Orlando, Fla.: Harcourt Brace Jovanovich, 1982.

Brock, Gerald W. *The Telecommunications Industry*. Cambridge, Mass.: Harvard University Press, 1981.

Cheah, Chee-wah. "An Econometric Analysis of TDF Regulation." *Transnational Data Report* 8 (1984): 475–479.

Coursey, Don, R. Mark Isaac, and Vernon L. Smith. "Natural Monopoly and Contested Markets: Some Experimental Results." *Journal of Law and Economics* 27 (1984): 91–114.

Joskow, Paul L., and Roger G. Noll. "Regulation in Theory and Practice: An Overview." In *Studies in Public Regulation,* edited by Gary Fromm. Cambridge, Mass.: MIT Press, 1981.

Kinsley, Michael E. *Outer Space and Inner Sanctums: Government, Business, and Satellite Communication.* New York: Wiley, 1976.

Knieps, Günter, Jürgen Müller, and Carl Christian von Weizsäcker. *Die Rolle des Wettbewerbs im Fernmeldebereich.* Baden-Baden: Nomos Verlagsgesellschaft, 1981.

Neumann, Karl-Heinz, Urs Schweizer, and Carl Christian von Weizsäcker. "Welfare Analysis of Telecommunications Tariffs in Germany." In *Public Sector Economics,* edited by Jörg Finsinger. New York: St. Martin's Press, 1983.

Noll, Roger G. "The Political Foundations of Regulatory Policy." *Zeitschrift für die gesamte Staatswissenschaft* 139 (1983): 377–404.

Noll, Roger G., and Bruce M. Owen. *The Political Economy of Deregulation.* Washington, D.C.: American Enterprise Institute, 1983.

Peltzman, Sam. "Toward a More General Theory of Regulation." *Journal of Law and Economics* 19 (1976): 211–240.

Porat, Marc U. *The Information Economy.* 9 vols. Washington, D.C.: U.S. Department of Commerce, Office of Telecommunications, 1977.

Schumpeter, Joseph A. *Capitalism, Socialism and Democracy.* New York: Harper (Colophon Books), 1975.

Sharkey, William W. *The Theory of Natural Monopoly.* New York: Cambridge University Press, 1982.

Shepherd, William G. "'Contestability' versus Competition." *American Economic Review* 74 (1984): 572–587.

Snow, Marcellus S. *International Commercial Satellite Communications: Economic and Political Issues of the First Decade of INTELSAT.* New York: Praeger, 1976.

———. "Telecommunications and Media Policy in West Germany: Recent Developments." *Journal of Communication* 32, no. 3 (1982): 10–32.

———. "Telecommunications Deregulation in the Federal Republic of Germany." *Columbia Journal of World Business* 18, no. 1 (1983): 53–61.

———. "Telecommunications: The Big Picture." *Telephony,* June 25, 1984, 64–70. (a)

———. "Competition by Private Carriers in International Commercial Satellite Traffic: Conceptual and Historical Background." Paper presented at Tracing New Orbits Conference, Research Program in Telecommunications and Information Policy, Graduate School of Business, Columbia University, November 30, 1984. (b)

———. "A Comparison of Telecommunications in Seven Industrialized Countries: Report of a Workshop." *Journal of Information Science* 9, no. 2 (1984): 57–66. (c)

———. "Arguments for and against Competition in International Satellite Facilities and Services: A U.S. Perspective." *Journal of Communication* 35, no. 3 (1985).

Stigler, George J. "The Theory of Economic Regulation." *Bell Journal of Economics and Management Science* 2 (1971): 3–21.

Two

Free Entry into Telecommunications?

Carl Christian von Weizsäcker

VALUE-BASED VERSUS COST-BASED PRICING OF SERVICES

Economic theory understands well two polar cases of efficient and nondiscriminatory pricing. One case is the model of perfect competition. Here competition, including free entry and exit of firms, enforces a uniform price for a homogeneous good. This price corresponds to the marginal cost of production and, with free entry, the long-run average cost of production. It ensures an efficient allocation of resources. The case at the other extreme is the Lindahl theory of burden sharing of the pure public good. An efficient production level of a public good is characterized by the equality of its marginal cost of production with the sum of the marginal benefits derived from the public good by the different citizens. If the public good is produced at constant marginal cost, and hence marginal cost and average cost are the same, then it can be financed by contributions of each citizen that are equal to their marginal benefits times the quantity of the public good. This financing scheme, proposed by Lindahl, is called Lindahl pricing of public goods. It ensures an efficient outcome and corresponds to the principle of equivalent burden sharing (the principle of equivalence) in that each citizen shares in the total financing burden to an extent that is equivalent to his marginal benefit from the good. The problem with Lindahl pricing of public goods is that it is not feasible: Citizens have no incentive to reveal their benefits derived from the public good if their financial burden is computed in accordance with these benefits. For most cases, this unfeasibility is not substantially changed by the recent discovery of incentive-compatible mechanisms (see Green and Laffont 1979).

Between these polar cases of the competitive market for private goods and the Lindahl scheme of financing and producing pure public goods lies the case we are concerned with here: pricing (tariffs) for services of a public utility producing with nonnegligible economies of scale. Without these economies of scale we basically could leave the pricing issue to the private market, and it would essentially be decided according to the competitive polar case mentioned above. If, however, the marginal cost of providing its different services (which are private goods) is zero—if, in other words, the economies of scale are very substantial—then the availability of the services is like a public good, and if it were feasible, it could be handled best by the Lindahl scheme. People would contribute to the financing of the service availability in accordance with their benefit and would receive the service itself free of charge.

The extent of economies of scale will determine whether the equivalence principle derived from the Lindahl scheme or the marginal-cost principle derived from the competition model is more convincing as a guideline for public utility pricing. I shall discuss the implementation of the two principles, starting with the equivalence principle.

THE EQUIVALENCE PRINCIPLE OF PUBLIC UTILITY PRICING: VALUE-BASED PRICING

If a public utility enterprise has to cover its costs by selling its services and if there are economies of scale, it will have to charge prices above marginal cost. Most public utilities are multiproduct firms. A telephone enterprise sells telephone services at different locations of origin and destination of any call, and it sells the services at different moments in time. Even ignoring other services (e.g., telex, data communications), it is thus able to price its telephone services as a function of call location and time. The question then arises how to price different services in such a way as to obtain a good implementation of the equivalence principle. There is obviously no need to charge a uniform percentage markup over marginal cost. The equivalence principle is best implemented by so-called value-based pricing. This means pricing in proportion to the value of the service to the user. Thus, services of high value to the average user will be priced much above their marginal cost, and services of lower value to the user will be priced barely above marginal cost.

Note that this pricing strategy requires information about the value of a service to the users, just as the Lindahl scheme requires the corresponding information. Whereas a precise knowledge of each consumer's value of the service is clearly impossible, an estimate of the average value for large user groups is feasible in many cases. Common sense, experience, and market research will help in forming a reasonable estimate. Thus, the difficulty with the Lindahl scheme concerning revelation of preferences to a large extent disappears if the supplier is content with average preferences of large groups, and if small errors in those estimates do not matter too much. Obviously, the world is not perfect; decisions have to be made under incomplete information. In this somewhat incomplete way the implementation of the equivalence principle is possible. Without access to more accurate information, of course, one does not know how far off the mark any given scheme of prices is, if compared with an ideal implementation of the equivalence principle. Certain additional sources of information concerning this question may in principle be available, but they can be obtained only if one is prepared to deviate from value-based prices.

Value-based pricing, if understood as a proper implementation of the equivalence principle, will not ignore marginal costs of production. The marginal-cost component of the price for a service reflects the fact that the service is a private good, and there exists no efficiency or equity reason not to charge the consumer of this private good its attributable marginal cost. The value to the consumer only plays a role in the allocation of the cost exceeding marginal-cost prices.

A well-known formulation of optimal prices for public enterprises is the Ramsey–Boiteux theory as further developed by Baumol and Bradford (see Baumol and Bradford 1970; Boiteux 1971; Ramsey 1927). Without going very much into detail, it can be described as follows: A multiproduct enterprise is confronted with a cost structure implying economies of scale. Thus, we are talking of a natural monopoly situation. The firm tries to maximize social welfare subject to certain constraints. As it turns out, the Ramsey–Boiteux theory is very closely connected with the philosophy of value-based pricing.

Let x be the vector of outputs of the monopoly. Let $k(x)$ be the (scalar) cost function, and let $x(p)$ be the demand vector as a function of the price vector p. Let $U(p)$ be the consumer's net utility (consumer surplus) in money terms derived from the commodities provided by the natural monopoly. Ignoring income effects, it can be derived (by classical theorems in price theory) that

$$\frac{\partial U}{\partial p_i} = -x_i(p) \quad i = 1, 2, \ldots, n$$

Here, n is the number of different commodities supplied by the monopolist, p_i is the price of good i, and x_i is the quantity of good i demanded on the market at those prices. The profit of the public enterprise is $x(p)p - k(x(p))$. The social objective function L is a weighted sum of consumer welfare and enterprise profit

$$L = U(p) + \lambda(x(p))p - k(x(p)) \qquad \lambda > 0$$

where λ indicates the importance of the firm's profit as compared to consumer welfare. The weight could be greater or smaller than unity (i.e., the weight of enterprise profits could be greater or smaller than the weight of consumer welfare). In a situation in which monopoly profits go to a rich private monopolist, there may exist distributional reasons for making λ small. If we are concerned with a public enterprise obliged to cover its costs, then we have a Lagrangian problem of maximizing subject to a constraint. The λ is the Lagrange multiplier to be determined endogenously. If, due to natural monopoly, marginal costs are always below average costs, then one can show that λ will be greater than unity in the constrained optimum. We can thereby conclude that this constrained optimum problem is embedded as a special case in the following problem. If the government runs the monopoly, it can expect that monopoly profits can be transformed one to one into government revenue. Given government expenditures, this means that taxes can be lowered whenever those monopoly profits can be raised. The distortive effect of taxation implies that in an optimal taxation framework an additional dollar (or deutsche mark or franc) of government revenue (of a lump-sum kind or from the monopoly in question) is worth more than a dollar of private income. This is because the one-dollar tax reduction made possible allows the creation of more than one dollar of additional after-tax income. This is so because the distortive effect of taxes can be reduced. We can then interpret λ to be the ratio of the value of one dollar (lump sum) of government revenue to one dollar of private income, where now $\lambda > 1$.

Differentiation of L with respect to prices p_i implies for the optimum

$$\frac{\partial L}{\partial p_i} = -x_i + \lambda\frac{\partial \pi}{\partial p_i} = 0 \quad \text{if} \quad p_i > 0$$

where π is the profit of the monopoly enterprise. We can then show that for any i, j such that prices p_i, p_j are positive, the following holds at the optimum:

$$\frac{\partial \pi}{\partial p_i} \Big/ x_i = \frac{\partial \pi}{\partial p_j} \Big/ x_j \text{ or } \frac{\partial \pi}{\partial p_i} \Big/ \frac{\partial U}{\partial p_i} = \frac{\partial \pi}{\partial p_j} \Big/ \frac{\partial U}{\partial p_j}$$

This formula says that a small change in the price of good i implies the same ratio of contribution to profit to contribution to consumer benefit as does a small change in any other price.

This can be expressed in terms of elasticities of demand. Assuming for simplification of exposition that demand for each good depends only on its own price and not on the prices of other goods supplied by the monopolist, we can express

$$\frac{\partial \pi}{\partial p_i}$$

as follows:

$$\frac{\partial \pi}{\partial p_i} = x_i + (p_i - k_i)\frac{\partial x_i}{\partial p_i} = x_i(1 - m_i\varepsilon_i)$$

where k_i is the marginal cost of production of good i,

$$m_i = \frac{p_i - k_i}{p_i}$$

is the price–cost margin of good i and

$$\varepsilon_i = \frac{\partial x_i}{\partial p_i} \cdot \frac{p_i}{x_i}$$

is the absolute value of the price elasticity of demand for good i. Substituting this formula into the optimality condition yields

$$\frac{(1 - m_i\varepsilon_i)x_i}{x_i} = \frac{(1 - m_j\varepsilon_j)x_j}{x_j}$$

or

$$m_i\varepsilon_i = m_j\varepsilon_j$$

In the optimum the price–cost margin of any good thus is inversely proportional to the price elasticity of demand. The more elastic the demand for a good or service, the lower is its optimal price, given its marginal cost of production.

To show the relation between this rule of optimal pricing and value-based pricing I assume linear demand functions. Thus,

$$x_i = a_i - b_i p_i \qquad i = 1,2,\ldots,n$$

or

$$p_i = \frac{a_i}{b_i} - \frac{x_i}{b_i}$$

With linear demand functions the consumer surplus from good i for a given price p_i can be computed to be

$$U_i = \int_0^{x_i(p_i)} (p_i(z) - p_i(x_i))\mathrm{d}z = \int_0^{a_i - b_i p_i} \left(\frac{a_i}{b_i} - p_i\right)\mathrm{d}z$$

$$= \frac{1}{2b_i}(a_i - b_i p_i)^2 = \frac{1}{2b_i}x_i^2$$

We also can compute the price elasticities

$$\varepsilon_i = \left|\frac{p_i}{x_i}\,\frac{\partial x_i}{\partial p_i}\right| = \frac{p_i}{x_i}\,b_i$$

and thus obtain

$$\frac{U_i}{p_i x_i} = \frac{x_i^2}{2b_i}\,\frac{1}{p_i x_i} = \frac{1}{2}\,\frac{1}{b_i}\,\frac{x_i}{p_i} = \frac{1}{2\varepsilon_i}$$

In the Ramsey–Boiteux optimum we are then able to write

$$\frac{U_i}{(p_i - k_i)x_i} = \frac{1}{m_i}\,\frac{U_i}{p_i x_i} = \frac{1}{2m_i\varepsilon_i} = \frac{1}{2m_j\varepsilon_j} = \frac{U_j}{(p_i - k_j)x_j}$$

Now the expression $(p_i - k_i)x_i$ is the contribution of consumers of service i in excess of the cost attributable to the provision of service i ($k_i x_i$ = marginal cost of service i times quantity), i.e., it is the contribution of those consumers to the nonattributable costs of the enterprise and to its profits. We thus see that in the Ramsey–Boiteux optimum the ratio of net benefit U_i and "contribution" $(p_i - k_i)x_i$ is the same for all services. In this sense the equivalence principle (motivated by considerations of justice and equity) and the Ramsey–Boiteux rule (motivated by considerations of efficiency) lead to the same result.

This coincidence—as a mathematical theorem—hinges on the assumption of linear demand functions. (Within the class of linear demand functions it can be generalized to the case of nonvanishing cross-price elasticities.) It will be only approximately true for nonlinear demand functions. Given the substantial uncertainties about the shapes of demand functions, however, we should not be too worried about this fact.

An important point about this philosophy of public enterprise pricing has to be mentioned. It is the issue of *competition* with the public enterprise. If there are economies of scale involved in the public enterprise, a competing privately offered service without substantial economies of scale reduces the profitability of the public enterprise. It is not difficult to show that, assuming no effect on production efficiency, a merger of the competing industry into the public enterprise would enhance welfare, if the constraint is that the public enterprise has to avoid losses. In the Ramsey–Boiteux rule, price and margins are determined by demand conditions. Generally, the optimal price structure of the merged enterprise will imply a positive price–cost margin for the formerly competitive branch of its business. This optimal price structure was not feasible before the merger. This shows that the merger has raised total welfare, given the constraint that total costs of the enterprise must be covered. Thus, there exist good reasons why public enterprises tend to demand the exclusion of directly competing services from the field in which they offer their services.

This constraint on competition looks odd in a market economy, and we therefore have to analyze it a little bit. Take an example: If transportation by private automobile competes with an urban or metropolitan transportation system, should the latter have the right to exclude transportation by private automobile within the area or on certain routes within the area?

First, we should note that there are better ways to accomplish the same goals. If the automobile drivers were taxed appropriately and the tax revenue were used to subsidize the public transportation system, its customers would not have to pay higher prices, and the freedom of the automobile drivers would be less constrained. But note that this improvement now works with a relaxation of the cost-covering constraint for the public enterprise. This cost-covering constraint was understood as a consequence of the equivalence principle, whereby the users and beneficiaries of a public service should finance it in accordance with their benefits. If we apply the Lindahl scheme of financing public goods to several public goods simultaneously, it still remains true that each of them separately should be financed by the Lindahl contributors. For, in the optimum, the sum of the marginal benefits of each public good must equal its marginal cost. But deviations from the cost-covering constraint are justified if one recognizes that the tariffs for services are only rough approximations of the Lindahl scheme. Thus the provision of a fairly homogeneous service with little potential for price discrimination, but with substantial economies of scale, may not be feasible without a deficit or at least may reduce its use substantially, if prices are much above marginal cost. Frequently the availability of such a service at a low price enhances the welfare of people who do not use that service at all. Mass transit systems, for example, have a substantial positive impact on land values in areas with access to the system. Financing the system in part by land taxation is efficient and in accordance with the equivalence principle.

Since optimizations over a broader scale are not politically easy to accomplish, however, the cost-covering constraint does play a dominant role in the provision of service by public enterprises. The resistance against competition is a universal tendency among public enterprises (as it is among private ones), and it derives its justification very much from the principle of value-based pricing with a cost-covering constraint. Competition will then frequently be subsumed under the heading "cream skimming": a profitable activity that exploits the possibility of luring away some beneficiaries of the public good or service availability by offering more favorable prices, thereby enabling those beneficiaries to avoid paying their benefit-related contribution to the financing of the public good.

Some theoretical research shows the possibility that rational value-based price structures (with the cost-covering constraint) may not be sustainable if competition arises (see Baumol, Bailey, and Willig 1977; Faulhaber 1975). But it is implausible that these nonsustainability conditions are frequently fulfilled in practice. The real justification for excluding competition is that this exclusion is a substitute for a politically infeasible rational financing scheme, like taxing landowners. Even if we accept these reasons for the exclusion of competition, problems may arise because the pressure on the public enterprise to implement rational prices is weak without competition. Indeed, political pressures may not only prevent the rational measures, thereby justifying exclusion of competition; they may exclude competition in order to prevent a shift toward rational tariffs. Politically strong groups may benefit from a tariff structure that involves internal subsidization incompatible with rational tariffs. Here, the exclusion of competition serves in a socially inefficient way the purposes of special interest groups.

For this last reason, it is particularly important to consider substitutes for the exclusion of competition, such as contributions by competitors to the overhead costs of the public enterprise. But such contributions cannot be discussed before we understand cost-based tariffs.

COST-BASED PRICING

As stated, covering total cost is inconsistent with marginal-cost pricing if economies of scale prevail in the relevant output range. Thus the competitive ideal, namely prices that provide the marginal-cost signal to the consumer, is not available without modification. It is therefore necessary to discuss cost-based pricing in some detail.

Consider the case of a multiproduct supplier whose total costs k depend on certain activity levels $x_1, x_2, \ldots, x_n$, so that we can write

$$k = k(x_1, x_2, \ldots, x_n)$$

We assume that each activity level x_i can be varied independently of the other activity levels. We furthermore assume that the function k is differentiable. This implies that we can define marginal costs of each activity by the partial derivative of costs with respect to that activity. Writing k_i for marginal costs, we define $x_i k_i$ as the costs attributable to activity i. The totality of attributable costs is

$$Z = \sum_{i=1} x_i k_i$$

Note that cost-based pricing in the sense that price equals per unit attributable costs is equivalent to marginal cost pricing. The question now arises which proportion of total cost is attributable. The answer depends only on the degree of economies of scale. Let s be the index of scale economies. We define it as follows. For given $x_1, \ldots, x_n$ let $F(\lambda)$ be defined by

$$F(\lambda) = k(\lambda x_1, \lambda x_2, \ldots, \lambda x_n)$$

Upon differentiation of F with respect to λ at $\lambda = 1$ we get

$$F'(\lambda)|_{\lambda=1} = \sum_{i=1} x_i k_i = Z$$

We define the index of scale economies as

$$s = \left.\frac{F(\lambda)}{F'(\lambda)}\right|_{\lambda=1} = \frac{k}{Z}$$

Thus, the proportion of attributable cost to total cost, say a, is

$$a = \frac{Z}{k} = \frac{1}{s}$$

and thus inversely proportional to the index of scale economies. The proportion of nonattributable or overhead costs to total costs is thus

$$1 - a = 1 - \frac{1}{s}$$

If we accept the cost-covering requirement, we have to find an approximation to the marginal-cost pricing principle. One possibility is proportionality between prices and marginal costs and hence a proportionality between the contribution of an activity to overhead cost and its attributed cost.

Before continuing the elaboration of cost-based pricing of public enterprises, we should note its relation to pricing under competitive conditions. If there are no important economies of scale, competition is workable, and it leads to prices close to long-run marginal costs. Competition also works if there are economies of scope (without economies of scale) so that a firm will supply several different products. The marginal-cost pricing rule still applies to the extent that marginal costs are well defined.

If two or more products have to be produced in fixed proportions, then only a joint marginal cost is defined. Under conditions of competition, the prices of the products are such that their (appropriately weighted) sum equals their joint marginal cost and that each price makes demand equal to supply of the corresponding product. In the absence of economies of scale the competitive process will thus always lead to definite pricing results. These resulting prices have the property that they or their appropriately weighted sum is equal to marginal costs, wherever marginal cost is defined.

One example of different services offered with fixed proportions is services that require a substantial capital investment and that cannot be stored. Thus, availability of a certain level of services at one time of the day (or year) implies its availability at any other time of the day (or year). Under perfectly competitive conditions, peak-load pricing ensues so that capacities are fully utilized all the time, except at times where even a (net) price of zero does not allow full-capacity utilization.

Using these results from competitive analysis, we generalize the concept of cost-based pricing accordingly. If economies of scale are present, the proposed rule of proportionality of price and marginal cost must be understood in the following way: Wherever a separately priced service has a well-defined marginal cost, the price of the service is in proportion to that marginal cost. Where only a group of different services have a joint marginal cost, their prices as a weighted sum must be proportional to the joint marginal cost. The individual prices must be chosen so as to equate demand for each of the services to their jointly determined supply quantity.

Note that this scheme of cost-based pricing can be considered nondiscriminatory. Each buyer pays a price that corresponds to the direct (marginal) cost caused by his utilization of the service plus a percentage markup that is equal for all customers of the public enterprise. Moreover, this way of implementing nondiscriminatory pricing allows admittance of competitors, if these competitors are charged a "tax" that corresponds to the percentage contribution of the different services to nonattributable overhead costs induced by economies of scale. With this tax or charge to finance overhead costs of the public enterprise, a competitor can enter the market successfully and compete for the business of a service of his own choice whenever his costs in providing this service are lower than the attributable cost of the public enterprise. In contrast, a competitor with costs above those of the public enterprise in any given service will not be successful and will incur losses. The overhead charge levied on the competitor is thus a device that allows screening of the socially beneficial competitors from the rest, who could live only on socially unproductive cream skimming. The total social cost of providing any given level of service would then be reduced by the entry of a competitor.

Cost-based pricing is thus modeled after competition and is compatible with competition. In this respect it is different from value-based pricing, the effectiveness of which suffers from competition. To the extent that competition fosters progress by innovation and flexibility, cost-based pricing thus has advantages over value-based pricing. Nevertheless, it must be emphasized that value-based pricing has static allocational advantages over cost-based pricing, since, after all, the Ramsey–Boiteux theory shows us that value-based pricing maximizes welfare given the cost-covering constraint.

It is worthwhile at this point to study the issue of *price discrimination*. Equity and efficiency considerations are used to support the *equivalence principle*, as discussed above. We have seen its similarity to the Ramsey–Boiteux optimal tariff. But equity considerations, as well as administrative and political expediency, have also led to the *principle of uniform price*. The same service is to be offered at the same price, even if there exist substantial unit-cost differences in offering this service. Thus, telephone calls are charged in proportion to their length of time and as a function of the distance of the call, but the same price applies in rural and in metropolitan areas, in spite of the fact that per-call costs of the PTTs are much lower in densely settled areas than in rural areas. The principle of price uniformity is used as another argument against admitting competition, which would of course concentrate on those segments of the market where costs are low. This cream skimming would be incompatible with the implied internal subsidization of high-cost user groups who benefit from the uniformity of price. Strong resistance by these groups against competition can therefore be expected.

But even if we ignore the issue of admitting competition, a difficulty arises in telecommunications tariffs because of a contradiction between the equivalence principle and the uniformity principle. This contradiction is now discussed.

Economists are well trained in the model of the price-discriminating monopolist. The monopolist who is able to split up his market into different segments, such that customers in different segments are unable to trade with one another, will charge different prices for different customer segments. Low elasticity of demand of a customer segment implies a high profit-maximizing price. A high elasticity of demand for a different customer segment implies a low profit-maximizing price. But note that price discrimination in principle could also be one way to apply the equivalence principle in public enterprises. Indeed, to the extent that segmentation makes discrimination feasible, value-based pricing will require price discrimination and thus will violate the principle of uniform price.

This contradiction between two principles derived from equity considerations so far has not been widely discussed. I believe this is because of the unclear meaning people attach to the word *discrimination*. It is worth the effort to clarify the meaning of discrimination. By this I mean a definition of discrimination that is objective and that does not depend on opinions of the customers affected by the decisions. If two services are priced differently, but people consider them to be basically the same service, they tend to talk of discrimination. If they do not consider the two services the same service, they may not think of this situation as one of discrimination. If two services have the same price and are considered the same service by those concerned, they will not talk of discrimination. If they consider them to be different services, and if they know that the unit cost of provision is substantially different, they tend to consider the identical price a discrimination against the users of the low-cost service.

In both these examples the same objective situation will be called discriminatory or nondiscriminatory, depending on the subjective view of the homogeneity or heterogeneity of the two services. Thus, we need an objective criterion for deciding whether two services are really the same service or are different. I propose to call two services economically homogeneous if their costs per unit are the same. Thus, pricing will be nondiscriminatory if prices correspond to the attributable cost of production.

The principle of tariff uniformity is thus really discriminatory rather than the opposite. Only the public lack of attention to the costs of production makes it possible to view it as a nondiscriminatory policy. Nor is uniformity of price necessarily a good implementation of the equivalence principle. There is no reason to expect that value-based prices for telephone services in urban and rural areas lead to equal or similar prices. Obviously, there are administrative and informational limits to nonuniformity in prices. But clearly they cannot be used to defend the universal uniformity of prices for telephone severices as currently observed.

THE CHANGING BALANCE IN TELECOMMUNICATIONS: FROM VALUE-BASED TO COST-BASED PRICES

Value-based pricing as a second-best strategy has advantages over cost-based pricing in terms of static efficiency and in terms of equity. This is shown by the Ramsey–Boiteux theory of optimal prices and by the relation between value-based pricing and the principle of equivalence. But value-based pricing is superior to cost-based pricing only if it is applied optimally and not substantially distorted by political pressure. Moreover, it almost automatically leads to the exclusion of competition with the public enterprise.

In contrast, cost-based pricing, as outlined above, allows the admittance of private competition to public enterprises. This makes it more open to innovation, and in general to the discovery of new solutions for given problems. From the point of view of progress rather than static efficiency, it is therefore superior to value-based pricing. Moreover, by admitting competition, cost-based pricing limits the possibility that some users will be exploited by politically strong special interest groups. The exploited groups have an option to end the exploitation by obtaining their services from competing suppliers. The pressure to adhere to the rules of rational tariffs is thus substantially greater than it would be if competition were excluded.

The welfare loss incurred by cost-based pricing in terms of static allocative inefficiency will rise in proportion to the importance of economies of scale.

In this section I want to argue that for the telecommunications sector, the case for value-based tariffs has become much weaker and the case for cost-based tariffs has become much stronger as a result of certain interrelated changes in the structure of this sector. They are as follows:

1. The technology applied in the sector is rapidly changing and opens many opportunities for innovation and progress. The benefits from competition have thus risen substantially.
2. Because of changes in the technology and the overall growth of the sector, economies of scale have changed their character and have generally diminished in importance.
3. The rapid change in the cost structure together with the inertia of tariffs have created substantial distortions in the tariff structure. They are difficult to overcome politically; admission of competition may speed up this process.

I now discuss these three developments.

INNOVATION AND COMPETITION

Hayek's (1968) description of competition as a process of discovery is particularly useful. In the context of innovation we may describe this process as follows: The incentives for a bureaucracy to innovate are limited. An innovation is always risky, and there are always important counterarguments against innovation. Only if the top management decides to go ahead with the innovation will the organization support it. The top management usually gets the relevant information from within the organization, and thus to a large extent it will decide in accordance with the prevailing view of the members of the organization. Lacking competitive pressure, the majority view tends to favor the status quo. Change causes inconvenience and upsets de facto property rights in certain jobs and positions within the organization.

A competitive market with free entry has no shield against the innovative initiative of one of its suppliers or an outsider. An attempt at innovation does not need approval of a majority in the industry. Individuals or small groups of individuals and some financial backing by venture capitalists is sufficient to make an attempt to innovate. Many such attempts are failures, but those that succeed usually provide social benefits much beyond the private benefit to the innovator. An organizational setup fostering innovation, therefore, is socially highly beneficial. This is one of the great dynamic advantages of competition. The superiority of competition in fostering innovation is strikingly documented by the fact that practically all economically important innovations in the twentieth century have been implemented in market economies, whereas the centrally planned economies are peculiarly non-innovative and purely imitative. Their growth merely builds on imitating Western technological achievements (see Kornai 1971).

The dynamic advantages of fostering innovation in an economic sector are greater whenever the potential to innovate is greater. The technologies available by now in telecommunications create a substantial innovative potential. The overall reduction in telecommunications costs makes possible a great variety of new applications. The competitive process would be best suited to discovering which new applications should be implemented.

It should be noted here that competition, if it raises the speed with which new telecommunications applications will be implemented, also benefits the growth of the demand for network services and thus should not be looked at simply as competition with the estabilished PTT network. Indeed, it can even be considered complementary to the PTT network, since it may enhance the demand for its services.

ECONOMIES OF SCALE

The greater the economies of scale, the more convincing is the case for value-based pricing and the case against cost-based pricing. The development of economies of scale in telecommunications is thus of great interest to this question of tariff policy.

Economies of scale in telecommunications networks are the result mainly of six factors, which I will now enumerate and then try to evaluate:

1. Economies of scale resulting from better distribution of research and development (R&D) costs. As in any R&D-intensive industry, it is an advantage to manufacture products for a large market, since per-unit R&D costs are thereby small.
2. Economies of scale in manufacturing. They are again a common phenomenon in many industries. Note that neither Factor 1 nor Factor 2 as a rule implies the need to replace a private market by a public enterprise.
3. Economies of scale that reflect the neighborhood effect in the network. As in all public utility networks, the cost of establishing network links with each customer falls as the number of customers increases, if many customers are close neighbors. The lines to neighboring customers can be bundled together, and thereby costs can be saved. Moreover, a denser population of customers implies a better possibility of installing switching systems of optimum size near the customers, which saves switching costs as well as line costs.
4. Economies of scale resulting from the exploitation of the law of large numbers. Line utilization can be greatly increased if certain lines can be used by many customers. This is already partly taken account of in the neighborhood effect under Factor 3. In addition, lines between switching systems, in particular long-distance lines, make use of these effects.

The larger a system is, the better it can make use of these bundling advantages.

5. For a customer, access to a large network is of more value than access to a small network. Thus, each additional telecommunications customer tends to create a benefit for all other customers.
6. There exist economies of scale in the intensity of use of transmission facilities for any given customer.

The significance of these several sources of scale economies changes through time. Whereas Factors 1 and 2 were of some importance in the past (as well as in the present), they should not influence our thinking about tariffs very much. It is reasonable, as has been done in the past, simply to reckon with the actual per-unit costs of equipment. This is particularly true of those countries in which R&D and manufacturing are not part of the public enterprise running the telecommunications network.

Factors 3, 4, and 5 have been important in the past as long as the telephone was not yet installed in the majority of households. As we now begin reaching the stage of nearly full connection in highly industrialized countries, the situation has somewhat changed. The neighborhood effect (Factor 3) remains valid in the sense that the average cost per customer is lower with an efficient local monopoly network than with two or more suppliers with overlapping networks. Up to now, it therefore remains true that the cost structure implies a local natural monopoly. But note that this is only a local natural monopoly. Factor 3 does not imply cost disadvantages if two cities each run their own public enterprise to provide telephone services instead of being part of a common national telephone enterprise.

Factor 4 partly contributes to the local natural monopoly structure. But beyond that, the cost advantages of scale that accrue from the law of large numbers and bundling are by now almost fully exploited in highly industrialized countries. Competing suppliers of long-distance transmission services in high-volume traffic areas probably have no substantial cost disadvantage as compared to a single supplier. The new transmission technologies tend to reduce the importance of scale economies due to Factor 4.

Factor 5 intrinsically is important only as long as a large fraction of potential users is not yet connected with the network. The importance as an economies-of-scale factor disappears in a highly developed network that has penetrated its potential market. Thus it is clearly no longer an important factor with regard to the telephone. It is important for the incipient stage of new services, such as videotex or teletext. But those latter services are—as regards tariffs—not of great importance because their tariffs will be adapted to the tariffs of the (telephone) network that they use. They are value-added services built on existing networks, and their tariffs thus have to be harmonized with the existing network tariffs. As a result, although it is interesting to think about how to promote these new services, we are not so much concerned with it here.

Factor 6 remains important and may gain increased importance in the future. Two effects are involved. A large proportion of the value of the installed network cannot make use of the law of large numbers and thus is idle whenever the customer connected to it does not use the network. A higher use intensity will thus raise the network cost less than proportionately, because parts of the network equipment are more fully utilized. The second effect is that installation of a larger bit rate capacity for a customer does not raise the investment installation cost proportionately. This will become particularly important after the large-scale introduction of optical fiber channels.

For tariff evaluation of this cost structure, it is important to distinguish between fixed (monthly or installation) charges and volume charges. Costs induced by the installation and maintenance of any particular customer's connection should be covered by the fixed charges. This would be so with value-based or with cost-based tariffs, unless Factor 5 is still important. Assuming that it no longer is (for the telephone, this assumption is correct), we can thus work with the hypothesis that fixed charges are not very much affected by the choice between value-based or cost-based pricing. The main difference lies in the volume-dependent tariffs.

Costs covered by volume-dependent tariffs are the costs of operating and installing equipment jointly used by many customers (i.e. equipment that is not customer specific). But here, we have argued, economies of scale are no longer very important (Factors 4 and 5), so cost-based tariffs seem to be quite appropriate.

DISTORTIONS OF PRICE STRUCTURE

As a result of technological developments, the cost structure of the telecommunications system has changed substantially. Thus, long-distance transmission in particular has declined as a cost component, as has (or will) the switching function. The relative cost of long-distance telephone calls has thus declined. This is not yet reflected in the price structure and thus constitutes the first distortion in the price structure.

The second distortion comes from the difference in day–night tariffs. It was reasonable and appropriate to introduce peak-load pricing in the telephone sector. But the substantial growth of private household telephone ownership and the attractive evening or night tariffs led to a shift of the user peak into the evening, when rates are low. So now some telephone networks are faced with the paradoxical situation of having to invest substantial sums of money in order to avoid bottlenecks at times of day when the rate is low. This distortion again is very difficult to get rid of politically.

The third distortion is the uniformity of rates in both densely settled and rural areas in spite of the fact that costs of providing the services are much lower in densely settled areas than in rural areas.

A high rate of technical change leads to rapid adaptations of prices if competition prevails. The computer industry is a striking example of this proposition. The political process is much too slow to be able to maintain a rational tariff structure if conditions change rapidly. Interest-group resistance to changes is the main reason. The need for competition to overcome price inertia is thus particularly strong for the telecommunications sector.

SOME INSTITUTIONAL IMPLICATIONS FOR THE TELECOMMUNICATIONS SECTOR

Rational tariff policy is difficult to implement if the institutional structure is not appropriate for it. Above, I have argued that the balance has shifted from the case for value-based tariffs to the case for cost-based tariffs. In a more static environment with substantial economies of scale, the traditional natural monopoly argument for value-based tariffs and—as a second-best strategy—for the exclusion of competition is strong. Declining importance of scale economies, rapid technological change, and increasing political distortions of tariffs make it more appropriate to switch over to cost-based tariffs as they were outlined above. In particular, there is no need to prevent competition. As was shown, if any private competitor with the public enterprise network pays a proportionate contribution to the nonattributable overhead cost of telecommunications, then the right incentives for entry exist: Firms with efficiency superior to the public network enter, and those without an efficiency advantage do not enter.

Opening up competition in the telecommunications network means a substantial institutional change for this sector. This in itself leads to the expectation that resistance against this change will be strong. As was shown above, one of the implications of competition would be that tariff uniformity cannot be maintained across regions if costs differ substantially from region to region. We can expect strong resistance from regions that benefit from the present tariff structure.

Whether or not it is possible to compensate rural areas for any disadvantage they might suffer from the de-averaging of rates is a political rather than an economic question. Clearly the de-averaging in order to obtain cost-based tariffs is a move in the direction of efficiency. Thus, by well-known compensation principles in economics, it is possible to compensate the losses out of the gains of the winners and thereby to make everybody better off. But the political bargaining preceding such a move could be formidable.

It is, of course, conceivable to maintain the subsidies for rural areas, even with the admission of competition. This solution, although less efficient, is perhaps politically more feasible. Competing suppliers would then have to pay a certain percentage of their telecommunications revenue into a fund to be used for subsidizing telecommunications services in rural areas. Such an arrangement might still have efficiency advantages because it still would enable society to use the competitive mechanism for the discovery of useful and cost-effective new applications of telecommunications. This dynamic function of competition would thus still work to a certain extent.

The substantial surplus of revenue over costs generated in many European PTTs is a source of high allocative inefficiency. One reason for this surplus is the idea that the PTT as a whole, including the postal service, should cover its costs. Since in most countries the postal service by itself incurs high deficits, these tend to be covered by the telecommunications surpluses. An organizational and financial separation of the postal and the telecommunications part of the PTT seems to be a useful institutional step in the context discussed here. I believe it is possible to design a tariff structure for the postal service so that it becomes financially independent from subsidies. But major tariff structure reforms would be required, and they would not be popular. In any case, this is not the topic of the present chapter.

There exists an activity that is somewhat related to competition with the network but does not involve actually setting up competing hardware. I want to call it *rate arbitrage*. Firms buy telecommunications from the network and sell them again in a somewhat different form. These rate arbitrageurs, to the extent that they are admitted, can perform some of the functions that a direct competitor would fulfill. In particular, if they offer a value-added service, they can explore new methods of using telecommunications. Such value-added activity is the mildest form of competition with the network. It is not only competition but actually can be complementary to the network and can stimulate demand for the network service. It can be viewed in analogy to the relation between a wholesaler and a retail trader. The two might conceivably compete; more important, however, they perform complementary services, each of which depends on the other. It is therefore quite likely that the PTTs will not strongly resist such value-added suppliers, even though so far they have considered themselves as providing the retail function.

Admittance of rate arbitrage does not necessarily enforce cost-based tariffs, but it does enforce—to a degree at least—harmonization of tariffs. Different services that can be transformed from one into the other by a customer would have to have rates that are in harmony. Thus, for example, a firm could obtain leased lines and organize a network of such leased lines that—together with appropriate PBX equipment—could be used by its customers like the public dial network. If the latter's rates are not in harmony with the rates of leased lines, then this arbitrage sets in: The public network traffic will be eroded unless rates are changed accordingly.

Political processes generally make it difficult to change tariffs of enterprises not exposed to competition. Cost-based tariffs might actually change very quickly if we took seriously the concept that prices should represent social costs of production of goods and services. In telecommunications, services are offered that have a very low short-run variable-cost component. Ideally, whenever demand drops off from the normal rate of capacity utilization, prices should go down substantially. This idea, so far, has been exploited in the introduction of peak-load pricing. Rates depend on the time of day. But, as mentioned, it was politically not feasible to avoid the shift of the peak to the low tariff period and, thereby, "wasteful" expansion of capacity for "off peak" users. Another form peak-load pricing could take would be instantaneous-feedback pricing.

Whereas traditional peak-load pricing implies a fixed tariff (only varying through the day according to a predetermined pattern), instantaneous-feedback pricing creates an instantaneous feedback from the current actual capacity utilization to the price charged. In this way, if an appropriate functional relation between capacity utilization and the price charged is chosen, capacity utilization can be continually stabilized. This instantaneous-feedback pricing is sometimes also referred to as Vickrey pricing, after the economist W. Vickrey, who first proposed it. We should note that Vickrey pricing is not necessarily the ideal method of pricing; it involves additional resource costs because the customer somehow has to be informed about the current prices charged, which can change every minute. These additional costs may not be worth the benefit if the traditional method of peak-load pricing is handled skillfully and flexibly. This is because usage patterns as a function of time of day are rather stable and thus, say, a semiannual updating of the tariff to changed demand patterns may be sufficient to stabilize capacity utilization reasonably well.

But note that we have to compare Vickrey pricing with an actual pricing method that is politically very inert and thus leads to substantial waste in the system. Moreover, in highly industrialized countries the additional resources required for the information feedback are insubstantial. A small part of TV broadcasting capacity, such as teletext, is basically enough to inform the user about the present price. Clearly some additional technical problems would have to be solved. Nevertheless, I believe that the cost of closing the feedback loop by providing this information is low.

The benefits of such a pricing scheme are, as mentioned, the better capacity utilization and the automatic rather than political adaptation of price to the supply of and the demand for telecommunications. This makes the system much more flexible and reduces substantially the political inertia of present-day tariff policy in telecommunications.

A PRAGMATIC BEGINNING

A more cautious approach to competition would be the following: The PTTs admit competing suppliers who, either as value-added service suppliers (or rate arbitrageurs) or with their own hardware, offer their services. They would have to pay an access fee to the PTT, which allows them to connect with the PTT network. The PTT goes on to provide service with uniform tariffs, thereby continuing the internal subsidization of those customer groups that obtain the service at relatively high costs from the PTT. The access fee can be viewed as a contribution to the financing of the overhead of the telecommunications system and the financing of the ongoing subsidization of certain customer groups. The access fee would be adjusted in such a way as to stabilize the market share of the competition at a predetermined level of, say, 10 or 15 or 20 or 30% of total telecommunications network revenue. The access fee would be raised as a fixed percentage of the private supplier's net telecommunications revenue. The net telecommunications revenue is the supplier's revenue from supplying telecommunications network services minus the telecommunications network services that the supplier buys from the PTT or other competing network service suppliers.

The access fee can thus be seen in analogy to the value-added tax. We can think of it in this way: The PTT pays a notional fee to itself for the financing of internal subsidies and the unattributable overheads. The fee finally paid by the end user of telecommunications network services should be the same (i.e., independent of who his supplier is). Therefore, an independent supplier pays the fee on his revenue but is refunded the fee paid by his own telecommunications network supplier.

This proposal of course does not imply full-blown competition. But the scheme allows making use of some advantages of competition and should meet less political resistance because internal subsidization continues. The advantages of competition that can be gained are the following: Private suppliers are free to introduce new products and services, which should also have stimulating effects for innovation in the terminal equipment market. For business users, it would create additional possibilities of exploiting opportunities for lower costs and for speeding up new uses of telecommunications, particularly in the context of broadband networks. Private households as well may be able to use their TV cables for other telecommunications services. Entrepreneurial initiative for the offering of such services may speed up their introduction. A further advantage of this sort of competition is that the competitive sector will provide reference points for the evaluation of costs and tariffs of the PTT. This puts additional pressure on the PTT to increase its internal efficiency and flexibility.

If that proposal merits a more detailed analysis, two questions will have to be answered. First, what is a reasonable target market share for the competitive sector of the network? Too small a market share may limit the competitive fringe to activities that are relevant only for highly specialized customers; thus, the overall network picture may not be changed much. Also, the pressure imposed on the PTT may be too small. Too large a target market share—at least in the initial decade of the operation of such a scheme—may not be attainable with a positive access charge and thus may erode the revenue base of the PTT substantially, thereby causing problems of political resistance similar to those met by proposals of completely free competition. We must be aware of the fact that the independent suppliers will engage in cream skimming, the horror word that is the main counter-argument against the admission of competition. To overcome that political resistance it is necessary to adopt a sufficiently restrictive target market share so that the access fee corresponding to that share and paid by the independent suppliers does generate a certain fiscal compensation for the PTT's lost market share (see Figure 2.1).

A second question that would have to be investigated in the context of the proposal is the following: What are the dynamics of adapting the access charge to actual market shares? Actual market shares react with a time lag to changes in access charges. To have a reasonably stable system, and in the interest of efficiency in planning, access charges cannot be changed too

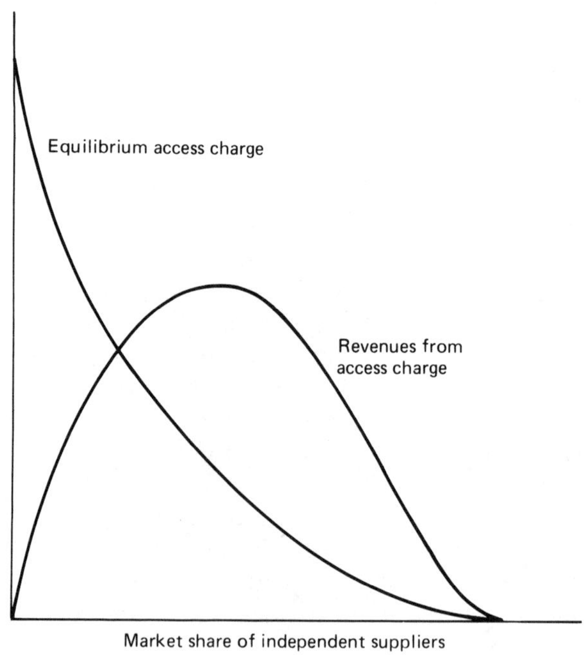

Figure 2.1

rapidly. Too large an inertia in access charges, however, may imply too large a deviation of actual market shares from the target market share.

REFERENCES

Baumol, W. J., E. E. Bailey, and R. D. Willig. "Weak Invisible Hand Theorems on Pricing and Entry in a Multiproduct Natural Monopoly." *American Economic Review* 67 (1977): 350–365.

Baumol, W. J., and D. Bradford. "Optimal Departures from Marginal Cost Pricing." *American Economic Review* 60 (1970): 265–283.

Boiteux, M. "On the Management of Public Monopolies Subject to Budgetary Constraint." *Journal of Economic Theory* 3 (1971): 219–240.

Faulhaber, G. R. "Cross-Subsidization: Pricing in Public Enterprises." *American Economic Review* 65 (1975): 966–977.

Green J., and J. Laffont. *Incentives in Public Decision Making*. Amsterdam: North-Holland, 1979.

Hayek, F. *Wettbewerb als Entdeckungsverfahren*. Kiel, Germany: Kieler Vorträge, N.F. 56, 1968.

Kornai, J. *Anti-Equilibrium*. Amsterdam: North-Holland, 1971.

Ramsey, F. "A Contribution to the Theory of Taxation." *Economic Journal* 37 (1927): 47–61.

Three

The Political and Institutional Context of Communications Policy

Roger G. Noll*

All nations, regardless of how their political and economic systems are organized, exercise considerable political control over the communications sector. In all but a few countries, ministries or government enterprises provide broadcast and telecommunications services, and even in countries that rely on the private sector to supply such services, government bureaus exercise considerable control over the industry.

For technical and economic reasons discussed in this book, communications policy is undergoing transition and reevaluation in most developed countries. Whether deregulation, privatization, or decentralization, change is everywhere apparent. Yet each country has relatively little experience with alternative institutional arrangements of the communications sector. One potentially valuable use of international comparative studies is to provide a more comprehensive analysis of the relationship between the performance of policy alternatives and the institutional and political environment in which they must be embedded. This can provide some basis for constructing reasonable, informed expectations about the likely consequences of changes in domestic policies in the absence of any domestic experience or evidence that is directly pertinent.

With opportunity comes danger, however, for international comparative studies inspect institutions and performance in diverse political

*This chapter was prepared while the author was a Guggenheim Fellow and a Fellow at the Center for Advanced Study in the Behavioral Sciences. The author thanks the John Simon Guggenheim Foundation, the Center, and the National Science Foundation for financial support.

settings. To the extent that the performance of the communications sector depends in subtle ways on the interactions between political institutions and market organization, these factors must be taken into account in comparative analysis.

The purpose of this chapter is to provide a general conceptual framework for examining the role of political and institutional structures in shaping the performance of the communications sector. The ultimate objective is to contribute to enhancing our understanding of the factors that affect the growth and direction of change of the sector, and especially to identify the key policy levers available to public decision makers. The more proximate objective is to provide a framework for organizing data collection and analysis that will enable us to ask and answer the right questions about how institutions—political and economic—affect the performance of the industry; the efficiency of the price signals it sends to its customers; the extent to which its services match the economic and other demands of the society; the efficiency of its technology and the rate at which it innovates; and the distributional gainers and losers from its operations and practices.

Successful international comparisons for the purpose of examining the relationships between institutions and performance depend on solving a number of difficult data problems. Most obvious are those related to basic economic and technical variables. Prices, costs, and quantities of service must be measured consistently through time and between countries. In addition, data must be collected in a way that enables some measurement of the extent to which accounting practices within each country not only affect data comparability but create incentives affecting the truthful revelation of accurate information—and even the technical choices among methods of delivering services (and, therefore, indirectly the costs of providing service). These problems illustrate one important way—but not the way examined in this chapter—that institutional arrangements and practices affect performance.

The remainder of this chapter examines other connections between institutional arrangements and performance. The principal working hypothesis is that the performance of the communications sector—indeed, of any part of the economy—depends on the political and economic environment in which it operates. Here, the political and economic environment is taken to mean the kinds of organizations that make decisions affecting prices, technology, service, and other important variables; the relationships among these organizations; the rules governing these relationships; and the nature of the process for changing these rules. To understand the process driving the performance of the sector requires an accurate characterization of this environment and a theory for relating these characteristics to performance. I divide this task into two components, each of which is assigned a section in this chapter. The section that follows deals with the supply environment: the range of alternative ways to organize the sector that provides communications services. In the next section I deal with the political environment: how the political system affects the policy choices of political officials and the objectives they seek. This section also discusses interactions between the two: how the supply and political environments interact to shape the performance of the industry.

CHARACTERIZING THE SUPPLY STRUCTURE

Numerous economic variables are likely to be associated with the performance of the communications sector, regardless of its institutional structure. These obviously must be taken into account in any assessment of the sector's performance. Among these are macroeconomic conditions, the country's trade policies, and the state of the country's technical know-how. But the importance of communications arises in part because these variables are also affected by the performance of the sector, which in turn is affected by the sector's structural characteristics. The two most important structural characteristics are the organizational forms of the participants and the number and ease of entry of suppliers.

The range of structural possibilities can be relatively easily comprehended by depicting it in a two-dimensional diagram (Figure 3.1). The vertical axis represents ease of entry as an institutional (rather than technical) variable. That is, it measures the extent to which government policy is favorable to entry. The origin represents a government policy that prohibits entry. The upper bound of the vertical axis represents an absence of policies that inhibit entry, combined with policies, like antitrust, that attempt to prevent entry-foreclosing strategies of incumbents (except through superior efficiency).

The horizontal axis arrays the various institutional forms and market structures that might develop. In reality, this dimension collapses two distinct concepts into one measure. The first is the traditional market structure variable: how many entities operate in the market. The second is the degree of reliance on the private sector versus direct government control. These two concepts are amenable to combination because of their high degree of correlation. Specifically, one rarely finds government ownership combined with a multiorganizational structure, nor separate regulatory institutions for overseeing either ministries or competitive private industry. Nevertheless, there are exceptions: Australia's competing airlines (one private, one public); the Postal Rate Commission, which regulates the U.S. Postal Service, a government corporation that is a monopolist in many services but faces unregulated competitors in express service and small-package delivery; and economic regulation of trucking in

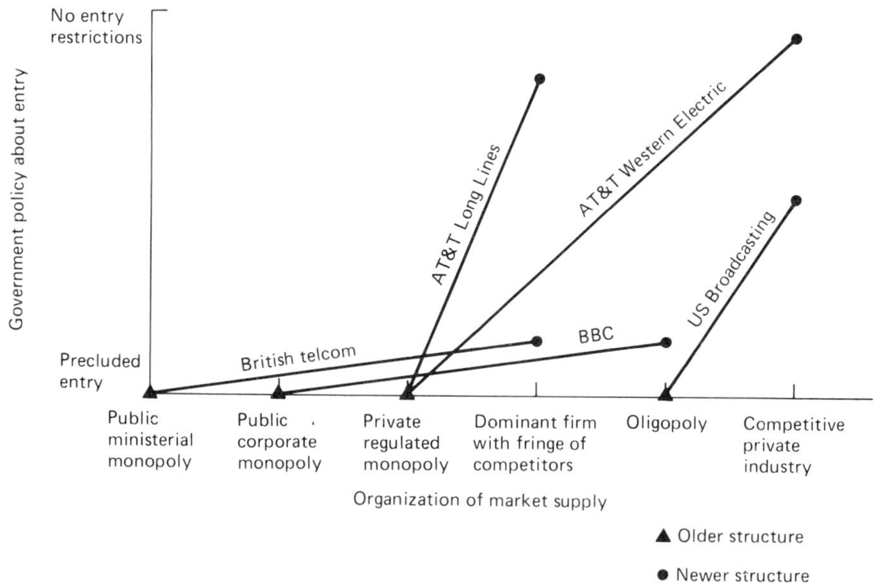

Figure 3.1

several countries. Here the exposition in two dimensions is for ease of representation and the approximate accuracy it brings to the organizational choices that have emerged in the communications sector. On the horizontal axis, by combining the degree of concentration of the supply of service and the extent of direct government management, we measure the degree of government involvement in the management of firms in the industry.

The principal use of the diagram is as a device for analyzing alternative forms of industry organization in terms of the extent to which they are subject to effective political control. The origin represents the minimum in structure and the maximum of political control: the ministerial department that provides a monopoly service from which potential competitors are banned. Next along the horizontal axis come other monopolistic forms that have less direct political control: the independent government corporation, like the BBC before entry was permitted by private competitors, and the private regulated monopoly, such as AT&T in the United States before the procompetitive regulatory and court decisions of the 1970s.

To explicate the meaning of the diagram, several well-known organizations in the communications sectors have been located on it. In each case, these organizations have been located twice—in an "early" and "late" incarnation, where the intervening period covers the changes between, say, the 1950s and the 1980s. Undertaking this exercise, of course, emphasizes the extent of the transition that the communications sector is now experiencing. The general tendency is a movement away from the origin in both dimensions—toward more competition.

As entry becomes easier and the number of firms increases, two phenomena occur. First, the number and diversity of competitors make the industry more difficult to control politically because of the sheer magnitude of the attendant informational and enforcement problems. Second, the competitive interactions among firms give the political actors less opportunity to alter their performance in directed, politically useful ways. A competitive environment creates less slack (monopoly profits or inefficiencies of operation) that can be redistributed politically. The least potential for political control resides in the upper-right-hand portion of the figure, where numerous organizations supply service and entry is easy.

The theoretical significance of these two dimensions is sufficiently straightforward to be summarized quickly. Economic theory postulates that private firms seek to maximize profits; bureaucratic theory posits the maximization of bureau size and authority (Downs 1967; Niskanen 1971; Wildavsky 1964). The profit motive is derived from the objectives of private sources of capital to the firm, which are transmitted through the incentive structure of the firm: Profit-seeking behavior by employees at all levels is rewarded. The desire to increase bureau size and authority is derived from the incentives of bureau managers, whose power and rewards are positively related to the importance of the bureau. For private firms and for bureaus facing an elastic demand curve, these motives produce technical efficiency—the organization will minimize costs for whatever level of service it provides (Baumol 1967). For bureaus facing inelastic demand, bureau size (measured by inputs) is maximized by adopting cost-enhancing technologies—means of providing service that require more inputs. Finally the behavior of a regulated private monopoly is roughly similar to the behavior of the bureau, although with some significant and subtle differences that depend on the method chosen for calculating allowed profits and for setting prices.

In all instances, supply organizations are likely to possess information about technology, costs, and demand superior to that commanded by political actors seeking to control the suppliers. The extent of this informational superiority will depend in part on the degree of separation of the supply organization from the means of political control and in part on the resources government officials allocate to monitoring performance of supply organizations (Noll 1983). The gap is smallest for ministerial agencies and greatest when a regulatory bureau must cope with a heterogeneous group of competitive, private suppliers. Hence, the possibility for strategic use of information to serve organizational objectives depends on the structure of the supply side of the industry (Noll and Owen 1983). Somewhere along the middle of the horizontal axis lies the point at which strategic possibilities are maximal: The structure is not sufficiently competitive for interactions among supply organizations to force efficient operations by eliminating excess profits and inefficient technical choices, but the informational superiority of the suppliers gives them significant autonomy from political control. Entry policy also affects manipulability: Easy entry serves as a threat against inefficient operations, whereas precluded entry provides suppliers with more possibilities for benefiting from information manipulation.

The preceding summary of the theoretical arguments relating structure to performance is focused on so-called static efficiency: Given current technical knowledge, how efficiently does an industry operate? Of at least equal significance in the long run is dynamic efficiency: How does the industry perform in developing new technologies that lower costs and/or expand the number of services that produce net societal benefits?

Theory is less well developed about dynamic efficiency, but some propositions have emerged (Klein 1977; Mansfield 1977; Nelson and Winter 1982; Reinganum 1984). First, the most innovative industries seem to be those with a few highly rivalrous firms in which entry is also relatively easy. Second, large, established firms normally account for relatively steady incremental change, while entrants normally account for radical departures from established technology. Third, in the most progressive industries the rank order of firms by sales, profits, and other measures of success tends to be unstable, as do measures of market concentration. Apparently the possibility of experiencing meteoric rises and falls in fortune provides the incentive to maintain a large R&D effort and a willingness to innovate and take risks. Thus, relatively free entry, in the absence of controls on market shares, and some degree of significant competition all appear to be important factors affecting technical progress. Nevertheless, there are important exceptions, so such generalizations must be hedged. In the United States, for example, telecommunications was monopolized from approximately World War I until the early 1970s; technical progress, however, was quite rapid. However, the period of competition (recent years and the period before World War I) also experienced high rates of progress (Brock 1981). Whether progress was more or less rapid during the period of monopoly is an issue on which there is relatively little information, and it is not likely ever to be convincingly resolved. Technical progress also seems to have been quite rapid in Japan, which has had monopolized service but rivalrous equipment manufacturing with some political entry barriers, the latter reflecting the practices of the Ministry of International Trade and Industry, but with a general movement in the direction of more competition.

The general guideline relating structural aspects of the supply side to performance appears to be as follows: Whereas monopoly and foreclosed entry hold the possibility of capturing economies of scale and scope and of exercising closer political control, they increase the opportunities for monopolistic inefficiencies and probably, on balance, mitigate against dynamic efficiency. Rivalry among large firms with easy entry probably enhances short-run and long-run efficiency, but attenuates political control.

CHARACTERIZING THE POLITICAL STRUCTURE

The preceding analysis discussed the relationship between the supply structure and the feasibility of political control, but without mentioning what political control might be used to achieve. Obviously, political actions can serve numerous goals relating to economic efficiency, equity, social cohesion, and technical progress, not to mention narrower, self-interested political objectives of politicians. The purpose of this section is to outline the various political objectives that might develop, and how they are likely to be related to the political structure of a country—that is, how a country's political institutions may shape its political objectives in communications policy.

In comparison to the microeconomic issues raised in the preceding section, theory is less settled on the question of political behavior. Several approaches are currently in use, and their relative popularity among research scholars varies considerably among countries. Consequently, the presentation here is eclectic, attempting to summarize the principal arguments of each school of thought. I chose this tactic for two reasons. First, reflecting the state of development of the field, no approach is clearly superior for explaining all facets of political choice, and each can legitimately claim to shed light on some aspect of political behavior. Although I have my preferences regarding where new insights are most likely to be found, these are at present more intuitive than scientific. Second, regardless of the intrinsic scientific merit of alternative approaches, each has faithful adherents who are not likely to be reached by analysis that does not connect to their favored theoretical construct. Consequently, as a framework for inducing more research into international comparative studies of communications policy, this book would unnecessarily limit its potential audience and impact by being too doctrinaire in the choice of a theoretical framework.

For ease of exposition, political theories are herein divided into four distinct categories. Each is rather broad, encompassing a number of approaches that probably are not comfortable being classified together. These are Atomistic Democratic Theory, Statist Theory, Pluralist Theory, and Institutional Theory.

Atomistic Democratic Theory

This class of models of political behavior abstracts from the effects of political institutions and, in many cases, from the presence of serious conflicts of interest. In some cases, it presumes the existence of something called "the public interest," which is the policy that, in a world of complete information and efficient institutions, would be adopted by consensus. In other cases, democratic theory focuses on the positive theory of democratic processes in which there is a stable majority-rule winner (Buchanan and Tullock 1962; Downs 1957). These theories are also individualistic, in that normative judgments are based on consequences in terms of the welfare of the members of the polity. In welfare economics, for example, the public interest is derived from a "social welfare function" that is a weighted sum of functions relating individual welfare to consumption and wealth (Bergson 1966).

Two concepts command most of the attention of this approach. The first is economic efficiency: producing at minimum cost, optimizing the rate of technical change, and providing exactly the right amount of every commodity and service for which the net consumer benefits from use exceed the net social costs of production. Normatively, efficiency is interesting because of its consistency with the utilitarian objective of the greatest good for the greatest number (e.g., maximizing economic welfare). As a positive theory of political behavior, the argument rests on its internal logic—a move to enhance efficiency is Pareto-improving, at least in principle, in that the extra goods from improved efficiency can be divided among all citizens to make everyone better off.

The second dominant concept is distributional equity. Normatively, distributional equity rests on egalitarian or utilitarian foundations; if the latter, it is derived from the plausibility of the assumption that people are roughly equal in their ability to enjoy economic well-being. Positively, both political philosophy and institutionless, one-dimensional (economic welfare) formal positive political theory support the conclusion of egalitarian tendencies. Rawls (1971), for example, argues for the collective rationality of distributional equity as the social norm if distributional questions were decided by citizens before they knew their identities (abilities, inherited status, tastes, etc.).

The economist's normative theory of the democratic state presupposes the separability of the two issues. For example, Samuelson (1954) proposed separating public debate into two issues: the ideal distribution of income and then, once that is settled, the efficient operation of the economy, both public and private.

Unfortunately, of course, these goals are not separable to the extent that not all distributions of income are consistent with all possible combinations of efficient production of goods and services. Put another way, redistributing income to the desirable extent cannot be achieved without cost, including costs owing to distortions of the incentive structure conveyed through markets. Moreover, to the extent there is disagreement about distributional goals, one must either allow people to attempt to achieve distributional objectives at each significant decision point about allocation or make the political decision process authoritarian in that some allocative choices are not susceptible to normal democratic influences. In any case, when choices must be made over a set of issues that span more than one dimension (e.g., distributional equity and the quantity of a public good to be provided), majority-rule democracy does not, in general, produce an equilibrium, or even a normatively interesting outcome (Arrow 1951; McKelvey 1979).

The usefulness of atomistic democratic theory is not so much that it is an accurate theory of the behavior of political actors but that it focuses attention on certain summary questions of economic impact. Efficiency and equity (or distributional effects) matter, even if they are not determinative of the policy choice in a concise, utilitarian way. Moreover, much of the public debate—especially as enunciated by civil servants and other analysts—is cast in these terms. Not only economists, but lawyers, engineers, and other professional groups have relatively well developed concepts of efficiency and equity within their frameworks of analysis. Presumably such "objectivist" input to the political process has value, or else political actors would not actively seek it.

Applied to communications policy, this world view is relatively straightforward. It tends to raise economic efficiency to the level of a social imperative. Judgments among alternative arrangements are made according to their relative efficiency, perhaps with, but more likely without, attention to distributional considerations, although as Feldstein (1972) and Willing and Bailey (1981) show, this latter characteristic is inessential to the basic idea. Moreover, there is often the implicit (rarely explicit) assumption that political processes will produce efficiency if only technical analysts do a good job presenting the facts. This was argued, with some caveats, in Breyer's 1982 analysis of regulatory reform in the United States.

The indeterminacy of majority rule undermines democratic theory as a good device for predicting policy; however, it also introduces the opportunity to include the role of political leadership in the theory of policy formation. For example, Riker (1982), using the example of the debates over slavery and states' rights in the United States in the first half of the nineteenth century, shows how political entrepreneurs made systematic use of the instability of the status quo to enhance their power—and change policy. Although telecommunications issues are not likely to achieve sufficient salience to become the focus of a great national debate, they can be swept along by larger, destabilizing movements, like deregulation in the United States or decentralization in France, which may be predictable and may (or may not) lead to performance-enhancing changes in policy.

Statist Theory

The statist view of national policy making focuses on the state as a decision-making entity that is separable analytically from its constituent parts. States have sovereignty over geographic areas, organizations, and people, and they have objectives that they pursue through combinations of coercion and inducement.

Statist theory is a heterogeneous category of methods of analyzing national policies, sufficiently so that, for many purposes, the category would be too broad to be useful. Much of this category is essentially political philosophy, asking what a state ought to do, how it ought to do it, and under what conditions it ought to command the loyalty of its citizens; and examining the constitutional and other legal rules of the society to ascertain whether they conform to these normative criteria (see Eckstein 1979). Other statist approaches view the state as allocating power within the society for the purpose of serving the interests of a particular class or group, as, for example, Marxist or elitist theories (e.g., Duvall and Freeman 1983; Lukes 1974; for curmudgeonly comparisons of these forms of statist theories with pluralism, to be discussed below, see Manley 1983 and Polsby 1980). A similar approach posits that the state is analogous to a business in that it seeks to maximize the wealth and power of state officials (North 1981). But the most common approach is to assume that the state pursues the "national interest." Among economists, especially of the Chicago tradition, national interest is usually equated to present and future national income, and the conclusion is to foster internal and external economic liberalism (e.g., Friedman 1981; Johnson 1967). Political scientists, however, adopt a broader definition of national interest, incorporating internal and external stability (Howard 1979) and the positive assertion of national power in the international community (Aron 1966; Morgenthau 1948). Indeed, the preeminence of the nation-state as the dominant organizational unit in human society is attributed to its superiority in these largely noneconomic domains (Tilly 1975). The most significant implication of this work is that the design of optimal policy requires that tradeoffs be made between purely economic values (both national wealth and distributional equity) and the objectives related to power, security, and stability (Gilpin 1981; Katzenstein 1977; Krasner 1976). One source of tradeoff is, of course, the direct requirements of the noneconomic objectives, but another is that the state, in order to retain its power and sovereignty, must cut deals with potentially threatening groups of constituents that, in the short run, detract from economic objectives and, perhaps, even objectives relating to international power, but that are essential to retaining internal stability (e.g., Mahon and Mytelka 1983; Martin 1979).

The most important unsolved puzzle in all statist theories is the magnitude of the relative weights assigned to various national objectives and the process by which they are derived. Only Marxists have an explanation for this, which is the linkage between ownership of the physical resources used in production and the distribution of political power. A critique of this view is not within the scope of this chapter; suffice it to say that most scholars find the Marxist account to be at best incomplete. In any case, the absence of an endogenous process for establishing national objectives makes empirical research primarily an *ex post* search for explanations of policy changes, running the risk of spurious correlation and tautological argument. Another difficulty is the absence of much concrete analysis about the connections between state actions and internal stability: For example, how, specifically, does a particular domestic policy affect the legitimacy of the state's claim to loyalty from the citizenry?

Because of the incomplete state of development of statist theory, it is hazardous to use this theory to predict a policy environment for any sector on the basis of expected economic, technological, and political changes. But this may reflect the nascent stage of development of the theory when applied to domestic economic policies, rather than necessarily the absence of intrinsic merit in the approach. In any case, the form of the analysis would bc as follows.

To explain developments in an area of microeconomic policy, such as communications, statist theory indicates that the relevant facts are the linkages between the sector and policy, on the one hand, and the purpose of the state, on the other. Policy will favor the enhancement of groups and sectors viewed as essential to the maintenance of state power, internal stability, and the structure that supports it, as well as of national wealth. An industry that could become an important source of political instability will be protected if it is inefficient in world markets, and in any case it will not be seriously tinkered with unless it is threatened with decline. An industry seen as potentially threatening to the established state structure will be constrained or even prohibited, regardless of the economic growth potential it provides.

Telecommunications and broadcasting are important to the state because of the role of communications in maintaining social cohesion and the importance of communications systems and technologies to national security and the rest of the economic system. Hence, statists view as natural a persistent government policy to promote the sector, including its protection against domination by foreigners or potentially disruptive internal groups. The purpose of government policy will be threefold: (1) to assure that the sector does not become a barrier to the development of other favored economic activities; (2) to promote developments that support the state's overall economic and political objectives; and (3) to make sure that the use of the communications network is consistent with the goal of promoting state social and cultural interests.

Superficially, privatization and deregulation appear inconsistent with statist doctrine; however, this is not necessarily the case. Both are consistent with state interests if the state is certain that forces supportive of the state will control them. A trend toward these policies, then, would be viewed as caused by increasing confidence by the state in the supportiveness of the groups that would control the sector.

Pluralist Theory

The pluralists might otherwise be regarded as a type of atomistic democratic theorist. Their focus is on the aggregations of individuals by economic interests, with explicit recognition that interests are in conflict and that different interests may be represented in the political system with differing degrees of effectiveness. As used here, the term refers to political theories that are individualistic (although they may never disaggregate the population further than by economic interest groups), that focus on the resolution of conflicts of interest, but that are stripped of significant attention to the role of most political institutions—as also are the two preceding theoretical schools.

Pluralists are also a heterogeneous lot, so this category should be viewed as quite loose. Some pluralists are antireductionist sociologists who would reject my calling this school individualistic, for they regard the disaggregation of interest groups into individual members as necessarily entailing a significant loss in the potential explanatory power of group behavior. Nevertheless, they would agree that the group acts to achieve self-interested ends for its members, and in this sense the theory is individualistic. Other pluralists are economists who build theories of group behavior by using game theory to analyze the interactions of members of the group (Olson 1965). Some pluralists also believe that the policy emanating from interest-group interactions has important normative significance—a political legitimacy arising from the legitimacy of the process that produced it, such as a democratic political process (Bentley 1908). Others take a less sanguine view, analyzing perversities of the solutions to interest-group games. These include Dahl (1982) and Lindblom (1977), who are explicitly pluralist; and Becker (1983), Peltzman (1976), and Stigler (1971), who exemplify the closely analogous Chicago school of public policy making.

The basic structure of pluralist theories is largely the same for all, and easily characterized. Each group in the political process can be viewed as receiving some payoff from every contemplated movement of public policy, and in particular of having a most desired direction for policy to move—the direction with the highest payoff to the group. In addition, each group has a cost of effective representation of its cause in the political process. These costs depend on the difficulty of organizing the group, getting its members to support group activities, and reaching a group consensus on how the group should act. Holding the total stakes of each group member constant, these costs should increase with the size and heterogeneity of interest of the group, because smaller groups face less difficulty in preventing some members from free-riding on others and in reaching agreement on the group's methods and objectives. The amount of political force a group can bring to bear on policy is then the difference between its stakes and its costs of maintaining cohesion. The policy outcome is the policy position where the forces being applied by all groups in different directions are mutually canceling. Hence, to measure the likely policy outcome, pluralist theory instructs us to measure the stakes, organization, membership, and effectiveness of the interests participating in the debate. And in particular, one group that can normally be ignored is the general public in the role of final consumer. The wealth and income side of each person's interests is more effectively organized than the expenditure side because of the diffuse, heterogeneous nature of the latter.

In terms of industrial policies, the pluralist school leads to the view that policy will work to preserve the existing sources and distribution of income, and to enhance the position of the groups already advantaged. This means relative passivity to expanding sectors, but protectionist interventions for contracting ones, especially if the latter are unionized and highly concentrated so that a few powerful, well-organized groups are exerting force on the political system. Applied to the communications sector, the outcome is not theoretically predetermined, for the sector has conflicting characteristics. It is rapidly expanding, so the welfare of existing interests is not usually threatened; however, it is also highly concentrated, and thus present workers and owners, especially if organized effectively, have a strong incentive to lobby for prohibitions against entry that will enable them to extract additional gains from expansion. The outcome, according to the pluralist view, should depend on the extent to which the sources of growing demand are organized to offset the demands of the industry for entry controls.

Another group that pluralists predict will have limited influence is foreign producers, because of their truncated opportunities for political participation. Free trade in an industry comes about only under two conditions: the industry is too poorly organized (or so advanced technically) that the net gains of working for protection (e.g., the difference between reduced sales by foreigners and the costs of obtaining political intervention) are not positive; or other, better organized industries with extensive foreign markets fear retaliation if the first industry is protected, and work to offset the political activities in support of protection. This would require some natural political or technical linkage between the two industries.

In the case of communications, the likely result is protection, especially if the most important linkage industries (computers, electronics) are weak, seek protection, and so do not have a big stake in foreign sales. Only a very inefficient communications sector, combined with a well-organized, long-suffering user group, could be expected to offset this protectionist tendency.

Institutionalist Theory

The new institutionalists take the position that the details of the political system—its rules and organization—matter in terms of the development of public policy. Like pluralists, institutionalist theories tend to be individualistic, seeing policy as the result of individual actions and as evaluated on the basis of individual effects. They also incorporate interest-group behavior into their models, and sometimes other, more general democratic forces (such as those outlined in atomistic democratic theories). But the key point is that the incentives and actions of groups and individuals are filtered through an explicit analysis of the effects of institutions. The defining idea of the school is that policy is the result of the incentives operating on political officials and that these incentives are the result of interactions between the political activities of constituents and the political institutions through which these activities must be channeled.

One focus of institutional analysis is the importance of the electoral system: the "electoral connection" between citizens and policy makers (Fiorina 1977; Fiorina and Noll 1979). The object of this analysis is to examine how the method of electing the government affects the way politicians make policy.

For simplicity, consider two questions concerning how the government is elected. One is the autonomy of the legislative and executive politicians. At one extreme, parliamentary systems do not have autonomous, independent legislative and executive branches; the parliament serves both functions, so the individual members cannot disassociate themselves from party and policy, whether of the government or of the opposition. At the other extreme is the U.S. government, with its separation of the legislative and executive branches (with separate elections) and further separation of the legislative branch into two coequal houses. Here, a legislator is independent of the executive, and, as one decision maker among many independent agents, can hardly be held accountable for the general state of policy emanating from government.

The second dimension of governmental structure is the nature of the constituencies from which legislators are elected. The extreme cases here are nationwide proportional representation and single-member geographic districts. In the former, voters cast ballots for parties, and parties run ordered lists of candidates for the legislature. The share of the party's representation is determined by its share of the total vote, and candidates on the party list are declared elected down to the point at which the party's legislative seats are exhausted. In the latter, each party nominates a candidate to fill a legislative seat representing a specific constituency. The ultimate winner can be either the candidate with a plurality of the vote in the first election or the eventual majority winner after a sequence of runoffs.

Both of these structural characteristics are illustrated in Figure 3.2, in which several legislative bodies are located for expositional purposes. The degree of legislative autonomy is the most difficult concept to grasp, and then to measure, for it depends on the rules governing the relationship between the branches of government. In France, for example, the branches are separate, but the legislature is relatively weak because the executive can dictate the legislative agenda. In most nations that practice separation of powers, the legislature controls its own agenda. Proposals from the executive branch have no standing unless introduced by a legislator; even then, they have no precedence over other proposals that have been introduced.

The significance of these factors is in the incentives and political behavior that they induce on voters and legislators. Generally, as a nation moves upward and to the right from the origin in Figure 3.2, the legislature is more likely to respond to pluralist demands for special-interest legislation. Under nationwide proportional representation, legislators do not receive personal votes; hence their ability to build an independent base of

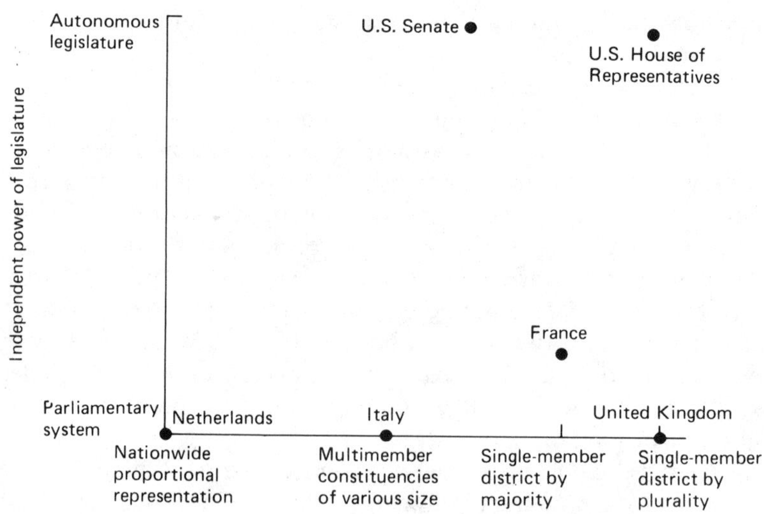

Figure 3.2 Method of election of parliamentarians

support—separate from the party—is vastly limited. Only at the level of the national party will interest groups gain recognition. And because specific industries or narrow economic interests are likely to be too small to provide a large enough electoral base to support a party, particularism is manifested through parties that represent either much larger affinity groups—labor, religious groups, ethnic groups, ideological groups—or broad coalitions of economic interests (Barry 1975). In contrast, the smallest support constituency for a legislator occurs in single-member districts in which elections are decided by plurality. Here, a legislator represents a tiny fraction of the total population and need not win even half the vote to be elected. At this level, narrow economic interests are far more likely to be the deciding force in legislative elections, as analyzed in Cox, McCubbins, and Sullivan (1983).

The significance of the autonomy dimension is in the ability of the legislature to carry out the preferred policies of its members against the wishes of the executive. In parliamentary systems, the conflict between the legislative and executive branches is minimized because the latter are chosen by the former, and in any case individual members have little opportunity to act autonomously. But an autonomous legislature representing narrow constituencies has the power and inclination to engage in distributional politics in the most particularistic form—as, for example, the famed "pork barrel" in the American legislature (Ferejohn 1974; Weingast, Shepsle, and Johnson 1981). Even in Great Britain, the structure of constituencies, despite the relative weakness of individual members, creates some opportunities for a legislator to develop an independent base of strength from the party through the British counterpart to pork barrel, called "dustbin" politics, as documented by Cain, Ferejohn, and Fiorina (1983).

In the pure pluralist model, the political equilibrium is for a degree of politics that actually reduces national income and wealth. The reason is that each group sees only its share of taxation as the cost of its favored program, but captures the full benefit. Interaction among interest groups seeking special favors, when modeled as a noncooperative game, leads to a prisoner's dilemma situation—an outcome in which all would be better off if no group received favors, but each group is better off joining the winning distributive coalition than attempting to undermine it. This situation is broken only when the degree of inefficiency of the distributive equilibrium is so great that the cost share of each group in its own program exceeds its benefits to that group (Weingast 1979), or when the national costs of distributive politics cause a political demand to alter the electoral institutions, such as a switch to proportional representation (Rogowski 1984). Because these are rather loose constraints, legislatures located in the upper-right-hand portion of Figure 3.2 will be relatively free to engage in highly inefficient distributive programs.

In contrast, party-list legislators and separately elected chief executives must win a large national coalition. Consequently, they have less of an incentive to engage in distributive politics. The reason is that national elections, whether presidential elections or nationwide proportional representation, force candidates and parties to offer simultaneously an entire package of distributive programs that voters must accept or reject as an entirety. This places a far more stringent constraint on the degree of inefficiency of the package: The tax share of the party's coalition must be smaller for all programs together than each group's particular benefit from its own program.

The resolution of the conflict between national political interests, represented by coalitions, parties, and chief executives, and particularistic interests, represented by autonomous legislators who represent narrow constituencies, is decided by the relative power of the two forces. Hence the rationale for the conclusion that the least degree of distributive politics is found in systems located at the origin of Figure 3.2.

Protection of industry, whether through international trade barriers or internal barriers to competition and free entry, is an example of distributive politics. It provides income and wealth to the favored economic interest, but reduces production efficiency. Consequently, the extent to which an industry-specific policy becomes protectionist should depend on the political structure of thc country. The same telecommunications industry organization, for example, should produce distinctly different results in, say, the United States, France, and the Netherlands. Moreover, if change does occur in the direction of less protectionism, its source is more likely to be in the executive branch and among party leaders than among legislators in any country in which legislative constituencies are relatively small. For example, in the United States, both Democrat Jimmy Carter and Republican Ronald Reagan were instigators of economic deregulation, and in both cases moved substantially faster than Congress wanted or would have done on its own (Derthick and Quirk 1985). The engine of change was executive appointments to regulatory bureaus and executive court actions, like the AT&T antitrust case.

The second institutional factor affecting policy is organizational: the forms of the organizations that connect policy makers to private industry. In part, this was discussed above in the analysis of the economic structure of the industry. The political system can exercise maximal control when political actors actually run an industry, as with ministerial public enterprise. This is an example of a more general phenomenon: The ability of the political process to direct economic activity in any area is greatest if the connection between elected officials and the industry's decision makers is direct and does not need to be mediated through another organization, such as a regulatory agency or some other bureau comprised of professional mediators, such as trade associations. Another example, besides ministerial public enterprise, is corporatism as practiced in some European countries and in some Japanese industries. Here, government ministries possess the means to control or at least strongly to influence private decisions (such as in controlling credit or the allocation of research) and implement their plans through direct contact with officials of industry. This, of course, is a more attenuated form of control than a ministerial public enterprise. Corporatism is closer in form to an independent public enterprise that must have important elements of its budget approved by the political system (such as the Tennessee Valley Authority or the U.S. Postal Service).

When intermediating organizations are present, the degree of political control over the target industry depends on the structural features of the intermediating agency. Several factors influence whether the intermediating agency transmits government policy effectively, acts relatively independently of either government or the private sector, or serves largely as a conduit for the interests of the target industry (Noll 1983).

1. Is the authority of the agency narrowly defined in law, or does it have a broad instruction to develop policy in an ill-defined public interest? Vague mandates invite autonomous bureaus or capture by the private sector.
2. Who runs the organization, and how are the leaders appointed? Do they serve at the pleasure of political leaders (or private groups), or are they long-term, secure employees, such as career civil servants or judges? The latter invites independence, and the development of policy according to the professional norms of the kinds of people who populate the agency.
3. What procedures must the organization follow for reaching decisions? Does it bear a difficult burden of proof, or can it act relatively freely of evidentiary requirements? Are its processes open to participation by anyone, or are they closed to groups strongly affected by them, or perhaps even to everyone other than the target industry? Generally, a high evidentiary burden and a relatively open process favor autonomy; a high evidentiary burden and a closed process favor industry (because only industry can supply the evidence needed to support a decision); and a low evidentiary burden makes the process more unpredictable.
4. Does the intermediating agency possess rich or poor resources relative to the scope of its authority? Understaffed organizations are obviously going to be more dependent on outsiders for direction.
5. What is the nature of formal, external review of the role of the mediator? Is the organization advisory to political actors, to industry, or to both? Is it decisive, but subject to extensive judicial review? Or is the only check on decisions the response of the political process to its performance? These alternatives are ordered according to increasing

autonomy, of course; the nature of the review will determine whether it tips in favor of political control or industry control. Industry, for example, is likely to benefit from extensive reviews—unless the opposition is well organized, such as is the case in matters of environmental policy. But in communications policy in a setting of monopolistic supply, opposition is not likely to be well organized, so extensive external review opportunities will favor the monopolistic supplier.

In summary, the organizational aspects of institutional analysis deal with the extent to which pluralist and other politically effective interests can attain their ends for reasons related to the structure of the relevant decision-making environment. Of course, political actors probably are in some sense aware of these distinctions; hence their choice of an institutional mechanism for implementing policy will also reflect the political forces giving rise to policy (Fiorina 1985; McCubbins 1985). To undertake a protectionist policy, but to implement it through an independent organization staffed by, say, economists practicing a norm of efficiency, is to attenuate vastly the protectionist bent of the process. Indeed, in the United States, precisely such a move was undertaken in the 1930s when economists in the U.S. Treasury were given a key role in determining tariffs (Goldstein 1983). Thus it would be a mistake to think of these organizational factors as completely independent in affecting policy. But, for analytical purposes, categorizing them separately serves a useful function for understanding how the existing institutional structure is likely to push policy.

CONCLUDING OBSERVATIONS ABOUT COMMUNICATIONS

Suppose that the topic of interest to policy analysis is to examine institutional alternatives in terms of their contributions to national objectives as the latter emerge from democratic or statist theories, but in a setting in which pluralist forces are at work, though with varying degrees of impact owing to institutional factors. We can then offer some hypotheses about how communications policies might evolve and perform using the theoretical perspectives offered in the previous section.

Communications is a relatively important sector from both the democratic and statist perspective because individual users derive so much economic well-being from these activities; because telecommunications especially is important to the development of other sectors of the economy; and because of the role of communications in serving noneconomic national objectives. Thus, from a pluralist perspective, the sector is more likely than others to be the focus of significant political attention from groups other than the suppliers of services. One would not expect a pure protectionist policy to be stable, given the importance of the sector.

Nevertheless, the communications sector tends to be highly concentrated and well organized, so it, too, should be a potent political force. Because history has brought us to a position of relatively high concentration, movements toward less centralized control must overcome considerable political inertia. How fast this takes place depends on three things: (1) the extent to which a less centralized regime actually serves interests other than those of the supply side; (2) the institutional structure in which change is taking place; and (3) whether telecommunications can be tied into a currently salient general political issue.

A discussion of the economic and technical merits of decentralized control is beyond the scope of this chapter, except to cite the nature of the debate. The technical argument for centralized control is economies of scale and scope: Costs allegedly will be lower and service better if production is centralized. The opposing argument is that in most advanced countries the size and diversity of demand for communications services has long since passed the point at which it is provided most effectively through a centralized structure. More diversity of supply, it is argued, will cause services to be better tailored to specific user needs, and will enhance innovation, so any possible economies of centralization will be more than offset.

Suppose that the argument for greater diversity is technically correct, so that, on balance, democratic, statist, and other pluralist forces will favor it. Then the following *ceteris paribus* hypotheses should flow from some combination of the four theoretical models described here.

1. The speed of reform should be greater in nations with relatively advanced sectors that make extensive use of the telecommunications system and that are relatively concentrated or otherwise politically well organized. For example, nations with strong computer industries should move toward reform more rapidly than nations relying almost completely on imported computers.
2. The speed of the reform should be more rapid in countries in which the performance of the industry is least efficient, thereby imposing the greatest cost to users. Of course, in the real world the *ceteris paribus* element is likely to be violated between this and the first hypothesis; countries with highly progressive computer and electronics industries usually have very advanced communications systems that encourage these developments. Nevertheless, the independent effects of an advanced user industry and an advanced supplier industry ought to be in the opposite direction.
3. The speed of reform should occur more rapidly in countries in which reorganization to improve the performance of the domestic economy is, in some form, a salient political issue.
4. Countries that are most vulnerable to their position in international trade should evolve more quickly in the direction of efficient reform, as

should countries in which there is the strongest demand for national identity, whether expressed as social cohesion or a strong national defense.

5. Politicians with national constituencies ought to view reform more favorably than leaders with localized constituencies. Thus, in countries with independent executive and legislative branches, the executive branch ought to be more reformist; meanwhile, legislatures composed of representatives from separate geographic constituencies ought to be the most reluctant to change.
6. In countries with strong, independent legislators, reform should be more effective the greater is the distance of the legislature from the details of communications policy making, attenuating particularistic control by pluralist forces. In all societies, creating an intermediating technical bureaucracy between the government and the telecommunications sector should produce a more efficient industry than would a structure in which political control is exercised through direct contacts between political leaders and industry decision makers.

More generally, the problem of developing effective national interventions by governments at the level of industries and companies is more severe in relatively self-sufficient, diverse societies and in nations with political structures that tend to fragment decision making among political leaders with separate constituencies. Effective regulation or industrial policy, therefore, ought to be more difficult in Britain or the United States than, say, in Japan, with West Germany and France in intermediate positions. (But for the same reasons, other forms of policies—infrastructural investments, for example—should flourish more in the former.)

These hypotheses provide some insight into why communications was ripe for reform circa 1980. A favorable political climate was created by disruptions in trade and by the deterioration in the economies of advanced industrialized states that began in the 1970s. This gave rise to structural reorganization of the institutions controlling the economy as a salient political issue. At the same time, the microelectronics revolution substantially increased the demand for communications services, as well as the supply of new, more efficient equipment to provide them. Both factors undermine the political ability of supply organizations, whether private corporations or public monopolies, to maintain protectionist policies.

The first condition contributing to the reform environment is far more likely to disappear than the second. A restoration of economic stability and growth would cause the issue of national economic management to slip on the list of salient national political issues. But the relatively balanced conflict between users and suppliers in the communications sector will remain. This conflict should work toward efficient performance as long as the institutional structure makes use of the conflict to guide policy. The primary threat is that the competing interests will reach accommodation and present a united front through merger or a cartel-like agreement. Such a threat is most likely to emerge, again, in relatively self-sufficient, diverse economies with decentralized political systems that maximize pluralist influence.

REFERENCES

Aron, Raymond. *Peace and War*. Garden City, N.Y.: Doubleday, 1966.

Arrow, Kenneth J. *Social Choice and Individual Values*. New York: Wiley, 1951.

Barry, Brian. "Review Article: Political Accommodation and Consociational Democracy." *British Journal of Political Science* 5 (1975): 477–505.

Baumol, William J. *Business Behavior, Value and Growth*. Orlando, Fla.: Harcourt Brace Jovanovich, 1967.

Becker, Gary S. "A Theory of Competition among Pressure Groups for Political Influence." *Quarterly Journal of Economics* 98 (1983): 371–400.

Bentley, Arthur F. *The Process of Government*. Chicago: University of Chicago Press, 1908.

Bergson, Abram. *Essays in Normative Economics*. Cambridge, Mass.: Harvard University Press, 1966.

Breyer, Stephen. *Regulation and Its Reform*. Cambridge, Mass.: Harvard University Press, 1982.

Brock, Gerald W. *The Telecommunications Industry*. Cambridge, Mass.: Harvard University Press, 1981.

Buchanan, James M., and Gordon Tullock. *The Calculus of Consent*. Ann Arbor, Mich.: University of Michigan Press, 1962.

Cain, Bruce E., John A. Ferejohn, and Morris P. Fiorina. "The Constituency Component: A Comparison of Service in Great Britain and in the United States." *Comparative Political Studies* 16 (1983): 67–91.

Cox, Gary W., Mathew D. McCubbins, and Terry Sullivan. "Policy and Constituency: Reelection Incentives and the Choice of Policy Intervention." *Working Papers on Institutional Design and Public Policy*. WP-02. Department of Government, University of Texas, May 1983.

Dahl, Robert. *Dilemmas of Pluralist Democracy*. New Haven, Conn.: Yale University Press, 1982.

Dahl, Robert, and Charles E. Lindblom. *Politics, Economics and Welfare*. Chicago: University of Chicago Press, 1976.

Derthick, Martha, and Paul J. Quirk. "Why the Regulators Chose to Deregulate." In *Regulatory Policy and the Social Sciences*, edited by Roger G. Noll. Berkeley, Calif.: University of California Press, 1985.

Downs, Anthony. *An Economic Theory of Democracy*. New York: Harper & Row, 1957.

———. *Inside Bureaucracy*. Boston: Little, Brown, 1967.

Duvall, Raymond D., and John R. Freeman. "The Techno-Bureaucratic Elite and the Entrepreneurial State in Dependent Industrialization." *American Political Science Review* 77 (1983): 569–587.

Eckstein, Harry. "On the 'Science' of the State." *Daedalus* 108 (1979): 1–20.

Feldstein, Martin S. "Equity and Efficiency in Public Pricing." *Quarterly Journal of Economics* 86 (1972): 175–187.

Ferejohn, John A. *Pork Barrel Politics*. Palo Alto, Calif.: Stanford University Press, 1974.

Fiorina, Morris P. *Congress: Keystone of the Washington Establishment*. New Haven, Conn.: Yale University Press, 1977.

———. "Group Concentration and the Delegation of Legislative Authority." In *Regulatory Policy and the Social Sciences*, edited by Roger G. Noll. Berkeley, Calif.: University of California Press, 1985.

Fiorina, Morris P., and Roger G. Noll. "Majority Rule Models and Legislative Elections." *Journal of Politics* 41 (1979): 1081–1104.

Friedman, Milton. *Capitalism and Freedom*. Chicago: University of Chicago Press, 1981.

Gilpin, Robert. *War and Change in International Politics*. New York: Cambridge University Press, 1981.

Goldstein, Judith. "A Reexamination of American Trade Policy: An Inquiry into the Causes of Protectionism." Ph.D. dissertation, University of California, Los Angeles, 1983.

Howard, Michael. "War and the Nation-State." *Daedalus* 108 (1979): 101–110.

Johnson, Harry. *International Trade and Economic Growth*. Cambridge, Mass.: Harvard University Press, 1967.

Katzenstein, Peter J., ed. *Between Power and Plenty: Foreign Economic Policies of Advanced Industrial States*. Special issue of *International Organization* 31 (1977).

Klein, Burton H. *Dynamic Economics*. Cambridge, Mass.: Harvard University Press, 1977.

Krasner, Stephen D. "State Power and the Structure of International Trade." *World Politics* 28 (1976): 317–347.

Lindblom, Charles E. *Politics and Markets*. New York: Basic Books, 1977.

Lukes, Steven. *Power: A Radical View*. New York: Macmillan, 1974.

McCubbins, Mathew. "Regulating the Regulators: A Theory of Legislative Delegation." *American Journal of Political Science* (1985).

McKelvey, Richard. "General Conditions for Global Intransitivities in Formal Voting Models." *Econometrics* 47 (1979): 1085–1111.

Mahon, Rianne, and Lynn Krieger Mytelka. "Industry, the State and the New Protectionism: Textiles in Canada and France." *International Organizations* 37 (1983): 551–582.

Manley, John. "Neopluralism: A Class Analysis of Pluralism I and Pluralism II." *American Political Science Review* 77 (1983): 368–383.

Mansfield, Edwin. *The Production and Application of New Industrial Technology*. New York: Norton, 1977.

Martin, Andrew. "The Dynamics of Change in Keynesian Political Economy." In *State and Economy in Contemporary Capitalism*, edited by Colin Crouch. London: Croom Helm, 1979.

Morgenthau, Hans. *Politics among Nations*. New York: Knopf, 1948.

Nelson, Richard R., and Sidney G. Winter. *An Evolutionary Theory of Economic Change*. Cambridge, Mass.: Harvard University Press, 1982.

Niskanen, William. *Bureaucracy and Representative Government*. Chicago: Aldine, 1971.

Noll, Roger. "The Political Foundations of Regulatory Policy." *Zeitschrift für die gesamte Staatswissenschaft* 139 (1983): 377–404.

Noll, Roger, and Bruce M. Owen. *The Political Economy of Deregulation*. Washington, D.C.: American Enterprise Institute, 1983.

North, Douglass C. *Structure and Change in Economic History*. New York: Norton, 1981.

Olson, Mancur. *The Logic of Collective Action*. Cambridge, Mass.: Harvard University Press, 1965.

Peltzman, Sam. "Toward a More General Theory of Regulation." *Journal of Law and Economics* 19 (1976): 211–240.

Polsby, Nelson. *Community Power and Political Theory*. New Haven, Conn.: Yale University Press, 1980.

Rawls, John. *A Theory of Justice*. Cambridge, Mass.: Harvard University Press, 1971.

Reinganum, Jennifer F. "Practical Implications of Game Theory Models of R&D." *American Economics Review Papers and Proceedings* 74 (1984): 61–66.

Riker, William H. *Liberalism against Populism*. San Francisco: Freeman, 1982.

Rogowski, Ronald. "Some Possible Effects of Trade and War on Representative Institutions and Party Systems." Department of Political Science, University of California, Los Angeles, 1984. Mimeo.

Samuelson, Paul A. "The Pure Theory of Public Expenditure." *Review of Economics and Statistics* 36 (1954): 387–389.

Stigler, George J. "The Theory of Economic Regulation." *Bell Journal of Economics* 2 (1971): 3–21.

Tilly, Charles, ed. *The Formation of Nation States in Western Europe*. Princeton, N.J.: Princeton University Press, 1975.

Weingast, Barry. "A Rational Choice Perspective on Congressional Norms." *American Journal of Political Science* 24 (1979): 245–263.

Weingast, Barry, Kenneth Shepsle, and Christopher Johnson. "The Political Economy of Benefits and Costs." *Journal of Political Economy* 89 (1981): 642–664.

Wildavsky, Aaron. *The Politics of the Budgetary Process*. Boston: Little, Brown, 1964.

Willig, Robert D., and Elizabeth E. Bailey. "Income Distributional Concerns in Regulatory Policy-Making." In *Studies in Public Regulation*, edited by Gary Fromm. Cambridge, Mass.: MIT Press, 1981.

PART 2

A Survey of Telecommunications Policy in Seven Countries

Four

Deregulation, Divestiture, and Competition in U.S. Telecommunications: Lessons for Other Countries

Alan Baughcum

This chapter is divided into six sections.

The first section reviews recent actions by the FCC in deregulating or "unregulating" terminal equipment, long-distance services, and the U.S. portions of international telecommunications markets. The roles of Congress and the states are discussed, particularly as they have affected the development of access charges.

Next comes a section containing a history of the divestiture of AT&T, including the 1956 Consent Decree and the 1982 Modified Final Judgment. This is followed by a discussion of attempts by Congress, beginning in the mid-1970s, to pass telecommunications legislation. By early 1984, both houses of Congress had passed legislation. Action by the FCC in postponing the imposition of access charges resulted in the suspension of congressional attempts at lawmaking in the telecommunications arena.

The succeeding section describes, in summary form, the current status of U.S. telecommunications markets in equipment, interstate services, and intrastate services. Next comes a section with observations on U.S. telecommunications for the purpose of drawing lessons for other countries. The critical nature of technology in eroding entry barriers is emphasized. Policymakers must deal with increasingly competitive telecommunications markets.

The last section is a summary of the chapter. It documents the institutional uniqueness of U.S. telecommunications, yet suggests that the general trend toward more competitive markets will leave no country's telecommunications industry unchanged. Finally, the appendix reviews the history of U.S. regulation in broadcasting and cable.

THE FEDERAL COMMUNICATIONS COMMISSION AND DEREGULATION

In general, the Federal Communications Commission (FCC) has moved consistently in recent years to open markets to competition. By making it easier to interconnect with the Bell network, by opening the long-distance market to competition, and by attempting to allow AT&T to enter the computer market, the FCC has endeavored to eliminate significant barriers to entry. Congress has expressed concern about the effects of such deregulation; that concern has delayed the imposition of access charges, which is vital to industry restructuring. Moreover, the FCC's requirement that AT&T enter unregulated markets through separate subsidiaries may have reduced overall market efficiency. Detailed discussions of this history can be found in Baughcum and Faulhaber (1985), Brock (1981), Meyer (1980), and U.S. Congress, House (1981).

The FCC's attempts to "unregulate" the U.S. portion of international communications markets has raised concerns on the part of European PTTs and INTELSAT. Developments in this sector are simply a reflection of the same forces that have moved U.S. communications markets toward competition. Nonetheless, just as with Congress in the domestic arena, there are institutional pressures attempting to slow this movement.

Deregulation as a policy issue in the United States is now moving into the jurisdiction of state regulatory commissions. Already, several states have allowed the certification of non-telco and non-AT&T companies for the provision of interLATA communications services. State regulatory commissions (and legislatures) must also consider the extent to which intraLATA competition will be permitted.

This section considers these developments in turn. Detailed discussions of this history can be found in Baughcum and Faulhaber (1985), Brock (1981), Meyer et al. (1980), and U.S. Congress, House (1981).

Terminal Equipment

Traditionally, major telephone companies in the United States have been vertically integrated. In particular, AT&T owned Western Electric, which produced, purchased, and warehoused the majority of equipment purchased by Bell operating companies. Similarly, GT&E and United owned their own suppliers, Automatic Electric and Northern Electric, respectively. The equipment provided to the telephone companies encompassed not only network switching and transmission equipment but also the telephone instruments and PBXs typically offered to residential and business customers.

Under traditional regulation, the telephone company tariffs limited terminal attachments to company-provided, leased equipment. In 1955, the FCC refused to permit Hush-A-Phone Corporation to sell cuplike devices that attached to telephones in order to provide privacy to the speaker. Decisions by the D.C. District Court of Appeals over the next 2 years instructed the commission to consider subscribers' rights to use the telephone as long as the exercise of those rights was not harmful to the public at large.

The next 20 years saw the FCC consider issues such as the following: the Bell tariff restricting customers' use of a device to connect an ordinary telephone to a mobile radio transmitter; the FCC's conclusion that the tariff was unreasonably discriminatory; and the FCC's order instructing AT&T to file tariffs allowing customers to attach devices to the network that did not actually cause harm to the network. Bell was allowed to specify technical standards for interconnecting equipment. The FCC instituted a registration program to approve interconnect equipment for network attachment. It was not until 1978 that court challenges to this registration program at the FCC were finally cleared away. Indeed, it was only in early 1984 that the U.S. Supreme Court upheld a lower court's decision awarding $278 million in damages to Litton resulting from Bell's imposition of tariffs requiring so-called protective interface devices.

Basically, the FCC preempted state regulation of the interconnection of FCC-registered terminal equipment. By the late 1970s, the FCC had effectively created markets for interconnect equipment vendors in providing residential telephones and in providing key systems and PBXs to businesses.

The FCC, in its *Computer II* decision, ordered that local service and terminal equipment charges be itemized separately and required that AT&T offer new terminal equipment through a separate subsidiary. Separation was required in order to restrict AT&T from using its monopoly power in regulated markets to provide unfair or anticompetitive advantages over its competitors in unregulated markets.

It is somewhat surprising that the FCC would order that AT&T enter unregulated markets through a separate subsidiary. The concern about misuse of monopoly power can be traced to the classic Averch–Johnson (1962) model. However, there is no analytical basis to believe that a change in organizational form will counter the efficiency distortions of rate-base/rate-of-return regulation. Indeed, the very existence of AT&T's monopoly power in the long-distance market can be questioned when the FCC is actively engaged in eliminating entry barriers in that market. Fisher, Greenwood, and McGowan (1983) demonstrate conclusively that such market power depends on the presence of entry barriers. Another approach is taken by Willig (1985), who argues that the presence of even one *potential* competitor can assure competitive results under certain circumstances. The long-distance market does not lack for competitors.

It is possible to develop methods that will encourage regulated firms to perform efficiently (e.g., to price on the basis of cost). For example, Baughcum and McGowan (1982) propose a method for transferring customer premises equipment out of the rate base to the unregulated market that encourages efficient behavior without the probably significant costs associated with traditional regulation or with constraints on organizational form. The key ingredient is to utilize the forces of the market, typically by reducing or eliminating entry barriers, to price or value products and services even in traditionally protected markets.

The requirement that AT&T operate through a separate subsidiary may be seen as a political solution to the alleged fears of AT&T competitors. More cynically, the requirement that AT&T operate through a fully separate subsidiary adds significant costs to that firm's operation. Not the least of those costs were delays of 1 to 2 years in AT&T's ability to function in terminal equipment markets. A major effect of such restriction has been to hamper AT&T's timely entry into competitive markets, at the same time making it easier for competitors to increase their market shares. The effect on the consumer has probably been some loss in price and quality that would have been present had AT&T been free to move more quickly or flexibly in serving the market.

Long Distance

Just as with terminal equipment markets, AT&T has traditionally held a monopoly in domestic long-distance communications markets. In 1959, however, the FCC issued its *Above 890* decision granting private microwave systems access to a dedicated portion of the radio spectrum and allowing the construction of such systems regardless of their economic effects on the established common carrier.

AT&T, responding to the prospect that large users might build their own microwave facilities, filed new tariffs, effectively discounting services to those users. TELPAK reduced private-line rates for bulk lease of channels. WATS (Wide Area Telecommunications Service) offered reduced rates to large users of long-distance voice services.

A combination of these reduced rates and regulatory slowness in dealing with entry applications delayed the opening of long-distance markets until the 1970s. In 1963, Microwave Communications Inc. (now MCI) filed to seek authorization to operate as a specialized common carrier (SCC) offering private-line service between St. Louis and Chicago. The FCC, in its 1971 *Specialized Common Carrier* decision, ordered a policy of allowing entry of new carriers into this specialized communications field. The FCC also opened entry into domestic satellite communications in its 1972 *Domsat* decision. (As with the later *Computer II* decision, the FCC handicapped AT&T by excluding it from the market for 3 years.) The early 1970s also saw the FCC authorizing entry of value-added carriers, firms that leased facilities and enhanced basic channel capacity to provide additional service features.

MCI later sought to offer Execunet, a service equivalent to message telephone service (MTS). The FCC sought to restrict MCI to the service allowed in its SCC decision. The courts overturned this restriction as an attempt to grant AT&T a monopoly in the long-distance market without undertaking proceedings to determine that such a monopoly was in the public interest. By 1978 the FCC, in its MTS/WATS proceeding, effectively found that competition in intercity message markets was in the public interest.

The next few years saw several additional deregulatory moves by the FCC. In Docket No. 97–252, it effectively exempted telecommunications services provided by the new competitive carriers such as MCI, Southern Pacific Communications, and other SCCs. In October 1980, the FCC also extended the provision of resale and shared use of private lines to the public switched network.

The FCC has yet to open the long-distance market completely to deregulation. Plans are under consideration, however, as to how this might best be accomplished. Hesitation in allowing complete deregulation seems to rest on the notion that there are firms possessing market power that must be constrained in order to protect the competitive process. In particular, AT&T was required in the FCC's *Second Computer Inquiry* decision in 1980 to offer "enhanced" communications services (and terminal equipment) through a fully separated subsidiary.

The FCC, in its CC Docket No. 93–1147, is examining the long-run regulation of AT&T's domestic interstate services. AT&T recently filed a request in that docket for regulatory forbearance, which included lifting tariff regulation, facilities regulation, and rate-of-return regulation. AT&T argues that the development of a competitive long-distance service market makes traditional regulation unnecessary.

Restrictions on AT&T and the hesitation to open markets fully to competition may be traced to many factors. It may be that such regulations result from the desire of competitors such as MCI to protect themselves from complete competition while they attempt to build networks and a market share. More charitably, regulations may reflect a genuine concern on the part of policy makers that consumers will not benefit from unfettered competition between an elephant (AT&T) and several mice (AT&T competitors).

Unfortunately, economic analysis has been misused in deliberations regarding telecommunications deregulation. Economists have documented the large share of AT&T in long-distance markets and in the existing base of terminal equipment. Whether measured by traditional concentration ratios, Herfindahl indices, or Lerner indices, telecommunications markets seem to exhibit a concentrated market structure consistent with market power on the part of "dominant" firms. Such calculations encourage a cautious policy toward deregulation.

However, such calculations are valid, if at all, only if these static measures of market characteristics are likely to persist. It is the essence of telecommunications markets that technology is rapidly eliminating distinctions between markets, industries, and lines of business. Static measures simply cannot capture the richness of this Schumpeterian "creative destruction." Policy based on such static measures will probably be counterproductive and will not facilitate an adjustment to efficient markets.

International Regulation

International telecommunications regulation differs from domestic regulation in several ways. First, voice and nonvoice communications have been more segmented in international markets; second, markets have been segmented by technology (e.g., satellite and cable); and third, international markets depend heavily for their regulation on the actions of independent nation-states. Nonetheless, international regulation is similar to domestic regulation in that the United States has tended toward deregulation with restrictions on major common carriers.

Before 1962, AT&T provided voice services, and IRCs (international record carriers) provided nonvoice services, both over submarine cables. In 1962, Congress established the Communications Satellite Corporation (Comsat) to act as a carriers' carrier with regard to the provision of satellite channels for international telecommunications service. INTELSAT was formed to create a global satellite system.

In 1976, the FCC issued an order permitting AT&T to offer Dataphone service in the international market. Dataphone is a service permitting users to employ message toll telephone service to send data, facsimile, and other record traffic with the use of appropriate terminal equipment. In 1979, the FCC's *Datel* decision removed a comparable restriction on voice traffic over IRC facilities by allowing voice as a permissive or secondary use. Also in 1979, the *Gateways* decision of the FCC permitted expansion of the IRCs' direct record service to additional U.S. cities.

In the same year, the FCC allowed Western Union to offer overseas record services in the form of telex service to Canada and Mexico. (It actually took congressional legislation to allow Western Union into international markets.) The FCC required that IRCs be allowed to interconnect with domestic telex services and required carriers to unbundle their rates.

Three developments at the FCC have been especially disturbing to international observers. First, in the FCC's *Notice of Proposed Rulemaking for International Resale and Shared Use of Services and Facilities,* the FCC has considered extending the resale and shared use of private lines leased for international service. Second, the FCC, in its *Second Computer Inquiry,* has extended the effect of its decision to international service. Apparently, foreign administrations worry that the deregulation of enhanced services will effectively permit resale and shared use. Additionally, the basic–enhanced dichotomy created by the FCC seems to create differences in ISDN configurations in the United States vis-à-vis the rest of the world. Finally, the United States is considering the applications of several private companies, including Orion Satellite and ISI, for orbital slots to provide international satellite capacity and service between the United States and Europe. Foreign administrations, Comsat, and INTELSAT have objected that this contravenes their previous understanding of the U.S. commitment to a single global satellite system. A White House statement in late 1984 gave qualified approval to such competition with INTELSAT.

In short, the United States has adopted measures that extend competition to international service markets and is considering additional measures that are opposed by most foreign administrations.

Access Charges and Congress

The history of access charges is now several years old and continuing. It is a history involving Congress, state commissioners, AT&T and its competitors, and the FCC. Because the history is complex, this account proceeds chronologically so that the reader can develop a feel for the multitude of interests at work, as well as the time-consuming nature of the political process.

On December 22, 1982, the FCC adopted access-charge rules, originally scheduled to become effective on January 1, 1984. By that time, local carriers were to bill interexchange carriers and end users for access to the local exchange for interstate and international calls. For a legal history, see Bruce (1985).

The FCC defined access costs as "costs assessed by local telephone companies for the use of their facilities to originate and terminate interstate calls." These costs "encompass all services and facilities that will be included in the rates to be filed by the new Bell Operating Companies for the origination and termination of interstate calls."

The FCC listed four goals that the access-charge plan should satisfy: (1) continued assurance of universal service; (2) elimination of unjust discrimination or unlawful preferential rates; (3) network efficiency; and (4) prevention of uneconomic bypass.

The FCC divided costs into two categories: non-traffic-sensitive (NTS) charges and traffic-sensitive charges. NTS charges do not vary with usage. They include customer premises equipment, inside wiring, outside wiring, subscriber loop plant, and costs assigned to interstate service for a universal service fund. The universal service fund is "designed to ensure continued availability of quality telephone service in high-cost and rural areas."

In the first year, the FCC's rules would impose NTS access charges on both customers and interstate carriers. The customer charges, which account for about $4.3 billion in the first year, average $4 per customer line. These charges will be collected by local telephone companies through a combination of flat and usage-based charges subject to two rules: (1) the flat-rate portion must be at least $2 for residential rate payers and $4 for businesses; and (2) the maximum bill must not exceed the private-line rate. In the first year, interstate carriers will pay about $4.2 billion in access charges. About $1.4 billion will be charged to AT&T for premium access. (The $1.4 billion was chosen, apparently, as an administrative convenience. It happens to equal 1984 customer premises equipment costs.) The remaining costs will be collected from all carriers utilizing access services, based on their volume of usage.

After the first year, carriers will continue to pay NTS access charges for the universal service fund. Carriers will also be assessed NTS charges for CPE and inside wiring (total 1984 costs—$1.6 billion) if they are not removed from regulated service.

The remaining carrier charges in the first year plus additional costs due to inflation, additions to plant, or other factors will be converted to customer charges over a 5-year period. In particular, the FCC defines a residual requirement (per line) as

$$\begin{aligned}\text{Residual} = {} & \text{Total Revenue Requirement} - \$4 \\ & - (\text{CPE} + \text{Universal Service Factor} \\ & + \text{Inside Wiring})\end{aligned}$$

All of the residual will be charged to carriers in the first year. In subsequent years, the proportion of the residual charged to carriers will be reduced by 20 percentage points per year, and will thus be phased out at the end of the fifth year. Over the same period, the maximum that can be charged to any specific customer will be reduced by 10% per year. At the end of the seventh year, all customer access charges must be flat-rate charges.

Traffic-sensitive charges will be assessed for interstate carriers, based on costs generated by three categories of plant and equipment: (1) dedicated facilities to access local plant; (2) common network trunk facilities and associated equipment used for both long-distance and local access; and (3) originating and terminating central office equipment.

The revenue requirements for the traffic-sensitive charges are $2.5 to $3 billion in 1984. These charges will be per-minute charges, calculated from revenue requirements and total minutes of usage estimates. Two categories of traffic-sensitive charges are specified: Category 1 (FX/CCSA, ENFIA-A, and ENFIA-C services); and Category 2 (MTS, WATS, and ENFIA-B services).

On July 28, 1983, the FCC voted to allow local telephone companies to charge residential customers a *maximum* of $2 per month in 1984 for each telephone line connected to a long-distance service. The maximum residential access charge would be raised to $3 and then $4 per month, per line, in 1985 and 1986 and would continue to be phased in until 1989, when it would equal an estimated national average of $5.42 in 1983 dollars.

This reduction in previously proposed residential access charges was made possible by increasing business telephone customer access line charges (CALC) to $6 per month in 1984 (or less if the full cost of their connection is less). All business customers would be paying their full connection costs by 1986.

In August 1983 the FCC issued a memorandum opinion and order in its reconsideration of the access charge decision in Docket No. 78–72 Phase II. The major item of interest in that order was the FCC's calculation of the premium access charge to be levied on providers of traditional message-toll and wide-area telephone services (e.g., AT&T). The FCC eliminated the premium access charge to be paid by AT&T as a "separate rate element." Instead of this charge, the FCC specified the factors to be applied to the relevant minutes of nonpremium usage in order to compute the differential between AT&T and other common carrier (OCC) per-minute line charges.

The FCC determined that the differential reflecting the competitive advantages of premium access between the per-minute charges assessed AT&T and the other common carriers was 35%. This 35% differential was a less generous discount than the OCCs had received under previous regulation. The differential is valued at $2.17 billion and, according to the FCC, should be identical to the amount that a hypothetical nonpremium carrier having AT&T's market share would be willing to pay to become the premium carrier.

The FCC has focused on costs that could be avoided by a carrier that has premium access and on the revenue loss that would result if AT&T were not able to offer its customers superior-quality communications as a result of inferior access. The estimate of the value of the premium differential stemmed largely from estimates of the cost of conversion if all Bell rotary telephones were converted to touch tone operation ($275–408 million annually) and the value of the technical superiority of AT&T interconnections itself (between $432 million and $1.08 billion).

The FCC declared that the premium charge should be phased out at the same rate at which equal interconnection is provided. In the event that the schedule set by Judge Harold H. Greene in the Modification of Final Judgment (MFJ) for the BOCs' offerings of equal access proves to be too ambitious for these companies to achieve, the FCC set up "default differentials." According to the FCC, the default differential on the MFJ schedule should be 23% for 1985, 12% from January 1 to August 31, 1986, and zero thereafter.

On October 3, 1983, AT&T filed with the FCC for the largest telecommunications rate reduction in history. AT&T reported that the new rates would save users $2 billion in 1984. Accompanying the filing were statements by AT&T officers that the proposed congressional action to delay or eliminate access charges would force AT&T to revise its plans to cut interstate rates, which it hoped to put into effect on January 1, 1984.

The rates filed by AT&T would reduce MTS by 10.5%. A 75-cent interstate directory assistance charge for MTS and outward WATS provided by AT&T was introduced with an allowance for one free call per month. AT&T's WATS usage rates were proposed to be reduced 10.7%. Private-line service rates, however, would be increased by 9.4%.

On October 18, 1983, the FCC signed a nine-page memorandum opinion and order that approved suspension of their access charge and proposed interstate tariffs to April 3, 1984. On October 19, the chief of the FCC tariff division said at a press briefing that the action was taken based on the commission's review of the tariffs themselves. In particular, the FCC faced the difficulty of reviewing 43,000 pages of new tariffs and more than 160,000 pages of supporting documentation.

The FCC was also concerned that AT&T had used the occasion for filing interstate tariffs to restructure completely its private-line service rates rather than merely reduce its rates overall. For example, the access charge proposed by the FCC would reduce AT&T's interstate revenue requirements by $3.3 billion. However, the interstate rate reduction in AT&T's filing would result in a $1.75 billion reduction in revenues. Thus AT&T's application for new interstate rates would not offset the effect of increased access charges but would in fact increase AT&T's revenues.

On January 25, 1984, the FCC voted to delay the imposition of residential telephone access charges until mid-1985. The vote reflected pressure from Congress, which was ready to legislate a delay in the imposition of access charges in the event of FCC inaction. The FCC also voted to place a $4 ceiling until 1990 on monthly access charges imposed on businesses with single telephone lines as well as on residential customers. For other business users, a $6 per month charge was to take effect in April.

In late February 1984, the FCC issued an order that made the actual imposition of access charges on April 3 problematic. The FCC found significant elements of the National Exchange Carrier Association's (NECA's) local access tariffs unlawful and sent the NECA staff members back to the drawing board to revise them.

AT&T took strong exception to an FCC order issued 2 days before the FCC's action on NECA tariffs. In that order the FCC had provided its latest formula for calculating the per-line charges to be paid by interexchange carriers for access. MCI Communications estimated that the $235 it now pays for a connection would rise under the FCC formula to somewhere between $335 and $355. AT&T estimated that MCI's access charge would rise from approximately $260 to about $380, while its own "premium access" charge would be $830 for an access line used 9000 minutes monthly. In a filing to the FCC, AT&T has formally asked the regulators to reconsider their order. AT&T said the net effect of the agency's new access-charge order would be to reduce its rate of return on interstate long-distance service from roughly 11% to less than 5%. That would leave it with net earnings on interstate service of $450 million on $26.6 billion of revenue, a result AT&T called confiscatory, intolerable, and illegal.

AT&T is likely to be opposed at the commission by the same companies that have been requesting the FCC to impose a high premium access charge on AT&T. Those companies include U.S. Transmission Systems, MCI, U.S. Telephones, GTE Corp., SBS, Western Union, EMX Television, and Lexitel Corp.

On March 21, 1984, the FCC responded to AT&T's filing and to complaints by AT&T customers and competitors by delaying until June 13 the imposition of access charges on multiline business customers. The FCC cited the need for additional information to ensure that proposed access tariffs would be generally responsible and workable.

In an announcement on March 21, AT&T Chairman Charles L. Brown indicated that the company would not earn enough money to cover its first-quarter dividend of 30 cents per share. Mr. Brown blamed the earnings problem on the FCC's delay in imposing access charges and thereby relieving AT&T of the financial burden of subsidizing local service.

On April 9, 1984, more than 175 members of the House of Representatives urged the FCC to postpone business access charges at least until mid-1985. The letter to Chairman Mark Fowler noted: "We feel strongly that the FCC was right to defer imposition of access charges for residential and single-line businesses. We urge you to give the same consideration to businesses with more than one line."

The FCC announced it would reexamine the 12.75% authorized rate of return for AT&T and Bell operating company exchange carriers. As a result of that reexamination, the FCC ordered AT&T to implement an across-the-board reduction of 6.1% in MTS and WATS tariff rates. This reduction, the largest since 1970, resulted from the FCC's reducing proposed carrier common-line access charges to interexchange carriers plus other FCC adjustments in AT&T revenue and cost forecasts. Specifically, for exchange carriers, the FCC directed that carrier common-line charges be reduced by 8.5% both for AT&T and its competitors, thereby preserving the discount for MCI and others. The FCC ruled that in the absence of these changes, AT&T would have earned 18.64%, well in excess of the authorized 12.75%.

As a result of the FCC's decisions, the first end-user access charges became effective on May 25, 1984, and will apply to multiline business subscribers. The FCC put a cap of $6 per month on those charges, but FCC Chairman Fowler suggested that those charges will actually average about $4.75 per month. "Grandfathered" Centrex system customers (systems in place or ordered by July 27, 1983) will begin paying $2 per month on that same date. Access charges for other users were reexamined by the FCC in December 1984.

As of this writing, access charges have yet to become generally effective. Congressional pressure and competing claims of impending financial disaster by AT&T, MCI, Sprint, and others have delayed their imposition. This delay is a major problem, since the adoption of a system of access charges is vital to the restructuring of the U.S. telecommunications industry. Access charges will replace much of the present separations and settlements system for interjurisdictional cross-subsidies. Long-distance markets in particular will not be characterized by cost-based rates until the requirement that those rates bear current proportions of overhead contribution is lifted.

The States' Role

State regulators have been active in soliciting the U.S. Congress to pass legislation that would delay or proscribe the FCC's imposition of end-user access charges. They fear that ratepayers will associate FCC-mandated increases in access rates with their public service commissioners. Many also seem genuinely to be concerned that various ratepayers (e.g., the poor, the elderly, and the handicapped) will lose communications services with the advent of deregulation, divestiture, and access charges.

Studies by economists and staff at the FCC and NTIA seem to show, without exception, that disconnection as a result of increased access charges is not likely to be significant. Furthermore, it is perfectly reasonable to institute budget or lifeline rates with low access charges and call allowances to minimize or even eliminate the problem. It might well be a useful exercise in political economy to develop a model that would explain why such a large public outcry has developed over rate increases that are so seemingly small.

State legislators share the concerns of state commissioners. The California Assembly has passed legislation requiring that customers be informed of FCC responsibility for rate increases, that lifeline rates be available to needy ratepayers, and that intrastate telecommunications revenues be "taxed" to create a pool of revenues to provide communications service to the poor.

State regulatory commissions and legislatures face additional policy issues. Regulators are being confronted with requests for certification by carriers wishing to offer intrastate services, both interLATA and intra-LATA. Various states may find their regulatory statutes inadequate; it may be necessary to write new statutes allowing commissions to grant such certification.

State regulators and legislators will also be faced with pricing issues. As competition moves rates and prices toward underlying cost structures, traditional reliance on flat and averaged rates will no longer suffice. Carriers will no doubt offer a variety of pricing structures in the intrastate market, similar to those with which AT&T has been experimenting at the national level. In particular, off-peak discounts of various sorts offer carriers ways of increasing revenues with minimal increases in costs. Similarly, pressure for the adoption of measured service rates for local service will not disappear.

The United States may face significant problems as telecommunications regulation and deregulation move to the state arena. Neither regulatory commissions nor legislative staffs generally have sufficient experience with telecommunications. To the extent that state policy makers respond only out of fear of short-term rate increases, the long-run costs to the U.S. economy may be significant.

Summary and Conclusions

This section has reviewed recent actions of the FCC in deregulating or unregulating telecommunications markets. These markets include terminal equipment, long-distance services, and international services. The FCC's actions and congressional responses with regard to access charges were also discussed. Finally, the increasingly important role of state regulators and legislators was noted.

In general, the FCC has acted to remove entry barriers in telecommunications markets. New entrants are typically exempted from the traditional regulatory requirements imposed on common carriers. However, the FCC has continued to impose facilities, tariff, and profit regulation on AT&T. AT&T's participation in unregulated markets is generally required to occur through separate subsidiaries.

The FCC has attempted to end the process of interjurisdictional separations and settlements that has historically minimized local rate increases at the cost of reduced long-distance tariff decreases. The FCC chose to end this so-called cross-subsidy by recovering revenue in the form of flat-rate access charges on end users. Congress and state regulators have objected strenuously to the imposition of any charges on end users, favoring instead charges imposed on inter-exchange carriers. Inter-exchange carriers have objected to the differential premium charged for the costs of trunk-side and line-side interconnection with the local exchange. Access charges have yet to be implemented.

State regulators and legislators are largely unprepared for the decisions regarding entry certification, competitive policy, and pricing now facing them. The quality of their response in the form of regulations and statutes will have much to say about the cost of telecommunications deregulation to the U.S. economy.

THE DIVESTITURE OF AT&T

This section reviews the 1956 Consent Decree limiting AT&T to the provision of common-carrier communication services; the Modified Final Judgment ending the U.S. Department of Justice's antitrust suit against AT&T and removing the restrictions of the Consent Decree; and the course of divestiture since January 1, 1984.

The 1956 Consent Decree

AT&T's history is marked by significant antitrust activity, beginning with the Kingsbury Commitment in 1913 and antitrust and patent litigation in the 1920s and 1930s regarding radio communications, broadcasting, and motion pictures. In 1949, the U.S. Department of Justice brought an antitrust case against AT&T. That suit charged Western Electric and AT&T with a conspiracy to restrain trade in violation of section 1 of the Sherman Act and charged Western Electric with monopolizing the market for telephones and related equipment in violation of section 2 of that act. The Justice Department asked for an end to AT&T's ownership of Western Electric and for the dissolution of agreements between AT&T, the Bell operating companies, and Western Electric. The suit essentially sought the separation of regulated monopoly services from unregulated equipment supply.

Following years of legal and political maneuvering, negotiations between AT&T and the Attorney General led to the Consent Decree of January 1956. The decree left the Bell System structure unchanged and effectively left AT&T oversight to regulators and legislatures. However, two provisions of the decree restricted the scope of Bell System activities and required liberal licensing of Bell System patents.

AT&T was "enjoined and restrained from engaging, either directly, or indirectly through its subsidiaries other than Western and Western subsidiaries, in any business other than the furnishing of common carrier communication services." Western Electric was similarly enjoined.

The second substantive provision of the decree was a requirement that all patents controlled by the Bell System be licensed to others on request.

Licenses under all patents, except for those involved in the cross-licensing agreements reached in previous decades among General Electric, RCA, AT&T, and Westinghouse, were required to be issued to any applicant at a "reasonable royalty." AT&T was also required to provide technical information along with patent licenses on payment of reasonable fees. (Although it is not known how many such licenses have been issued since 1956, there is anecdotal evidence that Bell licenses were important to the formation and growth of the U.S. semiconductor industry and to the development of the Japanese telecommunications and electronics industry.)

The Modified Final Judgment

On January 8, 1982, the U.S. Department of Justice announced that it had reached agreement with AT&T on the terms of a modification of the 1956 AT&T Consent Decree. The government and AT&T attempted to dismiss by stipulation the government's pending monopolization case against AT&T. On August 24, 1982, a Modification of Final Judgment (MFJ) between AT&T and the U.S. Department of Justice was entered by Judge Harold H. Greene of the U.S. District Court for the District of Columbia. The acceptance by the parties concerned of modifications to the agreement imposed by the court enabled Judge Greene to dismiss the government's case against AT&T.

The key to AT&T's power to impede competition, according to the court, has been its control of local telephone service. AT&T has allegedly used its control of this local monopoly to keep competitors (long-distance carriers and equipment manufacturers) at a disadvantage in two principal ways. First, it has attempted to prevent competing long-distance carriers and competing equipment manufacturers from gaining access to the local network, or to delay that access, thus placing them in an inferior position vis-à-vis AT&T's own services. Second, it supposedly has used profits earned from the monopoly local telephone operations to subsidize its long-distance and equipment business in which it was competing with others.

Under the MFJ, local Bell operating companies providing local-exchange telephone services were to be divested by AT&T. AT&T would continue to own a nationwide intercity network composed of its Long Lines Department and the intercity facilities of the Bell operating companies, and would retain ownership of Bell Telephone Laboratories and Western Electric.

The MFJ removes restrictions imposed by the 1956 Consent Decree on AT&T that prevented AT&T from entering computer, computer-related, and information services markets. These restrictions are no longer necessary because of the divestiture of local telephone companies and the presence of other large and experienced firms in the computer industry. However, the court did preclude AT&T from entering the field of electronic publishing for a period of 7 years, until the risk of its domination of that field had abated. AT&T could still distribute information provided by others, but it would not be allowed to generate (i.e., publish) information *and* transmit that information.

The monopoly possessed by local Bell operating companies also required, in the court's opinion, that these companies be prohibited from providing long-distance and information services, and from manufacturing equipment used in the telecommunications industry. However, the monopoly power of local telephone companies was not deemed to extend to the marketing of customer premises equipment and the production of the Yellow Pages advertising directories; hence these lines of business are permitted.

The local Bell operating companies are required to avoid discrimination between AT&T and other interexchange carriers and equipment manufacturers. In particular, all inter-exchange carriers would be provided "equal access" to the local exchange. The details and timing of equal access (as well as other matters) were to be contained in a required filing by AT&T of a plan of reorganization due within 6 months of the entry into force of the MFJ.

AT&T filed its plan of reorganization with the court on December 16, 1982. Judge Greene filed his order after hearings and deliberation on July 8, 1983. In its reorganization, AT&T would divest its ownership interest in the Bell System's exchange operations by January 1, 1984, by contributing its stock in the reconfigured companies to seven newly created regional holding companies and then spin off these seven companies to existing AT&T shareholders. No officer, director, or employee of one regional company will serve in any of those capacities in another regional company, for a local company in another region, or for AT&T or for any of its subsidiaries. Each regional holding company had approximately 100,000 employees and from 15 to 25 million installed telephones as of the end of 1982; they are each comparable in size to a major European PTT.

Other elements of Judge Greene's order included:

1. Suits such as that brought by Litton against AT&T and its subsidiaries (there was a $276.8 million award in Litton's favor) resulting in judgments against the Bell System would have damages apportioned among AT&T and the operating companies on the basis of each firm's relative net investment.
2. AT&T would retain ownership of Bell Systems patents, with operating companies to be granted royalty-free licenses to current patents and to those issued in the 5 years after divestiture.
3. The MFJ was to create a central staff organization (now called Bell

Communications Research, Inc.) to be owned by the seven regional holding companies; the CSO would provide network planning services, systems engineering, applied engineering services, applied research, and information systems support.

On August 5, Judge Greene issued a nine-page memorandum and a brief order putting into effect an amended plan of reorganization of AT&T. AT&T would be allowed to use the Bell name and logo in connection with Bell Labs and AT&T's foreign operations; domestically, the operating companies would have the right to the Bell name and logo. Chairman Brown of AT&T announced that the company would employ the next best-known designation, AT&T, and a new logo.

In a later order, Judge Greene ruled that the operating companies may route all interLATA traffic to AT&T from subscribers who do not otherwise designate an interexchange carrier. He did not order divested operating companies to route undesignated traffic to AT&T, but authorized them to do so if they so chose. This ruling will be of importance for the interim period until September 1, 1986, during the equal access phase-in.

On December 12, 1983, the U.S. Supreme Court, without comment, affirmed the decision of Judge Greene in the settlement of *United States* v. *AT&T*. This affirmation cleared away legal challenges to the January 1, 1984, breakup of AT&T.

Judge Greene and Access Charges

Judge Greene defined equal access as access with overall quality equal within a reasonable range that is applicable to all carriers. He rejected a more stringent definition that would have yielded identical technical quality (i.e., identical values for loss, noise, and echo, and identical probability of blocking). Apparently, access will be provided through state-of-the-art, four-wire digital tandem switches.

It is Judge Greene's view that the costs of providing equal access should be covered by charges imposed on inter-exchange carriers. AT&T, as the largest inter-exchange carrier, will thus pay the bulk of those costs. He does not see the threat of bypass by those carriers or by large business customers as sufficiently great that end users should be charged for such costs.

Summary and Conclusions

This section has reviewed the 1956 Consent Decree limiting AT&T to the communications industry. Additionally, the 1983 Modified Final Judgment was examined. The MFJ freed AT&T from the restriction of the 1956

Decree. However, the price was high. AT&T was broken up into seven regional holding companies with Long Lines, Bell Labs, and Western Electric remaining with AT&T.

THE U.S. CONGRESS

Congress has been trying to pass legislation to guide telecommunications policy for most of the past decade. From the Consumer Communications Reform Act of 1976 to H.R. 4102 and S. 1660 of 1983, all such attempts have been futile. This section reviews that history; it is interesting to note that the sponsorship of legislation has shifted from AT&T's attempts to retain its monopoly to attempts by AT&T's competitors and customers to protect their interests against AT&T.

Legislative Attempts: Pre-1983–1984

AT&T, backed by independent telcos such as GT&E, sought passage of the Consumer Communications Reform Act in 1976. The bill sought to roll back measures adopted by the FCC to that date, increasing competition in the long-distance service market. AT&T's monopoly would have been in effect endorsed by legislation. Terminal equipment would have been regulated at the level of the state utility commissions; the FCC's registration program would have been terminated.

In the late 1970s, Representative Lionel Van Deerlin (chairman of the House Communications Subcommittee) took the lead in introducing legislation that would have set telecommunications policy in a direction different from that advocated by AT&T. The Van Deerlin bill would have reduced regulation by the FCC, replaced much state regulation with FCC oversight, established an access fund to subsidize local service, divested Western Electric, and abrogated the 1956 Consent Decree.

The 1976 proposed legislation was opposed by such groups as the Justice Department, the Computer and Business Equipment Manufacturers Association, the Public Interest Research Group, and the FCC. The later Van Deerlin legislation was opposed by AT&T and most of the telephone industry. As a result, it was not possible to gain a consensus on the basic direction of telecommunications policy that could be written into legislation and enacted into law.

Legislation in 1983–1984

H.R. 4102 and S. 1660 were each named the Universal Telephone Service Preservation Act of 1983. Each seemed to be motivated by proposed FCC regulations on access charges and by the fear that local telephone rates would rise significantly if those charges were imposed.

There were differences in the two pieces of legislation, however. First, the House bill prohibited the imposition of end-user access charges on residential and single-line business subscribers. Second, the House bill explicitly provided for a contribution by private telephone system bypassers. Third, the reimbursement schedules for exchange carriers differed with regard to a universal service fund. Also, the House bill provided for the creation of nonprofit associations of residential telephone consumers within each state. These associations would appear before state commissions and collectively before the FCC in telephone proceedings.

S. 1660 simply provided that no flat charges for interstate access service be recovered from residential and single-line business users by exchange carriers until January 1, 1986. The bill also set up a universal service fund to offset non-traffic-sensitive costs for high-cost exchange carriers. Apparently, the fund would be financed by charges on interexchange carriers and bypassers, although the bypass language was not as explicit as that in the House bill.

It is worth noting that the Reagan administration opposed these bills, as did AT&T, regional holding companies, the FCC, and large business customers of telephone carriers. Nonetheless, the House passed the legislation on November 10, 1983; the Senate, on January 26, 1984, tabled S. 1660 by a 44 to 40 vote after the FCC delayed imposition of access charges on residential and single-line business customers to June 1985.

There seems to be no doubt, based on comments and actions of Congress since the tabling of the proposed legislation, that Congress is willing to attempt legislation again if the FCC adopts regulations opposed by representatives and senators. Congressional pressure has been responsible for most of the delay in the imposition of access charges.

Summary and Conclusions

This section has reviewed the attempts by Congress to enact telecommunications legislation. In AT&T's attempts to pass the Bell bill to retain its monopoly, and in attempts by competitors and customers to impose their will on AT&T, Congress has been unable to achieve a consensus making legislation possible. Only the threat of access charges at the FCC seemed able to provoke successful legislation in 1983–1984. The FCC delayed access-charge imposition, and Congress tabled its legislation. Future legislation will be attempted if the FCC tries to impose end-user access charges.

TELECOMMUNICATIONS MARKETS IN THE UNITED STATES

The thesis of this section is that many telecommunications markets in the United States are now largely competitive. The remaining markets will become competitive, certainly by the 1990s.

Long Distance

Traditional measures of the competitiveness of markets use market-share data or concentration ratios. (For a concise sample of the debate on whether long-distance markets are now and will remain competitive, see Katz and Willig 1984 and Morris and Preece 1984.) Those who argue that the long-distance market is not yet competitive support that claim by citing AT&T's 95% market share (*Wall Street Journal*, May 2, 1984, 4). Major competitors such as MCI and GTE Sprint have much smaller shares, 2.5% and 1.5% respectively.

There are at least three major problems with such statistics. First, there are measurement problems. AT&T claims that, in the overall toll-call market, which includes long-distance traffic carried by the Bell operating companies within LATAs, it has a 61% market share. Second, a large market share (whether 95% or 61%) may or may not imply an uncompetitive industry organization. For example, if AT&T's pricing, investment, and diversification decisions are heavily regulated by commissions and courts, then the firm will not be free to exercise its market power, assuming that such market power exists. Finally, market-share statistics are static measures of industry organization; in the case of telecommunications, the erosion and disappearance of entry barriers is critical. AT&T has a large market share and will for some time to come, but it is also likely that AT&T's market share will be reduced over time as regulatory commissions at the federal and state levels eliminate barriers to entry. Such entry constrains the large firm's pricing, investment, and diversification decisions even in the absence of legal regulations.

The scheduled implementation of equal access will facilitate increasing competitiveness in long-distance service. As customers become free to choose among competing interexchange carriers by dialing the same number of digits, much of AT&T's current advantage will be eliminated. AT&T will still have a facilities advantage, but the investment schedules of MCI, GTE Sprint, and others are quite large. Garfinkel (1984) indicates that AT&T's new competitors will invest approximately $1 billion in new capacity, compared with AT&T's construction budget of roughly the same amount. While there may be short-term capacity problems, as recently experienced by GTE Sprint, these difficulties are not likely to persist, since the incentive to add to profits by expanding facilities is very clear.

Equipment Markets

Western Electric can be characterized as a firm in a competitive industry. Market-share data support such a characterization; Congress (1981) found that Western had a 60 to 80% share of the PBX market in 1973, while a report in the *Wall Street Journal* (February 10, 1984, 29) found that Western's share had dropped to 29.1% in 1983.

There is almost no segment of the equipment industry that is not competitive. Even with large central office switches, where R&D costs for a new generation of equipment total $1 billion, the problem is one of oversupply, not of constrained capacity. At the opposite end, the market for simple telephones has become so crowded that phones can be purchased on the streets of New York for $3 to $4 per instrument.

The key development in this market, just as with long-distance markets, was the erosion and elimination of entry barriers. Market power cannot be maintained if entry is opened. A large market share cannot be sustained with open entry unless such a share reflects underlying cost advantages. Entry will tend to push prices to reflect those cost realities so that customers will benefit even if one firm supplies most of the product.

Intrastate Markets

State commissions must now approve or refuse to certify inter-exchange carriers for intrastate interLATA traffic and for intraLATA traffic. It is likely that interLATA traffic will join interstate traffic as a competitively provided service. Such competition is already a reality, even with existing entry barriers. For example, office developers are at present building or installing their own telecommunications systems. As of January 1984, 58 buildings were having such systems installed. Olympia and York has entered into a joint venture with United Telecommunications to install shared communications in Olympia and York buildings in 40 cities and to link them by satellite.

Commissions are likely to be more cautious about opening intraLATA markets to competition because of regulators' concerns that certain local subscribers will experience large rate increases.

Telecommunications traffic distributions are highly skewed. It is typically the case that a very small percentage of customers, particularly business customers, provide a large percentage of total revenues. Additionally, for LATA traffic, those large users are usually concentrated in a very small geographical area (e.g., the financial district of a major city). Thus, two or three blocks of buildings can contain customers who generate a quarter to half of an operating telephone company's local business revenues.

When one combines this skewed distribution with new technological opportunities such as Digital Termination Systems (DTS), cellular radio, and cable, one can understand the concerns of regulators and local telephone company management. Local cable operators, microwave radio system owners, and new cellular radio vendors constitute a major potential source of competition. (For a full discussion of these possibilities, see chapters by Lucas, Long, Jackson, Hatfield, and others in Baughcum and Faulhaber 1985.)

IntraLATA communications will probably never be completely competitive. There will not be vendors willing to duplicate the local central office and distribution plant in its entirety. However, many profit opportunities will attract competition. These profit opportunities will operate, as they have in other telecommunications markets, to motivate firms to seek to erode or eliminate regulatory entry barriers.

General Principles

The dynamics that have operated to open U.S. markets to competition will also operate to open telecommunications markets in other countries. Equipment markets will open first, with service markets to follow. Great Britain and Japan have already begun this process. While continental European countries are resisting such trends, there are signs of liberalization there as well, as Chapters 5 (France) and 6 (West Germany) describe.

There are two basic reasons for believing that competitive markets will be the rule worldwide in telecommunications. First, the combination of new technologies and traditional rate structures means that there are opportunities for cost savings for customers and profits for potential vendors. Those opportunities will motivate efforts to achieve financial reward by eroding or eliminating existing entry barriers.

Second, policy makers will find it increasingly expensive to maintain autarkic telecommunications policies. In equipment, it is simply too expensive for each major economy to support its own central office switch manufacturer. On the service side, the proliferation of technologies and service options will effectively make it impossible for a single vendor to satisfy the myriad demands of customers. This will be exacerbated by multinationals who obtain services in country A and find it difficult to obtain them in country B. Pressure will mount on B's policy makers to allow the firm to supply itself or to allow other vendors to enter. (For a fuller discussion of the costs a country will impose on itself by not developing its telecommunications sector, see Baughcum and Pittman 1983.)

OBSERVATIONS ON TELECOMMUNICATIONS IN THE UNITED STATES: LESSONS FOR OTHER COUNTRIES

This section reviews the major forces at work in U.S. telecommunications markets for the purpose of identifying trends or lessons that might be useful for PTTs. Technology is the driving force in telecommunications, whether from the spread of microelectronics or from the emergence of new transmission media such as fiber optics. Competitors seek profit from the opportunities created by technological advance; customers seek improved performance–price ratios from their telecommunications expenditures.

The resulting pressure will erode traditional regulations and institutions outside the United States just as they have domestically.

Technology creates opportunities for profit taking and cost savings because existing tariffs are increasingly out of alignment with underlying cost structures. These opportunities are the incentive that motivates firms such as MCI to invest in the legal and political activities that will erode or eliminate entry barriers to desirable markets.

The basic trend of interest to PTTs, therefore, is that toward competitive markets. The only way to resist this trend successfully without incurring unacceptable costs is to restructure tariffs, services, and institutions toward underlying cost structures. The basic lesson of use to PTTs is that resistance to this change brings costs that are quite high and are rising.

Technology

Technological change has affected both equipment and service markets. Consider the equipment market first.

Telecommunications equipment is typically subdivided into three areas: (1) central office switching; (2) transmission; and (3) customer premises equipment. One of the effects of technological change is to blur the lines even between these three basic groupings. For example, multiplex equipment traditionally discussed under the heading of transmission can now, with digital switching equipment, be incorporated into central office switches. Similarly, advances in microelectronics and in digital switching technologies have made it possible to extend intelligence to terminal equipment instead of concentrating it in the central office switch.

With the development of electronic and digital switching, central office switches and computers are increasingly indistinguishable. This offers the telecommunications network the ability to add new services by writing new and improved software programs. It also allows telecommunications to take advantage of microelectronic technology yielding cost reductions with each new generation of technology. However, it does mean that the cost of developing new generations of switches has risen to historically high levels. The cost of developing the most recent generation of digital switches has ranged from $0.5 to $1.0 billion for each producer. At least half of the cost seems to go toward developing the necessary software.

Two other changes are worthy of note with regard to switching technology. First, the labor required in hardware manufacture is only about 16% of that needed for electromechanical switch manufacture. Software manufacture may or may not significantly offset this reduction in labor requirements. Second, it takes a long time to get a switch to the market, probably 5 to 10 years. Both factors mean that it is increasingly costly for PTTs to rely on one or more domestic manufacturers when there are so many switching manufacturers in world markets now. Switzerland, for example, recently decided to bypass its domestic manufacturer, Hasler, in favor of the international marketplace.

In contrast to switches, the salient property in transmission is probably diversity. Competition occurs among manufacturers and among technologies. Satellite, microwave radio, and optical fibers are each areas in which technological advances are continuing to result in reduced transmission costs. While the R&D costs of transmission equipment are not so high as in switching, the costs of insuring autarky across all technologies will still be significant. Again, it probably makes sense to rely on the international marketplace, particularly since certain manufacturers will no doubt develop significant comparative advantages in such markets. The United States, with its long distances required for transmission links, is an example.

If it is desirable to maintain diversity in supply for transmission, then diversity in supply is certainly useful in customer premises equipment as well. The application of microelectronics has resulted in a proliferation of increasingly intelligent equipment available to the business and residential customer. Business customers can buy PBXs with new features such as call forwarding, automatic callback, and conference calling that were not previously available. Similarly, residential customers can purchase telephone answering devices, telephones with memory for storage of frequently called numbers, and other features.

It is the prospect of foregoing this diversity that raises the costs of protectionism in telecommunications markets. In particular, as users (including American multinationals) organize into groups capable of effectively presenting their views to PTTs and ministries, much of the political dynamics that has occurred in the United States will be reenacted overseas.

Just as technological changes in telecommunications equipment make the cost of maintaining monopoly supply excessive, so also will the traditional monopoly structures and regulations in service provision be costly to support. Indeed, since the provision of services occurs over facilities consisting of combinations of the equipment categories previously discussed, changes in equipment technology of the magnitude being experienced must inevitably cause service changes as well.

Service costs have been reduced with each new generation of transmission media. From coaxial cable to microwave to satellite to fiber optics, long-distance costs have fallen significantly as the capacity provided by each medium has increased. Transmission costs over these media have also become more insensitive to distance. Satellites costs are indifferent to calls within their "footprint," whether next door or long distance. With fiber optics, engineers are continuing to increase the distances required between repeaters.

Local service costs have not had the same attention paid them as have long-distance systems. The pattern of regulation has repaid technology applied to the latter market segment rather than the former. However, as the current bypass discussion makes clear, there is no shortage of ideas about how local service costs might be reduced by using digital termination systems, cable for data, and cellular radio.

It should be noted that the digitalization of networks is also an important factor in reducing service costs. Modems for voice–data modulation–demodulation will become obsolete. Increased capacity can be coaxed out of all facilities, including local distribution plant, by digital techniques and equipment.

In short, the direct costs of major equipment such as switches; the indirect costs of assuring diversity of supply (transmission and CPE); and indirect costs, such as those foregone by slowness in network digitalization, mean increased pressure on PTTs in meeting customer needs. Insistence on monopoly supply may result in intolerable cost burdens on those organizations.

Costs, Tariffs, and Profits

The basic point is quite simple. Just as in the United States, PTTs have built various cross-subsidies, intentionally and unintentionally, into their tariff structures and service offerings. Typically, longer-distance calling subsidizes local calling, with international calling being particularly profitable.

Both users and potential competitors are sophisticated enough to see opportunities for cost savings or profit taking, respectively. European PTTs may, in some instances, be surprised at the aggressiveness of, say, MCI in pursuing profit and new sales. PTTs face the choice of attempting to supply the needs of their customers themselves, in which case they will gradually change their tariffs and service offerings in the direction of costs, or of opening their markets to competitors who can supplement the offerings of the PTT. In either case, the customer benefits. It is probably the case, however, that attempting to maintain a monopoly supply is the higher cost option.

Entry Barriers

If, as I believe, the costs of maintaining monopoly supply are large, the PTT may find it advisable to reduce or eliminate entry barriers in the supply of various equipment or services. Just as in the United States, I would expect that terminal equipment and long-distance (international) services would be areas where PTTs might find this advisable in the near term. (In many cases, European PTTs were in advance of the United States in eliminating entry barriers in the sale of terminal equipment.)

It is worthwhile reiterating that entry barriers are critical to the exercise of market power. A firm or PTT can exercise market power (i.e., raise price above cost) only if other firms are prohibited effectively from arbitraging the price–cost differential. This can generally be accomplished by employing the power of the state to erect and maintain entry barriers.

Entry barriers, in this instance, carry within them the seeds of their own potential destruction. Knowledgeable customers and potential competitors can judge the size of the price–cost differential being charged. They will then have the incentive to spend the amount of resources that will eliminate the entry barrier supporting the market power. Lawyers, consultants, and lobbyists are paid in many instances as an investment in eliminating entry barriers in the United States. It is likely that a similar phenomenon, subject to cultural, legal, and social differences among countries, will take place in Europe and other important markets.

Trends toward Competitive Markets

Technology is forcing telecommunications in the direction of increasingly competitive markets in the United States. Technology will operate in a similar fashion in other countries. This trend will proceed in other countries in a manner different from that in the United States because of cultural, legal, and social differences among countries. In general, however, the United States is a useful laboratory for study, as the basic phenomenon will work itself out there first.

Just as the United States offers positive lessons, however, it also offers some cautionary ones. In particular, if a government decides to deregulate telecommunications, it should be careful in its treatment of the PTT. Imposing special requirements such as separated subsidiaries, profit regulation, tariff regulations and entry–exit proscriptions should be evaluated carefully. Many of these requirements have been imposed in the United States not for reasons of economic efficiency but for political and competitive reasons.

Similarly, peculiar institutional factors in the United States have resulted, in my judgment, in progress toward competitive markets in an uncertain, slow, and inefficient fashion. Current modest progress toward deregulating long-distance communications markets is not well served by the delays and uncertainty in settling access charges caused by disputes between the FCC and Congress.

PTTs, as government agencies, may have an advantage over the United States in this regard. Because of their monopoly position, they might be able to move quickly and surely toward greater efficiency without the costly and time-consuming transitions required in the United States.

Conclusions

This section reviewed the basic forces at work in telecommunications markets in the United States. Technology acting in conjunction with traditional tariff structures creates opportunities for profit taking and cost saving. Despite institutional differences, there is no reason to expect other countries to be exempt from this phenomenon.

PTTs have the choice of adopting more cost-based structures or eliminating entry barriers and opening markets. The former may not be as efficient as the latter, given the diversity of customer needs and the technologies required to meet those needs.

PTTs that seek to resist the basic trend toward more competitive telecommunications markets will incur high costs. These costs will consist of the direct costs of autarky and the indirect costs of foregone diversity.

To the extent that PTTs seek lessons from the U.S. experience, they should consider carefully the restrictions imposed on AT&T in domestic markets. Separate subsidiaries and other requirements may be political solutions with significant efficiency costs. In particular, the PTTs should avoid imposing delays and uncertainties on major service and equipment suppliers.

SUMMARY

This chapter has reviewed the role of the FCC, Congress, the courts, and state legislators and commissions in the deregulation of telecommunications markets in the United States. In general, the trend has been to open markets to the forces of competition. However, the concerns of AT&T's competitors and policy makers have led to delays in the introduction of access charges and to restrictions on AT&T as it enters unregulated markets.

The evidence in support of concerns about anticompetitive behavior on the part of unregulated carriers and in support of the proposition that competition must lead to losses in telephone subscription seems weak. Indeed, the organizational solutions (i.e., separate subsidiaries) seem to have little or no relationship to the analytical problem of Averch–Johnson effects. Furthermore, the evidence is now overwhelming that competition and access charges need not lead to loss of universal service.

The political process whereby the United States is adjusting to competitive markets therefore seems slow and costly. The impatience of an economist with political solutions, however, is not a new phenomenon. It should probably not be surprising that the dismantling of an industry organization and a system of regulation and control that have been in place for more than half a century takes a fair amount of time. In particular, time will be required given the many opportunities that interested parties have to affect policy (FCC, Congress, courts, state commissions).

U.S. telecommunications markets are not unique. The same forces of technological change will conflict with out-of-date rate structures and costly entry barriers in other countries. The effect will be to create incentives for entry and for opening of markets to multiple vendors.

Obviously, no two countries' political institutions are identical. Countries outside the United States may take longer or move more quickly than the United States in opening markets. For example, the opening of telecommunications markets in the United Kingdom occurred almost abruptly with a change in government, as Charles Jonscher indicates in Chapter 7. Alternatively, France seems to be dedicated to an entirely different approach, as Jean-Paul Voge argues in Chapter 5. Its directed and planned development in telecommunications seeks to take advantage of new technologies and to offer new services to customers, just as competitive markets are meant to do in the United States. Yet, French resistance to relying on open markets may make it difficult and costly to achieve this.

The analysis and history in this chapter suggest three lessons for policy makers in other countries:

1. *The United States is unique in its institutional detail.* Surely no other country would knowingly and willingly impose such a complicated mix of regulatory agencies, courts, and legislatures on dynamic telecommunications markets.
2. *The United States is a leader in the phenomenon of increasingly competitive telecommunications markets; other countries will follow.* The conflict between technological change and traditional regulatory structures is eroding entry barriers in a manner that will be repeated in other countries.
3. *The U.S. approach is not necessarily a prescription for other countries to follow.* Other countries should think carefully about the delays and uncertainties in the progress of U.S. policy makers toward deregulating markets and developing access charges. Also, they should be careful about imposing requirements such as separated subsidiaries on the major suppliers. The costs in both cases are probably quite high.

APPENDIX: BROADCASTING AND CABLE DEREGULATION IN THE UNITED STATES

The Origins of Regulation

Regulation was a response to the problem of frequency assignment in radio broadcasting. Initially, the Department of Commerce simply licensed aspiring radio broadcasters as they applied. Not surprisingly, interference became a significant problem.

In 1927, Congress passed legislation establishing the Federal Radio Commission, empowering it to assign wavelengths and to determine the power and location of transmitters. In 1934 the Federal Radio Commission became the Federal Communications Commission with additional responsibility for the regulation of telecommunications.

Broadcasting regulation differs from telecommunications regulation generally in that the FCC cannot regulate the rates or profits of broadcasters. Instead, the FCC grants licenses for a definite period of time that are renewed on the basis of the public interest. Congressional action regarding the method of regulation indicates that competition was intended to have a greater role in broadcasting than in other regulated industries.

Additionally, the FCC has been required by Congress to grant licenses with an eye to geographical distribution so as to provide equality of radio broadcasting service. This requirement became known as the "local service" objective (i.e., locating stations in as many areas as possible). The FCC also seeks to promote diversity of program content and to fulfill broadcasting's public-service role.

The local service objective had major effects on broadcasting. In order for each city to have as many stations as possible, the FCC did not encourage powerful regional broadcasters except in the sparsely populated areas of the mountain states. This policy, combined with the scarcity of VHF spectrum allocated to television, meant effectively that there would be three networks based on local stations. The alternative would be four networks with more emphasis on regional broadcasting stations and fewer local stations.

The spectrum-scarcity problem was exacerbated by the deliberate pace with which UHF and VHF competition was resolved. It was not until the all-channel receiver act of 1962 that TV sets could be expected to receive both UHF and VHF broadcasts, and not until the 1970s that large numbers of sets became available to receive UHF stations. UHF still suffers technical disadvantages in that it is difficult to receive a good UHF picture outside a radius of a few miles from the transmitter.

As a result of its concern with localism, the FCC developed a set of rules regarding ownership. Specifically, the FCC limited group owners to no more than seven AM, seven FM, and seven television stations, only five of which could be VHF stations, although this rule has been recently relaxed. Also, the FCC has discouraged the ownership of two stations in the same area.

The evidence seems to be clear that local service has had limited benefits. Indeed, Noll, Peck, and McGowan (1973) make a good case that the consumer would have been better served by six networks with regional broadcasters than by three networks based on local broadcasters.

Cable Television

In contrast to its policies of encouraging local broadcasting, FCC policies have retarded the development of cable television for much of the past several decades. It was the FCC's prohibition of cable carrying distant signals from distant communities into major metropolitan areas that limited cable's audience. Cable can obviously provide dozens of channels, but the FCC's regulation limited the diversity of program choice that cable could offer and hence limited the attractiveness of cable to subscribers.

Restriction of cable paradoxically can be defended on the grounds that competition from cable will reduce the profit of local broadcasters and hence harm the FCC's aim of maintaining local service. As Noll, Peck, and McGowan (1973) have shown, however, fears of injury are not valid. Furthermore, the loss of the competitive spur from cable may entail significant costs in technological progress. It is also paradoxical that cable should be restricted, since the first accomplishment of cable was to bring television to communities unable to receive TV signals because of terrain or distance from TV transmitters.

The FCC and the courts in the 1970s have effectively deregulated the cable television industry; the result has been dramatic growth in cable subscriptions and intense competition for municipal franchises. First, the FCC's order in 1976 (57 FCC 2d 141) permitted cable systems to choose their signals from stations without regard for their location. The development of low-cost satellite interconnection resulted in several "superstations" (major-market independent stations) transmitting programming via satellite to local cable franchisees. Second, in 1980 the FCC repealed its distant signal carriage and syndicated exclusivity rules (79 FCC 2d 663). Thus, cable systems are now free to import as many signals as they wish, from any location, and need not delete programs for which local stations have obtained contracts.

Finally, cable development was aided by the Home Box Office case in the mid-1970s. That case struck down the FCC's so-called anti-siphoning rules, which severely restricted the showing of feature films that had been in theatrical release for less than 2 years and prohibited the broadcasting of sports events regularly televised by local broadcasters during the past 2 years. It is not surprising that the major reason for subscription to cable systems is the demand for movie viewing and sports programming.

Unregulation in Broadcasting

The FCC, as it has in telephony, has recently adopted policies to open up broadcasting markets by reallocating spectrum and eliminating entry barriers. Among the various steps taken to promote competition are the following:

1. The creation of a new broadcast service, low-power television; the demand for such licenses has been so great that the FCC is using a lottery to select potential franchisees randomly
2. The creation of direct-to-home broadcast systems (DBS)
3. Revision of the rules for Instructional Television Fixed Service (ITFS) to allow the lease of excess capacity for commercial service; some ITFS spectrum has also been reallocated to Multipoint Distribution Service (MDS), resulting in thousands of applications
4. Consideration of its restrictions on group ownership limitations to 7-7-7 stations; its rule prohibiting network ownership of cable systems; elimination of its rule that an owner of two stations cannot own a third within 100 miles of the first two; relaxation of ownership requirements to encourage minority ownership of stations
5. The deregulation of radio broadcasting with regard to programming and consideration of doing the same with TV broadcasting

Telephone and Cable

Telephone companies are still prohibited from owning cable systems within their own service areas, with certain exemptions granted in selected rural areas. Telephone companies are free to build and operate cable systems outside their own service areas.

Telephone companies can build systems in their own service area if they lease the facilities to a cable operator and retain no control over programming. A proposal to cable the District of Columbia with Chesapeake and Potomac Telephone Company building the system is currently before municipal authorities, for example.

MCI and Cox Cable have proposed a system in Nebraska in which the cable system would collect traffic for MCI's network. The Nebraska Public Utilities Commission has prohibited such an arrangement to date.

Effects on the Marketplace

It is interesting to observe the effect of these regulatory changes. As recently as 1977–1978, the three TV broadcast networks had 91% of the viewing audience. By 1983–1984, that share was below 80% and is projected to drop below two-thirds in 1990 (*Wall Street Journal*, May 11, 1984, 33). Cable is projected to increase its share to above 10% by 1990, with independent TV stations—those not affiliated with the three broadcast networks—increasing their share to 23%.

Customers are also finding that programming choices have increased through new technologies such as videocassette recorders (VCRs). Decisions in the courts with regard to copyright will no doubt spur further growth in the acceptance of VCRs.

Conclusions

The FCC has adopted a policy in broadcasting of protecting VHF stations. Over time, that policy has restricted the growth of UHF stations and cable systems in the name of promoting local service. There is evidence that such policy has cost the consumer significantly without promoting program diversity.

More recently, the FCC has extended its policy of unregulation to broadcasting and has eliminated entry barriers and reallocated spectrum to foster more competitive markets. As a result, the share of the viewing audience held by the three TV networks has declined, and the consumer has benefited from a wider choice in programming.

As in telephony, much of the change in regulation is a result of technological change (cable, satellites, VCRs), but the resistance of policy makers to that change is impressive. Cable deregulation has required 10 to 20 years. Television has yet to be deregulated. Expectations as to the rate of change in policy based on purely technological criteria must be tempered by political realities having to do with interests of policy makers and parties affected by regulations.

REFERENCES

Acton, J. P. "An Evaluation of Economists' Influence on Electric Utility Rate Reforms." *American Economic Review: Papers and Proceedings* 72 (1982): 114–119.

Ainsworth, J., and G. Johnston. *A Discussion of Telephone Competition*. Chicago: International Independent Telephone Association, 1908.

Alleman, J. H. *The Pricing of Local Telephone Service*. OT Special Publication 77–14. Washington, D.C.: U.S. Department of Commerce, Office of Telecommunications, April 1977.

———. *Bibliography of Source Material, USITA*. Ad Hoc Measured Service Committee Bulletin No. 2–82 (1982).

Anderson, G. W. *Telephone Competition in the Middle West and Its Lessons for New England*. Boston: New England Telephone Company, September 1906.

Artle, R., and C. Averous. "The Telephone System as a Public Good: Static and Dynamic Aspects." *Bell Journal of Economics and Management Science* 4 (1973): 89–100.

Auray, R. R. "Customer Response to Changes in Interstate MTS Rates." In *Assessing New Pricing Concepts in Public Utilities*, edited by H. M. Trebing. East Lansing, Mich.: Michigan State University Press, 1978.

Averch, H., and L. Johnson. "Behavior of the Firm under Regulatory Constraint." *American Economic Review* (December 1962): 1052–1069.

Baseman, K. "Open Entry and Cross-Subsidization in Regulated Markets." In *Studies in Public Regulation*, edited by G. Fromm. Cambridge, Mass.: MIT Press, 1981.

Baughcum, Alan, and Gerald Faulhaber, eds. *Telecommunications Access and Public Policy*. Norwood, N.J.: Ablex, 1984.

Baughcum, Alan, Jerry Hausman, and Timothy Tardiff. "The Demand for Optional Local Measured Service in Adjusting to Regulatory, Pricing, and Marketing Realities." *Proceedings of the Institute of Public Utilities Fourteenth Annual Conference*. East Lansing, Mich.: Michigan State University Press, 1983.

Baughcum, Alan, and John J. McGowan, "Valuing AT&T's Transferred Assets: A Proposal." *Public Utilities Fortnightly*, October 14, 1982.

Baughcum, Alan, and Robert Pittman. "The Impact of Telecommunications Investment on Economic Development in the Pacific." Paper presented at the Pacific Science Congress, Dunedin, New Zealand, February 1983.

Baumol, W. J. "Quasi-optimality: The Welfare Price of a Non-discriminatory Price System." In *Pricing and Regulated Industries: Theory and Application,* edited by J. Wenders. Denver, Colo.: Mountain States Telephone and Telegraph Co., 1977.

Baumol, W. J., and D. F. Bradford. "Optimal Departures from Marginal Cost Pricing." *American Economic Review* 60 (1970): 265–283.

Baumol, W. J., J. Panzar, and R. Willig. *Contestable Markets and the Theory of Industry Structure.* Orlando, Fla.: Harcourt Brace Jovanovich, 1982.

Baumol, W. J., and R. Willig. "Fixed Costs, Sunk Costs, Entry Barriers, and Sustainability of Monopoly." *Quarterly Journal of Economics* 96 (1981): 405–431.

Bolter, W. G. "The FCC's Selection of a 'Proper' Costing Standard after Fifteen Years—What Can We Learn from Docket 18128?" In *Assessing New Pricing Concepts in Public Utilities*, edited by H. M. Trebing. East Lansing, Mich.: Michigan State University Press, 1978.

Bonbright, J. *Principles of Public Utility Rates*. New York: Columbia University Press, 1961.

Breyer, S. *Regulation and Its Reform*. Cambridge, Mass.: Harvard University Press, 1981.

Brock, G. *The Telecommunications Industry: The Dynamics of Market Structure*. Cambridge, Mass.: Harvard University Press, 1981.

Brooks, J. *Telephone: The First Hundred Years*. New York: Harper & Row, 1976.

Bruce, Robert B. "Entering and Exiting the Access Labyrinth: Regulatory and Judicial Background and Policy Initiatives for the Future." In *Telecommunications Access and Public Policy*, edited by Alan Baughcum and Gerald Faulhaber. Norwood, N.J.: Ablex, 1984.

Charles River Associates. *Demand for Local Telephone Service Upon the Introduction of Optional Local Measured Service (LMS)*. July 1982.

———. *Impacts of the AT&T Divestiture on Innovative Behavior*. Draft of final report prepared for the Office of Technology Assessment, U.S. Congress, December 5, 1983.

Cornell, N. W., and M. D. Pelcovits. "Access Charges, Costs and Subsidies: The Effect of Long Distance Competition on Local Rates." Paper presented at Columbia University Business School Conference on Regulation and New Telecommunications Networks, Arden House, New York, 1982.

Danelian, N. *AT&T: The Story of Industrial Conquest*. New York: Vanguard Press, 1974.

Duvall, J. B. "The Conceptual Framework of Common Carrier Policymaking at the Federal Communications Commission in Recent Years: An Economist's Perspective." *Proceedings of the 1981 Rate Suspension on Problems of Regulated Indutries*. Columbia, Mo.: University of Missouri Extension Publications, 1981.

Evans, David S., ed. *Breaking Up Bell: Essays on Industrial Organization and Regulation*. Amsterdam: North-Holland, 1983.

Faulhaber, G. "Cross-Subsidization: Pricing in Public Enterprise." *American Economic Review* 65 (1975): 966–977.

Faulhaber, G., and S. Levinson. "Subsidy Free Prices and Anonymous Equity." *American Economic Review* 71 (1981): 1083–1091.

Faulhaber, G., and J. Panzar. "Optimal Two-Part Tariffs with Self-Selection." Bell Laboratories Economic Discussion Paper No. 74, January 1977.

Federal Communications Commission Network Inquiry Special Staff. *New Television Networks: Entry, Jurisdiction, Ownership and Regulation*. Vol. 2. Final report. 1980.

Ferris, C. D., and D. Kelley. "The Transition to Structural Telecommunications Regulation." In *Challenges for Public Utility Regulation in the 1980s*. East Lansing, Mich.: Michigan State University Press, 1981.

Fisher, Frank, Joen Greenwood, and John McGowan. *Folded, Spindled, and Mutilated: Economic Analysis and* U.S. *v*. IBM. Cambridge, Mass.: MIT Press, 1983.

Garfinkel, Lawrence. Paper presented at plenary session of the Twelfth Annual Telecommunications Policy Research Conference, Airlie House, Airlie, Virginia, April 23, 1984.

Garfinkel, Lawrence, and P. B. Linhardt. "The Revenue Analysis of Local Measured Telephone Service." *Public Utilities Fortnightly*, October 9, 1980, 15–21.

Griffin, J. M. "The Welfare Implications of Externalities and Price Elasticities for Telecommunications Pricing." *Review of Economics and Statistics* 64 (1982): 59–66.

Hazelwood, A. "Optimum Pricing as Applied to Telephone Service." *Review of Economic Studies* 18 (1950–1951): 67–78.

Joskow, P. L. "The Determination of the Allowed Rate of Return in a Formal Regulatory Proceeding." *Bell Journal of Economics and Management Science* 3 (1972): 632–644.

———. "Pricing Decisions of Regulated Firms: A Behavioral Approach." *Bell Journal of Economics and Management Science* 4 (1973): 118–140.

———. "Inflation and Environmental Concern: Structural Change in the Process of Public Utility Price Regulation." *Journal of Law and Economics* 17 (1974): 291–327.

Joskow, P. L., and R. Noll. "Regulation in Theory and Practice." In *Studies in Public Regulation*, edited by G. Fromm. Cambridge, Mass.: MIT Press, 1981.

Kahn, A. E. *The Economics of Regulation*. Vols. 1 and 2. New York: Wiley, 1971.

Kahn, A. E., and C. A. Zielinksi. "New Rate Structures in Telecommunications." *Public Utilities Fortnightly* 97 (1976): 19–24.

Katz, Michael L., and Robert D. Willig. Paper presented at the Twelfth Annual Telecommunications Policy Research Conference, Airlie House, Airlie, Virginia, April 26, 1984.

Kelley, D. *Deregulation after Divestiture: The Effect of the AT&T Settlement on Competition*. FCC Office of Plans and Policy Working Paper No. 8. April 1982.

Levin, Harvey J. *Fact and Fancy in Television Regulation*. New York: Russell Sage Foundation, 1980.

Littlechild, S. C. "Two-part Tariffs and Consumption Externalities," *Bell Journal of Economics* 6 (1975): 661–670.

______. "The Role of Consumption Externalities in the Pricing of Telephone Service." In *Pricing in Regulation Industries: Theory and Application*, edited by John T. Wenders. Denver, Colo.: Mountain States Telephone and Telegraph Co., 1977.

______. *Elements of Telecommunications Economics*. Stevenage, England: Peter Peregrinus Ltd., 1979.

MacAvoy, Paul W. *Deregulation of Cable Television*. Washington, D.C.: American Enterprise Institute, 1977.

MacNeal, H. *The Story of Independent Telephony*. Chicago: Independent Pioneer Telephone Association, 1934.

Margeson, A. "Public Policy Issues of Network Access Pricing." In *Issues in Public Policy Regulation*, edited by H. A. Trebing. East Lansing, Mich.: Michigan State University Press, 1979.

Meyer, J. R., et al. *The Economics of Competition in the Telecommunications Industry*. Cambridge, Mass.: Oelgeschlager, Gunn & Hain, 1980.

Mitchell, B. M. "Optimal Pricing of Local Telephone Service." *American Economic Review* 68 (1978): 517–537.

______. "Alternative Measured Service Structures for Local Telephone Service." In *Issues in Public Utility Pricing and Regulation*, edited by M. Crew. Lexington, Mass.: Heath, 1980. (a)

______. *Economic Issues in Usage-Sensitive Pricing*. Rand Paper Series No. P-6530. Santa Monica, Calif.: Rand Corporation, 1980. (b)

______. *Local Telephone Costs and the Design of Rate Structures*. Rand Paper Series No. P-6617. Santa Monica, Calif.: Rand Corporation, 1981.

Morris, R. L., and R. S. Preece. "Negotiating for Improved Interconnection between U.S. Telcos and Their Competitors." *Telecommunications Policy* 6 (1982): 179–198. (a)

______. *Negotiating for Improved Interconnection: The Incentives to Bargain*. FCC Office of Plans and Policy Working Paper No. 7. Revised April 1982. (b)

Noll, Roger, Merton J. Peck, and John J. McGowan. *Economic Aspects of Television Regulation*. Washington, D.C.: Brookings Institution, 1973.

Oi, W. Y. "A Disneyland Dilemma: Two-Part Tariffs for a Mickey Mouse Monopoly." *Quarterly Journal of Economics* 85 (1971): 77–96.

Ordover, J. "Understanding Economic Justice: Some Recent Developments in Pure and Applied Welfare Economics." In *Economic Perspectives: An Annual Survey of Economics*, edited by M. B. Ballabon. New York: Harwood, 1979.

Ordover, J., and J. Panzar. "On the Nonexistence of Pareto-Superior Outlay Schedules." *Bell Journal of Economics* 11 (1980): 351–354.

Ordover, J., and R. Willig. "An Economic Definition of Predation: Pricing and Product Innovation." *Yale Law Journal* 91 (1981): 8–53. (a)

———. "Notes on Non-Price Anticompetitive Practices by Dominant Firms." Paper presented to the Telecommunications Policy Research Conference, Annapolis, Maryland, 1981. (b)

———. "Local Telephone Pricing in a Competitive Environment." Paper presented at the Columbia Business School Conference on Regulation and New Telecommunications Networks, Arden House, New York, June 3, 1982.

Owen, Bruce M., Jack H. Beebe, and Willard G. Manning, Jr. *Television Economics*. Lexington, Mass.: Heath, 1974.

Owen, Bruce M., and R. Braeutigam. *The Regulation Game: Strategic Use of the Administrative Process*. Cambridge, Mass.: Ballinger, 1978.

Park, R. E., and B. M. Mitchell. "Optimal Peak-Load for Local Telephone Calls." Paper presented at the Telecommunications Policy Research Conference, Annapolis, Maryland, April 1982, and the International Forecasting Conference, Paris, June 1982.

Peltzman, S. "Toward a More General Theory of Regulation." *Journal of Law and Economics* 14 (1976): 109–148.

Posner, R. A. "Taxation by Regulation." *Bell Journal of Economics and Management Science* 2 (1971): 22–50.

———. "Theories of Economic Regulation." *Bell Journal of Economics and Management Science* 5 (1974): 335–358.

Preece, R. "A Club-Theoretic Approach to Telephone Access Externalities." Unpublished FCC staff paper, n.d.

Preece, Robert, and Roy L. Morris. Paper presented at the Twelfth Annual Telecommunications Policy Research Conference, Airlie House, Airlie, Virginia, April 26, 1984.

Roberts, K. W. S. "Welfare Considerations of Nonlinear Pricing." *Economic Journal* 89 (1979): 66–83.

Rohlfs, J. "A Theory of Interdependent Demand for a Communications Service." *Bell Journal of Economics and Management Science* 5 (1974): 16–37.

———. *Economically Efficient Bell System Pricing*. Bell Laboratories Economic Discussion Paper No. 138. 1979.

Scherer, F. M. *Industrial Market Structure and Economic Performance*. New York: Rand McNally, 1980.

Selwyn, L. L., and G. F. Borton. "USP: Will USP Really Decrease Local Service Costs?" *Telephony*, January 28, 1980, 36–38.

Sherman, R., and M. L. Visscher. "Rate-of-Return Regulation and Price Structure." In *Problems in Public Utility Economics and Regulation*, edited by M. Crew. Lexington, Mass.: Heath, 1979.

Spence, M. "Nonlinear Prices and Welfare." *Journal of Public Economics* 8 (1977): 1–18.

Squire, L. "Some Aspects of Optimal Pricing for Telecommunications." *Bell Journal of Economics and Management Science* 4 (1973): 515–525.

Stigler, G. G. "The Theory of Economic Regulation." *Bell Journal of Economics and Management Science* 2 (1971): 3–21.

Taylor, L. *Telecommunications Demand: A Survey and Critique*. Cambridge, Mass.: Ballinger, 1980.

U.S. Congress. House. Subcommittee on Telecommunications, Consumer Protection, and Finance of the Committee on Energy and Commerce. *Telecommunications in Transition: The Status of Competition in the Telecommunications Industry*. Washington, D.C.: Government Printing Office, November 3, 1981.

White, L. J. "On the Welfare Effects of Resale in the Context of a Nonlinear Pricing Schedule." *Bell Journal of Economics* 13 (1982): 280–285.

Willig, R. D. "Pareto-Superior Nonlinear Outlay Schedules." *Bell Journal of Economics* 9 (1978): 56–69.

———. "Customer Equity and Local Measured Service." In *Perspectives on Local Measured Service: Proceedings of the Telecommunications Industry Workshop,* edited by J.A. Baude et al. Kansas City: Telecommunications Workship Organizing Committee, 1979. (a)

———. "The Theory of Network Access Pricing." In *Issues in Public Utility Pricing and Regulation*, edited by M. Crew. Lexington, Mass.: Heath, 1979. (b)

———. Paper presented at the Twelfth Annual Telecommunications Policy Research Conference, Airlie House, Airlie, Virginia, April 26, 1984.

———. "Market Structure and Government Intervention in Access Markets." In *Telecommunications Access and Public Policy*, edited by Alan Baughcum and Gerald Faulhaber. Norwood, N.J.: Ablex, 1984.

Zajac, E. E. *Fairness or Efficiency: An Introduction to Public Utility Pricing*. Cambridge, Mass.: Ballinger, 1978.

Five

A Survey of French Regulatory Policy

Jean-Paul Voge

Telecommunications

ORGANIZATION (LES TÉLÉCOMMUNICATIONS FRANÇAISES 1982)

French Telecom

The telecommunications branch of the French PTT is the Direction Générale des Télécommunications (DGT). Throughout this chapter, the DGT will be referred to as French Telecom.

By law, telecommunications in France is a monopoly of the Ministère des Postes, des Télécommunications et de la Télédiffusion (PTT Ministry). Article L.33 of the Code des PTT (PTT Code) states: "No telecommunications installation shall be established or employed for the transmission of correspondence except by the Minister or with his authorization."

It should be noted that the law does not oblige the minister (through his departments) to do everything himself. Nevertheless, nothing can be done without his agreement. As a consequence, telecommunications in France is the responsibility of a state administration that is part of the PTT Ministry.

This administration is French Telecom. Its general mission is to implement and operate all telecommunications networks and services. Depending on the circumstances, this mission is performed by the administration's own employees or is delegated in part to other parties.

French Telecom has a complex structure, based essentially on the following hierarchical levels:

A headquarters team known as the General Directorate

One or two intermediary management levels, in the form of departments organized either on a geographical basis (Regional Directorates and Operations Directorates, each covering part of the national territory) or to satisfy special needs (so-called External Departments with nationwide activities)

A bottom level of departments for job execution (exchange maintenance, customer service, etc.)

French Telecom is one of the two traditional branches of the PTT Ministry, the other being the Direction Générale des Postes (French Postal Department). The head of French Telecom is the Directeur Général des Télécommunications (Director-General of Telecommunications). Since January 1980, the PTT Ministry has also been responsible, by delegation of authority by the prime minister, for Télédiffusion de France (TDF), the national broadcasting authority (see the Audiovisual Media section of this chapter).

French Telecom includes a major research organization, the Centre National d'Etudes des Télécommunications (CNET), or National Telecommunications Research Center. The CNET performs fundamental research, applied research, and development work in telecommunications and related areas. As well as pursuing R&D determined by French Telecom's internal needs and objectives, the CNET provides expert advice and assistance to outside companies and organizations.

In 1982, French Telecom had a total staff of around 164,000, including 4300 at the CNET. In the same year, its revenues were 54 billion francs, the number of main telephone lines reached 19.5 million, and the number of telephones 29.6 million. Between 1972 and 1982, the number of main lines grew at an average annual rate of 16%. Finally, the R&D budget was 2.2 billion francs in 1982, including internal R&D by the CNET plus R&D contracts awarded to outside companies and organizations.

Subsidiaries of French Telecom

French Telecom does not act directly in all its areas of responsibility. In some cases, it acts through a separate entity or subsidiary. This is usually a Société d'Economie Mixte (mixed investment company), a company constituted in accordance with private law but in which a large part or all the capital is owned by the state, giving the latter total control.

Most of these subsidiaries are in fact controlled by the Compagnie Française de Câbles Sous-Marins et de Radio, more commonly known as France Câbles et Radio (FCR), itself controlled by the French state since 1945. The FCR Group has two main kinds of subsidiaries:

Foreign subsidiaries. In most countries, the law forbids activities by companies other than those constituted under local law. This is why FCR has set up a large number of such subsidiary companies (20 at the beginning of 1980), in both French-speaking countries (including Senegal and the Central African Republic) and non-French-speaking countries (e.g., Portugal, Greece, Israel, and Lebanon). These companies typically operate submarine cables, satellite ground stations, or both. Special mention should be made of France Telecom, Inc., in the United States.

French subsidiaries (i.e., entities constituted under French law). These are five in number, including two quite large companies: EGT and Télésystèmes. Entreprise Générale des Télécommunications (EGT) procures, markets, installs, and maintains equipment such as telephone answering machines, Eurosignal paging receivers, automatic mobile telephones, and facsimile machines. Télésystèmes is a leading computer services and software company.

There are also subsidiaries of French Telecom partly controlled by the FCR Group. They range from small to large enterprises, and include the following:

Transpac, a company that operates and markets the packet-switched data network of the same name. The French state holds at least 67% of its capital; main network users hold at least 28%.

Société Française d'Etudes et de Réalisations d'Equipements de Télécommunications (SOFRECOM), which provides technical assistance and engineering services for foreign customers. Its main lines of activity are network planning, consulting engineering for specific networks and facilities, supervision of contract execution, assistance in operation and maintenance, and training services. Its capital is divided between the French state (33%) and a number of major French banks.

Société Mixte pour le Développement de la Technique des Télécommunications (SOTELEC). Among other activities, SOTELEC publishes the technical journal *Commutation & Transmission*, in separate French and English editions.

The Industrial Environment

French Telecom acts through its own departments and through its subsidiaries, the latter being legally separate entities in which the administration nevertheless has a power of control.

This being said, the world of telecommunications in France does not consist exclusively of French Telecom and its subsidiaries. There are many other companies whose business lies partly or totally in the telecommunications sector. French Telecom has no direct control over these companies, but strong ties necessarily exist because of the administration's role as a customer. They fall into three main categories: manufacturers, civil engineering and installation firms working for French Telecom, and "independent installers."

Manufacturers

With the exception of a few low-volume items to meet rather specific requirements (e.g., traffic recording machines), French Telecom has never manufactured equipment. Instead, equipment is procured from private industry, using general procedures for state procurements.

Orders from French Telecom account for some two-thirds of the output of the French civil telecommunications industry. The remaining one-third corresponds to:

Orders for private equipment in the home market (e.g., PABXs, which in France are purchased directly from the manufacturers or their agents)

Export orders

At a time when issues of employment and the balances of trade and payments are of great importance, the following figures give an idea of the size of the French telecommunications manufacturing industry:

People employed in 1982: 72,000

Total 1982 sales: 21 billion francs, of which 24% were export sales and 76% were sales to the home market

The industry has set the target of exporting at least one-third of its output.

About 40 companies of significant size in France manufacture telecommunications equipment, but around 90% of total production is achieved by five large groups. The largest three of these groups were nationalized in 1981:

The Compagnie Générale d'Electricité (CGE) Group, which includes CIT–Alcatel, Télic–Alcatel, and Les Câbles de Lyon

The Thomson Group, the most important members of which (in the telecommunications sector) are Thomson–CSF and Lignes Télégraphiques et Téléphoniques (LTT)

Compagnie Générale de Constructions Téléphoniques (CGCT), formerly a subsidiary of ITT

It has recently been decided to merge the civil telecommunications activities of the CGE and Thomson groups into a new company, Alcatel–Thomson.

The other two large groups, neither of which is nationalized, are:

The G3S Group, which includes Compagnie des Signaux et d'Entreprises Electriques (CSEE), Société d'Applications Générales d'Electricité et de Mécanique (SAGEM), and Société Anonyme des Télécommunications (SAT)

Télécommunications Radioélectriques et Téléphoniques (TRT), a subsidiary of Phillips

Other big companies are also playing a growing role in telecommunications in France. They include the Matra Group, in which the French state has a majority holding, and the Jeumont–Schneider company, a subsidiary of the Empain–Schneider Group. Mention should also be made of two computer companies that have a significant involvement in the development and growth of data communications and telematics: Bull (formerly CII–Honeywell Bull), a nationalized company and Europe's second largest computer manufacturer, and IBM–France.

The breakdown of industry sales by category of product in 1980 was as follows:

Switching	50%
Radiolink (including microwave)	14%
Cables	7%
Transmission equipment	13%
Other (subscriber premises equipment, telegraph and telex equipment, data communications equipment, etc.)	16%

Civil Engineering and Installation Firms Working for French Telecom

Although French Telecom has hardly ever manufactured equipment, it has always installed equipment and continues to do so. Nonetheless, it has at all times contracted certain kinds of work (e.g., laying large cables) to specialized companies for an agreed price. The following figures give an idea of the volume of work entrusted to such firms:

Total value of contracts in 1980: 5.5 billion francs

Percentage of total line work carried out by outside firms: 80% (but 100% for civil works)

Number of companies executing civil engineering and other line work on behalf of French Telecom: about 1650

Unlike equipment manufacturers, these companies are numerous and usually small.

Independent Installers

Alongside equipment manufacturers and firms performing installation work for French Telecom on a contract basis, there are so-called independent installers. These are companies that sell or rent equipment directly to customers; they also install the equipment, including PABXs, key telephone systems, and data communications equipment. This is because, despite its monopoly, French Telecom allows customers, especially professional and business customers, to procure their on-premises telecommunications equipment directly. In this regard, the French situation differs significantly from that in many other countries.

As a general rule, the installers do not manufacture equipment themselves, their role being limited to supply (as agents of manufacturers), installation, and maintenance. Not just any company can set up as an installer in France; an authorization from French Telecom is necessary. At present, there are some 500 authorized installers in France. But the real situation is somewhat more complex. It is possible for a company to act as an installer without being authorized by French Telecom, provided it is answered for by an authorized installer or a manufacturer. The independent installer business employs a total of around 15,000 people and has a turnover of around 2 billion francs. Finally, it should be noted that an independent installer may also perform installation work under contract for French Telecom.

CURRENT REGULATORY POLICY AND TRENDS (DAMLAMIAN 1983)

In the area of telecommunications, deregulation is often presented as the necessary condition for efficient development of the new kinds of networks and new services made possible by technological progress, notably by giving freer play to the synergy between telecommunications and information processing. According to its supporters, deregulation has the potential to satisfy the needs of customers better, to enhance quality, and to reduce costs.

In this context, a state monopoly of telecommunications is often presented as an obstacle to the development of new services. However, monopoly is not synonymous with sclerosis. There is no single solution that is automatically the best for all countries, whatever their size, level of industrialization, existing telecommunications resources, history, and so on. The truth is that monopoly and liberalism are everywhere closely mixed, but in varying proportions.

This is especially true in France. Although certain legal and regulatory texts may give the impression that there is a very strict monopoly based on law, the real situation is characterized by rather flexible application of these principles. Over the years, the monopoly has as a concept and as a practical force been adapted to changes in the technologies of telecommunications. A good example of such evolution is the law of July 29, 1982, on audiovisual communication, discussed later in this chapter.

Reasons for Deregulation

Three sorts of reasons are usually given for deregulating telecommunications: (1) technical reasons; (2) economic or industrial reasons; and (3) political reasons.

Technical Reasons

Over the past 20 years, the technologies of telecommunications and information processing have been converging. In many countries, the first of these sectors has been totally regulated, while the second has been totally unregulated. This situation could not last, and new arrangements have become increasingly necessary.

In addition, telecommunications networks were in the past very rigid, all the interfaces between network elements being more or less defined once and for all, with only a small degree of adaptability. This helped consolidate the existing monopolies and led to a certain confusion between the concepts of the network, the service, and even the terminal. The single term *telephone*, for example, refers not only to the telephone set at a subscriber's home, but also to the telephone network, and to the telephone service.

More recently, technological advances have permitted the insertion of computer-like systems in telecommunications networks. The interfaces between network elements have become increasingly explicit and increasingly flexible, thanks to progress in international standardization and the growing use of software rather than hardware for many functions.

Networks as a whole are evolving slowly but surely toward integrated service digital networks (ISDNs). On the one hand, we therefore have a trend toward the unification of networks; on the other hand, there is a diversification of terminal equipment and services. For some people, all this means that there is now a place for newcomers, a place made free by deregulation. This is certainly true for terminal equipment and services.

Concerning the networks, however, there is a very strong trend toward less diversity than in the past, toward a single network one day using optical fibers to provide not only telephony, data communications, and telematic services but also television and other videocommunications services.

Economic and Industrial Reasons

Before deregulation, structures for the operation of telecommunications services were similar in all countries of the world. There was either a legal monopoly exercised directly or indirectly by the state or a natural monopoly exercised by a private company under the supervision or control of the state. In the first case, the justification was political: Telecommunications is a public-service activity that must not escape the direct control of the state. In the second case, the justification was economic, but it was then necessary for the state to impose public-service obligations and tariff constraints on the private company exercising the monopoly.

The economic reasons for deregulation mainly concern countries like the United States, where the situation was that of a natural monopoly exercised by a private company. The new reasoning consists of shifting the frontiers within which market forces act so that new competition is created without altogether eliminating the situation of natural monopoly. The argument, which remains to be proven, is that this added competition will result in lower tariffs. In any case, a mechanism must be provided for guaranteeing a minimum service to all citizens without discrimination.

It should be noted that the deregulatory zeal of the U.S. authorities has not yet gone so far as to eliminate the natural monopoly of the new regional companies spawned by AT&T. And these companies operate networks comparable in size to the national telephone networks in European countries such as Italy, the Federal Republic of Germany, the United Kingdom, and France.

Beyond the economic reasons mentioned above, there are reasons of national industrial policy. By means of deregulation, new manufacturers and service companies are given access to business that in the past was compartmentalized and therefore overly protected from competition. This reasoning is that of the U.S. authorities, for example: The clash between AT&T and IBM, not to mention other U.S. and foreign companies, is expected to improve the competitiveness of U.S. companies over companies in other parts of the world.

These reasons are perhaps valid in the United States, but are much less valid in Europe, at least in the current situation. The U.S. domestic market is very large. There is no equivalent market in a European country on which local companies can develop their strengths. While promoting the progressive and balanced emergence of a European market, as opposed to a set of national markets in European countries, it is therefore necessary when considering deregulation to take into account the economic and industrial interests of each country.

Political Reasons

For some countries, including the United States and a few countries in Europe, deregulation is motivated at least in part by political ideology. The idea here is to reduce the role of the state in matters considered to be best regulated by free market forces. This is not the policy of the French government.

The Situation in France

What is the situation in France today? The answer is a mixture of monopoly and liberalism. Whereas for the postal service, the state has by law the exclusive right to exercise certain activities, this is not the case for telecommunications. As explained, there is no longer an inflexible legal monopoly in France for telecommunications.

The current law allows the PTT minister to authorize the ministry or a third party to establish and make use of telecommunications facilities. The arrangements for telecommunications in France are thus characterized by a power of authorization given to the PTT minister, representing the State, and not by a strict monopoly.

Moreover, this power is not arbitrary. Instead, it is governed by precise legal rules that guarantee, under the control of the legal authorities, identical treatment for all users, within the context of a neutral and permanent public service.

Finally, it is undeniable that the minister's power of authorization has, since the end of the nineteenth century, been exercised in a very flexible and liberal manner. It is true that networks are usually directly financed, built, and operated by the PTT. But the situation is very different for terminal equipment, where a large degree of competition has been introduced in the market since 1920.

Mention should be made of PABXs in particular, where the PTT's role has always been limited to the supply and maintenance of very small exchanges. A large and thriving private sector exists in France for selling, installing, and maintaining customer premises equipment, employing over 15,000 people. The countries that today present themselves as champions of liberalism are, in this regard, only following, more than 60 years afterward, in France's footsteps.

The situation as it stands has produced most of the expected advantages of a monopoly:

A universal service, accessible to all and in all parts of the national territory

The existence of reliable and highly secure networks

Tariffs that are the same for customers in all parts of the national territory, that are designed to promote regional development, and that do not favor areas or routes of high traffic. (The reality of all deregulation, in contrast, is that of "cream skimming," in which the routes or types of traffic of interest to newcomers are those generating higher-than-average profits.)

Common standards, simplifying life for customers and producing economies of scale by avoiding interfaces between heterogeneous elements

These many advantages are not offset by an equally long list of negative effects of the sort attributed by some people to a natural or legal monopoly (lack of dynamism and innovation, higher-than-necessary costs, etc.). Tariffs in France are at present lower than in most other West European countries. And far from inhibiting innovation, the organization of telecommunications in France has stimulated it.

Three examples illustrate this point. The first is the development of digital telephone switching. The world's first digital time-division telephone exchange to enter commercial service in a public network was commissioned in 1970 in the Brittany region of France. In 1984, more than 25% of switching in the public switched network was digital, and this proportion has increased to 50% in 1986. It has paved the way for the forthcoming opening of a 144 kbit/s switched digital service, a major step along the road to an ISDN.

The second example is telematics and data communications, in which France is a recognized world leader. The Transpac packet-switched public data network was opened in 1978 and has become the world's largest X.25 network. Videotex is a fast expanding reality. After the "3V" home videotex trial, involving some 2500 households, began near Paris in 1981, a nationwide professional videotex network was inaugurated in 1982. General public videotex is being introduced at an accelerating rate in many parts of the country, in harmony with the electronic directory service. A further illustration is the *Telecom 1* communications satellite, launched in 1984. One of its missions will be to support a digital business network for customers in France and other European nations.

The third example is the recent go-ahead by the French government for the "recabling of France," using optical fibers and other advanced concepts to implement interactive cable television and videocommunications networks. French Telecom is to build, own, and operate these networks, as explained later in this chapter. Subscribers will eventually be able to receive, over a single line, a complete spectrum of narrowband and broadband services: broadcast television channels, including those distributed by satellite; interactive access to TV program banks and film libraries, and to audiovisual data bases; stereo sound programs; telephony (and perhaps later videophony); telematic and data services; remote security monitoring; and so forth. The cost advantages of such integrated networks are in themselves a strong argument in favor of a natural monopoly.

We next examine in somewhat more detail the measures taken by French Telecom for the development of the Transpac network and of videotex and the electronic directory service, because they afford a good illustration of the French administration's regulatory policy. The new cable television and videocommunications networks are discussed at some length later in the chapter.

The Transpac Network (Bonnetblanc 1984)

With more than 12,000 direct customer connections, Transpac is today the world's largest packet-switched data network. When the network was set up in 1978, its "godfathers" had to reconcile three sets of objectives and interests, by no means always complementary:

A *public service* mission of meeting the needs of all customers—from the smallest to the largest, from small companies to very large corporations and administrations—in all parts of the national territory, notably by accommodating a large range of transmission speeds, codes, and procedures

A *general economic objective* of establishing and marketing a profitable public network and at the same time stimulating growth in the French manufacturing and software industries, new data bases and data banks, and the development of advanced services for professional and business customers

The *special interests* of computer and data network manufacturers and vendors, computer service companies, and software houses, which tended to look on French Telecom as a competitor

For this reason, the network is owned and operated by a private company, Transpac. French Telecom holds two-thirds of the shares in this company, the remainder belonging to concerned private-sector partners. This is a good example of how the policy of separate subsidiaries allows French Telecom, in the case of new services relying on leading-edge technologies, to adopt more flexible and streamlined managerial and organizational arrangements than in the case of a public service run directly by the administration. It also has the advantage of establishing mutually profitable cooperation between the public and private sectors.

Videotex and the Electronic Directory Service (Bonnetblanc 1984)

Successful implementation of home videotex for the general public is possible only if the terminal price is that of a mass-market product sold in hundreds of thousands or millions of units. The difficulty lies in creating this mass market in order to achieve the cost reductions. In Great Britain, for example, 5 years after launching of Prestel there was a total of only 25,000 terminals. The French solution is now well known. French Telecom has specified and ordered in large quantities a minimal-cost videotex terminal known as the Minitel, and is introducing it in homes throughout the country as an "electronic telephone directory" to replace traditional paper directories. If things go as planned, the Minitel terminals will also be used for access to a broad range of videotex services. The interest for and effective use of each service will determine its economic feasibility and existence, but will certainly differ considerably from subscriber to subscriber. It is thus necessary to reconcile in a single project the fundamentally egalitarian nature of a public service, in which a need should be satisfied only if it is sufficiently widespread, and the particular requirements of relatively limited groups of users.

The compromise solution adopted by French Telecom has several original aspects in regard to the usual procedures for public services. The electronic directory service is being made available only to volunteer subscribers—others continue receiving paper directory books—and after wide-ranging coordination with all interested parties. In particular, the service is being opened in each region only at the request of its elected authorities, who thus in effect underwrite the economic interest of the service and share responsibility for its deployment with French Telecom. The coordination concerns the elected regional, departmental, and local authorities; the local populations; and potential service providers (including the local press). There is no formal agreement creating legally binding relations between the various parties, but the coordination promotes consensus. It also helps to protect the interests of each party and establish balanced participation by all concerned.

This being said, proper written agreements are, of course, necessary with the service providers and operators of host computer centers. They may be located in regions where the electronic directory service is open or in other regions, and obviously have an important role to play in promoting and marketing new videotex services.

French Policy for the Coming Years

The coming years in France will see a number of important developments, changing the terms of the debate between monopoly and deregulation. These will include the following:

1. Continued expansion of public data networks, the availability of higher-speed channels, and the integration of voice and data traffic. For example:

Continued rapid growth of the Transpac network, which will have some 50,000 customer connections by 1987.

Integration of telephone (voice) and data traffic in the *Telecom 1* satellite-based business network beginning in 1984. This network will offer customers a range of transmission speeds up to 2 Mbit/s.

Opening in 1985 of a 64 and 144 kbit/s switched digital service over the public switched telephone network, making use of digital local and transit exchanges and of digital transmission between exchanges. The tariffs for this service will be highly attractive, about twice those for the current telephone service.

Connection of PABXs to the PSTN by 2 Mbit/s and 512 kbit/s digital links.

Rapid extension of direct in-dialing (DID) to medium-size PABXs.

Possibility for digital PABXs to have slave-line connection or switching units at remote locations within the same PSTN charging area.

All these developments will facilitate the implementation of multi-service private-company networks using the infrastructures of public networks, and will reduce the relative importance of leased lines and circuits.

2. Implementation of a new tariff policy, involving a progressive convergence of user charges and actual costs for French Telecom. In the case of telephone service, this will involve a reduction in rates for long-distance national and international calls;[1] time-dependent charging for local calls; and a new system of time bands and reduced-rate tariffs for off-peak calling.

3. Measures favorable to the development of value-added services using public networks with the active but not exclusive participation of French Telecom and its subsidiaries. The idea here is twofold:

Develop all possible kinds and sources of traffic, so as to increase the profitability of networks.

Preserve national interests in the industrial, commercial, and even cultural areas by avoiding the continuation or repetition of certain aspects of today's situation. At present, French companies are forced to make use in some cases of foreign value-added services and facilities, quite simply because they are not available in France.

Examples include various data bases, mainly in the United States, and message switching on private networks (e.g., the General Electric network).

In this context, French Telecom is installing a videotex services access network with uniform tariffs spanning the entire national territory, and is placing Minitel terminals in homes and offices across France for the electronic directory service and other applications. In the French Telecom approach to videotex, it will not directly operate or manage any host computers, except those for the electronic directory service and other internal applications. Instead, the network is being made as open as possible, with maximum freedom for service providers to attach their computers. The French Telecom charges for use of its facilities are independent of the user–host distance. In addition, arrangements exist so that the service providers can obtain adequate payment for their services if they desire. All this adds up to an exceptionally favorable opportunity and environment for companies to develop and market added-value services.

4. An unchanging policy with regard to terminals and other customer premises equipment. The present policy is very liberal and will remain so. In the next few years, we may expect to see very strong growth in the markets for a second and even third telephone set in private households, and for cordless telephones and various telephone-line peripherals (e.g., answering machines). The net result will be increased traffic, to which French Telecom certainly has no objection, requiring only that the equipment sold to customers comply with a number of technical standards. It will, of course, encourage French companies to manufacture and sell products in these markets when they are of significant size.

In view of the preceding, French Telecom has little doubt of its ability in the coming years to continue reconciling the concept of a public service with economic dynamism and progress, without the need to modify the laws governing telecommunications in France.

Deregulation of International Traffic

The French position is very clear on deregulation of international traffic. Each country is free independently to modify the organization of its domestic telecommunications networks, but any change in the arrangements for international traffic requires a certain degree of coordination with other countries.

To take the example of the United States: The Federal Communications Commission (FCC) can introduce wide-reaching regulatory changes within the country itself, such as promoting competition in long-distance service. If, however, it wishes to approve new competition in carrying international traffic, then it must respect certain rules.

The French administration has no objection to competition between U.S. international carriers, including newcomers, provided this does not unilaterally threaten its own stake in international traffic handling and its interests in the development of intercontinental infrastructures. It follows that the FCC must oblige new U.S. international carriers to respect the unwritten rules of the past, which forbid the diversion of traffic between countries and traffic "pirating."

Until now, the infrastructures for intercontinental networks have been installed and administered by organizations with members from all the countries concerned: INTELSAT for satellites, and multination consortia for the construction, operation, and maintenance of submarine cable links. The FCC must not unilaterally authorize the launching and operation of a private transatlantic satellite, for example, without the explicit agreement of other administrations and operating companies in the zone to be covered. To do so would directly affect their interests and would dangerously weaken the financial integrity of INTELSAT, an organization governed by an international treaty signed by the United States. It is worth recalling that the U.S. government has several times invoked the same principle during recent years when opposing the launching of European or Euro-African commercial satellites.

Another important aspect of deregulation for international traffic concerns leased and private-line circuits, particularly freer arrangements for sharing, reselling, and price levels. Any general extension of such practices would be prejudicial to public telecommunications services.

Deregulation of Public-Sector Markets for Telecommunications Equipment

The French administration has come out firmly in favor of opening up the French Telecom market to foreign suppliers, provided the following two principles are respected:

Priority to manufacturers in member countries of the European Economic Community (EEC)

Reciprocity in all cases, based on lists of concerned equipment and, when appropriate, bilateral agreements (e.g., the recent agreement between France and the Federal Republic of Germany concerning cellular radiotelephone networks)

The creation of a European telecommunications market, as opposed to a set of national markets in Europe, would appear to be an essential preliminary step before worldwide negotiations, within the framework of the General Agreement on Tariffs and Trade (GATT), toward the deregulation of international trade in telecommunications equipment and services. Another prerequisite is uniform standards and approval procedures for equipment in Europe. This should be achieved by ongoing work within the Conference of European Postal and Telecommunications Administrations (CEPT) and the International Telegraph and Telephone Consultative Committee (CCITT) of the International Telecommunication Union (ITU).

Audiovisual Media

THE LAW OF JULY 29, 1982 (LA LOI SUR LA COMMUNICATION AUDIOVISUELLE 1983)

Until the law of July 29, 1982, was enacted by the French Parliament, radio and television were a monopoly of the state, for both programming and broadcasting. This being said, there had been since 1980 a sort of spontaneous proliferation of local radio stations; their transmissions were systematically jammed at first, but then tolerated while awaiting the promised new law.

The law of July 29, 1982, ended the monopoly on programming, proclaiming "the freedom to publish audiovisual messages intended for the public and distributed by radiowaves or by cable." The freedom of audiovisual communications remains, however, controlled in regard to broadcasting and distribution. Authorization from the state is needed to use the radiofrequency spectrum. Separate permission is required to set up broadcasting–distribution infrastructure and facilities whenever transmission goes beyond private premises to reach the public domain. Also, the publication of messages, although free in principle, must be covered by a prior declaration or even an authorization. A declaration is sufficient—after a period of transition ending in 1985—in the case of interactive communications services "in which each user personally consults a remote set of texts, sounds, images, or audiovisual documents or messages of any sort, to the exclusion of cinema productions, and receives in return only the requested elements."

In all other cases, a prior authorization will still have to be obtained, either from the government (i.e., the state) or, in the special case of local over-the-air audio broadcasting services (private local radio stations) and local cable television services, from the Haute Autorité de l'Audiovisuel (Audiovisual High Authority) instituted by the law.

The Haute Autorité de l'Audiovisuel has nine members appointed by the president of the Republic, the president of the National Assembly, and the president of the Senate. It is responsible, in particular, for guaranteeing the independence of the public radio and TV service from the political authorities (executive branch), and for issuing certain authorizations to the private sector.

A Parliamentary Delegation, a National Council, and regional committees on audiovisual communications have also been created by the law. The Parliamentary Delegation has supervisory powers and the right to publish opinions and recommendations. The National Council and regional committees have a purely consultative role.

More restrictive conditions apply to certain services. Any service involving over-the-air TV broadcasting and intended for the public at large (rather than a limited audience such as a professional group or the subscribers to a TV service in which the signals are transmitted in scrambled form) must be covered by a "public service concession" rather than a simple authorization. This implies the acceptance of the general and special rules applicable to the public service, and the establishment of a contract defining the arrangements for remunerating the service in question. Moreover, the distribution or broadcasting of cinema productions is the subject of specific rules aimed at protecting movie theaters from dangerous competition. A minimum delay, fixed by government decree, must be observed between the first release of a film to movie theaters and its availability on other audiovisual media. This delay has been set at one year in the case, for example, of the new Canal Plus pay-TV channel, which began broadcasting in November 1984.

One of the important issues addressed by the 1982 law is that of the contribution of advertising to the revenues of audiovisual media. In the case of the public radio and TV service, no ceiling is laid down by the law, but it is expected that the fraction of revenues from advertising will not go above about 25%. For private media, the law provides that this contribution shall not exceed 80%, but with the actual ceiling fixed when the corresponding authorizations are given. In practice, advertising may well be limited to a maximum of 25% on cable networks, so as to limit revenue losses in the local press.

Concerning local private radio stations, a draft law approved by the Council of Ministers on May 3, 1984, makes a distinction between stations owned and operated by nonprofit organizations and those belonging to commercial firms. In the latter case, advertising income will be authorized up to a certain proportion of the total operating budget, probably about 25%. In the case of nonprofit organizations, however, paid advertising will be forbidden, but the stations will be able to receive subsidies from the central government, from regional, departmental, and local authorities, and from public agencies.

The 1982 law was also concerned with strengthening the protection afforded to private persons involved in audiovisual communications: They will benefit from a right of response, and are guaranteed anonymity when choosing from the programs and information available for reception.

THE PUBLIC RADIO AND TELEVISION SERVICE

Before the 1982 law, radio and TV broadcasting were a state monopoly exercised through the Office de la Radio–Télévision Française (ORTF) until 1974 and through a variety of public-sector organizations after 1974:

> Télédiffusion de France (TDF), the national broadcasting authority, is a public establishment of an industrial and commercial nature. TDF designs, engineers, installs, operates, and maintains broadcasting and distribution networks.
>
> Radio France is in charge of the administration and programming of radio broadcasts.
>
> TF1, Antenne 2, and FR3 are the three companies in charge of administration and programming for the three national TV channels in France.
>
> Société Française de Production et de Création Audiovisuelles (SFP) produces TV programs and other audiovisual material.
>
> Institut National Audiovisuel (INA), a public establishment of an industrial and commercial nature, is responsible for maintaining archives, for personnel training, and for research on audiovisual production, creation, and communications.

Radio France, TF1, Antenne 2, and FR3 are Sociétés Nationales de Programmes (national program companies).

The new freedom introduced (under control) into audiovisual communications by the 1982 law does not eliminate the public radio and TV service. The seven organizations listed above have much the same functions under the new system as before the 1982 law. It is possible that other national TV program companies will be created. The INA has changed its name, becoming the Institut National de la Communication Audiovisuelle (INCA). A new Société de Commercialisation (marketing company) is being set up to sell audiovisual program material produced in France to foreign customers. Its capital will be divided between the state and various public organizations.

But the most important change in the public service is its decentralization, involving a progressive but deliberate policy of establishing regional radio and TV companies in metropolitan France and French overseas territories, with a view to stimulating local creation and giving greater coverage to local events. Specifically, plans call for setting up regional radio broadcasting companies (subsidiaries of Radio France), local radio stations, a national TV company with a regional mandate, and a total of 12 regional TV companies, which will be progressively given full independence in programming. This is for metropolitan France. For overseas territories, there will be a national company with subsidiaries in the form of regional TV companies, which will be progressively given full independence in programming. This is for metropolitan France. For overseas France, will be responsible for administering and programming world transmissions aimed, in particular, at French citizens in other countries.

A majority of the capital of the regional and territorial companies will be owned by the national companies of which they are subsidiaries, the remainder being held by the corresponding regional or other territorial elected authorities, directly or through their public establishments.

VIDEOCOMMUNICATIONS AND CABLE TELEVISION NETWORKS

The French government's plans for cable television and videocommunications networks are not yet finalized in all details, but they are a very good illustration of how it is intended to reconcile the new freedom in communications—enshrined in the July 1982 law—with the public monopoly of telecommunications and broadcasting. When the plans are examined closely, they also reveal another important concern: the desire to work closely with industry in order to prepare new markets, in France and abroad, for electronic equipment and audiovisual programs, where there is currently a high degree of dependence on foreign sources (particularly films and series from the United States).

At present there is virtually nothing in the way of cable television networks in France, just a few small collective antenna networks distributing only the French national TV channels plus, in frontier zones, foreign channels that are normally received over the air there. Permission was given in 1973 for the cable distribution of local programs in seven French towns, on an experimental basis. Only one of these towns (Grenoble) actually made use of this authorization. The corresponding trial was interrupted in 1976 because of the lack of interest on the part of viewers, perhaps due in part to inadequate local programming facilities.

The program adopted by the Council of Ministers on May 3, 1984, gives the initiative for the creation of cable networks to elected local authorities. In each case, the local authority is required to establish a Société Locale d'Exploitation du Câble (SLEC), or local cable services company. This company will be responsible for programming on the cable channels, for commercial management and operation, and for relations with persons subscribing to distributed cable services. However, the actual cable network will be owned and operated by French Telecom, which will make channels and facilities available for a fee to the SLEC. For its part, Télédiffusion de France (TDF) will be in charge of the design and operation of the head-end equipment (broadcast receiving station, control center, local programming and production centers, etc.).

Each SLEC may participate in the cost of building its cable network, through a reimbursable loan to French Telecom, representing a negotiated proportion of the capital costs. The SLEC will in each case be a Société d'Economie Mixte (mixed investment company), with a "blocking" (minority veto) or majority share of its capital held by the local authority. Its president will be an elected member of the authority.

Apart from the need to preserve the monopoly on distribution, the essential reason for leaving the ownership of and technical operating responsibility for the new cable networks in the hands of French Telecom is the intention of employing the networks for other than simple TV and sound channel distribution. They are expected to become increasingly interactive (two-way) and also to support telecommunications services, perhaps forming part, some time after 1990, of a nationwide, broadband ISDN. This long-term objective imposes a number of constraints. The networks must have a switched-star structure, rather than a tree structure like most existing cable television systems, in order to provide the requisite degree of interactivity and accommodate two-way services. Above all, it is necessary right from the outset to opt for optical fiber cables rather than coaxial cables for the terminal sections of the networks between households or offices and the distribution centers (addressable hubs) to which they are connected.

The government assigned French Telecom the ambitious target for the initial 1983–1985 period of installing networks reaching out to 1.4 million homes, with a budget of 6 billion French francs (plus 1 billion francs for R&D). State funds of about 2 billion francs will also be used in supporting the development of a programming industry. The concerned local authorities, for their part, will have to contribute some 1.5 billion francs, while the supplier companies (many of them nationalized) will spend perhaps an additional 1.5 billion francs on research and product development.

What will become of these ambitious plans? The first equipment orders have been placed by French Telecom. More than 150 local authorities have shown official interest for a local cable network, but they are also worried about the profitability (or potential losses?) of the networks.

Many issues remain to be resolved, notably concerning financing arrangements and the exact distribution of authority and responsibilities among the various partners. The government would appear to be having some difficulty in reaching the corresponding decisions and has not yet published all the decrees for application of the 1982 law. It would appear that use of optical fiber cables is still very expensive in comparison with coaxial cables, and the choice of an "all optical" design is being questioned in some quarters, where it is seen as too expensive when set against the amount subscribers are willing to pay, at least in an initial phase.[2] It is therefore too early to be sure of all the details of the future cable networks in France. Even so, the broad lines of the program for "recabling the nation," as of this writing, clearly illustrate how the French authorities intend to make intelligent use of cooperation—stimulated rather than spontaneous—between public, semipublic, and private partners, achieved through carefully controlled deregulation in a context of decentralization.

Computers and Information Processing

In the area of computers and information processing, the issue in France is not one of deregulation but on the contrary one of introducing appropriate legislation. All in all, the policy pursued in France during the 1970s was similar to that of most industrialized nations.

The law of January 6, 1978, was concerned with the implications of computers and data files for personal liberties. It provides individuals with a new set of safeguards on data files held by public and private organizations. Citizens now have a right of access to their personal data files, and the right to have errors corrected, under the supervision of a National Commission with regulatory powers. Restrictions have also been placed on the transmission of these data outside France. Finally, in 1983 France ratified the September 17, 1980, Convention of the Council of Europe, which extends protection on an international basis.

Other legal aspects of information processing are still under study or are the subject of evolving regulations: the public's right of access to administration documents and, more generally, "freedom of information"; the relations between the computer–information processing profession and users; copyright and property rights for data, programs, and software; protection of company files; the nature and value of computer data in international trade and for customs purposes; the necessary evolution in the law on evidence and the authentication of documents; and so on.[3]

Deregulation and Decentralization: Contradictory or Complementary Policies?

From the legal point of view, deregulation in France has so far concerned only programming for audiovisual media. In practice, this deregulation of programming turns out to be mainly a decentralization of the earlier state monopoly toward more local authorities. This is reflected in the planned regionalization of the public radio and TV service, and in the plans for new cable television networks.

The legal arrangements and system applicable to transmission, broadcasting, and distribution remain basically unchanged: The PTT minister has the right to grant authorizations or concessions. Only the future will show whether such waivers of the state monopoly will remain fairly limited, as in the past, or whether they will become increasingly common. Once again, liberalization appears more likely here at the local level rather than on a wider or nationwide basis. What is clear is that the state is playing a growing role in industrial policy: outright nationalization of the largest companies in the electronics industry (CGE and Thomson) or purchase of a majority share (Matra); a large financial involvement in the development of the French electronics industry; increased assistance to small- and medium-size companies and to entrepreneurs wishing to set up new companies; export assistance; and so on.

This strong intervention by the state in the electronics and telecommunications industries is in total contrast to the policy of deregulation in the United States. There, deregulation has been decided on in accordance with positions in favor of entrepreneurial freedom, competition, market forces, and the natural mechanisms of self-organization and self-regulation. It is considered necessary to minimize the regulatory activities of the state and cut back a government bureaucracy seen as overstaffed, inefficient, and wasteful of taxpayers' money.

The policies in France and the United States are therefore, in appearance, completely different, even though they have the same aim of promoting economic growth and making the economic crisis a thing of the past. To compare and judge these two policies properly, it is necessary to examine in greater depth the mechanisms of regulation and, more generally, of organization in industrialized societies. A first approach consists of trying to calculate, in quantitative terms, the evolution over recent decades in the costs of organization and regulation. A distinction is now possible between production costs and organizational costs, as Jonscher (1983) and I (Voge 1979) have attempted to demonstrate elsewhere. This distinction corresponds more or less to that established by Machlup (1962) and Porat (1977) between the two complementary sectors of production: (1) the sector of physical or material production; and (2) the sector of production (or distribution) of information.

This approach reveals a very strong increase in the costs of organization and regulation in comparison with those of production. At present, organizational costs represent close to 50% of the national product, against only 10% at the beginning of the century. It also reveals that the explosive growth in these costs—which has certainly played a role in the present economic crisis—is closely tied to the structures of political and economic organizations. These structures, which are almost universally centralized and pyramidal, are poorly adapted to communications between individuals. They make interactive (two-way) exchanges of information much too expensive, unlike the structures employed in electronic communications networks. The latter are in the main meshed or cellular structures, shown by theory and experience to be far more cost-effective (Voge 1983). Meshing does not exclude, of course, a hierarchy of meshed structures of different sizes, interconnecting, for example, increasingly large subsets of telephones (local, regional, national, etc.) by means of a parallel hierarchy of telephone exchanges.

The key difference between the two kinds of structure lies in the fact that meshed structures provide a large number of alternative paths for communicating between any two points, whereas pyramidal structures impose a single, hierarchical path. Also, in a meshed (telephone) network, calls tend to use the shortest possible path, only infrequently involving the top level of the hierarchy. It is clear that the transposition of such arrangements to human organizations implies a decentralization of the powers of choice and decision assigned to the various organizational levels.

The implementation of more cost-efficient organizational structures would thus seem to depend on two complementary conditions: (1) a plurality of alternative paths; and (2) decentralization of decision making in order to provide freedom of choice among these paths. U.S.-style deregulation is, at first sight, conducive to the creation of a plurality of paths and alternative solutions. However, our experience of what happened in the United States in the latter part of the nineteenth century shows that unbridled competition can instead lead to a proliferation of monopolies, of the sort associated with Rockefeller, Vanderbilt, Carnegie, and Pierpont Morgan. It was precisely to mitigate the negative effects of these "natural monopolies" that regulatory measures (e.g., the Sherman Antitrust Act) and the first regulatory commissions for transportation, communications, gas, and electricity were created in the early twentieth century. It is therefore rather astonishing to see these antitrust measures now weakened in the name of a deregulatory policy that pretends to be an attack on monopolies but that in practice eliminates the obstacles to a dividing up of the world market between cartels or the constitution of international trading companies of the Japanese variety.

The following question therefore arises: Does the quest for an optimal economy and optimal efficiency in economic organization not require a political "ecumenism" that preserves a proper balance between U.S.-style deregulation and the new French-style decentralization?[4] Such deliberate, imposed decentralization would be a more flexible and undoubtedly more realistic replacement for an antitrust policy, the difficulties and limits of which were illustrated by the long antitrust proceeding against IBM, finally abandoned under the Reagan administration. The breakup of AT&T is a good example of a solution that harmoniously combines decentralization (autonomy of the operating companies formerly part of the Bell System) and deregulation. Should the large multinational corporations not also be decentralized, by imposing the autonomy of their various national subsidiaries?

It is certainly too early to answer this question. But it is important to initiate, with no political or ideological prejudice, studies on the economic influence of organizational structures and on the role that can be played by regulation (or deregulation) and decentralization.

It may be noted that deregulation tends to act in favor of industrial competition; decentralization is aimed at restoring traditional social and political solidarities at the level of the basic, human-scale divisions of society and within large corporations. A judicious blend of deregulation and decentralization is thus equivalent to seeking, much as for sporting activities, the best balance between the spirit of competition and that of cooperation or teamwork. A balance of the sort would seem to be a feature of Japanese society, perhaps explaining that country's recent economic successes.

NOTES

1. The medium-term "management charter" for French Telecom, approved by the Council of Ministers on February 2, 1983, stipulates an annual reduction of 3% in real terms in telephone service tariffs between 1982 and 1986.

2. In 1983–1984, about half the homes reached by new cable networks may be served by coaxial cables, using existing collective antenna facilities in the apartment buildings of areas with high population densities.

3. Since July 1980, magnetic tapes and microfilms have been accepted in French courts as evidence in matters concerning civil contracts of low value.

4. Since the time of Napoleon, the central state administration in France has been vested with autocratic powers. To change this situation, decentralization is one of the priorities of the present government, as illustrated by a number of recent laws voted by Parliament.

REFERENCES

Bonnetblanc, Geneviève. Unpublished report. French PTT, January 16, 1984.

Damlamian, J. L. "Monopole et Déréglementation." Unpublished report. French PTT, November 11, 1983.

Jonscher, Charles. "Information Resources and Economic Production." *Information Economics and Policy* 1, no. 1 (1983): 13–35.

La Loi sur la Communication Audiovisuelle. Paris: La Documentation Française, 1983.

"Les Télécommunications Françaises." Paris: Direction Générale des Télécommunications, 1982.

Machlup, Fritz. *The Production and Distribution of Knowledge in the United States.* Princeton, N. J.: Princeton University Press, 1962.

Porat, Marc. *The Information Economy*. 9 vols. Special Publication No. OT 77–12. Washington, D.C.: U.S. Department of Commerce, 1977.

Voge, Jean-Paul. "Information and Information Technologies." *Growth and the Economic Crisis* 14 (1979): 1–14.

———. "The Politics and Economics of Complexity." *Information Economics and Policy* 1, no. 2 (1983): 97–114.

Six

Economic Policy toward Telecommunications, Information, and the Media in West Germany

Karl-Heinz Neumann*

This chapter concentrates on institutional issues. A certain regulatory structure in one particular country and the behavior of the corresponding regulatory institutions are described and analyzed. This is done with reference to the theory of regulation. But the main task of this chapter is not to discuss the normative or positive theory of regulation or to make a contribution to it. Rather, its aim is to supply information that may be regarded as a first step toward (comprehensive) international comparative studies as described by Roger Noll in Chapter 3 of this book.

To my knowledge there are as yet no comprehensive performance studies showing which institutional setting best suits the changing technological and economic environment in the information, telecommunications and media sector. This is not surprising because in a transitional phase it is impossible to undertake empirical comparative performance analysis. Up to now, for instance, it is not obvious what the results of deregulation in the telecommunications sector will be in countries following this policy. Will there really be competition in the long run between the incumbent firms and new competitors, or will competition be only a transitional phenomenon that will be replaced in turn by a period of monopoly? These questions cannot be answered given the present state of knowledge. But comparative institutional approaches may give us some preliminary ideas.

*This chapter represents the views and assumptions of the author and not necessarily the official views of the German Bundespost. The author is indebted to Bernhard Wieland for stimulating discussions of an earlier version of the chapter.

INDUSTRIAL POLICY TOWARD INFORMATION TECHNOLOGY

The theory of regulation is basically a microeconomic theory. It focuses on the behavior of regulatory institutions and on rules of regulation. Regulatory theory is typically applied to specific industries. But technological and economic developments often cannot be regarded as being restricted to individual industries. Information technology can be seen as an example of such a basis technology. Progress in this technology changes the production process more or less in all industries, since information handling has become a factor determining the efficiency of almost all production processes. Although economic theory has not yet totally clarified the influence of information and communications on productivity and economic growth,[1] the existing empirical literature indicates a significant positive relationship between high standards of information handling and economic development (see, e.g., Jussawalla and Lamberton 1982; Saunders, Warford, and Wellenius 1983). At least since the pioneering work of Porat (1977), the macroeconomic dimension of information has become obvious. I do not want to subject the reader to figures on the various dimensions of the information sector in Germany. Instead, I wish to concentrate on industrial policy toward information technology, since the rapidly growing importance of information technology has caused some governments to formulate a kind of national strategy toward this technology.

In the second half of 1983 the federal government of West Germany evaluated the position of the German information technology industry in the world market and the usage of information technology in Germany. One result of this investigation was that the (aggregate) position of European and German manufacturers in microelectronics and information technology is weak compared to the position of their primary competitors. This can be shown clearly by the following fact: Although the European market for microelectronics and information technology represents about one-third of the world market, the world market share of European manufacturers amounts to only about 10%. Of course the position differs from market to market. The position of Japanese and American manufacturers in the semiconductor industry is very dominant. U.S. manufacturers also dominate the German personal computer market. Exports of the German telecommunications equipment industry are relatively stagnant in a growing world market; therefore, the German world market position has declined from second place in 1970 to third in 1980.

The Bundesbank, Germany's central bank, has confirmed these figures in its annual report for 1983. Although the general export position has stabilized, the Bundesbank found Germany's performance in the export of high-technology products over the past decade and especially in recent years less satisfying. The Bundesbank considered five main high-technology product fields (including data processing and telecommunications) and compared the performance of Germany to the performance of the five other main exporting countries in these sectors (France, Great Britain, Switzerland, Japan, and the United States). While Germany had a 26.3% share of the high-technology exports of these six countries in 1972, by 1983 the share had dropped to 17% (see Table 6.1). The shares of France, Great Britain, and Switzerland also fell during that period. Only the Japanese share continuously moved upward, doubling from 1972 to its 1983 share of 25%. Japan has pushed Germany from second to third place. The U.S. industry had the leading position both in 1972 and in 1983. Table 6.2 presents the German trade-balance position in the high-technology products indicated. This position is negative only in data processing and electronic tubes. Thus the German world market position is not weak in all high-technology sectors.

Although it has to be kept in mind that the products mentioned here make up only a small fraction (less than 10%) of Germany's total exports, they are among the fast-growing ones. So perhaps they characterize the future export position better than today's.

It seems obvious that the strong position of foreign competitors in the field of information technology can partly be attributed to more intense activities or even government financial help. The development of microelectronics and information technology in the United States, for instance, profits from the enormous government spending on defense and

TABLE 6.1 Export of High-Technology Products in Six Selected Countries

Country	1972	1976	1978	1980	1982	1983[a]
	Export Shares in %					
West Germany	26.3	21.7	21.6	20.0	17.0	17.0
Data processing	40.2	24.8	16.0	16.7	14.5	14.5
Telecommunications	22.8	19.1	20.2	19.6	16.5	14.5
Electron tubes, transistors	17.4	15.3	19.3	17.1	11.0	11.0
Measuring instruments	25.6	24.0	22.9	21.6	20.2	21.0
Medical technology	36.4	33.1	31.5	29.4	26.1	26.5
France	11.1	10.9	10.4	10.3	8.1	8.0
Great Britain	13.8	11.5	11.7	12.6	11.1	10.0
Switzerland	3.5	3.6	4.1	3.6	3.2	3.0
Japan	13.0	18.2	18.5	18.2	20.3	25.0
United States	32.2	34.1	33.7	35.3	40.2	37.7
	In US$ (Billions)					
Selected Countries Total	8.4	20.6	29.8	44.2	49.7	54.0
West Germany	2.2	4.5	6.5	8.8	8.5	9.0

Source: Deutsche Bundesbank.
[a] Estimated.

TABLE 6.2 West German Foreign Trade in High-Technology Products (in DM billion)

	1978	1980	1981	1982	1983[a]
Export					
Data processing	1.8	2.8	3.2	3.7	4.8
Telecommunications	3.6	4.0	4.5	5.0	4.8
Electron tubes, transistors	1.7	2.2	2.3	2.4	2.9
Measuring instruments	3.5	4.6	5.4	6.0	6.4
Medical technology	1.8	2.1	2.5	2.9	3.3
Total[b]	12.9	16.1	18.4	20.6	22.9
Import					
Data Processing	2.2	3.3	3.9	4.2	5.3
Telecommunications	1.8	2.2	2.6	2.7	2.8
Electron tubes, transistors	2.3	3.3	3.4	3.4	3.9
Measuring instruments	1.9	2.8	3.1	3.4	3.4
Medical technology	0.8	1.0	1.1	1.3	1.4
Total[b]	9.1	12.6	14.1	14.9	16.9
Trade Balance					
Data processing	−0.4	−0.5	−0.6	−0.5	−0.5
Telecommunications	1.8	1.8	2.0	2.3	2.0
Electron tubes, transistors	−0.6	−1.1	−1.1	−0.9	−1.0
Measuring instruments	1.6	1.9	2.3	2.7	3.0
Medical technology	1.0	1.1	1.4	1.6	1.9
Total[b]	3.8	3.5	4.3	5.7	6.0

Source: Deutsche Bundesbank.
[a] Provisional.
[b] Including nuclear reactors.

space programs. Japanese firms profit from the strategic interaction between state and industry. So it might be more than the competitiveness of the individual firms that determines their market position.

Given the relatively weak position of the German industry and the support of information technology in other countries, the federal government has developed an industrial strategy to promote the development of microelectronics, information, and communications technology. The program covers five different areas:

1. Improvement of the general competitive environment
2. Motivation of people to use information and communications technology, especially in the educational system
3. Future-oriented development of the communications infrastructure and innovation in the terminal equipment sector

4. Expansion of the technology basis for defense purposes
5. Intensification and government support of research and development on a larger scale than previously

In detail the program consists of 32 different projects amounting to DM 3 billion. Some important telecommunications projects include the following:

1. The European market is to become more transparent and homogeneous. Existing barriers to market entry are to be removed.
2. The Bundespost will introduce the Integrated Service Digital Network (ISDN) within the next 10 years. A broadband ISDN will begin operation in 1989 on an experimental basis.
3. An expert commission will investigate the central organizational and regulatory issues in telecommunications.

TELECOMMUNICATIONS

Organization of the Industry

To describe the organization of the German telecommunications industry's structure essentially means to present the key role of the German Bundespost in this sector of the economy. As in most other European countries, the PTT is responsible both for telecommunications and postal services. In addition to postal and telecommunications services the Bundespost offers a variety of banking services. The joint supply of these services by one administration dates back to 1876, when the telegraph service was added to the postal service. In 1877 the telephone was first used for intra-organizational purposes of the telegraph service. When the telephone began to be used for private purposes 1 or 2 years later, the postal and telegraphic administration expanded its mandate to this service without further discussion. So it became part of the unified PTT. Since then, the resulting organizational structure has changed only slightly. At present, posts and telecommunications are under the authority of the minister of posts and telecommunications. This organizational framework has far-reaching consequences for the supply of telecommunications services, as I explain later in dealing with rate-setting issues.

In contrast to other network carriers in Europe and especially in the United States, the Bundespost does not produce transmission and switching facilities or terminal equipment. This equipment is purchased from German telecommunications manufacturers and to a lesser extent on the world market. In addition, R&D activities in telecommunications are concentrated within the manufacturing industry. Economies of vertical integration between network operation and production of facilities are exploited within this industry structure by a special consultation process between the relevant firms and the Bundespost.

Legal and Institutional Background

According to the German constitution, the minister for posts and telecommunications is legally authorized to exercise telecommunications sovereignty. Where military services are concerned, however, this sovereignty belongs to the minister of defense. Sovereignty implies not only the power to regulate the telecommunications sector but also the power to provide all telecommunications services through a governmentally owned public enterprise. The minister is a member of the federal cabinet and the head of the Bundespost. Details of organization, responsibilities, regulatory constraints, and duties are prescribed in the Postal Administration Law of 1953. The scope of the telecommunications monopoly of the German Bundespost is set forth in the Telecommunications Act of 1928, which is still valid today.

I mentioned above that the Bundespost is directed by a ministry headed by the minister of posts and telecommunications, who is a member of the federal government. Although the Bundespost is part of the general federal administration, it is financially independent of the general federal budget. It has to cover its costs from revenues and receives no financial support from the government, although many social obligations have to be fulfilled. This also implies that there is no direct parliamentary control over the budget of the Bundespost. The minister, however, is not totally independent in his decisions. First, overall administrative guidelines come from an Administrative Council of the Bundespost, which in addition has certain control and supervisory functions over the Bundespost. Second, the minister of posts and telecommunications has to consult the other ministers in certain decisions.

The Administrative Council, whose main tasks are comparable to those of a board of directors in a private firm, consists of members of the federal parliament (Bundestag) and the federal council (Bundesrat), our second parliamentary chamber; representatives of Bundespost employees and private industry; and two experts in telecommunications and finance. Consumer or user groups are not directly represented in the council. The council has to approve the annual budget, tariff changes, and the introduction of new services.

The minister of finance also has to agree to the Bundespost budget, but the influence of the minister of economics is more important in formulating regulatory policy. He has to agree to all rates and charges, and there is often disagreement between the two ministries about the general direction of telecommunications policy.

Considering the very different regulatory background of telecommunications in the United States, it is worthwhile mentioning that the federal states and the local governments are not able to exercise direct influence on telecommunications policy. The federal states have only a very weak influence within the limited responsibilities of the Administrative Council. Thus telecommunications policy and regulation is only a federal matter. West Germany does not have the two-tiered regulatory scheme characterizing telecommunications regulation in the United States.

The legal and institutional framework characterized above gives the Bundespost an ambivalent institutional character. On the one hand, it is a financially independent (public) enterprise, which must earn revenues on the market like any other firm. On the other hand, it is an administration directly dependent on political orders and burdened with all the incentive problems that are typical of bureaucratic public organizations.

The minister is chief executive of the Bundespost as well as a politician who has to transmit political aims defining the public interest to the regulated firm. Thus there is no special regulatory body controlling the public enterprise and setting regulatory rules. It is conventional wisdom in Germany that public enterprises need not be regulated if they work under direct political control. Such control is regarded as a substitute for regulation.

The Bundespost is subject only to a few legal constraints. The most important one is that it be financially self-sufficient. It does not receive any governmental subsidies or additional capital to finance its growth. However, all profits can be used for internal financing.

There are no rate-setting rules directly prescribed by law. The minister must manage the Bundespost according to the economic principles of the federal government and must serve the interests of the German economy. It is up to him to give a precise meaning to these general objectives by means of rate-setting and business policy. Nevertheless, his freedom of action is limited by the political process. Although the parliament has no formal mandate to decide on business policy issues of the Bundespost, nearly every major change of organization, tariffs, and services is discussed in parliament. This is especially the case in rate setting. The Bundespost often has to change or adjust its tariff proposals in response to decisions of the Bundestag. This simply reflects the fact that posts and telecommunications are governmental matters. In this environment posts and telecommunications tariffs can be regarded as political prices. In practice this can be seen from the fact that major rate changes nearly always include schemes to compensate losers of structural tariff reforms (see Neumann 1984). The policy measures here are package deals. Increases in some parts of the rate structure are combined with decreases elsewhere. Structural reforms are combined with rate-level reductions, and so on.

The public and political dimension of the activities of the Bundespost also means that as a public enterprise vested with monopoly rights, it is subject to a number of social obligations. One of these is the obligation to serve every customer. According to a number of court decisions, however, the Bundespost may follow economic considerations to keep this obligation in detail. Other obligations concern restrictions in rate setting and social tariffs.

Supply of Network Services

The Telecommunications Act of 1928 endows the Bundespost with extensive monopoly rights in the provision of telecommunications services. Since the Bundespost is a regulatory body as well as a telecommunications carrier, it is possible to transfer these rights—or parts of them—to private firms. So, from a legal point of view, there are opportunities for a flexible handling of the telecommunications monopoly, which can be defined on four levels:[2]

1. Operation of public transmission and switching facilities
2. Utilization of public transmission and switching facilities
3. Technical design of the entire telecommunications system
4. Provision and maintenance of terminal equipment

There are differences in the extent to which the German Bundespost actually makes use of its legal monopoly rights in the different telecommunications activities. The most extensive monopoly position is exercised on the first level. The Bundespost is the only provider of switching and transmission systems. The private construction of telecommunications networks is not allowed. This general rule, however, does not affect the internal networks of the Bundesbahn (the German railway carrier), the energy public utilities, and the security network of the police. Furthermore, discussion is now under way regarding how private firms can be given a role in constructing cable television networks. Two corresponding models are currently being tested. According to one model, private firms may obtain a license from the German Bundespost to cable a certain area and to operate the network. In the second model, private firms may organize consortia with the Bundespost that cable greater areas and operate and manage the corresponding network.

The Bundespost also regulates the utilization of the network or network facilities. For instance, private firms can lease lines, but the Bundespost regulates whether third parties or which third parties can use these leased lines. In general, shared use and resale of leased facilities is limited according to certain restrictive criteria. Thus, not only competition on the basis of owned facilities but even service competition has been prohibited up to now. Nevertheless, private firms can establish private switched networks if they are only used for internal communications and if the basic transmission service is leased from the Bundespost. Third-party access to these private networks is allowed in the field of data communications if it amounts to no more than 50% of the usage of the networks.

The contestability literature (see Baumol 1982; Baumol, Panzar, and Willig 1982) tells us that, given some idealized market conditions, legal barriers to entry are not necessary (or are even harmful), especially if the incumbent firm is a natural monopoly. Why do we still have such legal barriers to entry when economic theory seems to tell us that this is nonsense? What is the basis of the legal and actual monopoly position of the Bundespost in telecommunications?

First, we do not know to what extent the telecommunications sector can be regarded as a natural monopoly or, to be more precise, which parts of the telecommunications system belong to the natural monopoly domain. We know that economies of scale and scope play an important role in the German telecommunications system. We also know (or think we know) that the extent of economies of scale in the German telecommunications system is greater than in the United States. Indeed, the scale of the German system is smaller than that of some of the seven new American regional companies established after the divestiture of AT&T. But we also know that economies of scale and scope in a (regional) telecommunications system are not simply proportional to the magnitude of the system but depend on the local and regional concentration of demand as well. Up to now there have been no empirical studies of economies of scale in the German telecommunications system.

Second, we do not know whether the cost structure entails sustainability. Thus, inefficient market entry may be possible. I think that unsustainability is a much more important phenomenon than the sustainability literature now supposes.[3] This is especially the case if one takes a dynamic and intertemporal point of view.

Third, a natural monopoly can be sustainable only if the firm chooses an allocatively efficient rate structure and earns zero economic profits. Later in this chapter we see that these conditions are not fulfilled in the German telecommunications sector today. The telecommunications business of the Bundespost has to earn profits and is obliged to cross-subsidize because of regulatory and political constraints.

Fourth, the mechanism of potential competition as applied by Baumol, Panzar, and Willig can fulfill its function only if there are no (economic) costs of market entry or exit. This idealized market condition is not given in the telecommunications sector. Substantial sunk costs can be found here that are an important barrier to entry. Under these conditions, the regulation problem is aggravated by the lack of the contestability property.

What are the consequences of these arguments and facts for the current monopoly organization of the German telecommunications system when we take them all together? Because economies of scale are more significant than in the U.S. system, it is questionable whether there would be a really competitive environment if market entry were allowed. A quasi-competitive situation under strong governmental regulation, like the one in the United Kingdom at the moment, would not be an improvement over the current situation.

The current rate structure offers many opportunities for profitable market entry, for instance in the long-distance market. But in most cases that would be inefficient market entry induced by the opportunities of cream skimming and rate arbitrage. If we regard it as the main task of competition and market entry to change distorted tariffs in the direction of allocatively more desirable tariff structures, it may be useful to allow competition. But in the case of the Bundespost the same results could be achieved by simply changing the current rate structure in the right direction. This could be done easily by a discretionary act. But if one regards the current rate structure and its distributional implications as being part of a social consensus, competition would bring this down.

I do not wish to argue that competition is impossible in the German telecommunications system. But as long as there is a broad consensus regarding the distributional aspects of the basic telecommunications infrastructure services, as there is now, it becomes difficult to allow competition. And basic service is defined in Germany in a broad sense. The attempts in the United States to distinguish between basic and enhanced services and establish different competitive and regulatory environments in each of these fields are not very encouraging.

Engineering considerations play the dominant role in discussions of the Bundespost's telecommunications monopoly, while economic arguments are much less influential. This naturally has an effect on the agenda and outcome of the debate.

It is conventional wisdom in Germany that the long-run development in telecommunications network technology is toward an integrated broadband network based on optical fibers and that this network will be used both for interactive telecommunications and for TV and radio distribution. It is also conventional wisdom in Germany that this network can only be operated by one carrier because of the growing importance of economies of scale and scope in optical fiber transmission. It is obvious that the transition to an optical fiber network will take decades. It is impossible for engineers to understand how network optimization during this transitional period can be carried out in a competitive environment.

The discussion of competition in the German telecommunications sector is not yet finished. It started when the Monopoly Commission published an inquiry on the role of the German Bundespost in telecommunications in 1981. Although the commission argued against competition in the provision of network facilities, it recommended service competition on the basis of leased lines in the form of resale and value-added services. The commission's recommendations were based on a study by Knieps, Müller, and von Weizsäcker (1981), who presented their conclusion against network competition as a tentative one.[4]

Supply of Terminal Equipment

It is widely believed that the position of the Bundespost in the terminal equipment sector is as monopolistic as it is in providing network services. But this is not really true. In my opinion the organization and regulation of the German terminal equipment sector have been more liberal than in the United States and the United Kingdom before liberalization started there. PABXs, for instance, have been allowed for decades.

The legal telecommunications monopoly includes the right to provide and maintain all customer terminal equipment. It is important to remember that the Bundespost does not (as other carriers do) develop or produce any terminal equipment, whether by itself or through a separate subsidiary. All equipment is manufactured by private industry and rented or bought by the customer. The potential supply monopoly in this field is exploited only to a small extent by the Bundespost. The role of the Bundespost and the market structure differs from service to service. It ranges from monopoly supply to absence from the market. The Bundespost has a legal and de facto monopoly position in providing simple main stations and modems.

PABXs and facsimile equipment are provided in competition with the manufacturers. Here the market share of the Bundespost amounts to about 20%. The Bundespost does not provide telex machines, but it does have the exclusive right to service them. In contrast to other telecommunications carriers, the Bundespost also does not supply any data communications equipment. At present it is being considered whether the Bundespost should supply teletypewriters.

The last example shows that the Bundespost today is not really free to decide on the extent of its engagement in the terminal equipment sector. At least since the report of the Monopoly Commission on the role of the Bundespost in telecommunications, the Bundespost's market position is controversial. The commission recommended that the Bundespost withdraw totally from the terminal equipment market with the exception of providing main stations, where, it stated, the Bundespost should maintain its monopoly position. At this point there was a fundamental difference with the Knieps, Müller, and von Weizsäcker report. These authors argued in favor of general market activities of the Bundespost in the terminal equipment sector: It should be up to the market to discover if there are economies of scope between the provision of the network and terminal equipment services. Furthermore, it would be illogical to exclude the

Bundespost from this market and thereby to impose higher costs on consumers, and at the same time to promote competition in general. Although heavily disputed, the commission's opinion has become the position of the federal minister of economic affairs. As a consequence, it is up to the Bundespost to find compromises in the political process in every individual case. It is obvious that from this institutional process no economically desirable market structure, conduct, and performance can be expected in this field.

It is difficult for me to understand why the Bundespost should be excluded from all activities in the terminal equipment sector. There are not only technical interdependencies between both parts of a telecommunications system but economic interdependencies as well. I cannot discuss this topic in detail, but want to concentrate on a particular aspect of this relationship. The joint supply of terminal equipment and network services can be justified by the strong complementarities between these entities. Demand for terminal equipment will be higher if network services are cheap, efficient, and innovative, and vice versa. The network provider is interested in low terminal equipment prices, so he has strong incentives to intensify the competition in this market. This at the same time favors the consumers' interests. Furthermore, if there are economies of scope between network services and the provision of terminal equipment, they cannot be realized if the network carrier is excluded from the terminal equipment market. A problem arises only if there are strong substitution effects between networks and terminals.

Tariff Policy in Telecommunications

Pricing issues are one of the main topics in the theory of regulation. The normative theory focuses on welfare-maximizing rate structures of the regulated firm or the public enterprise working under certain specified constraints. The political or economic theory of regulation has more far-reaching ambitions (see, e.g., Peltzman 1976; Stigler 1971). Its proponents argue that regulation is not a substitute for market failure. Regulation, in this view, has to be explained by the politician's attempts to use the rate structure of the regulated firm to get political support. The main instrument for this purpose is cross-subsidization. In this process the regulator or the politician is assumed to choose the rate structure that maximizes his utility (measured in votes, income, or reputation). This is not the place to discuss the relevance of normative and positive theories of regulation and their differences. But I would like to make a short tentative remark. I think the political theory of regulation cannot really explain the existence of regulation in some industries. The main argument against the hypothesis that regulation can be explained only by political considerations is that in almost every Western country the same industries are regulated regardless of political and economic structures. Nevertheless, the political theory of regulation might explain the persistence of certain rate structures that, under normative theory, would be expected to change.

Cross-subsidization can be found in all parts of the Bundespost's rate structure. If one regards redistribution as a legitimate aim of public pricing, then cross-subsidization may be considered as socially desirable if the groups that should be subsidized really are favored by the chosen rate structure and if the welfare losses resulting from distorted prices are not "too" high.

Germany's telecommunications tariffs are often criticized for being among the highest in the world. However, the difficulties in comparing prices of "identical" goods between different countries are well known. In telecommunications not only the currency conversion problem has to be solved. It is also more difficult here to find the suitable "basket" of services or rates that offers an adequate basis for comparisons of the whole rate structure. Nevertheless, German telecommunications tariffs range in the upper field regardless of the comparative base chosen.[5]

To a certain degree this high level of telecommunications tariffs may be explained by the fact that posts and telecommunications are integrated in one administration. For the past 10 years the same pattern of cross-subsidization between these services has been in effect: Telecommunications services subsidize postal services. In 1982 these subsidies amounted to DM 3 billion. In former years the subsidization stream has sometimes reached more than DM 4 billion annually. If these cross-subsidies were absent and the telecommunications division had to cover only its own costs (including a market rate of return for capital), the rates could be about 15% lower than they are today.

The substantial surplus of revenues over costs generated in the telecommunications business of the Bundespost is not only a source of high allocative inefficiency (I return to this topic later in the chapter); it is also unsatisfactory from the point of view of a rational innovation policy. Telecommunications and postal services to a large extent satisfy the same needs. Historically, the postal service represents the old traditional technology; telecommunications depends on modern innovative technology. To stimulate innovative activities, however, it would make more sense if the traditional technology earned profits that were used to subsidize the innovative technologies. There are, to be sure, important arguments against the subsidization of innovative technologies, so I will not stress this alternative. But in every case the subsidization streams slow down the economically desirable substitution process between posts and telecommunications.

The telecommunications business not only subsidizes the postal business within the Bundespost but also subsidizes the federal budget. This results from a special kind of payment the Bundespost has to furnish in lieu of taxes. Currently this payment amounts to 10% of total revenues (DM 4 billion in 1982). Some rough calculations show that these payments to the federal budget are higher than the taxes the Bundespost would have to pay if it were taxed as a private firm (see Heyden 1980). Therefore, these payments are a further source of the high level of telecommunications tariffs in Germany.

I wish now to turn to telecommunications tariffs, especially to their structure. I first describe the current rate structure briefly. As in most other countries, we have two-part telecommunications tariffs. The customer pays a fixed monthly amount for being connected to the network and then is charged a usage-sensitive tariff. The fixed charge is not differentiated between business and residential users. But there are reduced rates for poor and handicapped people. Tariffs for local calls depend on the number of calls and, since 1980, on the call duration as well. Together with introducing local-call timing, the Bundespost has enlarged local calling areas such that neighboring exchanges are now included in these areas. Long-distance calls are divided into three distance bands. The rates increase with distance and are roughly proportional to the duration of calls within each distance band. Rates are different by time of day and day of week.

This rate structure is a source of far-reaching distortions compared to allocatively efficient rates.[6] First, the current rate structure does not totally reflect the considerable decline in long-distance transmission costs. Therefore the rates are too distance sensitive. A second distortion arises from the current peak-load pricing practice. The substantial growth of residence demand and attractive tariffs in the evenings have led to a shift of the traffic peak to the evening when rates are low. The Bundespost first responded by investing large sums to remove bottlenecks occurring at low-rate periods, thus adding further distortions. Even though the peak-load pricing structure was changed in 1980, the fundamental problem of peak demand in periods of lower rates still exists. A third distortion results from the uniformity of rates in urban and rural areas in spite of the fact that costs are much lower in urban areas. To overcome this distortion, long-distance rates must be sensitive to distance, route, or density. To my knowledge the only carrier that has taken a first step to diminish this distortion is British Telecom, which has introduced reduced rates for the 100 highest-density routes. In Germany it would be politically very difficult to abandon the principle of uniform price. It is widely believed that this principle is an essential pricing element in regulated industries for regional and social considerations.

In a recent study by Neumann, Schweizer, and von Weizsäcker (1983), rough estimates of the welfare effects of different telephone rate structures have been worked out, and I present them here briefly. The calculations are based on the rate structure in 1979. They concentrate on the price distortions between local and toll calls. The calculations show that prices are set above marginal costs and that these distortions cause remarkable welfare losses. But even at the high level of profits in 1979 it seems possible to lower these losses considerably simply by restructuring telecommunications tariffs.

The calculations of marginal costs reveal that the price for local calls slightly exceeds the corresponding marginal costs, whereas the average price of a long-distance call exceeds marginal costs by a factor of 2.5. It is well known that deviations of prices from marginal costs cause welfare losses. These losses amount to DM 2 billion compared with the first-best solution of marginal-cost pricing. They are equivalent to 13.5% of revenues from call charges in 1979. The magnitude of these welfare losses is determined both by the level and the structure of the tariffs.

In the case of economies of scale, welfare losses are inevitable if the firm has to cover its costs or earn profits. Prices that minimize such inevitable losses are called *Ramsey prices.* These prices skim consumer surplus where demand is less price sensitive. But the prices in 1979 were not Ramsey optimal. Rather, they exhibited precisely the opposite properties of optimal prices. Although toll calls react significantly more elastically to price changes than local calls do, the tariffs for toll calls deviate more significantly from marginal costs than local-call tariffs do. In order to attain the profits earned in 1979 (DM 5 billion) at Ramsey-optimal tariffs, the price of a local call accordingly would have to have been increased by 93%, and the price of a typical toll call would have to have been reduced by 27%. A welfare gain of almost DM 1 billion would have been realized by the changeover to optimal tariffs.

The surpluses realized in the telecommunications sector are used to cover the deficit in the postal sector and for payments to the federal budget. Without considering the opportunity costs of financing the profits of the telecommunications business by taxes or other rate structures in the postal business, it is possible to estimate the welfare effects of telecommunications tariffs that just cover costs. Ramsey-optimal prices that exactly covered costs would have reduced the welfare losses substantially, to a level of DM 0.04 billion.

One may ask why the rate structure does not change when these substantial welfare gains are attainable. This may be a problem of information or political feasibility. The political aspect leads to the question whether restructuring the rates in the proposed direction might involve distributional consequences that are politically or socially unwanted. On the basis of the consumption patterns of representative household groups, I have calculated benefit–cost ratios (Neumann 1984) representing the income effects of the mentioned price changes (increasing local rates and decreasing toll rates). All benefit–cost ratios increase with income. This reflects the fact that the relative consumption shares of toll calls increase with income. Therefore, the proposed rate change would have regressive income effects. Apart from this, the analysis suggests that residential users as a group will suffer from that tariff reform. In contrast, business users will be the winning group. These distributional consequences may explain why the rate structure has not yet changed.

Economic analysis cannot stop at this point. A definitive treatment of the distributional consequences of distorted tariffs must also calculate the effects of the business users' net benefits to the customers. If there is competition among the firms, the net benefits to the business sector do not simply increase profits but lead instead to reduced product prices. Because of lack of data, however, these effects often can be calculated only with the help of arbitrary assumptions.

The model presented has to be further investigated to improve the validity of the results. In particular, the model must be further disaggregated to include the whole rate structure and not only a part of it. Nevertheless, some structural conclusions can be drawn that characterize the pricing policy of a public enterprise in a highly monopolistic sector. I summarize them as follows:

1. Although the Bundespost has a far-reaching legal and de facto monopoly position in telecommunications, this position is not used for setting monopoly prices. These prices would double the actual surplus of revenues over costs.
2. The actual rates are strongly distorted compared with allocatively efficient rates.
3. The price distortions cause substantial welfare losses.
4. Nevertheless, these losses are considerably lower than those of unconstrained monopoly prices.
5. The structural distortions can be explained by pursuing distributional objectives. Residential users are favored over business users, and low-income users are favored over high-income users.

One may argue that the calculations of optimal rates are based on rather weak data. This may be right. But the empirical economist always has to work with the data that are available to him. The results, if they are surprising, may provide incentives to produce better (or other) results based on more reliable data.

THE ORGANIZATION AND REGULATION OF THE MEDIA

To understand the specific organization and regulation of the media in West Germany it is necessary to differentiate between mass and point-to-point communications. The content of (electronic) mass communications is regulated in a sense that I shall describe immediately, whereas the content of individual communications is completely unregulated. The distinction between mass media and point-to-point communications is also relevant for regulatory responsibilities. The electronic mass media are under the jurisdiction of the 11 federal states, whereas the regulation of electronic point-to-point communications services is part of the telecommunications sovereignty of the federal government. Furthermore, the facilities for radio and TV transmission are provided by the Bundespost. In contrast, each state regulates and controls radio and television by its own broadcasting legislation.

This two-tiered regulatory scheme requires each new activity to be classified as mass or point-to-point communications. While this distinction might have been useful in former times, new developments in telecommunications technology make the application of such a classification scheme more and more difficult. A recent example is Bildschirmtext (interactive videotex). When the Bundespost considered introducing this service, we had an intensive debate as to whether it was a medium of mass or of point-to-point communications. This dispute was not settled because the debate revealed that a clear distinction was not possible. But the discussion complicated the introduction of the service. Finally, after intensive consultations, the federal states created their own legislation on the mass communications aspects of Bildschirmtext. The institutional setting has to adapt to this trend toward integration in technology, and the current structure should not be a factor delaying the introduction of new technology.

This regulatory structure causes a special link between media and telecommunications policy in Germany. The development of the so-called new media can be understood only if this link is kept in mind. The relationship between these policy issues is certainly different from the situation in other countries.

The development and organization of the German broadcasting system has to be viewed in a historical perspective. During the Nazi regime, broadcasting was under direct state control and was used for political and propaganda purposes. In the postwar period, the Allies themselves exercised the broadcasting sovereignty at first and then handed it over to the federal states.

The basic structure of the German radio and TV system consists of nine regional radio and TV stations. Their ownership structure is a little difficult to describe. They are noncommercial, public, but nevertheless not state owned, and are subject to the public-law jurisdiction of the federal states. The programs and the internal structure of the stations are controlled by boards that consist of representatives of political parties and the so-called socially relevant groups (churches, unions, entrepreneurs, local government representatives, and others).

The political parties have a far-reaching influence on the nomination of members of these boards. Because of the extensive power of the boards,[7] the broadcasting stations are strongly influenced by the political parties and their preoccupation with equal time. That is why the boards are often criticized for being another political arena rather than supervisory bodies.

The nine regional stations together produce one nationwide program, and each in addition provides one regional program. They also produce some radio programs. Since 1964, a second nationwide TV program has been provided by a separate central station (ZDF), which works under conditions similar to the regional stations. So, up to now, German households have been able to receive two nationwide programs and one or more regional programs, depending on location and the quality of the antenna. In addition, a household can receive programs from neighboring countries, also depending on location and antenna quality. No private commercial stations have yet been licensed.

The broadcasting stations are financed partly by uniform nationwide fees and partly by advertising. As advertising time is limited to 20 minutes a day, fees are the main financial source of the broadcasters.

What is, or was, the basis of the public broadcasting monopoly in Germany? An economic argument may give a first explanation. The electromagnetic spectrum used to transmit over-the-air radio and television in Germany is a scarce resource that can be allocated only to a few programs. It is worthwhile mentioning that the spectrum in Germany is more limited than it is in other countries. This is so because of the special geostrategic situation of Germany and the special demands of the allied forces for spectrum. Under these technical constraints, it was taken to be the duty of the state to organize the allocation process and regulate market entry.

But these economic and technological considerations do not totally explain the chosen special "public" organization of radio and television in Germany. It was common sense in postwar Germany that the mass media should not again come under the control of one social group or even the state. So our Basic Law involved a clause (Art. 5) guaranteeing freedom of the media. In addition to the general freedom of expression, Article 5 contains a special reference to freedom of the press and freedom of broadcasting (see Hoffman–Riem 1981). In the case of broadcasting this basic right is not only understood as a civil right that has to be defended against the state. According to some decisions of the German Federal Constitutional Court, this constitutional provision, moreover, obliges the state to play an active role in furthering pluralism within broadcasting.

In 1961 the Constitutional Court had to decide whether an attempt by the federal government to establish a new TV network over which it might have substantial influence was constitutional. The Court declared the attempt unconstitutional and formulated basic propositions concerning broadcasting in general. The Court justified the monopoly position of the existing "public" broadcasting stations. It argued that broadcasting had become one of the most powerful mass media. Because of the existing scarcity of frequencies, there was the danger of biased influence on public opinion if the medium was controlled by market forces. The public broadcasting system was regarded as a constitutional way to guarantee freedom of broadcasting. Pluralism should be guaranteed by internal boards on which all important political, ideological, and social positions should be represented. This concept has become the main basis of the German broadcasting system. Pluralism is not expected to be realized by competition of different institutions and different opinions but by representation of all opinions and interests within one monopolistic system.

Thus the Constitutional Court justified the existing structure of the broadcasting system on two grounds: (1) by the shortage of frequencies together with the large financial requirements to enter the market; and (2) by the existing influence of radio and television over public opinion.

The German mass media system is often held to be based on a fundamental separation and balance of power between the privately owned press and the publicly organized broadcasting system. In this view, the present broadcasting system could and should be a countervailing power to a rather concentrated press in order to guarantee pluralism within the mass media system as a whole. Therefore, many people argue that this balance of power could be undermined if private and commercial television were allowed. This result is foreseen particularly when powerful media conglomerates are allowed to enter the radio and TV market as well.

It is obvious that the ownership and regulation structure described above can survive only as long as the opportunities to transmit radio and TV programs are technically limited. Broadband cabling and satellite transmission have thus challenged the existing structure of the broadcasting system in Germany. But given the complex institutional framework, cable television cannot be regarded as an exogenous challenge. Broadband cabling is being discussed in Germany in the context of the desirability of more TV programs, especially if these are commercial programs. This discussion, which is a political one in Germany, has not yet stopped. It began in 1975 when an expert commission, which had analyzed the entire area of communications and telecommunications development in Germany, recommended the introduction of cable television. The commission stated that the final decision on cable television should be preceded by pilot projects that would test the demand for cable television and different organizational frameworks.

Some years later, the federal state governments had laid the legal and institutional basis to start these pilot projects for a 3-year period. Nevertheless, they first began operation in 1983 and 1984.

Beginning in the 1970s, the Bundespost constructed the first local cable television networks. Although suitable for transmitting many additional channels, these networks up to now are used only for improved reception of the traditional programs. The Bundespost first started broadband cabling on a small scale. This policy has been changed since 1982. Then the new government decided to cable Germany within the next 10 years. The Bundespost intends to invest DM 1 billion a year for this purpose. The remaining investment is to be provided by private firms.

At present, the legal barriers to private and commercial broadcasting in Germany seem to be breaking down. In a landmark decision of 1981 the Federal Constitutional Court had to decide whether a private applicant could obtain a broadcast license. The Court discussed conditions under which private broadcasting licenses might be granted in the future. In detail these conditions are rather restrictive. Some people doubt whether a private applicant could ever fulfill them. So this decision seemed to satisfy the needs of both sides. The supporters of private television emphasize that this is possible as a result of the Court decision. The supporters of the public broadcasting system, however, are convinced that any attempt to introduce private broadcasting is subject to restrictive guidelines of legislative and administrative supervision.

According to the Constitutional Court's decision of 1981, it is now up to the federal state parliaments to formulate the conditions under which private broadcasting will be allowed in each state. The first media laws are now under consultation in the parliaments of the federal states. Thus the focal points of the debate have changed. The essence of the media policy debate in Germany is no longer whether we should have private broadcasting but under what conditions or within what regulatory framework it should be introduced. The main topics of debate are:

1. How can pluralism within private broadcasting stations be realized?
2. How should the coexistence and/or competition of public and commercial broadcasting be organized?
3. Should joint ownership between the press and cable television stations be allowed?
4. How should private television be financed?

NOTES

1. See Stigler (1961) and Machlup (1962) as the first theoretical treatments and Jonscher (1983) for a new approach.

2. The distinction of the first two levels corresponds to the distinction of facilities and service competition as described by Charles Jonscher in Chapter 7 of this book.

3. Sharkey (1982) gives some illuminating examples for that.

4. For a detailed comparison of these two reports see Snow (1982, 1983).

5. In the international comparison of telephone rates in the United States, Japan, the United Kingdom, West Germany, France, Italy, Canada, Australia, and Sweden, Mitchell (1983) found the highest rates in Japan, West Germany, France, and Australia and the lowest ones in the United States.

6. For details, see Neumann (1984).

7. They supervise and control the program and decide partly on the personnel and on finance.

REFERENCES

Baumol, W. J. "Contestable Markets: An Uprising in the Theory of Industry Structure." *American Economic Review* 72 (1982): 1–15.

Baumol, W. J., J. Panzar, and R. D. Willig. *Contestable Markets and the Theory of Industry Structure.* San Diego: Harcourt Brace Jovanovich, 1982.

Deutsche Bundesbank (Federal Republic of Germany). *Geschäftsbericht für das Jahr 1983.* Frankfurt.

Heyden, G. von der. "Besteuerung, Abgabenpflicht und Befreiungen der Deutschen Bundespost—rechtliche und wirtschaftliche Bedeutung." *Archiv für das Post- und Fernmeldewesen* 32 (1980): 122ff.

Hoffman-Riem, W. "The Freedom of Communications and the Future of Broadcasting in West Germany." *Studies of Broadcasting*, no. 17 (1981): 49–70.

Jonscher, Charles. "Information Resources and Economic Productivity." *Information Economics and Policy* 1 (1983): 13–35.

Jussawalla, M., and D. M. Lamberton, eds. *Communication Economics and Development.* Elmsford, N. Y.: Pergamon Press, 1982.

Knieps, G., J. Müller, and C. C. v. Weizsäcker. *Die Rolle des Wettbewerbs im Fernmeldebereich.* Baden-Baden: Nomos, 1981.

Machlup, F. *The Production and Distribution of Knowledge in the United States.* Princeton: Princeton University Press, 1962.

Mitchell, B. M. "The Cost of Telephone Service: An International Comparison of Rates in Major Countries." *Telecommunications Policy* 7, no. 1 (1983): 53-63.

Monopolkommission (Monopoly Commission) (Federal Republic of Germany). *Die Rolle der Deutschen Bundespost im Fernmeldewesen.* Baden-Baden: Nomos, 1981.

Neumann, K.-H. *Gebührenpolitik im Telekommunikationsbereich.* Baden-Baden: Nomos, 1984.

Neumann, K.-H., U. Schweizer, and C. C. von Weizsäcker. "Welfare Analysis of Telecommunication Tariffs in Germany." In *Public Sector Economics*, edited by J. Finsinger. London: Macmillan, 1983.

Peltzman, S. "Toward a More General Theory of Regulation." *Journal of Law and Economics* 19 (1976): 211ff.

Porat, M. U. *The Information Economy: Definition and Measurement.* Special Publication no. 77–12. Washington D.C.: U.S. Department of Commerce, Office of Telecommunications, May 1977.

Saunders, R. J., J. J. Warford, and B. Wellenius. *Telecommunications and Economic Development.* Baltimore: Johns Hopkins University Press, 1983.
Sharkey, W. W. *Natural Monopoly.* Cambridge, England: Cambridge University Press, 1982.
Snow, M. S. "Telecommunications and Media Policy in West Germany: Recent Developments." *Journal of Communication* 32, no. 3 (1982): 10–32.
———. "Telecommunications Deregulation in the Federal Republic of Germany." *Columbia Journal of World Business*, 18, no. 1 (1983): 52–61.
Stigler, G. J. "The Economics of Information." *Journal of Political Economy* 69 (1961): 213–225.
———. "The Theory of Economic Regulation." *Bell Journal of Economics* 2 (1971): 3ff.

Seven

Telecommunications Liberalization in the United Kingdom

Charles Jonscher

OPTIONS IN TELECOMMUNICATIONS NETWORK STRUCTURE

All the world's major industrialized countries have undertaken a review of the future of the telecommunications and information processing industries during the past few years. The directions that government policies have taken following this review have been very diverse. The United States is introducing competition into almost every aspect of the telecommunications sector, whereas some European countries plan to construct integrated networks that provide a wide range of telecommunications services under the monopoly control of a government ministry. The British government has chosen a course somewhere midway between these two more extreme positions, by substituting a duopoly for the former monopoly of basic telecommunications network construction and allowing competition in some but not all aspects of data and other enhanced communications services.

The diversity of these government policies—in response to essentially the same set of technological developments—illustrates how controversial is the analysis of the economics of telecommunications industry structure. One school favors the breaking up of dominant or monopolistic firms, both horizontally and vertically, in order to realize the benefits of vigorous competitive industry behavior. Another argues that economies of scale, economies of scope, and the organizational efficiencies of vertical integration suggest the retention of dominant firms in many sectors of network construction and operation.[1] The purpose of this chapter is to present the relevant economic arguments and show how these issues have worked themselves out in the case of U.K. policy toward the telecommunications industry.

The particular feature of technological change in the communications sector that makes this industry a complex subject for economic analysis is the trend toward convergence of telecommunications and data processing technologies. This convergence is illustrated in Figure 7.1. Until the early 1970s telecommunications and data processing systems were relatively distinct; although data processing installations made use of telecommunications services for providing access to remote users, and telecommunications networks used computer technology for some switching and network management functions, the industries themselves were largely separate and were characterized by a quite different industry structure. Telecommunications networks throughout the world were provided by de facto or de jure monopolies, while data processing services and equipment were supplied on a competitive basis.

However, the trends toward distributed processing in the computing sector and toward digital networks in telecommunications systems have led to a blurring of the distinction between these two industries. Users are increasingly demanding that communications networks provide processing, storage, manipulation, and other "intelligent" functions in addition to

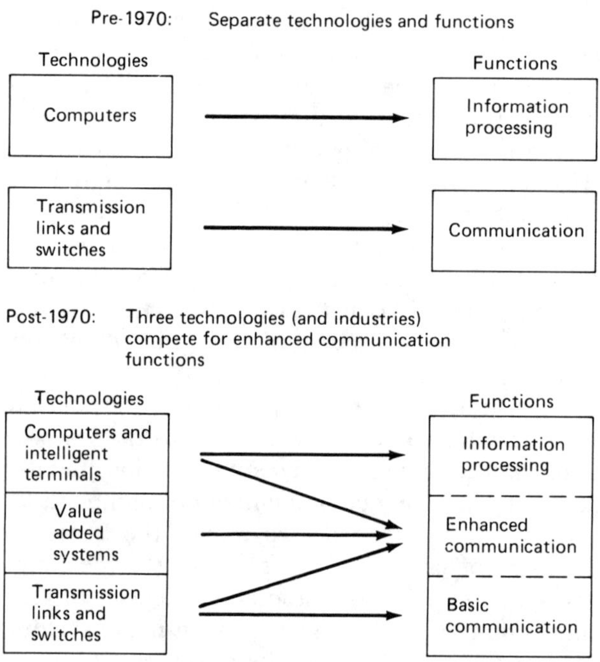

Figure 7.1

performing the basic transmission of messages between locations. These enhanced or higher-level processing functions can be provided in a number of different ways (see Figure 7.1):

1. By incorporating intelligent switches into the network operated by the telecommunications carrier
2. By an overlay network provided by a value-added carrier, who rents basic transmission facilities from the telecommunications carrier and installs switching or computing equipment at selected nodes of the network to perform the processing functions
3. By attaching intelligent terminal equipment to the termination of the telecommunications networks at the users' premises.

The two major industries of the information technology sector—telecommunications and computing—favor different solutions from this list. Option 1 will generally benefit the former and Option 3 the latter. Option 2 is provided by a relatively new industry, the value-added network operators, which will continue to play an important role in the sector.

Thus, in addition to the competition—which we label *horizontal* competition—that exists within the data processing service industry, there is developing a new axis of *vertical* competition between these two industry groups. The vertical axis is unusual because it represents competition not simply between different firms but between different technical solutions to the information processing problem. The way in which functions such as data communications are provided in a network will differ, depending whether a basic carrier incorporates these functions into the existing network switching points, whether an independent carrier provides them in the form of an overlay (e.g., packet-switched) network, or whether a computer manufacturer provides the data communications capability through the use of computers attached to the network as terminals.

Thus, when the government formulates a policy with regard to vertical competition, it is determining both an industrial and a technology policy. Moreover, it is not clear what rules governing the provision of data processing functions in communications networks would result in the greatest degree of competition. At first sight it would appear appropriate, in the interest of competition, to prevent the basic carrier from providing value-added services—or at least to exclude provision except through an arm's-length subsidiary. (This was the decision taken by the Federal Communications Commission in the United States in its *Second Computer Inquiry* decision of 1980.) This will encourage competition among value-added carriers and among terminal equipment providers. However, it is an open question whether a given function is most economically provided by equipment incorporated into the core of the telecommunications network and operated by the carrier or by equipment attached to the network and operated by the data processing industry or its customers. That competitive or technological tradeoff can be tested fairly only if the basic carrier is allowed to use its switching facilities to provide value-added functions; but in that case it is possible that value-added carriers, who cannot incorporate equipment into core network switches, will be unable to compete.

The government will lean toward one policy or another depending on where it sees the key axis of competition in enhanced services: Is it competition between firms in the telecommunications carrier industry or between the telecommunications and the computer industries? In the United States, is it between AT&T and MCI, or between AT&T and IBM? In the United Kingdom, is the key future axis of competition between British Telecom and Mercury, or between British Telecom and IBM?

These questions of optimal telecommunications network structure did not dominate the public debate in the United Kingdom that led to the current policy of liberalization. The policy of the Thatcher government toward the telecommunications industry has been driven by broader political goals and is a response to the conviction that "reform of the nationalized industries is central to economic recovery" (*The Conservative Manifesto* 1983). To date, the Conservative government has denationalized British Aerospace, Britoil, Cable and Wireless, British Steel, and a number of other public enterprises. The telecommunications industry was seen as being dominated by a large organization having two undesirable features: monopoly and public ownership.[2]

Since 1979, when the government announced its intention to follow up on the proposals made by the Carter Committee,[3] it has pursued its restructuring of the telecommunications industry in three major phases: (1) the liberalization of terminal equipment and value-added network services; (2) the licensing of Mercury as a second competitive basic telecommunications carrier; and (3) the flotation of British Telecom on the stock market. Each of these phases is explored in subsequent sections. We indicate the stated objectives of the government in each of these three areas; we describe the steps that have been taken to implement the policies; and we assess the extent to which the strategy has produced results consistent with the policy objectives. A chronology of major steps in the liberalization process is given in Table 7.1.

LIBERALIZATION OF VALUE-ADDED SERVICES AND TERMINAL EQUIPMENT

"It is the government's aim to promote consumer choice. Whenever possible, we want industrial and commercial decisions to be determined by the market and not by the state. We believe that consumers' choice and the

TABLE 7.1 Key Steps toward Liberalization of the British Telecommunications Industry

July 1980
Sir Keith Joseph, industry secretary, announces in House of Commons intentions to restructure the Post Office and relax the monopoly over terminal equipment and value-added services.

November 1980
The government publishes the Telecommunications Bill, seeking authority to divide the Post Office into two separate organizations: Posts and British Telecom.

April 1981
The government publishes the Beesley Report. It recommends full freedom for private-sector suppliers to use the national network to provide telecommunications services to third parties, at a flat rate.

October 1981
The Telecommunications Bill receives royal assent. It formalizes the split in the Post Office, establishes new responsibilities for the British Standard Institute (BSI), and sets up a subsidiary of the British Electrotechnical Approvals Board, the British Approvals Board for Telecommunications (BABT).

November 1981
Government steps in to hasten the process of equipment approval. It announces a formal timetable, calling for full liberalization by July, 1983.

February 1982
Mercury consortium receives a license to build and operate an independent network.

July 1982
Government introduces a white paper proposing the sale of 51% of British Telecom and the creation of a regulatory body, the Office of Telecommunications (OFTEL).

February 1983
Government accepts recommendation of a report by Professor Littlechild that BT's tariff increases for the 5 years after liberalization should be pegged below the inflation rate. Government also announces its intention to abolish BT's monopoly over the first telephone and to allow resale.

April 1983
Mercury launches telecommunications services in City of London.

July 1983
Telecommunications Bill reintroduced. It mainly sets up OFTEL and allows for the selling of BT.

November 1983
Government reaffirms its commitment to the liberalization of telecommunications in Britain, in a statement made by Kenneth Baker, MP, minister for information

TABLE 7.1 (continued)

technology. He confirms that by the end of 1984 the BT monopoly of supply and maintenance of the prime telephone instrument connected to BT systems will end for those customers who have a standard socket fitted by BT. Also, he confirms that maintenance of a newly installed call-routing apparatus should be liberalized completely by November 1986. Moreover, government has decided not to license operators other than BT and Mercury Communications Ltd to provide the basic telecommunications services for 7 years following the statement.

April 1984
The Telecommunications Bill receives royal assent on April 12, 1984. The government announces a radical revision in the standards-setting procedure so that all equipment may receive temporary approval provided it will not damage the integrity of the network. The purpose of the revision is to help companies, large and small, to market new products more quickly.

June 1984
The license under which British Telecom will operate telecommunications systems and provide telecommunications services is published.

Source: Adapted from Guy De Jonquieres, "World Telecommunications," *Financial Times*, FT Survey, October 24, 1983.

disciplines of the market lead to more stable prices, improved efficiency and a higher quality of service" (Jenkin 1982, 23).

This statement clearly laid out the strategy that the Conservative government intends to pursue. With respect to liberalization of the terminal equipment market and of value-added services, the government would provide a new and competitive forum in place of former policies that had constricted innovation and growth.

The opening up of the British terminal equipment market would take place in phases so as to protect the indigenous industry. By phasing in equipment competition, the Conservative government hoped to protect small suppliers from being overrun by British Telecom (BT), and, furthermore, to protect the British market from an influx of foreign suppliers.

The method by which Sir Keith Joseph proposed to protect the home industry was by setting standards for equipment. He made reference in July 1980 to changes in the procedure for the setting of standards; these were outlined again in the Telecommunications Bill published in November 1980. The bill, which was enacted in October 1981, delegated responsibilities formerly assigned to the Post Office to the independent, nonprofit British Standards Institute (BSI). This organization, which operates under Royal Charter and is partly financed by the government and partly by the selling of standards, was given the new responsibility to prepare mandatory standards for the Department of Trade and Industry (DTI). The testing of the equipment would be performed by the British Approvals Board for Telecommunications (BABT). This nonprofit organization, a subsidiary of the British Electrotechnical Approval Board (BEAB), was set up as a direct result of the Telecommunications Act. Its function is to test equipment in order to ensure the integrity of the BT network. Sir Keith Joseph stated that because standards would initially favor British manufacturers, the domestic industry would be given a period of grace during which it could prepare for international competition.

The opening of the market applied first to handsets and answering machines, second to automatic call makers and call diversion units, and third to PBXs. This progressive liberalization only really started to proceed a full year after the government announced its intention to carry it through. In November 1981, the government had to step in and establish an internal certification office serving as a surrogate standards board. This was in response to complaints voiced by other manufacturers, who felt that BT (a key participant in setting the technical standards) had stalled on setting up equipment standards at BSI so as to protect its own competitive edge.

Another area in which the Conservative government's industrial policy supported the idea of enhanced economic freedom, and therefore more consumer choice, was the provision of value-added network services (VANS). A report was commissioned from Michael Beesley (1981) of the London School of Business, which considered the costs and benefits of altering rules about resale of circuits, and the bearing of BT's monopoly power on this. The report's key findings were as follows:

1. In the home market there should be no restriction on the freedom to offer resale and value-added services to third parties, and the leasing of circuits should be at a flat rate.
2. Consumer benefits are likely to outweigh the projected loss of net revenues to BT (the revenue loss was forecast to reach 2% after 4 years).
3. International circuits should also be used more freely, but users should negotiate royalties with British Telecom.
4. An independent commercial communications network should be established in the United Kingdom because this would encourage true price competition in telecommunications services.

Professor Beesley's report was welcomed by the government and many of its recommendations subsequently implemented; technology had developed to the point where many VANS applications were possible, and the government argued that competitive provision in this area would benefit the consumer. Approximately a year later, after comments on the

Beesley report had been reviewed, the government restated its support and said that it "was attracted by his [Beesley's] free-market, please-the-customer approach . . . and therefore proposes to use the powers of the British Telecommunications Act to allow the private sector much greater freedom to use BT's inland network" (Baker 1982).

The licensing of VANS operators, like that of terminal equipment, was also to be progressive:

> The first step will involve licencing private operators to use BT circuits to supply any value-added network services which BT will not be supplying before 1 April 1982, that will take effect when BT takes over from the Post Office on 1 October this year [1981]. The second step, commencing at the beginning of 1982, will involve freedom for the private sector to use BT circuits to compete with BT in the supply of all kinds of services, provided that these services involve substantial elements additional to the basic network facilities. . . . A possible third stage might involve allowing the private sector complete freedom to use the BT network to supply services to third parties, including simple resale" (Baker 1982).

The liberalization process has met with some frustration. The approval and setting of standards have proved to be cumbersome and lengthy processes. Even the interim measures provided by the Department of Industry were flawed; the agency that did the testing of equipment, BABT, first needed the appropriate standards before it could carry out the appropriate tests. Until those standards were set (only 11 have been set to date) BT had to carry out the testing. Another problem, in the view of many industry participants, was that the Department of Industry set too high prices for BT's testing service. This discouraged smaller companies from submitting their equipment for approval.

The most recent steps taken by the government to speed up the approval process of terminal equipment were noted by John Butcher, junior industry minister, in his written parliamentary answer dated April 9, 1984. He has ordered an immediate change in equipment approval procedures: All apparatus will receive conditional interim approval for competitive sale, provided it passes the safety tests. Later on, the apparatus must pass a second set of tests, ensuring full accordance with existing standards.

The liberalization of value-added network services has progressed in a less troubled fashion. Since its introduction in October 1982, the General License has allowed 72 companies to be licensed to provide approximately 200 value-added services. The government hopes that, as more users appreciate the advantages that VANS bring to efficiency and productivity, the market will develop and more companies will be encouraged to enter the market (Marketing Solutions 1984).

THE LICENSING OF MERCURY

In February 1982 the government awarded an interim license to the Mercury consortium to operate an independent communications network in competition with British Telecom. Mercury was established as a joint venture of Cable and Wireless and British Petroleum (each with a 40% shareholding) and Barclays Bank (20%). Mercury hoped to attract business customers using its point-to-point leased-line service beginning in London. The license awarded to Mercury allowed it to offer a switched service for both voice and data. It will use optical fiber cables in a figure-of-eight network to be centered in Birmingham. The links in the optical fiber system will be of at least 10 fiber cables, each pair of fibers having an ultimate capacity of 540 megabits per second. It is hoped that initial customers will be businesses located within the city of London. The service must first attract these customers before being able to launch a full-scale attack on BT. According to some market forecasts, the area in which the service is competing—high-speed business communications—could grow up to 25% per year in real terms.

Another big problem faced by Mercury was the refusal of BT's engineers to link Mercury to its network. For various reasons, the Post Office Engineering Union (POEU) was against competition to BT. Until a court injunction forced the engineers to interconnect, Mercury was helpless. Not only did BT's POEU present difficulties, but BT itself stepped up its ability to compete. In response to BT's aggressiveness, Mercury made some adjustments in its service plans; it plans to introduce switching into its network as soon as possible so as to provide more services to a wider range of customers. Mercury hopes to expand geographically by leasing short circuits from BT and to obtain complete geographical coverage of the United Kingdom by leasing space on an INTELSAT V transponder.

The most important expansion of Mercury's services occurred in August 1983 when the government announced its decision to allow Mercury to provide international switched services. Though the Beesley report had recommended against competition in this sector, 2 years later the government saw no reason to protect BT's monopoly.

Mercury currently offers point-to-point leased links to several customers. It has taken a major step toward an alternative communications service in its completion of a 75-meter communications mast at Willesden Junction, London. This mast will form a link between London, Birmingham, and Manchester. It will act as a distribution node, thereby extending coverage in London; later on, the site will house a trunk access node linking the microwave system to the optical fiber network. For the trunk network, purpose-built towers or space on existing towers has been used to provide line-of-sight links for radio operation in the 13GHz band (maximum carrying capacity is 34mbps or 1000 simultaneous telephone conversations).

Mercury will shortly initiate international leased-line services between the United Kingdom and the United States. Mercury has leased an option on an INTELSAT V satellite and plans later on, when its services expand, to use the Telecom 1 satellite, Eutelsat's satellites, and possibly other independent operators. The ground segment is also being developed: Mercury has received outline planning permission for two satellite communications centers. The first is situated in London on the Isle of Dogs, which is about 5 or 6 kilometers east of the city, and the other is situated in Oxfordshire, just north of the city of Oxford. In London, the earth station will provide space initially for two dishes. Both dishes were supplied by Marconi Communications System Limited, at a cost of approximately £2 million.[4] One dish has an 8-meter antenna to provide TV distribution in the United Kingdom; the other dish has a 13-meter installation for transatlantic television and digital communications services. Another service that Mercury is now coordinating with carriers in the United States is switched services.

There is still no evidence as to whether Mercury will be a success. A government minister is quoted, anonymously, as saying: "It doesn't really matter if Mercury flops, it has already done its job of getting BT off its backside" (*The Economist*, March 15, 1983, 40). It is too early to tell whether this is all Mercury will have achieved. Its success remains heavily dependent on both its ability to attract a sufficient number of customers and on the government's competitive policies. It is not yet clear whether the U.K. telecommunications market can economically support two parallel long-distance communications networks.

PRIVATIZATION OF BRITISH TELECOM

"Unless something is done to change to capital structure and ownership of BT and to provide a direct spur to efficiency, higher investment could mean still higher charges for the customer. The government, BT and the general public would find that unacceptable. We need to free BT from traditional forms of government" (Jenkin 1982).

The Conservative government took several initiatives to provide for the "freeing" of BT. On July 19, 1982, the secretary of state for industry, Patrick Jenkin, made a statement to the House of Commons. This statement, published as a white paper, reflected the government's intention "to take the earliest opportunity to introduce legislation which, while keeping BT as a single enterprise, will enable it to be converted into a Companies Act company, British Telecommunications plc. The legislation will allow the sale of shares in that company to the public" (*Future of Telecommunications in Britain* 1982).

The Conservative government introduced into Parliament on November 17, 1982, a bill designed to promote the government's industrial policy of privatization. The bill (subsequently reintroduced in 1983 in largely unchanged form) is structured into seven parts:

> Part I provides for the secretary of state to appoint a director general of telecommunications, who in turn may appoint the staff of the Office of Telecommunications (OFTEL), the latter being established as the overall watchdog governing the functioning of the industry. It also gives the director the power to modify and to grant licenses (subject to approval of the secretary of state). This part also abolishes BT's exclusive privilege of running telecommunications systems and sets out the duties of the secretary of state and the director.
>
> Part II contains provisions so that telecommunications systems can be licensed and makes running a telecommunications system without a license a criminal offense. This section also sets out how the director may enforce license conditions, along with other regulatory powers. It empowers the secretary of state or the director to approve apparatus to be linked to telecommunications systems. Moreover, it allows the director to give consent for the making of orders for the compulsory purchase of land by public telecommunications operators and for the secretary of state to authorize or confirm such orders after the usual procedures.
>
> Parts III to VII outline the more general duties of the secretary of state and the director. Part V, it should be noted, allows for shares in BT plc to be sold. It also contains provisions allowing the financial structure of BT plc to be determined immediately.

It was the intention of the government to have the bill complete its passage by early 1984; it received the royal assent on April 12, 1984. The bill (now an act of Parliament) allows the secretary of state to impose his own timetable on introducing the telecommunications regulatory regime (whose focal point is OFTEL) and to determine when to sell shares in BT.

British Telecommunications plc's commercial activities are regulated under its new license, issued in June 1984 in accordance with the 1984 Telecommunications Act. An important feature of the license is that it will provide a regulated structure for BT's basic telephone-line rental and inland-call charges. Following the recommendations of a report by Stephen Littlechild (*Littlechild Report* 1983), BT's price increases for the first 5 years will be limited to "*x* percent" below increases in the retail price index

(RPI). After extensive consultation, the government determined that the value of x in this "RPI minus x" formula should be 3, implying that the real price of these BT services must fall by at least 3% per annum.

The license, which lasts for 25 years, will attempt to balance the concerns of the company, its customers, and its competitors. The draft license obliges BT to provide services in rural areas, ship-to-shore services, public call boxes, services for the disabled, and emergency services including maritime emergency services. Moreover, BT is obliged to continue to provide basic maintenance and installation services on a uniform scale of charges throughout the country. Under the license, BT also must provide universal service unless it is provided by a competitor.

Competitors of BT would like to have "fair trading" measures worked into the license. They claim that because of BT's dominant size, they will not be able to compete fairly without these clauses. However, BT expects to see obligations laid on its competitors in their licenses to match those laid on BT. The nature of the balance that has been struck between these objectives is discussed in the following section.

CONCLUSIONS

We noted in the opening section that there is a great deal of controversy whether the direction of technological change in the telecommunications industry is such as to require greater consolidation or greater fragmentation of network structures. The emergence of new transmission media such as optical fiber and satellite, and of a broader range of terminal equipment and value-added services, certainly provides scope for the construction of parallel networks and services on a competitive basis. Conversely, the increasing digitalization of the voice network is leading to the design of integrated services digital networks (ISDN), which provide transmission of voice, data, and video signals in one unified network, exploiting all the economies of scope that the new digital switching and transmission technologies have to offer.

Figure 7.2 summarizes the position toward which the U.K. government is leaning on the boundaries between competition and monopoly (strictly, duopoly) in the telecommunications service sector. The exact outcome will not be apparent until the wording of all relevant licenses—such as the general license for value-added network services—has been finalized. However, the following pattern appears to be emerging:

1. A boundary will exist (labeled *B* in Figure 7.2) below which service is restricted to the British Telecom–Mercury duopoly. This includes basic transmission and circuit switching of voice, video and data signals, and also packet switching of data.
2. A second boundary (labeled *A*) will be drawn, above which British

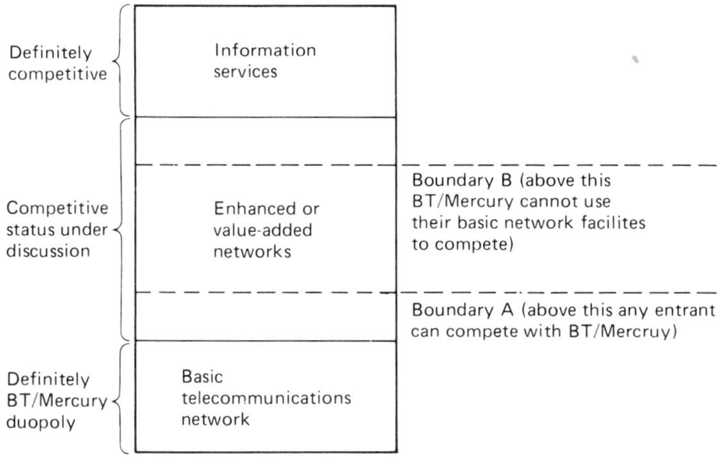

Figure 7.2

Telecom and Mercury cannot offer service in a manner technically integrated with their main switching and transmission facilities; they may compete in this field, but only through separately accountable divisions such as BT Enterprises, which deal with the parent corporation on an arm's-length basis.

Between these two boundaries is a region in which the three technical solutions to the provision of enhanced services listed in the first section of this chapter—provision through integrated networks, through overlaid value-added networks, and through intelligent terminal equipment—can compete freely. This region is likely to include financial networks, electronic mail services, various kinds of protocol conversion functions, and so forth. Insofar as there is a duopoly rather than a monopoly of basic transmission services, and insofar as there is some degree of consolidation and some of fragmentation in the vertical chain in Figure 7.2, the U.K. government can be said to have adopted a compromise position with regard to the structure of telecommunications networks. The United States has enacted a policy of almost maximum fragmentation of network architecture, by forcing the dominant carrier (AT&T) to provide all enhanced services only through a separate subsidiary rather than in a manner integrated with the core transmission and switching network. The countries of continental Europe are without exception excluding competition to the dominant state-owned long-distance carrier in basic transmission, and have varying degrees of restrictiveness governing competitive entry into value-added services.

It will be some years before the success or failure of the U.K. strategy becomes apparent. Some elements of the plan are widely welcomed. Perhaps the least controversial is the liberalization of terminal equipment, an area in which neither economic theory nor practical experience justifies the former monopolistic restrictions; indeed, all industrial countries are allowing a greater degree of competitiveness in this segment of the industry. The decision to allow enhanced vertical competition between BT's main network division and value-added service operators (i.e., to separate boundaries *A* and *B* in Figure 7.2) is in our view a good one, for it permits the coexistence of a variety of technical solutions to the provision of enhanced services. Time will tell whether this competition is rendered unworkable by predatory pricing behavior by the principal carrier, thus in effect justifying the U.S. policy decision to prohibit AT&T from direct participation in this market.

The most unusual element of the U.K. strategy has been the introduction of Mercury as the single licensed competitor in the basic transmission business. There is nothing in established economic doctrine to suggest that a legally enforced duopoly (and a widely unbalanced one at that) constitutes an optimal industry structure.[5] However, there is almost unanimous agreement that the emergence of Mercury has brought about a remarkable change in the behavior of BT; the latter company is perceived by its customers to be more responsive and flexible in meeting their needs, and perceived by competitors and suppliers as more aggressive and commercial in its stance. The increase in responsiveness and speed of service has been noted especially by customers in the financial sector of the City of London, where Mercury presents the greatest threat. Even senior BT officials are known to welcome the presence of the new competitor; it gives them a stronger hand in dealing with unions and middle management over the introduction of new and more efficient practices, and helps generally to instill a greater sense of commercial discipline into the organization.

It has been said that a market is well served if it contains one dominant firm of sufficient size to fund major new generations of products and to set de facto standards, and several smaller firms that keep the leader under constant pressure. (The U.S. mainframe computer industry, with its "IBM and the seven dwarfs" structure, has some of these characteristics.) Such a structure has some of the advantages of monopoly—efficient scale, sufficient resources to fund long-term developments—and some of competition. Introducing Mercury into the telecommunications industry is only a small step toward full competition along U.S. standards, but it may be the right move to make in that direction given the more limited size and wealth of the U.K. market.

DEVELOPMENTS IN CABLE TELEVISION AND SATELLITE BROADCASTING POLICY

In the years since 1980, U.K. government policy toward the broadcasting sector has been changing as rapidly as its policy in the field of telecommunications, especially with regard to cable television and satellite broadcasting systems. A chronology of the major policy developments in each of these two areas is given in Tables 7.2 and 7.3, respectively. The purpose of the brief discussion that follows is not to provide a detailed account of these developments but to draw attention to those that are most relevant to the future structure of telecommunications services.

During the 1960s and 1970s, the U.K. cable television industry experienced only modest growth, consisting almost exclusively of community antenna systems serving multiple-dwelling buildings or estates, and restricted by law to the retransmission to the three (now four) over-the-air broadcast channels. The otherwise unexciting developments of the industry during these years were punctuated by two experimental pay-TV trials; these took place in 1966, following recommendations put forward by the Pilkington Committee. The trials, which allowed viewers to see up-to-date films and other premium material by putting coins in a slot meter, were popular with subscribers until they were terminated by pressure from the British Broadcasting Corporation (BBC), the Independent Television (now Broadcasting) Authority (IBA), and the Post Office, each of which was concerned about the long-term threat that such developments posed to their monopoly or duopoly positions. The fact that the technology of the mid-1960s was quite capable of supporting pay-TV services is instructive, showing that the "cable revolution" has arrived at the time it has because the political climate is right and not, as is widely believed, because recent advances in information technology have made it possible.

The momentum toward liberalization began in 1980, with a statement by the government to the House of Commons that a pro-competition policy would be adopted and that twelve experimental pay-TV licenses would be granted. In July 1981 the government commissioned a report on cable systems by the Information Technology Advisory Panel (ITAP). This panel, reporting in February 1982, put forward a very optimistic and broad-ranging view of the future potential of cable television. The greater number of TV entertainment channels that might be carried by cable were seen to be only a small part of the new industry that would be created by the widespread dissemination of cable television networks. The principal benefits to society in the long term were seen to flow from the stimulus that would be provided to the adoption of every kind of information technology in homes and businesses.

The recommendations of the Hunt Committee (*Report on the Enquiry into Cable Expansion and Broadcasting Policy,* October 1982) set out detailed proposals for the institutional framework under which the cable industry would develop; a system of national franchising via a new cable authority was proposed. Government statements in the House of Commons in October 1982, and a white paper released in April 1983, largely confirmed the intention to implement the Hunt Committee findings.

The ITAP report, with its emphasis on advanced interactive services,

TABLE 7.2 Chronology of Recent Developments in Cable Television Policy

February 1981
There are 7 cable companies granted licenses in 13 areas, for pilot schemes to investigate the market.

July 1981
Government appoints Information Technology Advisory Panel (ITAP) to study future cable systems in the United Kingdom.

February 1982
ITAP report issued; recommends aggressive development of cable systems as the basis for a broadband infrastructure to supply information technology-based services to homes and offices.

October 1982
Hunt Committee appointed to investigate regulation, ownership, separation, finance, must-carry balance, morals, impartiality, exclusivity, foreign content, and related issues. Its report largely confirms ITAP findings and proposes franchising rules to be administered by a new cable authority; task of setting technical standards to be assigned to a technical working group.

April 1983
White paper issued by government, proposing a new statutory cable authority and describing franchising and licensing process.

September 1983
There are 37 applications received for cable franchises; 11 companies are offered interim licenses 2 months later.

December 1983
Cable and Broadcasting Bill introduced to Parliament; it states that cable authority should be set up by summer 1984.

March 1984
New taxation rules governing capital allowances announced in Chancellor of the Exchequer 1984 budget; widespread concern that these will undermine the viability of the (capital intensive) cable construction projects.

June 1984
Home Secretary extends proposed cable period from 12 to 15 years, responding to industry pressure to compensate for the adverse tax ruling of March 1984. Despite pessimistic mood of the industry, 40 groups are considering applying for cable licenses in the planned second round of applications.

represented one side of a controversy that was to dominate much of the subsequent debate on the future of cable systems in the United Kingdom. The other view was that cable television networks had to be seen primarily as entertainment systems—that only the demand for premium programming would provide sufficient revenue streams to recover investment costs.

TABLE 7.3 Chronology of Recent Developments in Satellite Broadcasting Policy

May 1981
Publication of paper on direct broadcast satellites by Home Office; very supportive of the concept of DBS services for the United Kingdom.

March 1982
William Whitelaw (then home secretary) allocates first two satellite channels to the BBC. The BBC announces that they will have a subscription service on one channel and "Window on the World" on the other. Later, in September 1983, the IBA was given a similar go-ahead.

March 1983
Home Secretary formally announces that Britain would have a national system of DBS. This would be based on a satellite system, Unisat, to be jointly owned by British Aerospace, GEC/Marconi, and British Telecom.

December 1983
BBC still uncertain about whether to launch DBS television channels, despite government authorization in 1982. Discussions between BBC and IBA initiated with a view to providing DBS services on a joint basis via Unisat satellite.

January 1984
First satellite commercial TV channel starts. Skychannel (Rupert Murdoch) operating in Swindon, Milton Keynes, and Greenwich.

March 1984
It is reported that BBC and IBA are close to agreement on DBS, since government is now prepared to accept preconditions, notably that IBA companies can have their franchises extended until 1997.

May 1984
Government gives go-ahead to BBC–IBA joint venture for use of Unisat transponders. IBA given the necessary powers to appoint other participants in the project. Advertisements appear in press inviting other participants to join IBA–BBC scheme. IBA to advise Home Secretary on those participants interested at the end of July 1984.

June 1984
A total of 15 applications for share in BBC–IBA project received. Unisat announces 2-year delay in schedule, now planning launch in 1988. IBA announces that joint venture is not tied to Unisat satellite, as previously configured, suggesting door may be open to other design proposals.

In reality, the controversy concerned timing rather than the ultimate structure of systems. Both sides agreed that, in the very short term, entertainment programming would provide the major income stream; in the long term, other service revenues would grow substantially. However, the question of the relative priority of the entertainment versus non-entertainment applications in the medium term proved to be an extremely awkward one, since fundamental technical choices, such as that between switched-star and tree-and-branch architectures, had to be settled on the basis of the level of priority to be given to two-way interactive services. On this issue the government took an intermediate position. While allowing the construction of systems without provision for the full range of interactive services, it encouraged the use of technologies compatible with such services through incentives designed to stimulate building of switched-star networks (notably, an increase in the license period from 12 to 20 years).

The nature of interactive services to be provided over cable remains unclear. While early proposals emphasized applications such as telebanking, teleshopping, and information retrieval, the lukewarm performance of videotex-based systems such as Prestel has caused the industry to become more sceptical about these prospects. Attention is now focused primarily on the possibility of using cable networks for voice telephony, by interconnecting with the new Mercury national telecommunications network. On the basis of current British Telecom local communications charges, it appears that cable television networks could profitably link up with Mercury to provide voice telephony services, especially to businesses. How resilient that strategy would be in the face of tariff revisions by British Telecom remains to be assessed. Meanwhile, Mercury and a number of cable companies are actively discussing the provision of such services.

Parallel with these developments in the cable industry, there has been an upsurge of interest in Direct Broadcast Satellite (DBS) services. Following the allocation of five DBS channels to each European country by the World Administrative Radio Conference (WARC) in 1977, the U.K. government was initially slow to follow up the opportunities available from this technology. In May 1981, however, the Home Office published a document entitled *Direct Broadcasting by Satellite*, which was to mark the beginning of an aggressive series of government moves in this area.

The desire to provide the public with a wider range of programming was undoubtedly a factor in the development of this policy (though in this respect the DBS services stood to compete with and hence hamper the growth of the new cable television networks); however, another key driving force behind the policy was clearly the goal of promoting British information technology, and in particular the U.K. satellite industry. Since the British Aerospace Dynamics Group was Europe's largest satellite manufacturer, this seemed one area of technology in which the United Kingdom could take a lead in future markets. At the instigation of the Department of Trade and Industry, British Aerospace, GEC/Marconi, and British Telecom formed a new company, United Satellite Limited (Unisat), which prepared plans for a high-power direct broadcast satellite to be launched in 1986. In March 1982 the home secretary allocated two channels on this system for use by the BBC.

Since that date, there has been increasing confusion and uncertainty concerning the future of the Unisat project. Studies showed that the satellite system would cost at least £250 million; despite the presence of some lower-power transponders for telecommunications applications, much of the cost would have to be recovered from the BBC through very high annual rental charges for its two channels. The BBC began to have doubts about whether the public would be willing to pay sufficiently high fees for the premium channels to cover these charges and yield a profit margin.

Furthermore, evidence began to emerge that technological advances were making the original high-power (200-watt) transponder specification unnecessary. Improvements in the performance of the low-noise amplifier and other critical components within domestic rooftop receiving equipment have progressed at such a pace that this equipment is currently able to receive signals from transponders of much lower power. A satellite providing such a weaker signal can be launched, or rented, for a per-transponder cost many times lower than that of the high-power Unisat project.

The government is by no means convinced of these technical arguments, and in any case is striving to keep afloat the original British Unisat design. It has now encouraged cooperation between the BBC, the IBA, and other commercial bodies to share the cost of the project. Officially, the Unisat satellite is still to be launched; privately, some industry observers have expressed doubts that it can survive uncertainties over market demand and costs. If launched, the satellite will provide additional satellite capacity in the United Kingdom for two-way telecommunications applications on its on-broadcast transponsers.

NOTES

1. Both schools of thought have support in economic theory. The idea that competition is usually to be preferred to monopoly is of course central to mainstream neoclassical economics. Writers such as Coase and, more recently, Oliver Williamson have emphasized the value of vertical integration as a means of reducing organizational inefficiencies and transaction costs (see, for example, Williamson 1975).

2. Steel and Heald (1982) describe four objectives of the government in its privatization policy: (1) to foster economic freedom; (2) to enhance efficiency; (3) to bring in line the wages of the public sector; and (4) to reduce the amount nationalized industries borrow from the government.

3. This report was commissioned in 1975 by the then Secretary of State for

Industry, Eric Varley, who had overall responsibility for the Post Office. The report, which was completed in 1977, was carried out by C. F. Carter FBA, vice chancellor of Lancaster University, who recommended that the Post Office should be prepared at that time to relinquish at least part of its monopoly, especially in the areas of new telecommunications services and subscribers' apparatus.

4. Mercury must first attempt to "buy British," but if British manufacturers cannot meet their needs, they will buy first EEC and then from anyone else.

5. See, for example, the comprehensive writings on the relationship between industrial structure and economic performance by Scherer (1980).

REFERENCES

Baker, Kenneth. Minister for Industry and Information Technology. *Hansard Parliamentary Debates*, Commons. London, July 30, 1982.

Beesley, Michael. *Liberalisation of the Use of British Telecommunications Network*. London: HMSO, 1981.

Carter, C. F. *Report of the Post Office Review Committee*. Cmnd. 6800. London: HMSO, 1977.

The Conservative Manifesto. London, 1983.

Future of Telecommunications in Britain. Report presented to Parliament by the Secretary of State for Industry by Command of Her Majesty. London: HMSO, July 1982.

Jenkin, Patrick. Secretary of State for Industry. *Hansard Parliamentary Debates*, Commons. London, July 1982.

Littlechild Report. Department of Industry. London: HMSO, February 1983.

Marketing Solutions Ltd. *Ringing the Changes*. London, 1984.

Scherer, F. M. *Industrial Market Structure and Economic Performance*. 2d ed. New York: Rand McNally, 1980.

Steel, David, and David Heald. "Privatizing Public Enterprise: An Analysis of the Government's Case." *Reports and Surveys,* 1982, 333–349.

Williamson, O. *Markets and Hierarchies: Theory and Antitrust Implications*. New York: Macmillan, 1975.

Eight

Developments in Canadian Telecommunications Regulation

Gordon E. Kaiser

Like many countries, Canada has experienced a dramatic change in its telecommunications industry in the past decade. The change results largely from the forces of competition in both equipment and service markets. Not only have the policies of the major monopoly carriers been radically altered by regulatory commissions, but the companies themselves have undergone significant structural change to meet the demands of the future. Inherent in these structural changes are significant changes in costing and pricing policies.

For years, Canadian telephone companies, like telephone companies around the world, regarded their mandate as rendering universal or end-to-end service to all subscribers. This universality presumed carrier ownership of transmission, switching terminal, and local loops. It also implied a lack of access and refusal to supply facilities to competing forms of transmission equipment.

While it can be said that competition in telecommunications has been the religious force behind these policy shifts, the underlying catechism of the new religion is the belief that there is no longer a natural monopoly in either the equipment or service markets.

This realization in turn results directly from technological developments over the past two decades. In the case of equipment, the growth of the computer industry in general and semiconductor technology in particular has increased both the demand for customer ownership of terminal equipment and the ability of new firms to develop products not available from the telephone company.

In the service sector, new technology—such as microwave in the 1950s, satellite transmission in the 1960s, and cellular radio technology in the 1970s—created similar pressures as new firms sought to offer services that competed with the telephone company's local and long-distance services.

Without doubt, the United States is the birthplace of this new religion. While Canada has lagged American developments, the Canadian policy has perhaps more closely followed American development than is the case anywhere else in the world. The differences in timing in the major policy developments are shown in Table 8.1.

TABLE 8.1 Timing of Major Policy Developments, Canada and the United States

	Canada	United States
Terminal equipment	1978	1968
Cable television access	1975	1975
Satellite access	1977	1972
Specialized common carriers	1979	1971
Radio common carrier access	1979	1968
Cellular telephone	1983	1982
Resale and enhanced service	1984	1984

INDUSTRY STRUCTURE

In spite of the lag of almost a decade, there is a remarkable parallel between Canadian and American telecommunications policies. This is explained in part by similarities in the telecommunications industry structure. Bell Canada, the largest telephone company in Canada, provides 70% of Canadian telephones. The (predivestiture) Bell System in the United States, the American Telephone & Telegraph Company (AT&T), through its Long Lines Department and 22 operating companies, accounted for over 80% of that country's telephones. Until 1947, 21% of Bell Canada's shares were owned by AT&T.

Equally significant is the fact that in both countries the monopolies in the service areas have been extended to equipment manufacturing by vertical integration, with the telephone company purchasing most of its equipment through its manufacturing subsidiary. Bell Canada purchases close to 70% of its equipment from its manufacturing affiliate, Northern Telecom, whereas, before its divestiture, AT&T obtained 99% of Bell System requirements from its manufacturing affiliate, Western Electric.

From 1914 to 1956 Western Electric owned 44% of the stock of Northern Telecom, with Bell Canada owning the remaining shares. The declining influence of AT&T and Western Electric over Bell Canada and Northern Telecom can be traced to the 1956 Consent Decree obtained by the American antitrust authorities.

In both countries, the directed purchasing policy of the telephone company has been supported by telephone company policies prohibiting subscribers from attaching subscriber-owned terminal equipment to the telephone company network. The AT&T policy was declared illegal in 1968; Bell Canada's similar policy was first challenged in 1978. The Canadian policy, as outlined later in the chapter, is currently under review.

It is also significant that the second largest telephone company in each country is General Telephone and Electronics (GTE). In the United States, GTE Telephone companies in 33 states serve approximately 8% of the nation's telephones. In Canada, the British Columbia Telephone Company, which is owned by GTE, accounts for virtually all the telephones in that province, representing 11% of the telephones nationally.

As in the case of AT&T and Bell Canada, the GTE organizations in both countries purchase large proportions of their equipment requirements from manufacturing affiliates. Vertical integration is therefore significant in both countries; 10.2 million telephones out of a total of 14.5 million are supplied by a vertically integrated structure in Canada. In the United States the two vertically integrated suppliers account for 146 million out of 162 million telephones. Vertical integration, of course, is not unique to North America. But the significant distinction between North America and Europe is the fact that the North American companies are privately owned. This fact alone has undoubtedly increased the vigilance of regulators in promoting the competitive entry policies of the last decade.

Finally, it is significant that both Canada and the United States are service economies. The essential ingredient in a service economy is information. The question is whether a monopoly or competition will more effectively reduce the cost of this essential information flow. The accepted wisdom as witnessed by the regulatory decisions in both countries is that competition promotes cost reduction and new technology. Monopoly, by contrast, is seen as safeguarding old technologies, particularly in the case of utilities with guaranteed rates of return on fixed-asset rate bases.

TECHNOLOGY

There are two basic reasons why Canadian policies have followed American events so closely. The first, as described above, is that the industry structure is similar.

The second rationale is the similarity of the technological pressures in the two countries that have had an impact on both transmission and equipment markets. The telephone companies' monopoly in transmission was challenged with the advent of microwave technology in the 1950s and satellite transmission in the 1960s. These new technologies permitted new firms to enter the industry by offering new services that competed with the telephone companies' local and long-distance services. In particular, both microwave and satellites have called into question the carriers' monopoly in long-distance transmission. In the future, the monopoly in local distribution may be challenged by fiber optics, interactive cable, and cellular radio technology.

New technology has also called into question the monopoly carriers' claims in equipment markets. The extension of monopoly from the service market to the equipment market turned on the twin policies—adopted by both AT&T and Bell Canada—of supplying their equipment needs from controlled equipment subsidiaries and prohibiting subscriber attachment of equipment to the telephone companies' facilities.

The growth of digital and semiconductor technology over the past 20 years has increased both the demand for customer-owned terminal equipment and the ability of firms to develop products not available from the telephone companies. This growth of user demand, along with the development of new supply capability, is the basis of the new North American terminal attachment policy.

While there may have been a lag in policy development between Canada and the United States, there is no indication of a lag with respect to the technology that underlies these policy changes. Microwave technology developed during World War II was first utilized in the transcontinental microwave system established in 1968 by the Trans Canada Telephone System, a consortium of all major Canadian telephone companies. This was followed by a transcontinental system established by CNCP, a consortium of the Canadian National and Canadian Pacific Railways, 3 years later.

In the United States, private microwave opened up as a result of a 1959 decision by the Federal Communications Commission (FCC) in the *Above 890* proceeding.[1] As in Canada, the railways were quick to take advantage of this option. Southern Pacific Railway, which ultimately established one of the largest specialized common-carrier networks, operated the largest private microwave system in the United States by 1961.

This technological history is similar with respect to satellites. Telesat Canada was formed in 1969 and launched its first domestic satellite in November 1972. The first domestic satellite in the United States was launched by Western Union in 1974 following the FCC's *Domsat* decision in December 1972.[2] Following this initial lag behind Canada, America allowed complete entry to the domestic satellite industry, resulting in the establishment of the Comstar System in 1976 and the RCA domestic system in the same year. The private digital system operated by Satellite Business Systems, originally a consortium of IBM, Comsat, and Aetna Insurance, is just starting initial operations.

Nor is there any evidence that Canada lagged in the development of semiconductor technology. In fact two Canadian firms, Northern Telecom and Mitel Corporation, made a significant contribution to the industry. Ten years ago, Northern Telecom's operations outside Canada were minimal. Now the company has 22 plants in the United States and 6 plants in other countries. By the end of the 1980s sales in the United States should exceed sales in Canada.

The growth of Mitel Corporation has been more dramatic. Starting in 1973 with a staff of 4 and sales of $12,000, the company reached a 1981 sales volume of $111 million. Eight of the company's 10 manufacturing plants are now outside of Canada. Sales outside of Canada account for approximately 80% of total sales.

COMPETITION IN EQUIPMENT MARKETS

The marketing power of AT&T and Bell Canada initially gained in equipment markets resulted from patents. Once these patents expired or were expunged,[3] the monopoly power that had been acquired in the equipment markets was maintained through vertical integration and the carriers' policy of prohibiting subscriber-attached terminal equipment.

Terminal Attachment

In 1953 both Bell Canada and British Columbia Telephone Company had identical rules in their regulations prohibiting customer-owned terminal equipment.[4] In 1955 the Bell Canada rules were tested in the *Sterl-A-Phone* case,[5] which was remarkably similar to the *Hush-A-Phone* case[6] decided in the United States the following year. In *Sterl-A-Phone*, Bell successfully prohibited the attachment of a harmless device to the telephone company's equipment. On essentially similar facts, the U.S. courts found in *Hush-A-Phone* that a tariff prohibiting a harmless attachment was "an unwarranted interference with the telephone subscriber's use of telephone in ways that are privately beneficial without being publicly detrimental."

Continuing controversy regarding the attachment of subscriber-owned equipment caused the Canadian Parliament to amend Bell Canada's Special Act of Incorporation in 1968,[7] the same year of the FCC's famous *Carterfone* decision.[8] The amendments provided that Bell could prescribe requirements for the attachment to its facilities and that any person who believed the requirements were unreasonable could apply to the Federal Regulatory Commission for determination of that reasonableness. The first application took place in 1975 when a member of the Ontario Legislature filed an application to permit the attachment of an automatic dialer.[9] The commission accepted Bell Canada's argument that as the company did not have a tariff, there were no requirements that the commission could judge reasonable or not. Accordingly, the commission took the position that it had no jurisdiction, and the 1968 amendments became meaningless.

The first breakthrough came in 1977 when a seller of mobile telephones challenged a new Bell tariff that denied the right of customer ownership of automatic mobile radiotelephones directly connected with the network.[10] The commission rejected the telephone company's argument that customer ownership would retard research and harm the integrity of the network. The commission held that the tariff should be suspended as an unjust discrimination against the complainant, Challenge Communications, subjecting the company to undue or unreasonable prejudice by the federal court of appeal. Leave to appeal to the Supreme Court of Canada was refused.

The *Challenge* case was similar to the *Carterfone* case in the United States 10 years earlier. One difference between *Challenge* and *Carterfone* was that the mobile radiotelephone in the Canadian case was located in automobiles on the streets of Toronto, while the Carterfone units of similar description were located on oil rigs in the Gulf of Mexico. The more important difference was that the commission in *Carterfone* required all AT&T tariffs to be modified to remove the prohibition against subscriber ownership. In *Challenge* a single tariff, the tariff for automatic radiotelephone, was reversed. It was not until August 5, 1980, that the federal commission enacted interim rules permitting all subscribers to attach terminal equipment to the network. Unlike the United States, the Canadian commission adopted a "primary instrument" concept reserving that instrument for the telephone company exclusively. The primary instrument concept, however, is now being questioned in a current proceeding before the Canadian commission.

Vertical Integration

Vertical integration between monopoly telephone companies and related equipment suppliers has been a long-standing issue in both Canada and the United States. In the United States that relationship between Western Electric and AT&T prompted the U.S. Department of Justice's antitrust action in 1949, which resulted in the 1956 Consent Decree.[11] The Consent Decree enjoined AT&T and Bell operating companies from engaging in any business other than furnishing common-carrier services. The decree also required Bell to license patents at reasonable rates upon request.

In 1971 the Federal Communications Commission instituted proceedings investigating the relationship between the Bell System and Western Electric. The commission decision 6 years later[12] rejected that trial operating companies should be given greater autonomy in the procurement of equipment. The commission ordered Bell to file within 90 days a proposal that would "satisfy our concerns regarding the lack of autonomy and independence both joint and individual given to Bell operating companies in equipment procurement." The AT&T proposal of May 1971 was rejected by the commission in March 1978, and the matter was left unresolved.

The third major development in the United States was the antitrust action launched by the Department of Justice in November 1974, seeking divestiture of both Western Electric and the Bell operating companies. After 51 days of trial a Consent Decree was entered into in January 1982. The settlement vacated the substantive provisions of the 1956 Consent Decree and substituted three new substantive requirements:

1. AT&T must divest itself of all 22 operating companies.
2. Before divestiture, the operating companies were to be reorganized to limit their activities to exchange telecommunications services or natural monopoly services actually regulated by tariff. The operating companies were prohibited from offering inter-exchange service or engaging in the supply of customer premise equipment.
3. The operating companies were required to provide all inter-exchange carriers and information service providers with exchange access of a type, quality, and price provided to AT&T on an untariffed basis.

Although AT&T was required to divest itself of the operating companies, and the operating companies were placed under strict limitations as to business activity, AT&T itself was freed from the 1956 Consent Decree. It was granted freedom in three important activities:

1. AT&T was freed from the patent licensing obligations imposed by the 1956 Decree.
2. Western Electric gained new freedom to manufacture and sell equipment outside the common-carrier field.
3. AT&T became free to engage in activities outside the common-carrier field with no limitations at all on the business in which it may engage.

In Canada, the relationship between Bell Canada and Northern Electric has been an issue before the Federal Regulatory Agency since 1938. Bell Canada acquisitions of significant regional telephone companies in the mid-1960s resulted in an investigation under the Combines Investigation Act, Canada's antitrust statute. The concern was that the acquisition of other significant carriers would increase the effect of vertical integration and further foreclosure of Canada's equipment market.

The result was a general inquiry under section 47 of the act, which began in June 15, 1977, and concluded 5 years later. After hearing 200 witnesses in the course of 228 days of hearings, the commission issued its final report on January 7, 1983. The director of investigation and research, who had originally taken the position that the appropriate remedy was divestiture of Northern Telecom from Bell Canada, argued in the end that the public interest would best be served by imposing a competitive bidding requirement on Bell Canada. The commission, however, recommended only that the CRTC review Northern's prices to Bell and that "Northern should be required to continue to sell to Bell at prices no higher than those offered to other Canadian customers."[13]

A competitive bidding order did, however, result from a 1979 proceeding before the Canadian Radio-Television Telecommunications Commission. In that case the British Columbia Telephone Company had applied for approval to acquire its manufacturing affiliates, Automatic Electric and Lenkurt. For years, B.C. Telephone Company and the two manufacturing concerns had been owned by the same parent, General Telephone and Electronics of New York. It was argued that the reorganization resulted in increased vertical integration. The commission's decision of September 1979[14] approved the acquisition on the condition that the British Columbia Telephone Company file a proposal for more open procurement, commonly known as competitive bidding. Accordingly, the telephone company filed a proposal providing for open tendering for the majority of equipment above certain minimum purchases.

With the variety of equipment increasing, and with increasing rates of technological obsolescence, shorter equipment lives, and increased costs of capital, it can be argued that vertical integration is not in the interests of the Canadian public, let alone competing manufacturers who stand to be foreclosed from markets. The standard justification of vertical integration, namely economies of scale, is questionable under the new technology. The new justification is economies of research and development.

It is also apparent that there are really three potential remedies with respect to monopoly in equipment markets: structural remedies such as divestiture and behavioral policies such as terminal attachment and competitive bidding. All three are being advanced by different governmental authorities in Canada and the United States.

Carriers in Competitive Markets

The advent of customer ownership of terminal equipment raises the question whether structural remedies are required to curtail potential abuse associated with carriers' participation in direct sale markets. In the United States, the Consent Decree would prohibit the Bell operating companies from engaging in the sale of terminal equipment at all. In Canada there is strong pressure that such activities should be carried out through a separate subsidiary.

The same issue exists with respect to carriers' participation in competitive long-distance services. The separate subsidiary concept was advanced by the Federal Communications Commission in its *Second Computer Inquiry*[15] with respect to these "enhanced services" as well as the provisioning of terminal equipment. In Canada the Federal Regulatory Agency is at present engaging in a lengthy cost inquiry to devise a mechanism by which the competitive activities can be isolated in an accounting sense to ensure that there is neither cross-subsidization from monopoly revenues nor predatory pricing, again to competing vendors.

COMPETITION IN SERVICE MARKETS

The pressure for competitive entry into the North American transmission markets resulted in large part from the advent of microwave technology during World War II. The first issue was the granting of frequencies for private point-to-point microwave.

The related issue was granting access from those communications facilities to the local distribution network of the telephone company. Access to the local exchange network has been the key to any meaningful competition. Litigation for access has involved four groups of competitors: cable television companies; microwave carriers; domestic satellite carriers; and radio common carriers. Each utilizes a different technology, but the request was the same: access to the telephone company's network in order that they might compete with the telephone company in certain areas.

It is important to understand the pressure of competition in terms of the identity of the potential entrants. Some of these potential entrants are unique to North America. This may explain the more rapid growth of competition in the North American telecommunications industry.

Cable Television

In Canada the cable television companies were the first to gain access to the telephone companies' facilities. The pressure from the industry undoubtedly resulted from the fact that Canada is one of the most heavily cabled countries in the world.

The history of the dispute dates from the late 1960s, when both Bell Canada and AT&T were prohibited from offering cable television services.[16] Telephone companies then sought to reduce the effectiveness of the cable television companies by prohibiting the attachment of the cables to the telephone company's poles. The first request took place in 1973, when nine cable companies requested the Federal Regulatory Commission to order attachment. While the first application was unsuccessful,[17] an application by a Quebec company 2 years later resulted in the commission's ordering Bell Canada to permit the cable operator to attach its cables to Bell Canada's poles in the licensed area:[18]

> It is not disputed that the telephone poles erected by Bell are its property, but as herein noted, the use or enjoyment Bell has of this property is subject to certain limitations imposed by law in the public interest. We believe that when one devotes one's property to a use in which the public has an interest, one, in effect, grants to the public an interest in that use, and must submit to be controlled by the public for the common good, to the extent of the interest one has thus created. We believe that Bell is in that position with respect to its telephone poles, which cease for this reason to be juris privity only.

The commission's decision resulted in the telephone company's filing tariffs for pole access, a result similar to a ruling by the FCC that same year.[19] The CRTC decision in Canada recognized that cable television was a potential competitor:[20]

> Although the two transmission technologies—coaxial cable and copper pair—provide distinct services into the home at present, new services may develop which may be provided by either technology. In such cases neither technology should be burdened with artificial tariffs preventing their development in a fair and reasonable manner.

Domestic Satellite Carrier

The major pressure for competitive solutions in Canadian telecommunications came as a result of satellite technology. The issue arose in an application by the monopoly satellite carrier, Telesat Canada, in 1977 for approval of an agreement whereby Telesat Canada would become a member of TCTS, a consortium of nine major telephone companies. The terms of the agreement gave TCTS control of Canada's sole domestic communications satellite.[21]

The telephone companies' rationale for the proposed agreement was that there was excess capacity on the satellite, resulting in poor economic results, which the telephone companies would seek to reduce if approval of the proposed merger was granted. In fact, the agreement guaranteed the satellite company a rate of return.

A number of intervenors opposed the proposal, arguing that the new technology would permit satellite messages to be transmitted directly to populated urban areas and that satellites would therefore represent, for the first time, a competitive alternative to the telephone company's terrestrial network. The agreement, it was alleged, would place a number of satellite users at a competitive disadvantage to the telephone company members of TCTS.

The commission agreed with the intervenors and turned down the application, arguing that the restrictions in the proposed agreement gave unwarranted advantages to the members of TCTS over all other potential Telesat users. In particular, the commission ruled that "a potential competitive situation in long-haul data, video and other private lines services may be restricted by the Agreement in a manner that does not appear to be justified."[22]

The commission's decision, however, was reversed on appeal to the federal cabinet.[23] Cabinet appeals are unique to Canada. Unlike analogous legislation in the United States, the National Transportation Act in Canada provides for the appeal of a regulatory decision either from the court or directly to the cabinet via a "political appeal."

In approving the agreement, however, the cabinet did so on the basis that it would not contravene any other act of Canada. Accordingly, in a recent application by Telesat Canada for approval of tariffs, the intervenors again alleged that the restrictive covenants were contrary to the Railway Act. Again the intervenors were successful before the commission.[24] The commission rejected Telesat's attempt to restrict the type of customers and also the requirement that any customer must purchase the whole radiofrequency channel.

Both restrictions discriminate against smaller carriers. The telephone company again appealed to the cabinet. This time the cabinet endorsed the commission by permitting broadcast undertakings to purchase directly from the satellite company and by allowing the sale of partial channels to approved common carriers.[25]

The Canadian solution was much more restrictive in terms of competition than is American policy. Ten years earlier, in 1972, the FCC had issued its *Domsat* decision[26] encouraging multiple entry of satellites. The FCC held that multiple entry would demonstrate whether satellite technology could provide specialized services on as efficient a basis as could terrestrial facilities. Furthermore, the commission recognized AT&T's advantage and prohibited the company from utilizing its own satellite for private-line services for 3 years.

There are two recent developments of note with respect to Canadian satellite services. First, broadcasters have been given the right to purchase services directly from Telesat rather than order them through regulated common carriers. Moreover, broadcasters now have the right to resell transponder capacity to other broadcasters.

Second, there has been development with respect to the ownership of satellite earth stations. Initially, ownership was restricted to Telesat Canada. In 1982 the Minister of Communications permitted subscribers to own receive-only earth stations. Recently this was further relaxed to provide that subscribers may own transmitter stations as well.

Specialized Carriers

In Canada it was the satellite case that first promoted serious thinking about competition in transmission markets. In the United States, however, the satellite decisions followed a pro-competitive decision taken 10 years earlier regarding microwave transmission.

In 1956, the same year as the *Hush-A-Phone* case in the terminal equipment market, the FCC began an inquiry regarding the feasibility of granting frequencies for private microwave systems. Before the 1960s, only the telephone companies and Western Union publicly offered private-line services, and those services were generally either telegraph or voice grade circuits. As in the case of the terminal equipment market, proliferation of computers in the 1960s created a demand for specialized private-line services not offered by the traditional monopoly. It was the development of microwave transmission facilities that proved an economical medium for meeting this new demand.

In its *Above 890* decision[27] authorizing private microwave, the FCC ruled that without clear evidence to the effect that microwave systems would adversely affect common carriers, it could not justify restricted licensing.

There was a similar response in Canada. In 1958 the Trans Canada Telephone System developed a transcontinental microwave system. In response, CNCP, a consortium of Canadian Pacific Railway and Canadian National Railway, applied to the federal cabinet and obtained approval to build a competing system. The Trans Canada Telephone System opposed the CNCP application on a number of grounds, including the allegation that it would result in higher telephone rates. The Canadian government acknowledged the importance of competition in this sector of telecommunications services by permitting CNCP to establish its Trans Continental System.

The license itself, however, was not sufficient. Access to the network was crucial. In the United States this permission had been granted by the FCC's 1971 *Specialized Common Carrier* decision.[28] The commission ruled that private-line microwave was a specialized, rapidly growing market not being serviced by the carriers. With respect to the allegations of revenue loss, the commission found no convincing evidence and noted that this particular market was a small percentage of the total AT&T market. The commission also dismissed the traditional economies of scale argument as not being persuasive in markets where technology and consumer demands are changing quickly.

The *Specialized Common Carrier* decision did not permit specialized carriers in the United States to provide message toll service. When MCI, which obtained microwave approval in 1969,[29] began to offer a message toll-equivalent service called Execunet, the commission ordered MCI authorization. This position was overturned in the U.S. Court of Appeals, however, and leave to the Supreme Court of the United States was denied.[30] Entry was further expanded when the FCC authorized value-added carriers in 1974 and permitted resale and sharing of private-line services 2 years later.

The result has been an explosion in the network in the United States. Participants in the market are now divided into two categories: network owners, such as MCI, Southern Pacific Communications, USTS, and Western Union; and resellers, the largest of which is U.S. Telephone Communications of Dallas, Texas. In 1981 these carriers had revenues of approximately $620 million, divided as follows:

MCI	$310 million
Southern Pacific	180 million
U.S. Telephone Communications	40 million
Western Union	10 million
All others	40 million

The most recent development has been the rapid growth of resellers, led by U.S. Telephone Communications. That company began operations in March 1980 with revenues of $3.4 million in that year. Revenues in 1981 were $40 million, and were near $80 million in 1982. U.S. Tel provides MTS-type service primarily through the resale of the facsimile lines and also resale of MCI network services and AT&T WATS lines. The company services the entire United States with a tiered rate structure.

Today there are about 180 resale carriers operating throughout the United States. There are also an increasing number of value-added carriers offering data communications services and electronic mail or voice mailbox services. Despite all this activity, competitive message service carriers represent only 2% of the total intercity market in the United States. The limited market share of these carriers, despite their exceptional growth, raises questions about the recent U.S. Consent Decree releasing the monopoly carrier from any constraints in intercity transmission.

Events in Canadian transmission markets are tame by comparison. Five years after the FCC's *Specialized Common Carrier* decision, the Canadian Pacific Railway filed an application before the CRTC seeking an order that Bell Canada "forward all reasonable and proper facilities for the receiving, forwarding and delivering of telegraphic and telephonic messages on or from telegraph systems and lines for the interchange or telecommunications traffic and for the interconnection of their respective telephone systems." A year later, the commission joined the Canadian National Railway to the proceedings.

For a number of years, CNCP competed with the Trans Canada Telephone System (TCTS) and various private-line and record message services. In 1976, the year of the application, CNCP provided 5.4% of the country's total telecommunications requirements. In the area of data communications, in which CNCP specializes, 44% of national requirements are provided by the consortium. The demand for data service was growing at a high rate: 25% per year between 1975 and 1980, and an estimated 17% per year between 1980 and 1985.

There was a history of competition between CNCP and TCTS. CNCP's introduction of telex in 1956 was met by the introduction of TWX in 1962 by TCTS. CNCP's introduction of broadband exchange services in 1967 was met by the telephone company's offering of MSDS, Multi-Com, and Voice-Com. The two carriers subsequently introduced competing digital data services, Infodat and Dataroute. Then, in 1977, CNCP introduced Infoswitch, a switched data system in competition with the telephone company's Datapak service.

Nonetheless, it was argued that competition could not continue without access to Bell's local distribution network. CNCP argued that effective competition in computer communications required that users be able to access the system through the telephone. In response, Bell Canada argued that granting interconnection to competing carriers would adversely affect its revenues by some $235 million. The commission found that this potential revenue loss had been greatly overstated and granted the application. The commission adopted the principle that regulated companies controlling essential facilities may not refuse to supply facilities to undermine competitors.[31] This was essentially the same language the FCC adopted in 1971 in the *Specialized Common Carrier* decision.[32]

It is significant in this regard that the CNCP decision strictly limited access to private-line services. Unlike the United States, the Canadian commission has been very careful to avoid development of competing message toll service.

Moreover, CNCP has to date been granted access to local loops only in Bell Canada and B.C. Tel territory. The provincially regulated carriers are united in refusing system interconnection. CNCP recently applied to the CRTC, asking the commission to order interconnection with Alberta Government Telephones (AGT). Understandably, this has met with a constitutional challenge.

The next major development in service competition in Canada occurred on October 25, 1983, when CNCP filed an application with the CRTC for orders permitting interconnection of its system with the public-switched telephone networks of Bell Canada and the British Columbia Telephone Company. If approved, the application will permit CNCP to compete with the telephone companies in the provision of long-distance public telephone service. As stated, CNCP already competes with the telephone company in the provision of various private communications systems.

CNCP filed its evidence in this proceeding on April 9, 1984, and the federally regulated telephone companies filed their evidence on April 30. Following an interrogation, a hearing commenced on October 2.

This proceeding was one of the most significant of all telecommunications proceedings in Canada. At issue was the extent of competition in long-distance communication. This raises serious costing and pricing concerns, given the extent of cross-subsidization of local service by long-distance revenues.

Radio Common Carriers

As radio common carriers began to compete with telephone companies in the supply of U.S. mobile communications, the FCC ruled in 1969 that telephone companies could not control dial-access interconnection or enjoy advantages not available to the radio common carriers.[33]

There has been a similar development in Canada. In 1978 Bell Canada began to offer and advertise wide-area dial-access radio paging service while denying to radio common carriers the facilities necessary to offer the same service. A group of radio common carriers applied to the commission, seeking an order directing Bell Canada to supply the selector-level telephone numbers that permit the dial access.

It was argued that the refusal contravened the Federal Railway Act and that Bell was granting itself undue or unreasonable preference. Upon hearing the complaint, the commission found that the refusal did contravene the Railway Act by discriminating against radio common carriers. It issued an injunction prohibiting Bell Canada from advertising its radio paging services until the matter had been resolved.[34] Subsequently, rates were set, although at a level six times the prevailing U.S. rates.

Since the decision of the CRTC, provincially regulated telephone companies in three provinces—Alberta, Newfoundland, and Nova Scotia—have elected to provide dial access to radio common carriers. There have been no decisions in Canada at either the federal or the provincial levels, however, which would permit the interconnection of two-way mobile services offered by the radio common carriers.

Cellular Telephones: Competition in Local Distribution

To date, competition and transmission have been restricted to intercity networks. There is every prospect that the future will see increased questioning of natural monopoly assumptions on the local distribution network. Again the examination will be fueled by new technology.

The two technologies evident in Canada are cable television and cellular radio telephony. Since Canada is the most heavily cabled country in the world, it is not surprising that it should be the focus of experiments in two-way interactive communications using existing cable systems. One of the leading developments allows subscribers to utilize cable television service to access software providing essentially a home computer function.

In the United States the growth of intelligent terminals has led to a wide variety of local network offerings. These systems either use fiber optic or coaxial cable to access proprietary terminals or employ the existing telephone network to access a wider variety and diversity of different terminals. The best example of the latter technology is Ethernet, a joint development of TEC, Intel Corporation, and Xerox. In Canada, the local distribution networks relying on existing telephone systems have been limited by current restrictions on resale and enhanced services.

The most dramatic development of local distribution networks involves the use of cellular radio telephony. This technology permits frequency allocations in the 800 MHz band to be split and reused with the result that capacity multiplies tremendously.

In both Canada and the United States, regulatory authorities have determined that there will be competition in the supply of cellular radio telephony. The FCC, in calling for applications in all major cities, stated that two licenses would be awarded in each city, with one license reserved for the "wireline" (telephone company) carrier. In Canada, the federal government has also adopted a policy of awarding two licenses in each of the 23 major metropolitan areas. One license is reserved for the serving telephone company, while the remaining license is awarded to a company called Cantel Communications. Cantel received the grant on December 14, 1983, following a review of applications by five major applicants.

On March 22, 1984, the CRTC issued an order setting out the standards of interconnection between the cellular telephone company and the existing land-line company, including guidance as to the negotiation of rates. The minister of communications also issued an order advising Bell Canada that it would not be entitled to a "head start" with respect to the new service. Bell had originally planned to begin service in September 1984, but this has been delayed pursuant to the ministerial order. The minister also indicated that the telephone company will be entitled to operate cellular services only after providing suitable interconnect arrangements to the competing nonwireline company. In addition, the telephone company has been ordered to provide the service through a separate subsidiary.

The cellular radio developments involved the Department of Communications for the first time as a major policy force with respect to competitive telecommunications. The department's initiatives in this regard were extended with the announcement on January 13, 1984, that the department intended to conduct a full-scale review of all telecommunications policy. The minister's statement in the House of Commons expressed the view that the introduction of more competition in the provision of communications products and services will have important implications for the structure of the telecommunications industry.

The minister further stated that in any restructuring of the telecommunications industry it would be necessary to ensure that the public's right to basic telecommunications services at reasonable rates would not be eroded. Any interested parties were invited to participate in the department's review by submitting written comments by May 14, 1984.

Enhanced Services

Pursuant to a public notice of November 14, 1983, the CRTC called for submissions regarding the provision of enhanced services in Canada. The issues before the commission included the following:

The definition of enhanced services

The regulatory treatment of enhanced services provided by parties other than common carriers

The regulatory treatment of enhanced services provided by common carriers

Resale and sharing for the purpose of providing enhanced services

Written submissions were filed by all interested parties on December 12, 1983, and reply comments were filed on March 6, 1984.

Resale of Telephone Services

The full development of competition in local distribution services requires the relaxation of the telecommunications company's traditional ban against resale. The commission concluded that it would hear the matter as part of the CNCP application for complete system interconnection.

In this regard the commission has identified a number of issues. Specifically, it has asked interested parties to distinguish in their comments among the following means of permitting increased market entry:

1. Resale and sharing of telecommunications services and facilities for the purpose of providing interexchange services other than message toll service (MTS) and wide-area telephone service (WATS) equivalents
2. Resale and sharing of telecommunications services and facilities for the purpose of providing interexchange services including MTS/WATS equivalents
3. Interconnection of telecommunications systems for the purpose of providing interexchange services other than MTS/WATS equivalents
4. Interconnection of telecommunications systems for the purpose of providing interexchange services including MTS/WATS equivalents
5. Interconnection of telecommunications systems and resale and sharing of telecommunications services for the purpose of providing intraexchange services

The commission noted that a major concern raised by the introduction of competition is the impact on existing pricing and accessibility of local telephone service:

> To the extent that competition results in an erosion of interexchange of revenues, there may be an impact on existing local service rates and accessibility. Competition may also be expected to affect the level of efficiency in the telecommunications services market. The impacts include the effects of entry on service quality and choice; network planning, design and provisioning; and research and innovation, both in terms of new services and the introduction of more cost effective technologies.

With respect to the impact on competition, interested parties were requested to indicate the advantages and disadvantages associated with various kinds of competitive entry in terms of their impact on the following:

1. The revenues of regulated common carriers
2. The rates for MTS and WATS, including the practice of rate averaging
3. Rates for other inter-exchange telecommunications services
4. The relationship among rates and different inter-exchange services
5. Rates for local telephone services and resultant implications for local service accessibility
6. Service quality and choice, supply and responsiveness, innovation, research and development, and supplier efficiency
7. The efficiency of telecommunications network planning and design
8. The long-run costs of supplying telecommunications services

With respect to regulatory implications, the parties were asked to comment on the following issues:

1. Alternative types of interconnection that could be furnished to competitors and the implications of each on network costs and the ability of competitors to compete on an equal footing with existing suppliers
2. The basis on which rates paid by competitors for interconnection should be established, including their relationship to (*a*) costs, (*b*) existing tariffs, and (*c*) the quality of interconnection
3. The extent, if any, to which competitors or others should contribute to the support of local service, and the manner in which such contribution should be determined
4. The extent, if any, to which distinction should be made among the kinds of services and facilities for which resale and sharing should be permitted
5. The nature of the regulatory treatment to be accorded to existing

suppliers in telecommunications services and to new entrants (excluding a consideration of service costing issues currently being deliberated in the commission's cost inquiry), and the consideration of the use of a structural separations approach.

STRUCTURAL CHANGE

To date, changes in Canadian telecommunications policy are directed largely to challenging the traditional telephone company rules prohibiting competition. These essentially fall into two categories: (1) rules prohibiting the attachment of equipment to the telephone company's facilities; and (2) rules preventing access to the telephone company's local distribution network. As was the case in the United States, however, the vertically integrated nature of the Canadian telephone company caused considerable inquiry into the need for structural change or divestiture.

Lengthy inquiries have been held in both countries on this matter, with the government usually proposing divestiture of the equipment affiliate.[35] Not much has resulted in Canada, however. In the end, the liberalized terminal attachment policies of the past decade, coupled with increased competitive bidding requirements in Canada,[36] have reduced the pressure for divestiture. In addition, semiconductor technology has made it much easier for new firms to enter telecommunications manufacturing and to challenge existing barriers.

The new competitive world has produced another structural issue, however. As telephone companies increasingly offer competitive services, there is concern that they may cross-subsidize those services with monopoly revenues, to the detriment of both subscribers and competitors.

In 1976 the CRTC initiated a cost inquiry to investigate the information requirements necessary to police against cross-subsidization and abuse of monopoly power:[37]

> This focus on service costing is largely a consequence of concern to carriers which operate in both monopoly and competitive markets and may price their competitive services below cost to the detriment of both their monopoly subscribers and their competitors.

The FCC identified the same policy problem in its 1979 cost allocation decision.[38] The matter is yet to be resolved in either country.

The uneasiness with costing rules, as well as the army of accountants required to determine and evaluate them, led Canadian and American regulators to examine the separate subsidiary concept. The matter first arose in Canada in 1973 when the Department of Communications recommended that carriers provide computer services only if they were made available through a separate subsidiary. The concept was also at issue in the Canadian terminal attachment hearings, but there the commission ruled that it would not be appropriate to require a carrier to conduct terminal equipment business for separate subsidiaries. A year earlier the Restrictive Trade Practices Commission came to the opposite conclusion on the same question.

The CRTC, however, intends to review the matter following completion of the cost inquiry. In the meantime, the CRTC imposed a requirement on carriers engaging in the sale of new terminal equipment that they not sell at a price lower than a "floor price." The floor price was to be filed in confidence with the commission and must be shown to be not less than "associated costs." Many of these same issues were considered by the FCC in its *Second Computer Inquiry*. In all likelihood, however, the relevance of the cost separations and separate subsidiaries has been superseded by the corporate restructuring of AT&T and Bell Canada.

On August 18, 1982, 6 days before Judge Harold Greene approved a settlement of the Justice Department's 1974 antitrust suit against AT&T involving the divestiture of that firm, Bell Canada's shareholders approved a major corporate reorganization paralleling the American move. The proposal was approved by the CRTC 8 months later.

The 1956 Consent Decree prevented AT&T from offering services and equipment outside of the common-carrier communications field. The quid pro quo for the restriction was a monopoly in traditional telephone services and equipment. Since then, new technology has changed the equipment, the services, and ultimately the industry boundaries.

New competitors emerged during the 1960s and 1970s, particularly in the long-distance service and terminal equipment business. As computer and telephone technology developed, industry boundaries blurred. It became clear that the real growth was outside the area of traditional telephony.

In return for being released from the constraints of the 1956 Consent Decree, AT&T agreed to divest itself of its operating companies. The New Consent Decree serves to settle the antitrust dispute and relieves AT&T of another 10 years of litigation. Furthermore, government antitrust lawyers were seeking divestiture of Bell Labs and Western Electric in addition to the operating companies. Under the Consent Decree, these were retained by AT&T. In the end, it was not a bad solution from AT&T's perspective, given the fact that the local telephone business had the lowest growth and profit forecasts.

From the government's viewpoint, divestiture of the operating companies removed the control of equipment markets as well as providing clear and fair access for competing transmission companies.

Against this history, the Canadian development is particularly interesting. Although competition developed in Canadian telecommunications as it did in the United States, it was much more limited and delayed by almost a decade. But, unlike AT&T, Bell Canada was not going to spend another decade fighting a losing battle.

Bell Canada, like AT&T, faced restrictions on its business activities. It is a statutory corporation and as such is limited strictly by the terms of the Special Act. It was argued that Bell Canada was limited in its business activities to traditional telephone activities. On two occasions, in 1968 and 1976, Bell Canada requested Parliament to amend the Special Act to eliminate these restrictions. On both occasions, Parliament refused.

The next attempt to expand saw Bell Canada enter new activities by creating subsidiaries of a small Ontario telephone company directly controlled by Bell. By the time of the reorganization, Capital Telephone had almost as many subsidiaries as telephones. Whether this was legal or not was much debated. But the prospect of illegality posed a real threat to Bell Canada.

The permissible scope of Bell Canada activities has been continually challenged over the past 20 years. In 1964 a cable manufacturer questioned the legality of Bell's ownership of Northern Electric (Northern Telecom). The challenge was unsuccessful on a technical ground: A telephone wire ran from the Bell facilities to Northern Electric's facilities in Montreal, and on this basis the Board of Transport Commissioners held that Northern was a part of the telephone operations. The issue was still being debated 20 years later, when in the course of the CRTC's 1981 Terminal Attachment hearings the commission sought submissions as to whether Bell Canada had the power under its Special Act to engage in the direct sale of terminal equipment in competition with interconnect vendors.

Bell's concern was undoubtedly heightened by a litigation introduced by CNCP whereby Telesat Canada's power to enter into the Trans Canada Telephone System Agreement was challenged as being beyond Telesat's Special Act. At the same time a Bell trademark action against a party using the term "Yellow Pages" was met with the defense that Bell Canada did not have the statutory power to engage in publishing directories.

Of equal concern was the "deemed dividend" policy developed by the CRTC in 1981. In an attempt to prevent cross-subsidization of competitive activities from monopoly revenues, the CRTC deemed dividends to the regulated company equal to a fixed rate of return of 15.5%. If the returns were below that amount, the income was nonetheless deemed to have flowed to Bell Canada for regulatory purposes. Bell Canada was directed to provide the commission with a proposal dealing with the reporting requirements arising from those directives before February 1, 1982.

These two problems—limitation on new activities and "deemed" income from unregulated subsidiaries—were solved by the reorganization. Before reorganization, all of Bell Canada's activities were carried out by subsidiaries of the telephone company. As a result, they are all subject to regulatory jurisdiction to one degree or another. These restraints were removed by creating a new holding company, Bell Canada Enterprises (BCE), and transferring most of Bell Canada's subsidiaries to the holding company. Before reorganization, Bell Canada had over 30 subsidiaries; thereafter, it had only 3.

In the process Bell Canada removed itself from the Special Act and the legal restrictions on its business activities. The corporate shuffle also eliminated the regulator's ability to deem dividend income from unregulated subsidiaries.

The real question, however, is whether the reorganization satisfies Canadian public policy concerns. Bell Canada initially took the position that the reorganization did not require regulatory approval and sought only court approval under the corporation statutes. On October 22, 1982, however, the federal cabinet issued an order requiring the CRTC to review the proposed organization.

Before the CRTC hearing, the Restrictive Trade Practices Commission, which had been holding hearings on the Bell–Northern relationship for over 4 years, issued a separate report on the proposed reorganization. This report expressed concern that the shareholders would receive the capital gain that resulted from the proposed reorganization, despite the fact that

> a strong case could be made that most of the increase in value of Northern's shares should accrue to the subscribers who, in a rate of return regulatory environment, are the real, if unknowing, risk takers in Bell's reliance on Northern as its principal supplier.

The commission noted that from 1975 to 1978, 83% of Bell Canada's equipment payments were made to Northern, and concluded:

> The Commission's major concern is with Northern. As described previously, Northern in fact provides a product jointly with the operating company, and the shareholders' risk in Northern is reduced because of Northern's relationship to Bell. The equity consideration that results concerning the flow of income is only one of the issues raised. As indicated above, Bell's managers will face a more serious divergence between shareholder and subscriber than currently exists when they make decisions in purchasing equipment. This problem, which is a very basic issue raised by vertical integration, will not disappear. Indeed it will be exacerbated.

Following 2 weeks of hearings, the CRTC issued its own report on April 18, 1983. The commission had been asked by the cabinet to study four questions:

1. Will the proposed reorganization result in increased rates for Bell

Canada's subscribers, and if it does, for what reason and to what extent?
2. Will the proposed reorganization impair the ability of the Canadian Radio-Television and Telecommunications Commission to exercise its mandate pursuant to the Railway Act, the National Transportation Act, and the Bell Canada Special Act? If so, specify how and to what extent.
3. If any impairment is identified in reponse to Question 2, what modifications would be required to the proposed reorganization to eliminate or mitigate such impairment?
4. If the proposed reorganization is implemented, should there be limitations such as those set out in Section 5 of the Bell Canada Special Act and the scope of activities that may be conducted by the Bell Group of companies? If so, specify these limitations.

With respect to the first question, the commission found that the proposed reorganization would not result in any increased rates for subscribers.

With respect to Question 2, the commission found that the reorganization might impair its ability to obtain information necessary to regulate Bell Canada. It recommended legislation to clarify its power to compel the production of documents and information from the new holding company (Bell Canada Enterprises) and from other Bell affiliates.

With respect to the commission's ability to monitor intercorporate transactions, the commission stated:

> provided the company furnishes it with quarterly reports of all significant intercorporate transactions, indicating the basis of valuation as to statements of fair market value where different valuation criteria are employed, together with copies of the Agreements and other documents relative to the transaction, the Commission should be in a position to ensure that such transactions comply with the *Railway Act.*

The commission rejected the recommendation by a number of parties that a minority shareholding interest be created in Bell Canada. Although the commission agreed that such minority shareholding could provide a significant incentive for Bell's directors to conduct the company's activities in the interests of both its subscribers and shareholders, it was not persuaded that such a shareholding should be established at that time. The commission did, however, recommend the enactment of legislation empowering the commission to make an order directing that a minority shareholding interest in Bell Canada be created, provided the commission were satisfied that it constituted a necessary, practical, and effective means of ensuring compliance with the applicable telecommunications regulatory legislation, including the Railway Act and the Special Act.

One of the most important areas studied by the commission was the potential for statutory limitations on the Bell Group. The commission recommended the following legislation:

1. Requiring that Bell Canada furnish telephones and telephone service on request under the same terms and conditions as in the Special Act
2. Prohibiting Bell Canada and other members of the Bell Group from applying for or holding a broadcasting license
3. Requiring Bell Canada to act solely as a common carrier, prohibiting it from controlling the contents and influencing the meaning or purposes of any messages it emits, transmits, or receives
4. Authorizing Bell Canada to prescribe reasonable requirements for the attachment to, or the use in connection with, its facilities of any equipment, apparatus, line, circuit, or device not provided by the company, empowering the commission to determine whether any such requirements are, in fact, reasonable, and if not, to take appropriate action
5. Prohibiting Bell Canada from acquiring or holding, directly or indirectly, any of the securities of any company engaged in research and development related to the company's objects that manufactures products for sale to the company or to other customers unless the company was a subsidiary of Bell in 1968
6. Requiring prior commission approval of any sale or other disposition of Bell Canada common shares by the company's controlling shareholders
7. Rescinding the Special Act provision requiring prior commission approval of the issue, sale, or other disposition of Bell Canada capital stock, except in the circumstances described in Paragraph 6.

The commission's recommendation that Bell continue to be prohibited from holding broadcasting licenses—including licenses to operate cable television systems—was based in part on the finding that the book value of Bell Canada's telecommunications assets alone was in excess of $10 billion, compared to the assets of approximately $1.2 billion for the entire Canadian private television, radio, and cable industries.

THE FUTURE

This chapter has attempted to record the developments in Canadian telecommunications policy over the past decade. Compared to the United States, the record is a conservative one. Compared to other countries, Canadian policy represents an aggressive approach.

In Canadian terms, there is no doubt that the industry has been radically reorganized, both in structural and policy terms. The implications are yet to be measured fully.

Moreover, the real brunt of competitive telecommunications is still to come. Proceedings currently before the CRTC involving enhanced services, resale, and complete system interconnection promise to be the most significant regulatory decisions in the country's history. The changes will benefit some consumers and hurt others. They may or may not adversely affect telephone company revenues. They will certainly create new opportunities for entrants and a variety of new service offerings.

These are very important policy developments to Canadians. Canada is a service economy, and the productivity of service economies depends increasingly on developments in telecommunications. More and more countries are looking to high-technology industries for growth prospects; Canada is not unique in that regard. To the extent that these matters can ever be measured at a given moment in time, the consensus would have to be that Canada is benefiting from these timely policy developments. There are always winners and losers in the reorganization of any industry as significant as telecommunications. It is clear, however, that the costs of standing still on these policy issues would have been even greater.

NOTES

1. Federal Communications Commission, *Above 890 Decision*, 27 FCC 359 (1959).

2. *Establishment of Domestic Communication Satellite Facilities by Non-Governmental Entities (Domsat)*, Federal Communications Commission, Docket No. 16495, 35 FCC 2d 844 (1972).

3. *Toronto Telephone Manufacturing Company* v. *The Bell Telephone Company of Canada*, 2 Exchequer 492 (1885); *In Re Bell Telephone Company and the Telephone Manufacturing Company and the Minister of Agriculture*, 7 OR 605 (1885). The Bell patents were declared void in Canada in 1885 on the grounds that the company refused to sell the telephone 2 years after the patent grant, contrary to section 28 of the Patent Act of 1872.

4. Bell Canada's Rules 7 and 9, which were enacted by the Board of Transport Commissioners pursuant to section 5 of the Railway Act, *Canada Gazette*, May 2, 1953, 1234, provide:

> 7. Except where otherwise is stipulated in its tariffs or by special agreement, the company shall provide and install all poles, conduits, plant wiring circuits, instruments, equipment, fixtures and facilities required to furnish service and shall be and remain the owner thereof and shall bear the expense of ordinary manufacture and repairs.
>
> 9. The company's equipment and wiring shall not be re-arranged, disconnected, removed or otherwise interfered with nor shall any equipment, apparatus, circuit, or device which is not provided by the company be connected with, physically associated with, attached or used so as to operate in conjunction with the company's equipment or wiring in any way, whether physically, by induction, or otherwise, except where specified in the tariff of the company or by special agreement. In the event of a breach of this rule, the company may rectify any prohibited arrangement or suspend and/or terminate the service as provided in Rule 35.

5. *Bell Canada* v. *United Sterl-A-Fone Corporation Ltd.*, OR 1 (1955).

6. *Hush-A-Phone Corp.* v. *United States*, 238 F.2d (D.C. Cir. 1956).

7. *Bell Telephone Company of Canada Special Act*, 16–17 Elizabeth II, Chap. 48, sec. 5(4), 5(5), and 5(6):

(4) Attachments. — For the protection of the subscribers of the Company and of the public any equipment, apparatus, line, circuit or device not provided by the Company shall only be attached to, connected to, or interconnected with or used in conjunction with the facilities of the Company in conformity with such reasonable requirements as may be prescribed by the Company.

(5) Transport Commission to determine if requirements reasonable. — The Canadian Transport Commission may determine, as questions of fact, whether or not any requirements prescribed by the Company under subsection (4) are reasonable and may disallow any such requirements as it considers unreasonable or contrary to the public interest and may require the company to substitute requirements satisfactory to the Canadian Transport Commission in lieu thereof or prescribe other requirements in lieu of any requirements so disallowed.

(6) Application to the Commission to determine reasonableness of requirement. — Any person who is affected by any requirements prescribed by the Company under subsection (4) of this section may apply to the Canadian Transport Commission to determine the reasonableness of such requirement having regard to the public interest and the effect such attachment, connection or interconnection is likely to have on the cost and value of the service to the subscribers.

8. *In the Matter of the Carterfone Device in Message Toll Service*, 13 FCC 2d 571 (1968).

9. *Re Dr. Morton Shulman*, CTC 244 (1975).

10. *Challenge Communications Limited* v. *Bell Canada* (*Telecom* decision), CRTC 787–11, October 7, 1977.

11. *United States* v. *Western Electric Company et al.*, Complaint filed February 14, 1949, Consent Decree reported at 1956 Trade Cases, para. 71, 134.

12. Federal Communications Commission, Docket No. 19129, Phase II, *In the Matter of the American Telephone and Telegraph Company*, March 1, 1977.

13. The Commission Report was issued in three phases: Restrictive Trade Practices Commission, *Telecommunications In Canada, Phase I, Interconnection* (September 19, 1981); *Telecommunications in Canada, Part II, The Proposed Reorganization of Bell Canada* (July 26, 1982); *Telecommunications in Canada, Part III, The Impact of Vertical Integration on the Equipment Industry* (January 7, 1983).

14. *British Columbia Telephone Company, Proposed Acquisition of GT Automatic Electric (Canada) Limited and of Microtel Pacific Research Limited* (*Telecom* decision), CRTC 79–17, September 18, 1979.

15. *Second Computer Inquiry Final Decision*, 77 FCC 2d 384 (1980).

16. 47 CFR 55, 63, 54–57. This ruling was upheld in *General Telephone Co.* v. *United States*, 449 F.2d 846 (5th Cir. 1971). In Canada, the 1968 amendments to the Bell Canada Special Act, 16–17 Elizabeth II, Chap. 48, sec. 5 (17), had similar effect.

17. *Bell Canada* v. *Transvision (Magog) Inc.* Canadian Transport Commission, October 15, 1975.

18. *Bell Canada, Tariff for the Use of Support Structures by Cable Television Licencees*, 3 CRT 68 at 785 (1977).

19. Federal Communications Commission, *Public Notice on Pole Attachment Formula*, November 10, 1975.

20. *Bell Canada, Tariff for Use of Support Structures by Cable Television Licencees*, 3 CRT 68 at 75 (1977).

21. Under the proposed agreement, the nine telephone companies of TCTS and Telesat would each have one representative on the TCTS board. All board decisions were required to be unanimous with the result that each member had a complete veto. The agreement provided that Telesat would lease only complete RF channels and then only to specified Canadian telecommunications common carriers.

22. *Telecom* decision, CRTC 77–10 at 56.

23. PC Order in Council 1977–3152, November, 1, 1977.

24. *Telecom* decision, CRTC 71–13.

25. PC Order 1981–3456, December 8, 1981.

26. *Establishment of Domestic Communication Satellite Facilities by Non-Governmental Entities (DOMSAT)* Docket no. 19495, 35 FCC 2d 844 (1972).

27. *Allocation of Frequencies above 890 Mc*, 27 FCC 359 (1959), 29 FCC 825 (1960).

28. *Specialized Common Carrier* decision, 29 FCC 2d 870 (1969).

29. *Microwave Communications Inc.*, 18 FCC 2d 953 (1969).

30. *MCI Telecommunications Corp.* v. *FCC* 561 F.2d 365, cert. den. 434 U.S. 1040 (1977).

31. *CNCP Telecommunications, Interconnection with Bell Canada* (*Telecom* decision), CRTC 79–11, at 124. Similar language was used by the Supreme Court of the United States in *Otter Tail Power Co.* v. *United States*, 410 U.S. 366 (1973).

32. *Specialized Common Carrier* decision, 29 FCC 2d 870 (1969).

33. Federal Communications Commission, Docket No. 16778 (1968), 12 FCC 2d 841 (*Guardband*), recon. den. 14 FCC 2d 209, affirmed subnom *Radio Relay Inc.* v. *FCC* 409 F. 2d 322 (1969).

34. *Collins Inc.* v. *Bell Canada* (*Telecom* decision), CRTC 79–12.

35. The U.S. vertical integration proceedings began with the antitrust complaint filed with the Department of Justice on February 14, 1949, seeking divestiture of Western Electric from AT&T. The resulting 1956 Consent Decree barred AT&T from non-telephone-regulated services and also required licensing of certain Western Electric and AT&T patents.

This was followed by Federal Trade Commission proceedings instituted in January 1971, which investigated the relationship between the Bell System and Western Electric. Despite the trial staff's recommendation of divestiture, the commission's decision 6 years later did not recommend divestiture, but ordered AT&T to file a proposal that would remedy the lack of autonomy of Bell operating companies regarding equipment procurement. Federal Communications Commission, Docket No. 19129, *Phase II, In the Matter of the American Telephone & Telegraph Company*, March 1, 1977. The Justice Department's recent antitrust action, which was initiated in 1974, resulted, after 8 years of discovery and procedural motions, in the 1982 Consent Decree.

In Canada, the wisdom of the vertical relationship between Bell Canada and Northern Telecom has been an issue before the CRTC and predecessor agencies since 1938. Extensive hearings began in 1977 before the Restrictive Trade Practices Commission pursuant to Canada's antitrust statute, the Combines Investigation Act. The Commission's Final Report, issued in 1983, ruled that neither divestiture nor competitive bidding was required in light of recent changes in regulatory rules such as the ability of customers to purchase and connect their own terminal equipment.

36. A 1979 application by the British Columbia Telephone Company, which is controlled by GTE, resulted in a CRTC decision approving the acquisition on the condition that BC Tel engage in competitive bidding regarding the acquisition of equipment. *British Columbia Telephone Company, Proposed Acquisition of GTE Automatic Electric (Canada) Limited and of Microtel Pacific Research Limited* (*Telecom* decision), CRTC 79–17, September 18, 1979.

37. *Bell Canada, Increase in Rates* (*Telecom* decision), CRTC 77–7, 3 CRT 87 at 106.

38. *In the Matter of the American Telephone & Telegraph Company, Manual and Procedures for Allocation of Costs*, 73 FCC 2d 629 (1979).

Nine

Telecommunications and Industrial Policies in Japan: Recent Developments

Youichi Ito

Three important telecommunications laws passed the Japanese national Diet in December 1984. This chapter deals with the content of those laws; the administrative, political, and economic context from which they emerged; comparisons with telecommunications regulatory developments in other countries, particularly the United States; and the implications of these new laws for communications theory.

The first law is the Telecommunications Business Law. It stipulates the basic principles and structure regarding telecommunications business in Japan. This law, among other things, abolished the monopoly enjoyed since 1952 by the Nippon Telegraph and Telephone Public Corporation (NTT) in domestic telecommunications and since 1953 by Kokusai Denshin Denwa Co., Ltd. (KDD) in international telecommunications. This withdrawal of monopoly naturally presupposes the introduction of competition into both domestic and international telecommunications businesses.

The second law is the Nippon Telegraph and Telephone Corporation Law. It converts NTT to a private joint-stock company and stipulates its aims and characteristics. The third law revises and adjusts certain existing laws so that they will be consistent with the principles and stipulations of the other two new laws.

These three new laws became effective on April 1, 1985. Together, they will drastically change Japan's traditional telecommunications system based on NTT's and KDD's monopoly by introducing competition into all the arenas of domestic and international telecommunications. Vice-Minister M. Koyama of Posts and Telecommunications of Japan called this change "revolutionary" and "Copernican" in his keynote speech at the Seventh Annual Pacific Telecommunications Conference held in January, 1985, in Honolulu (see Koyama 1985).

The two main actors in this chapter are the Ministry of Posts and Telecommunications (MPT) and the Ministry of International Trade and Industry (MITI). In the process of building consensus for the draft bill of the Telecommunications Business Law there were serious disputes and conflicts between these two government agencies. It is possible, of course, to explain these disagreements as a typical bureaucratic battle over territory; the bureaucrats' "territorial imperative" should certainly not be overlooked. The reason both MPT and MITI became so serious and involved with the outcome of this legislation, however, was that their institutional future, or at least their future policy, was at stake.

The change of NTT's management form did not cause conflict between MPT and MITI. MITI did not attempt to compete with MPT regarding conventional types of telecommunications such as telephone and telex. The MPT-MITI competition was over data communications and other related telecommunications and information services—the area called "enhanced services" in the United States. Communications and information service industries are expanding very rapidly in Japan and elsewhere, and are considered to be the industries of the future. MPT regards them as part of the telecommunications industry, while MITI considers them as belonging to the information processing industry. MPT views such services as an important object of its "telecommunications policy," while MITI considers them a vital part of its "industrial policy." We therefore do not discuss this problem simply as a "territorial battle," but instead consider it as a case study of competition between "telecommunications policy" and "industrial policy."

TELECOMMUNICATIONS POLICY

Definitions and Conceptualization

Telecommunications policy in Japan usually refers to policy made and executed by MPT in the telecommunications sector. Roughly speaking, those who have shown interest in telecommunications policy have been economists, lawyers, and communications scientists. These three kinds of specialists share many points of view, yet they differ in certain respects. In particular, they seem to differ in the priorities they accord to various policy goals. Economists tend to give priority to economic values, whereas lawyers and communications scientists give priority to social, cultural, and political values. It also appears that lawyers and communications scientists apply a broader spectrum of values in considering policy goals for telecommunications. However, economists and communications scientists are similar to one other as social scientists in their concern for the application of economic or communications theories and methodologies to explain and justify telecommunications policy, whereas the lawyers' approach is more normative.

These distinctions are interesting when we consider the differences in Japanese specialists' attitudes toward the current MPT-MITI controversies. Roughly speaking, economists have been more sympathetic to MITI, and lawyers and communications scientists have been more favorable toward MPT.

I consider myself a communications scientist, and my view of telecommunications policy reflects that perspective. In particular, I regard telecommunications policy as a kind of communications policy rather than a kind of economic policy.

What, then, is communications policy? I have defined it as "administrative, judicial and legislative measures taken to achieve social goals through communication" (Y. Ito 1982a, 272). Any policy involves objectives and measures to realize such objectives. Those measures are usually provided for the policy-making and policy-executing agency in the form of laws, regulations, ordinances, rules, and customs. Policy objectives are usually stated in those laws and ordinances. As discussed in Y. Ito (1982a), however, it would be more appropriate to consider these objectives as having been given to the administrative agency by society as a whole rather than as having been created by the administrative agency itself. For whatever cause, those policy objectives have seldom been systematically summarized and discussed.

Miura (1977), Tomita (1978), and Y. Ito (1982a) are among the few researchers in Japan who have collected and systematically discussed the policy objectives of communications policy. What characterizes these discussions is that such objectives cover a very wide range of social and individual values, including social welfare, local development, efficient information flow, privacy, ease of access to information, and enhancement of educational and cultural standards of the whole nation as well as local communities. This range of values is natural, since communication is related to a variety of human behavioral and social activities.

This application of a variety of policy objectives to actual policies can be seen in radiofrequency allocation and broadcasting license renewals. In these policies, many kinds of standards have been applied to each application in the light of comprehensive policy objectives. These objectives and standards are stated in the Broadcast Law (enacted in 1950), the Radio Law (enacted in 1952) and a dozen related ordinances, rules, and regulations. Because of their long experience, MPT officials have considered broadcasting policy as the basic model for telecommunications policy.

The same thing can be said about communications scientists and lawyers concerned with communications problems. Most of them entered this area from the study of mass media policies, particularly broadcasting. Thus they also have a tendency to consider broadcasting policy as a model for other telecommunications policies.

Most Japanese experts tend to think that the Japanese broadcasting policy and system have been fairly successful when compared with those of other countries (see M. Ito 1976, 1977, 1978; Y. Ito 1970; Sho 1963). The major reason is that Japanese broadcasting has developed with a good balance between the public network (Japan Broadcasting Corporation—NHK) and the commercial networks. The existence of commercial networks often prevented NHK from becoming dogmatic, inefficient, and bureaucratic. However, the existence of NHK has helped maintain a certain level of quality in Japanese radio and TV programs.

As a result, those lawyers, communications scientists, and MPT officials who consider broadcasting policy as a model for other telecommunications policies do not necessarily think (unlike economists, whose views we discuss in the next section) that completely free competition should be guaranteed in telecommunications. They believe that telecommunications other than broadcasting—particularly the so-called new media—can be used to influence not only economic values but also various other social, cultural, and perhaps political values, as in the case of broadcasting. They also hold that such values are generally better served by some degree of government regulation.

In the area of nonbroadcast telecommunications, however, such issues have not been seriously considered until recently. The reason is that nonbroadcast telecommunications have not traditionally had many social, cultural, or political implications. Policy objectives for telegraph and telephone have been relatively simple. Most of them have been of a technical or economic nature, such as eliminating the backlog of orders for installation of subscriber telephones, technical standardization, protection of privacy, and a few others. Only recently have nonbroadcast telecommunications begun to exhibit social, cultural, and political implications as wide as those of broadcasting. This change resulted from the emergence of new kinds of information and communications services and the so-called new media. For example, MPT declared the following in 1983 regarding the state of public telecommunications:

> The long-pending backlog of orders for installation of subscriber telephones was completely removed by 1978. At the same time, an automatic dialing system was completed throughout the country by that year. The telephone system in Japan has entered an age of pursuing qualitative improvement (Ministry of Posts and Telecommunications 1983, 49).

In addition to technical improvements, one of the directions in this "new age" was to use the telephone for various social purposes, as in the case of broadcasting. Several studies were conducted to explore such possibilities. For example, the Research Institute of Telecommunications and Economics (1977a, 1977b) and Takasaki (1975, 1977) examined how the telephone could contribute to improving the "quality of life" of the general public; Tamura (1977) studied how the telephone could contribute to the modernization of rural villages; and Y. Ito (1982b) discussed how the telephone is used for social purposes, such as personal consultation for crime prevention and information gathering. In addition there is Pool's well-known 1977 study of the social impact of the telephone.

Technical feasibilities as well as potential social functions of cable television were other subjects of investigation. That is why MPT sponsored the well-known Tama CCIS (Community Cable Information System) experiment (see Y. Ito 1982b; Ito and Dishi 1984; Kobayashi 1982; Masuda 1980; and Ministry of Posts and Telecommunications 1978). The same can be said about the CAPTAIN experiment and communications satellite experiments also sponsored by or conducted under the leadership of MPT.

MPT is now enthusiastically promoting the Teletopia Project (see Chiiki Joho Tsushin Kenkyu Kai 1984; Miraigata Komyunikeishon Moderu Toshi Koso Kondankai 1984). This is a social-development project exploiting new telecommunications media and services. Eleven different kinds of social development, such as international exchange, academic development, leisure and recreation, medical care, advanced farming, and community formation, are assumed, and 10 "model cities" are to be chosen on a competitive basis by evaluating applications from local communities. Then MPT will give priority in allocating resources (such as optical fiber, cable, videotex, and two-way cable television) and providing tax incentives and low-interest loans to promote the development and application of new media. In other words, this is a national project to back up local plans to utilize new telecommunications media for local needs. The reason MPT has adopted such a two-step policy is that "new media" have a variety of possibilities, and the ministry thought it better to back locally initiated social plans to realize various ways of utilizing them. This is an example of telecommunications policy as understood by MPT officials and communications scientists.

The achievement of traditional long-pending policy goals for the telephone and the emergence of various new communications media and services have enabled MPT officials to anticipate using these telecommunications media and services to carry out their policies for a wide range of social goals, as in the case of broadcasting. It would seem that they wanted to create, if possible, a system similar to the broadcasting system in the area of nonbroadcast telecommunications, namely competition between the public and private sectors. The problem for them, however, was that they did not have convenient tools like radiofrequency allocation and license renewal in the area of nonbroadcast telecommunications. Instead, they attempted, to the extent possible, to develop measures equivalent to them. Lawyers and communications scientists outside of MPT who consider broadcasting policy as a model for nonbroadcast telecommunications have generally approved these efforts by MPT. As a result of strong opposition by MITI, business circles, and economists, however, such a plan became extremely difficult to realize. Therefore, a compromise was reached between MPT and MITI, and regulation by MPT over nonbroadcast telecommunications will be very limited (though not nonexistent), as we see in more detail later in this chapter.

Historical Developments—Regulatory Agencies and Nonbroadcast Telecommunications

Modern Japan began with the Meiji Restoration in 1868. The following year, the telegraph was introduced to Japan. In those days the mail system was under the jurisdiction of the Ministry of Agriculture and Commerce (the predecessor of MITI), while telegraph and telephone were under the Ministry of Technology (the predecessor of MPT). As the result of a governmental reform in 1885, the Ministry of Communications was established to take over the mail system from the Ministry of Agriculture and Commerce and the telegraph and the telephone from the Ministry of Technology. When Japan initiated its telegraph in 1869, Japanese private industry was so feeble that no one felt this new technology should be operated by private enterprise. It began naturally as a direct government enterprise under the Ministry of Technology.

When the telephone was introduced in Japan in 1877, however, a number of business interests wished to enter the field. Certain sympathizers in the government—such as the Ministry of Finance, which was concerned about the huge investment required for this new enterprise—supported the idea. As a result, controversies over the management form of the telephone business lasted for several years. The government finally decided in 1889 that the telephone should be monopolistically operated by the Ministry of Communications, as was the telegraph. The Telegraph Law was enacted in 1900, prescribing that all wired telegraph and telephone services should be directly operated by the Ministry of Communications and managed as a complete government monopoly.

The major reasons for government monopoly were three:

1. Preservation of communications secrecy by military, police, and other government agencies was deemed important.
2. Under private management, investment would be made only in urban areas, and diffusion to rural areas would be delayed.
3. Telephones in most foreign countries (except the United States) were operated under a government monopoly.

In 1915 the Wireless Telegraph Law was enacted, under which anyone who had obtained government clearance could transmit and receive radio signals. Under these two basic laws, Japanese telegraph, telephone, and broadcasting steadily expanded and affected the nation's daily life.

During World War II, however, the Japanese telecommunications networks were almost completely destroyed by bombing. The reconstruction of telecommunications facilities was one of the most urgent tasks to which the postwar government had to devote itself. For this purpose, the government decided in 1949 to create a new ministry, the Ministry of Telecommunications, by dividing the Ministry of Communications into two new ministries: the Ministry of Postal Services and the Ministry of Telecommunications. At the same time, the government established the Advisory Council for the Reconstruction of Telegraph and Telephone to consider postwar telecommunications policies. This council published a final report in March 1950 recommending that the telegraph and telephone systems be operated by a public corporation instead of a direct government monopoly. Based on this recommendation, the Nippon Telegraph and Telephone Public Corporation (NTT) was established in 1952 for domestic communications and the Kokusai Denshin Denwa Co., Ltd. (KDD) in 1953 for international communications. As a result, a large part of the Ministry of Telecommunications was transferred to the newly created NTT and KDD, and the remaining regulatory sections were absorbed by the Ministry of Postal Services, renamed the Ministry of Posts and Telecommunications (MPT).

The Wire Telecommunications Law and the Public Telecommunications Law were enacted in 1953. Before that time, as mentioned, those who wished to install private telecommunication lines had to obtain permission from the Ministry of Communications. The new Wire Telecommunications Law prescribed that anyone could install private lines as long as they did not interfere with the public telecommunications system. Such a system had to be reported to MPT, but only when the lines would have some effect on the public telecommunications circuits were they required to be cleared by MPT. This was the first instance in Japan of "deregulation" regarding telecommunications legislation.

As a result of the development of wireless communications and the expansion of microwave networks, electric power companies and the Self-Defence Forces secured their own communications networks. In rural areas where the construction of facilities for NTT's private telephone system was delayed, the wired radio and telephone system expanded rapidly.

During the 1950s and 1960s, policy goals for telegraph and telephone were very simple. They were the reconstruction of facilities destroyed during the war, technical standardization, expansion of telephone networks, completion of automatic switching on a nationwide scale, and so forth. All these were technical problems, and they were left to NTT and KDD; consequently, MPT did not have much to do in this area.

In the late 1960s, however, various kinds of new telecommunications media, such as data and facsimile communications, began to spread, and together with the growth of the computer industry, a swift expansion of various forms of telecommunications and information services was projected. Rapid development of cable television in the United States and new ideas like the "wired city" caught the attention of the Japanese, and the first "CATV boom" occurred in the early 1970s as part of the "*johoka shakai* [information society] boom."

In order to cope better with this situation, MPT created the Telecommunications Policy Division in 1972 to plan and execute its nonbroadcast telecommunications policies. During its brief tenure, this division completed a number of well-known projects, such as the Information Flow Census (see Y. Ito 1981; Pool et al. 1984), the Tama CCIS (Community Cable Information Service) experiment, and the CAPTAIN (Character and Pattern Telephone Access Information Network System) experiment.[1] The division was later expanded and strengthened, and in 1980 it became the Telecommunications Policy Bureau.

As mentioned above, the restrictions on privately installed telecommunications circuits were eliminated by the enactment of the Public Telecommunication Law in 1953. Many other restrictions continued, however, such as those regarding equipment to be connected to NTT's lines, sharing of private leased lines, message exchange using private leased lines or cable television circuits, sublease of private leased lines, and interconnection of NTT's lines. These strict rules have been justified from the viewpoint of the security of public telecommunications networks, technical standardization, protection of communications privacy, and protection of NTT's monopoly. Complaints about these restrictions were seldom heard while telecommunications services were limited to telegraph, telephone, and telex. The complaints became loud, however, particularly in business circles, when data and facsimile communications spread rapidly in the late 1960s.

With the rapid increase of data (or computer) and facsimile services, users soon found that such restrictions were serious hindrances to free and efficient communications and information processing. MPT naturally understood the problem, and in 1971 it amended the Public Telecommunications Law by lifting several of the restrictions mentioned above. Moreover, MPT changed minor rules and regulations in 1972 and 1973, and many applications that had been prohibited before 1971 became possible.

For example, the deregulation from 1971 through 1973 permitted the connection of computers, information-receiving equipment, and facsimile equipment to NTT's telephone lines. Thus, after 1971, many private information service companies emerged. These companies provided stock market information to brokerage firms, data processing and storage services for small-scale companies, literature information for researchers, and so on. Sharing of private leased lines is now permitted on the condition that the parties involved have business transactions on a regular basis. Message exchange through private leased lines is also permitted on the condition that the messages have something to do with the data being exchanged.

Changes in the technology and in business practices, however, proceeded much faster than the rate of deregulation. For example, message exchange through cable television had not been permitted, and a new service connecting different kinds of computers and relaying unspecified combinations of data communications (VAN—value-added network) emerged. Faced with strong demand, MPT permitted VAN service for small-scale businesses in 1982 and message exchange through cable television in 1983.

These measures, in fact, amounted to an erosion of NTT's monopoly in public telecommunications. Thus, by the late 1970s and early 1980s most experts in this area came to agree that fundamental consideration and possibly a drastic change in the traditional public telecommunications order were needed.

Unlike AT&T, NTT had provided data communications service since 1968 and facsimile service since 1973 as a part of its public telecommunications service. NTT was thus already active in so-called enhanced services. Japanese business circles and MITI (their advocate) began to argue that NTT's activities should be confined to conventional services such as telegraph and telephone, and that new areas such as data and facsimile communications should be left to free competition by private businesses.

NTT, however, did not want to be confined to conventional areas. It stated that it would prefer to grow in the new areas even if it were to lose its traditional monopolistic position in conventional services. Thereafter there was no reason for MPT to insist on NTT's monopoly.

MPT decided to abolish the Nippon Telegraph and Telephone Public Corporation Law (enacted in 1952) and the Public Telecommunications Law (enacted in 1953) and replace them by two new laws, the Nippon Telegraph and Telephone Corporation Law and the Telecommunications Business Law. We discuss these laws in detail later in the chapter.

Historical Developments: Broadcasting

In the early 1920s, stimulated by the advent of broadcasting in the United States and Europe, radio fever gradually developed in Japan. Those who showed the greatest enthusiasm toward broadcasting were manufacturers and distributors of electrical equipment, radio amateurs, newspaper publishers, and news agencies. Many of them began to favor commercial broadcasting. According to the Wireless Telegraph Law enacted in 1915, anyone who had obtained government clearance could transmit and receive radio messages.

Investigation and research concerning the broadcasting system were begun in 1922 by the Ministry of Communications, and a draft of the general principles with respect to broadcasting was adopted by a special committee established in the ministry. The first question concerned the nature of the managing agency. Those in favor of public management—as prescribed in the Telegraph Law of 1900—argued that it should also be applied to broadcasting. In contrast, those in favor of private management stressed various differences between common carriers and broadcasting, and insisted that the principle of private management in ordinary business activity should be applied to broadcasting. After long discussions, the Ministry of Communications concluded that broadcasting in Japan should be managed by private enterprise under strict supervision by the government. Broadcasting was to be considered a system of radiotelephone privately established under special authorization of the government within the framework of the Wireless Telegraph Law of 1915. This system continued in effect for many years, until the enactment of the Broadcast Law in 1950.

Even in the Ministry of Communications there were those who strongly favored permitting broadcasting by private profit-seeking enterprises. A compromise was finally reached in 1924, and three nonprofit broadcasting stations began service in Tokyo, Osaka, and Nagoya. In 1926 the three stations were merged to form the Nippon Hoso Kyokai (NHK), a corporate juridical person.

Although NHK was managed privately, it was also a monopoly under strict government supervision. For this reason, it functioned as though it were a government monopoly, particularly under the totalitarian regime of the late 1930s and during World War II. In those years NHK was a propaganda machine for the government to dominate public opinion.

After the war, therefore, one of the most urgent tasks was to "democratize" Japanese broadcasting. Drastic reform of the system was inevitable. Then, as in the early 1920s, various mass media and other business groups began to apply for broadcasting licenses. Some argued that NHK should be dissolved or dismantled and replaced by a purely commercial system. The Occupation administration and the Japanese government, however, agreed that there was nothing wrong with NHK itself if its independence from the cabinet were secured.[2]

The Occupation administration attempted to transplant the American FCC system. The Broadcasting Committee, which was independent of the cabinet, was established in 1946. Then it was reformed, and the Radio Regulatory Commission (an organization very similar to the FCC) was established in 1950. Although the Japanese government agreed that

NHK's independence from the cabinet was necessary to "democratize" Japanese broadcasting, it felt that the Americans had created too many independent "administrative commissions" to be able to carry out consistent, integrated policy.[3] Thus, after Japan regained independence in 1951, the Japanese government abolished many administrative commissions created under the strong influence of the Occupation.[4] The Radio Regulatory Commission was one of those commissions; it was absorbed by MPT to become a part of it, as the Radio Regulatory Bureau, in 1952.

Meanwhile, the demand for broadcast licenses by private companies had become very strong. Newspaper publishers in particular were very enthusiastic, as they had been in the early 1920s. Both the Occupation administration and the Japanese government agreed that granting broadcast licenses to private applicants other than NHK would contribute to the diversification of broadcast programs and to the "democratization" of Japan. Thus, independent, American-style commercial radio stations commenced service in 1951 for the first time in Japan. Two years later, Japan's first commercial TV station began broadcasting.

Since then, both NHK and commercial broadcasters have developed steadily. Today, two NHK TV channels (general and educational) and at least two more commercial channels are available in most parts of Japan. In densely populated locations such as the Kanto (Tokyo-Yokohama) and the Kansai (Osaka-Kyoto-Kobe) areas, 8 to 10 TV channels are available. In radio, three NHK networks (AM general, AM educational, and FM mostly music) and five or six commercial stations are available in most parts of the country. As of 1982, the annual budget of NHK was 281,150,000,000 yen ($1,171,458,000), and the total sales of 121 commercial broadcasting companies amounted to 1,161,200,000,000 yen ($4,838,333,000). The latter amount is thus about four times as large as NHK's budget. Considering the fact that this is a comparison between 1 organization and 121 companies scattered all over Japan, however, one can say that NHK and commercial broadcasters as a whole are equally powerful, a relationship unique to the Japanese broadcasting system.

In Europe there is strong public broadcasting and weak commercial broadcasting. In the United States, by contrast, there is strong commercial broadcasting and weak public broadcasting. Y. Ito (1970) compared the broadcasting systems of Japan, Great Britain, and the United States and concluded that the Japanese system might be closest to the ideal. This is because both public and commercial systems have strengths and weaknesses, and these two systems complement each other most effectively when they are equally powerful.

The diversity and richness of NHK's educational radio and TV networks could never be realized under the commercial system, which even Japanese commercial broadcasters admit. Apart from its unique educational and cultural program services, NHK has generally been popular among older people, conservatives, and those in rural areas. Commercial stations have appealed to the younger generation, liberals, and urbanites. Generally speaking, Japanese policy makers, mass media, and the public seem to have been satisfied with the existing Japanese broadcasting system.

Since the early 1970s and as recently as 2 or 3 years ago, MPT's view of cable television had been negative and pessimistic. The rather disappointing results of the Tama experiment mentioned in the previous section might have been one of the reasons for this attitude. MPT almost seemed to think that the sole value of cable television systems was as a retransmission service; this view implies that cable television systems will probably disappear as the number of "free" UHF stations increases or as direct satellite broadcasting service begins. This has actually happened a number of times in Japan. Many cable television systems went bankrupt or were dissolved soon after new UHF stations entered the market. In May 1984 Japan began the world's first commercial direct satellite broadcasting service, and as a result two cable television systems were dissolved. For these reasons, MPT's policies toward cable television had long been more restrictive than encouraging.

About 3 years ago, however, MPT apparently changed its policy toward cable television. The reason for the change was that throughout the 1970s cable television was regarded as a kind of broadcasting and considered within the framework of broadcasting policy. The basic idea was that if the Japanese public is satisfied with the existing broadcasting order (many public opinion surveys indicated that it was), why bother to encourage the development of cable systems that might confuse the established order? Now, however, cable systems are considered an "integral part of the new information and communications order" rather than a "cause of confusion."

In the late 1970s various new media and new transmission technologies emerged, some of which were closely related to cable television. These new telecommunications technologies, taken together, were held to be the cause of the "new information and communications order," although no one knows yet exactly what that order will be like. Since no one knew what kind of order would emerge, MPT decided that it should be determined through free market competition. Thus, MPT has gradually lifted traditional regulations for cable television and is trying to allow these new media to compete with each other. MPT thinks that the new information and communications order will emerge by itself as a result of such competition. This does not mean, however, that MPT wishes to adopt a "hands-off" attitude. Its policy is to accelerate this process. In other words, it will promote the development of all these new media (as seen in the Teletopia Plan mentioned in the previous section), let them compete with each other, and then evaluate the results.

The diffusion ratio of cable television in Japan against the total number of households in March 1983 was 12%. This figure is much lower than in Canada, the United States, and smaller European countries such as the Netherlands, Belgium, and Denmark, but higher than in major Western European countries such as Great Britain, France, and Germany. The diffusion ratio in Japan is steadily increasing, however. In 1978 Japan launched an experimental direct broadcast satellite. In 1983, after 5 years of experimentation, Japan launched a commercial broadcasting satellite, and in May 1984 became the first country in the world to offer commercial TV by direct satellite broadcast. It is very likely that conventional broadcasting will face severe competition from cable television and direct satellite television in the near future.

INDUSTRIAL POLICY

Definitions and Conceptualization

Japanese "industrial policy" has now become famous—or notorious—among the world's major industrial countries, although a definition of the term is not clear. In Japan it is roughly understood as a kind of microeconomic policy pursued by MITI.

Every country has a macro economic policy to control inflation, recession, unemployment, and so forth. Those policies are typically carried out by fiscal and monetary means. The target of industrial policy, however, is each industry rather than the economy as a whole. That is why industrial policy is considered as a kind of microeconomic policy. Under Japanese industrial policy, while various incentives for expansion are extended to certain promising industries (such as high-tech industries), reverse incentives for contraction or retreat are offered to various targeted industries, such as oil and aluminum refining, coal mining, and petrochemicals.

In most industrial countries, this kind of microeconomic policy exists to some extent. The reason Japan is so well known in this area, however, is that industrial policy there has been more systematic and thorough, and therefore more effective, than it has been in most other industrial countries. In the United States, for example, tax, tariff subsidy, loan, and various other incentives have been provided to save particular industries. Alternatively, huge amounts for research and development have been provided by the U.S. government for certain industries. In the case of the United States, however, these industrial or microeconomic policies have usually been ad hoc and lacking integration, interagency coordination, long-term viewpoint, and theory. In contrast, Japanese microeconomic policies seem to be better integrated, coordinated, and carried out with more of a long-term viewpoint and greater attention to theoretical considerations. Recent American attitudes toward Japanese industrial policy have often been schizophrenic. On the one hand, Americans condemn it for being unfair; on the other hand, they admire it and insist that an American version of MITI (which they call DITI—Department of Industrial Trade and Industry) be created.[5]

Industrial policy, according to Ozaki (1970, 879), is

> an indigenous Japanese term not to be found in the lexicon of Western economic terminology. A reading through the literature suggests a definition, however: it refers to a complex of those policies concerning protection of domestic industries, development of strategic industries, and adjustment of the economic structure in response to or in anticipation of internal and external changes which are formulated and pursued by MITI in the cause of the national interest, as the term "national interest" is understood by MITI officials.

Here we simply define *industrial policy* as the policy planned and executed by MITI to influence the management of private enterprises in a particular industry.

Japanese industrial policy, according to Johnson (1982), consists of two kinds of policies. One is *sangyo gorika seisaku*, "industrial rationalization policy"; the other is *sangyo kozo seisaku*, "industrial structure policy." Johnson (1982) summarized MITI's *Industrial Rationalization White Paper* (Ministry of International Trade and Industry 1957) and outlined "industrial rationalization" as follows:

(*a*) The rationalization of enterprises, that is, the adoption of new techniques of production, investment in new equipment and facilities, quality control, cost reduction, adoption of new management techniques, and the perfection of managerial control.

(*b*) The rationalization of the environment of enterprises, including land and water transportation and industrial location.

(*c*) The rationalization of whole industries, meaning the creation of a framework for all enterprises in an industry in which each can compete fairly or in which they can cooperate in a cartel-like arrangement of mutual assistance.

(*d*) The rationalization of the industrial structure itself in order to meet international competitive standards. (This definition was included before the concept of "industrial structure" had been invented by MITI. After about 1960 it was no longer included in the concept of industrial rationalization.)

Thus, *industrial rationalization policy* means any policy to facilitate the realization of these different kinds of "rationalization" in Japanese industry.

The Sangyo Kozo Chosakai, or Industrial Structure Investigation

Council, was organized within MITI in 1961. What researchers did at first was to define a number of economic indicators, such as the degree of concentration, capitalization, and export ratio, and compare these indices of Japanese industrial structure with those of other major industrial countries. Once such comparisons had been made, they began to consider how the industrial structure should be changed to strengthen Japanese industry's international competitiveness.

Thus the Sangyo Kozo Shingikai, or Industrial Structure Council, was established in 1964 as a permanent advisory committee to the Minister of International Trade and Industry. In 1983 the council consisted of 20 sections and about 300 members. Its members represent various fields of Japanese society, such as industry, banking, academia, journalism, labor, and the consumer. The number of reports published by the sections of the council varies from year to year. In 1982 there were 4, and in 1983 about 20. These reports recommend to the Minister of International Trade and Industry how the Japanese "industrial structure" should be changed—which industries should be fostered as "strategic industries" and from which industries Japan should retreat. They also recommend what kind of policy should actually be followed to make such "structural changes." Although the reports are published under the name of the council or one of its sections, the first draft is usually prepared by MITI officials. All that the members of the council do is discuss the draft prepared by MITI officials and make any desired changes. Therefore the council, like many other bodies of this kind, can be said to be used by MITI officials to justify and legitimize its policies.

Just as MPT tends to depend on communications scientists, electrical engineers, and lawyers specializing in communications law for advice, MITI tends to draw on economists, whose role in MITI's policy making is therefore an important one. Many university professors of economics are in the Industrial Structure Council.

Historical Developments

As mentioned, Japanese industrial policy began in the early 1960s as an attempt to compare and approximate the Japanese industrial structure to those of more advanced industrial countries. The purpose was of course to catch up. The models to be pursued already existed in the United States and Western Europe.

In the late 1960s and early 1970s, however, the Japanese began to make their own models. The most important one was *johoka*, or "informationalization." Umesao (1963), Kohyama (1968), Hayashi (1969), and many other scholars and social critics advocated new ideas regarding *johoka* and *johoka shakai* (information society).[6] Thus, in the late 1960s and early 1970s an intellectual movement called the "*johoka shakai* boom" occurred in Japan. A number of American scholars, including Machlup (1962), Kahn and Wiener (1967), Brzezinski (1970), and Bell (1973), contributed to it as well.

This boom naturally had a strong impact on the Industrial Structure Council. In 1967, only 3 years after the creation of the council, an Information Industry Section was formed as part of it. This began with 20 members, representing trade associations, academics, journalism, and manufacturing companies. This section published its interim report in 1968 and final report in 1969. The latter was entitled *Tasks for* Johoka—*Report on the Development of Information and Information Processing Industries.* This report statistically compared the degrees of *johoka* in the United States, Japan, England, West Germany, and France (Industrial Structure Council 1970). According to the statistics, Japan's degree of *johoka* in the mid-1960s was about the same as that of Great Britain, West Germany, and France but was far behind that of the United States.[7] The report recommended that many policies be pursued to promote the "informationalization" of the Japanese economy and society.

The Information Industry Section of the Industrial Structure Council has been flexible in its activities. Each time it receives a policy question from the minister of international trade and industry, it creates three or four subcommittees or task forces consisting of 12 or 13 members. These subcommittees actually examine the issue and submit the interim reports, which are later collected and published as final reports of the section, usually in book form. Thus, the first final report was published in 1969, the second in 1974, and the third in 1980 (Ministry of International Trade and Industry 1974, 1982). Although final reports have not been published frequently, interim reports, in monograph form, have been issued almost every year since 1969 by one or two of the section's subcommittees.

Policies based on these recommendations have in general been called *johoka seisaku*, or "informationalization policies." Such policies have apparently succeeded in strengthening the Japanese computer industry, microelectronic industry, and other information and communications related industries. What MITI actually did at an early stage of "informationalization policy" was to provide tax and investment incentives, relaxation of monopoly regulations, and other initiatives to assure a coordinated computer development effort among government, research institutions, and industry. According to Bowes (1981), however, "more important than specific tax incentives and laws in the evolution of a Japanese information society has been the Japanese societal character which fosters consensual, cooperative effort among private industries, the government and research agencies" (p. 701).

In the early 1970s the emphasis of informationalization was on computers and microelectronics. In the late 1970s, it shifted to telecommunications and information and communications services. In order to achieve fully MITI's goal of informationalization it has become necessary for the ministry to exert some influence over these industries. Telecommunications services, however, have traditionally been under the jurisdiction of MPT. Therefore, MITI and its constituencies began to demand drastic deregulation in the field of telecommunications, meaning in effect a liberation from MPT's control. Serious conflicts occurred between MITI and MPT, corresponding to competition between industrial and telecommunications policies.

THE NATURE OF COMPETITION BETWEEN TELECOMMUNICATIONS AND INDUSTRIAL POLICIES

We have touched briefly on the nature of competition between MPT and MITI. Various groups discussed these problems and published their views in the late 1970s and early 1980s. Each ministry had its own point of view. MITI's outlook tended to support the present American system. It divided telecommunications services into *basic services* and *enhanced services*, insisting that in basic services the property of natural monopoly applied; therefore, legal monopoly and monopoly control by the government was permissible. In enhanced services, however, the property of natural monopoly did not apply; therefore, free entry and free competition should be guaranteed as a rule. In order to prevent cross-subsidy, it was insisted that one exception to this free entry principle was necessary. Accordingly, entry to enhanced services by business entities enjoying monopolistic status in basic services should not be permitted.

These policies have actually been adopted in the United States and advocated by economists who maintain that there are theoretical grounds for such policies. They insist that in this way resources will be best allocated, each business entity will be most efficient, and the telecommunications industry will be best organized. The voluntary policy advisory group Seisaku Koso Forum (Policy Study Forum), composed of economists specializing in economic policy and industrial organization, published a report favoring this approach in March 1984. Their recommendations were well covered by the mass media and had a significant impact on the MPT—MITI controversies.

Although this pro-competitive tone sounds very reasonable, we must pay attention to its political implications. Competition is advantageous to MITI and its constituencies (private businesses) but is disadvantageous to MPT, NTT, and KDD. This is so because it implies that MPT, NTT, and KDD should stay in the field of basic services—the market for which has already been saturated—whereas MITI should concern itself with enhanced services, which are expected to expand greatly in the future.

However, MPT does not like to distinguish rigorously between basic and enhanced services. It prefers instead to regard both simply as telecommunications businesses, to make it clear that they are both under MPT jurisdiction. In the new Telecommunications Business Law drafted by MPT, all telecommunications businesses are first classified as Type 1 or Type 2, and Type 2 businesses are then classified into Special Type 2 and General Type 2.

Type 1 telecommunications business refers to the "business which provides telecommunications service by establishing telecommunications circuit facilities" (Art. 6[2]). *Type 2 telecommunications business* is defined simply as "any telecommunications business other than Type 1 telecommunications business" (Art. 6[3]). In other words, Type 1 and Type 2 are classified according to *whether or not the business owns "telecommunications circuit facilities"* as defined in the law.[8]

Special Type 2 refers to the "telecommunications business which provides for the use of communications by many and unspecified persons of telecommunications facilities which exceeds in scale the standards stipulated, in terms of the capacity for accommodating telecommunications lines, in the applicable cabinet ordinance; or Type 2 telecommunications business which provides telecommunications facilities designed for communications between Japan and foreign points for the use of communications by others" (Art. 21[3]). General Type 2 is defined simply as "Type 2 telecommunications business other than Special Type 2" (Art. 21[2]). In other words, "Special" and "General" are classified according to the scale of facilities or coverage area and the kinds of customers. These classifications are shown in Table 9.1.

TABLE 9.1 Classification of Telecommunications Businesses in Japan

		Type 2	
Facilities	Type 1	Special	General
Own	Yes	No	No
Lease	No	Yes	Yes

According to the original MPT draft, firms wishing to operate as Type 1 or Special Type 2 entities needed to obtain permission from MPT. Those wishing to operate as a General Type 2 entity were merely required to notify MPT. Based on the principle of communication sovereignty, the draft stipulated that applications by foreigners, foreign companies, or companies more than 50% of whose top executives or voting rights are foreign could be rejected.

MITI and its constituencies did not oppose the entry restrictions imposed on Type 1 entities. But they strongly resisted the entry restrictions—including those on foreign capital—against Special Type 2 entities. They also claimed that there was no need for General Type 2 entities to notify MPT of their entry.

The U.S. government also criticized this draft strongly and demanded that any restrictions against foreign capital be eliminated. For many years, MITI and the U.S. government had disagreed over trade issues. Ironically, their interests coincided as far as this problem was concerned, and they cooperated with each other to put pressure on MPT to eliminate MPT regulations to the extent possible. A high-level official of MPT was reported to have complained that there was a conspiracy between MITI and the U.S. government.

Although MPT avoided the terms *basic* and *enhanced*, as far as MITI was concerned Type 1 roughly coincided with basic services and Type 2 with enhanced services. As mentioned, MITI regards enhanced services, or Type 2, as information processing and not telecommunications. MITI therefore argued that such services should be under its own jurisdiction and wanted to eliminate possible influence by MPT in this area. That is the main reason why MITI resisted any form of regulation by MPT so strongly.

MPT began as an agency very similar to European PTTs, and it is still like them in many respects. It directly operates the mail system, post office savings, and some insurance business. In Japan, however, the status of government agencies called *jigyo kancho*, or "business operating agencies," has for some reason been regarded as lower than that of *sesaku kancho*, or "policy agencies." This cannot be the only reason, but perhaps it is one reason why, since World War II, MPT has tended to phase out its business operating sections and become more like a policy agency. In order to be a *sesaku kancho*, MPT must change as follows:

1. MPT must be liberated from the burden of business management in mail, saving, insurance, and telecommunications. It should eliminate these business functions and make them independent public corporations or private companies.
2. At the same time, MPT must wield as strong an influence as possible over as many industries as possible.
3. It should exert this influence not by direct control but indirectly through subsidies, regulations, *gyosei shido* ("administrative guidance"), tax incentives, consulting, and so on.

After April 1985, MPT lost its traditionally strong and direct influence over NTT and KDD. If new companies enter the telecommunications field by adopting competitive policies, however, MPT's areas of jurisdiction will expand. As mentioned repeatedly, new telecommunications and information service industries are growing rapidly. Promising new services, such as VAN, are emerging, and MPT wants them under its jurisdiction. In exchange for giving more freedom to NTT and KDD, MPT wants to secure some influence over these newly emerging and promising telecommunications and information services. After all, it would not be too far from the truth to say that what MPT plans to do in the field of telecommunications is what MITI has been doing in other industries.

The confrontation between MPT and MITI became so heated that the leaders of the ruling Liberal Democratic party finally intervened and forced these two agencies to reach a compromise. As a result, the entry restrictions, including those against foreign capital in the Special and General Type 2 categories, became milder. "Permission" in Special Type 2 was changed to "registration," meaning that MPT must permit entry as long as the applicant satisfies the standards stipulated by the Telecommunications Business Law or ordinances based on this law. "Notification" in General Type 2 remained, but it was made clear that MPT must accept notification without any reservations. Entry restrictions against foreign companies in Type 1 remained, but the definition of "foreign" changed from 50% to one-third of top executives or voting rights.

One might think that Type 1 roughly corresponds to basic services and Type 2 to enhanced services in the United States. In practice, this view might turn out to be correct in the future, but we cannot predict this as yet. Theoretically, however, this view is not correct by any means, because it is possible for Type 1 to provide enhanced services and for Type 2 to provide basic services. The matrix between the Japanese and American classifications and the policy for each combination is shown in Table 9.2.

TABLE 9.2 Regulations for Telecommunications Businesses in Japan

			Type 2	
		Type 1	Special	General
Basic Services	Entry	Per.[a]	Per.[b]	Per.[c]
	Pricing	Per.[a]	Per.[b]	Per.[c]
Enhanced Services	Entry	Per.[a]	Reg.	Ntf.
	Pricing	Per.[a]	Ntf.	Fre.

Key: Per. = Permission by MPT is necessary.
Reg. = Registration at MPT is necessary (close to permission).
Ntf. = Notification to MPT is required (close to no regulation).
Fre. = Free. No regulation.

[a] "Foreign" companies as defined in Article 11 of the Telecommunications Business Law are not allowed to enter the Type 1 area.

[b] Since no company would enter the telegraph business, this actually means simple resale of leased lines for telephone service. There were strong arguments at the national Diet that simple resale of leased lines for telephone service should not be permitted. The policy for this problem has not yet been established.

[c] Permission by MPT is necessary to provide any service that uses radio waves.

The definition of "foreign" in Table 9.2 is as follows:

(*a*) Any person who does not have Japanese nationality.
(*b*) Any foreign government or its representative.
(*c*) Any foreign juridical person or association.
(*d*) Any juridical person or association which is represented by any person or body set forth in the preceding three items, or one-third or more of whose officers are such persons, or one-third of whose total voting rights is exceeded by the aggregate of voting rights directly held by such persons or bodies, where voting rights are calculated in accordance with the provisions of the applicable ordinance of the Ministry of Posts and Telecommunications (Art. 11).

Except for entry into the Type 1 area, there are no discriminatory restrictions against foreign capital. This means that foreign investors are not allowed to construct and own telecommunications circuit facilities. As long as they rent circuit facilities, however, they can enter any telecommunications business—even basic services such as telegraph and telephone.

THEORETICAL CONSIDERATIONS

As Y. Ito (1984) discusses, one of the major challenges facing communications policy research is to find a mechanism of change in communications policy or the communications system. By finding such a mechanism, we can explain various kinds of changes in communications policy or the system using simple models. Moreover, we may be able to predict future trends or changes in the policy or system.

In this book Noll (Chapter 3) proposes two interesting models. The first has to do with political processes and ideologies that are thought to affect communications policy making. He suggests the following four models: (1) naive democratic theory; (2) statist theory; (3) pluralist theory; and (4) institutionalist theory.

Reading a draft of Noll's contribution, I wondered which model would be best suited to the Japanese case outlined in this chapter. Major attention has been focused in this chapter on interactions between MPT and MITI. This might give readers an impression that the Japanese case best fits the institutionalist model, which argues that decision making in communications policy is the result of interactions among established political institutions such as government agencies and political parties.

This view is not exactly correct. Although space limitations prevent my discussing them in detail, pressures from outside the Japanese government, particularly from the mass media, the U.S. government, and the business community, had significant influence on the contents of the three new laws.

Japanese mass media, particularly newspaper publishers, thought recent developments in new media technologies a good opportunity to expand and earn profits. They therefore gave editorial support to MITI, insisting that entry into telecommunications should be liberalized and that traditional regulations should be lifted as much as possible.

The U.S. government, which suffers from a huge trade deficit with Japan, adopted the same view as the Japanese media. MITI is usually a tough negotiating partner for the U.S. government. As far as this problem is concerned, however, the interests of MITI and the U.S. government coincided, and both demanded deregulation of Japanese telecommunications. Mike Mansfield, the U.S. ambassador to Japan, expressed on many occasions his strong concerns, dissatisfaction, suggestions, and expectations regarding the draft bill of the Telecommunications Business Law. As a result, entry restrictions against foreign capital in the first draft of the bill were drastically eased.

Another actor is the Japanese business community. Keidanren, the Federation of Economic Organizations,[9] basically supported MITI and demanded drastic deregulation as soon as possible. At the same time, however, it expected mild regulation by the government, apparently to avoid too much competition. Keidanren also supported MPT's original idea of restricting the entry of foreign capital.

In considering this drama, which has changed the Japanese telecommunications system so drastically, one could observe that the leading actors were MPT and MITI, and that the supporting cast included the mass media, the U.S. government, and the business community. Political parties, NTT management, and the NTT labor union also played roles, but they did not have any significant influence on the content of the new laws.

Considering all the roles played by major actors in the drama, Y. Ito (1984, 91) suggested a "pragmatic model to explain deregulation" (see Figure 9.1). Since this is a general model, it can be applied not only to the decision-making process behind the telecommunications reform but also to the introduction of commercial broadcasting in the early 1950s discussed earlier in this chapter. In Chapter 4 of this book, Baughcum writes that "both users and potential competitors are quite sophisticated enough to see opportunities for cost saving or profit taking respectively. European PTTs may, in some instances, be surprised at the extent of the aggressiveness of, say, MCI in pursuing profit and new sales."

This description and prediction fit well in the model in Figure 9.1. We can say that what Baughcum predicted there has occurred in Japan, where such "aggressiveness" was expressed through the behavior of MITI. Therefore, after all, it seems that the recent deregulation of Japanese telecommunications can be best explained by the combination of "pluralist theory" and "institutionalist theory" suggested in Noll's chapter.

Another interesting theoretical scheme is Noll's Structural Map of

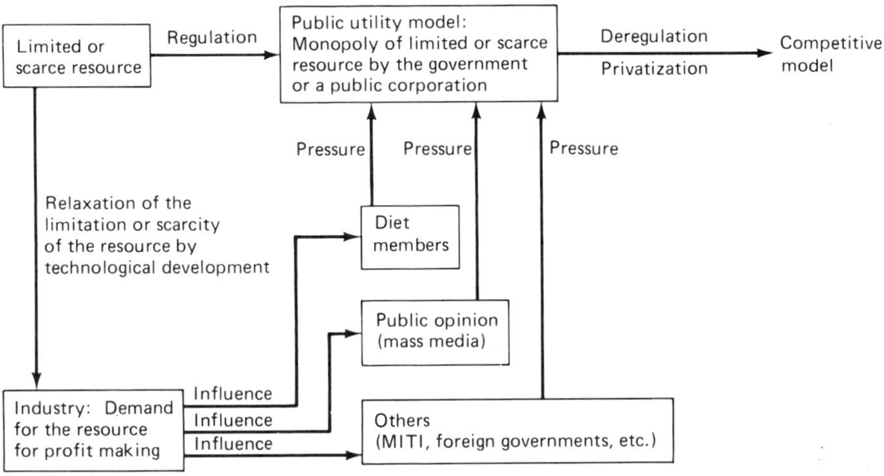

Figure 9.1

Communications Industries, shown as Figure 3.1 in Chapter 3 of this book. It indicates that as time passes, entry into the telecommunications industry becomes easier and the market becomes more competitive. According to Noll, this has been a general historical trend observed among advanced industrialized countries. As to why industrialized countries share this common trend, he implies that technical progress has something to do with it. But he does not discuss in detail the mechanism behind such a trend.

Y. Ito (1983a) discusses a similar topic. Using the diagram shown in Figure 9.2, he argues that as time passes, technology develops; as technology develops, available resources become more abundant; and as available resources become more abundant, deregulation of policy occurs. He indicates that this has happened in Japan not only in telecommunications but also in transportation, shipbuilding, textiles, iron and steel, and banking. Then he explains the mechanism behind such a trend, using the diagram shown in Figure 9.1.

SUMMARY

The traditional domestic telecommunications order in Japan changed drastically after April 1985. A major purpose of this chapter has been to analyze some of the primary driving forces that have brought about this change. In the late 1960s and early 1970s, when MITI and the business community demanded drastic deregulation in telecommunications, both MPT and NTT strongly resisted it because their traditional territories or monopolistic surplus might be lost. In the early 1980s, however, both MPT and NTT changed their minds because the telephone market had been almost saturated by then and the telegraph business had been declining for

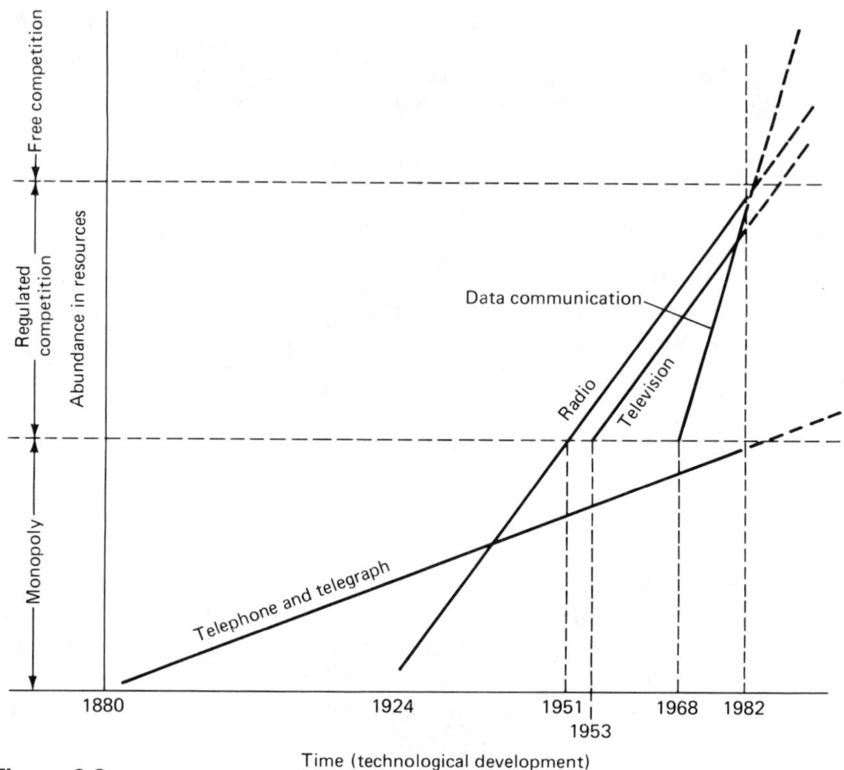

Figure 9.2

many years. In order for NTT to grow, it had to enter the newly emerging areas, namely "enhanced" telecommunications and information services. This was difficult in the traditional framework. Therefore, NTT, like AT&T, decided that it would give up traditional privileges if it were allowed freely to expand into this promising new area.

In contrast, MPT had a peculiar motivation. As previously pointed out, MPT has long been regarded as a *jigyo kancho*, or "business agency," and its prestige has been lower than that of a *sesaku kancho*, or "policy agency," such as MITI, the Ministry of Finance, the Ministry of Welfare, or the Ministry of Agriculture, Forestry and Fishery. MPT wanted to catch up with these agencies in policy-making abilities, social and political influence, and prestige. The current telecommunications revolution or "new media" revolution seemed to MPT a very good chance to achieve such a goal. Among other government agencies, MITI seemed the model to pursue. As pointed out, what MPT plans to do in the field of telecommunications is in the final analysis what MITI has been doing in other industries.

Since the late 1960s, MITI had developed its *johoka seisaku*, or "informationalization policy," as part of its industrial structure policy.

During the late 1960s and early 1970s, *informationalization* meant "computerization" to MITI. In the late 1970s, however, "computer communications" began to occupy an important part of its *johoka seisaku.* In order to push its informationalization policies further, it was necessary for MITI to eliminate many traditional regulations in the field of telecommunications. In other words, many laws and ordinances constituting the traditional telecommunications order became serious obstacles to promoting MITI's *johoka seisaku.*

The same thing can be said about the business community represented by Keidanren. When it tried to build more efficient and economical communications networks or start new profitable communications or information services, the traditional regulations protecting NTT's monopoly posed serious obstacles. For this reason, Keidanren joined other groups in demanding drastic deregulation of Japanese telecommunications. It is said that its demands were faithfully reflected in the recommendations of the Provisional Commission for Administrative Reform, because the chairman of the commission was the Keidanren president. The commission published its final report in July 1982, recommending thorough deregulation, free entry of private companies into telecommunications, and the divestiture and privatization of NTT.[10]

The mass media considered this transformation to be a good chance to expand their business. Many of them planned to establish new information services using the "new media." The United States saw an opportunity for American communications and information service companies to penetrate the Japanese market. Thus, both the Japanese mass media and the U.S. government demanded drastic deregulation.

With all these powerful actors moving in the same direction, dramatic reform of the traditional telecommunications system was inevitable. The Nippon Telegraph and Telephone Corporation Law and the Telecommunication Business Law were drafted by MPT. Serious conflict occurred between MPT and MITI over their respective areas of jurisdiction. Another reason for their conflict was the difference between the nature of communications policy and that of industrial policy.

Both communications policy and industrial policy are concerned with social welfare, local development, and the improvement of cultural and educational levels. As a result, their goals tend to overlap considerably. Industrial policy, however, attempts to achieve such goals through industrial development; communications policy attempts to achieve them through the improvement of communications or information flow. The latter approach to communications policy tends to be more varied than the former, because improvement of communications and information flow can directly affect a wider variety of processes than can industrial development. It therefore appears that industrial policy makers may concentrate on industrial development, whereas communications policy makers will have to pay more attention to other goals as well, such as political goals (e.g., freedom of speech, free flow of information, democratization), social goals (e.g., community development, social security), and cultural goals (e.g., preservation and fostering of traditional and local cultures). Such differences in policy goals were reflected in the difference of approach to the new laws and reinforced the conflict between them.

Furthermore, these developments were related to theoretical models suggested by Noll, and it was concluded that the recent deregulation of Japanese telecommunications could be best explained by a combination of pluralist theory and institutionalist theory. Finally, the general trend of regulatory policy in telecommunications, the mechanisms behind this trend, and the relationships between technological development, resource abundance, and regulatory policy were discussed.

NOTES

1. CAPTAIN is the Japanese videotex system. For details of the experiment, see Y. Ito (1982b).

2. One of the important reasons for the Occupation's decision to preserve NHK was that they wanted to use NHK, an established nationwide organization with two national radio networks, to carry out their Occupation policies efficiently. In other words, although NHK during the totalitarian period was an undemocratic organization, the Occupation wanted to use it for the "democratization" of postwar Japan.

3. This is not without grounds. Lack of coherence and consistency, overlapping of jurisdiction, interagency frictions caused by such overlapping, and policy differences have often been cited as problems in the American administration system. In the field of telecommunications as well, the "need for bundling the communications policy function into a single agency where long-term problems involving these disparate and varied interests" could be dealt with (Branscomb 1977, 220) has been pointed out. In 1978, furthermore, Congress attempted to transfer all spectrum assignment responsibilities from the FCC to the executive branch.

4. The Japanese government did not abolish all the administrative committees, however. They admitted the need for the cabinet to remain independent in some cases. The Fair Trade Commission, for example, which regulates unfair trade practices and executes antimonopoly, anticartel policies, remains in its original form.

5. In April 1984, for example, the Banking Committee of the House of Representatives published a report insisting on the need for the introduction of a Japanese-style industrial policy. At one point, in fact, the question whether the U.S. government should introduce industrial policy became an issue in the 1980 presidential election. The Democrats insisted on the necessity of such a policy, but the Republicans did not because, according to them, industrial policy should be determined by the marketplace.

6. For the details of these concepts, see Y. Ito (1981).

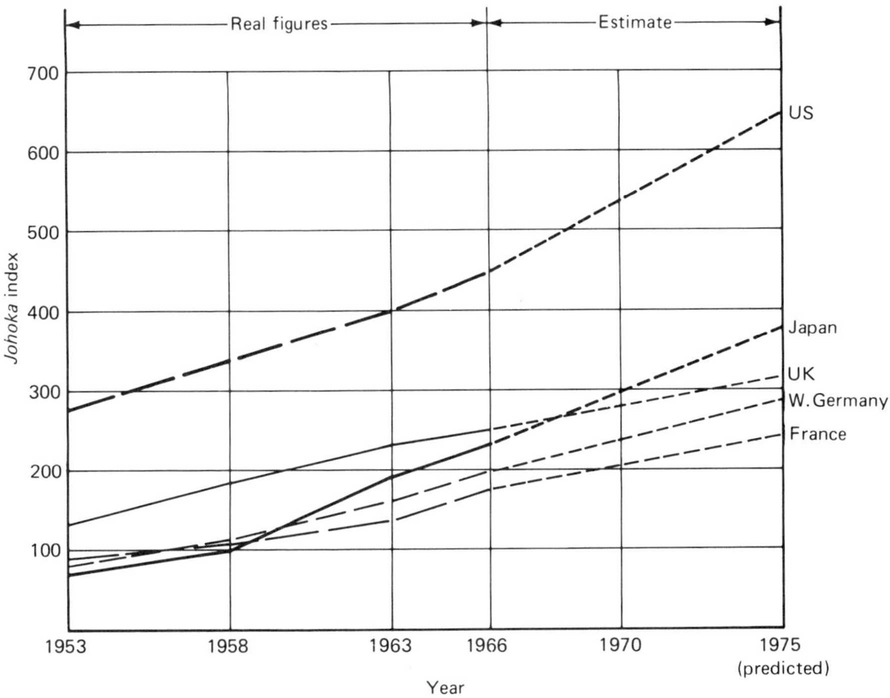

Figure 9.3

7. More sophisticated international comparative studies regarding the degree of *johoka* were conducted by researchers at the Research Institute of Telecommunications and Economics. See RITE (1968, 1970), Y. Ito (1981). See also the accompanying figure.

8. According to the tentative standard set by MPT, Special Type 2 means those entities that have more than 5 operating centers in Japan and that operate using more than 500 circuits (with 1200 bits per second).

9. The political role of Keidanren is similar to that of the U.S. Chamber of Commerce or the National Association of Manufacturers in the United States.

10. For the details of this recommendation, see Y. Ito (1983b).

REFERENCES

Araki, I. "Advent of a New Medium with Two-way Communication—The Case of the Hi-OVIS." In *Shakaigaku no Gendaiteki Kadai* (Contemporary problems of sociology), edited by Fudeya Minoru Hakushi tsuito Rombunshu Henshu Iinkai, Tokyo: Horitsu Bunka-sha, 1983.

Bell, D. *The Coming of Post-Industrial Society*. New York: Basic Books, 1973.

Bowes, J. "Japan's Approach to an Information Society: A Critical Perspective." In *Mass Communication Review Yearbook,* edited by G. C. Wilhoit and H. de Bock. Vol. 2. Beverly Hills, Calif.: Sage, 1981.

Branscomb, Anne W. "Bundling Communications Policy for the New U.S. Administration." *Telecommunications Policy*, June 1977.

Brzezinski, Z. *Between Two Ages: America's Role in the Technotronic Era.* New York: Viking Press, 1970.

Chiiki Joho Tsushin Kenkyu Kai, ed. *Teletopia Senryaku* (Teletopia strategy). Tokyo: Shuppan Kaihatsu-sha, 1984.

Communications Study Group (Ministry of Posts and Telecommunications), eds. *Japanese Legislation of Telecommunications.* Vol. 1, *Telecommunications Business Law*, and Vol. 2, *Nippon Denshin Denwa Kabushiki Kaisha Law.* Tokyo: Denki Tsushin Kyokai, 1984.

Edelstein, A. S. *Comparative Communication Research.* Beverly Hills, Calif.: Sage, 1982.

Edelstein, A. S., J. E. Bowes, and S. M. Harsel, eds. *Information Societies: Comparing the Japanese and American Experiences.* Seattle: University of Washington Press, 1978.

Hai Teku Kenkyukai, ed. *Denden Sampoh* (Three laws on telecommunications). Tokyo: Keigaku Shuppan, 1985.

Hayashi, Y. *Johoka Shakai* (Information societies). Tokyo: Kodansha, 1969.

History Compilation Room, Radio and TV Culture Research Institute, Nippon Hoso Kyokai. *The History of Broadcasting in Japan.* Tokyo: NHK, 1967.

Industrial Structure Council. "Johoka eno Kadai" (Tasks for informationalization). *Juristo* 450 (May 15, 1970): 92–97.

Ito, M., ed. *Hoso Seido: Sono Genjo to Tembo* (Broadcasting system: present state and perspective). 3 vols. Tokyo: Nihon Hoso Shuppan Kyokai, 1976, 1977, 1978.

Ito, Y. "Monopoly and Competition in the Broadcasting Industry." Master's thesis, School of Public Communication, Boston University, June 1970.

———. "The *Johoka Shakai* Approach to the Study of Communication in Japan. In *Mass Communication Review Yearbook,* edited by G. C. Wilhoit and H. de Bock. Vol. 2. Beverly Hills, Calif.: Sage, 1981.

———. "Komyunikeishon Seisaku" (Communication policy). In *Gendai Masu Komyunikeishon Ron*, edited by I. Takeuchi and K. Kojima. Tokyo: Yuhikaku, 1982(a).

———. "Urban Community Media in Japan." Unpublished report submitted to the division of Development of Communication Systems, UNESCO, 1982(b).

———. "Recent Trends in the Japanese Telecommunications Policies." In *PTC '83,* Pacific Telecommunications Conference: Papers and Proceedings, edited by D. J. Wedemeyer. Honolulu: Pacific Telecommunications Council, 1983(a).

———. "Recent Trends in Telecommunications Regulation and Markets in Japan." In *Forum 83*, *Fourth World Telecommunications Forum*, *Part 3*, *Legal Symposium on International Information Networks.* Geneva: International Telecommunication Union, 1983(b).

———. "Kagakuteki Komyunikeishon Seisakuron no Tame no Shiron" (Toward a scientific study of communication policy). *Joho Tsushin Gakkai Nempo* 1 (1984): 83–97.

———. "Implications of the Telecommunications Policy Reform in Japan." *Keio Communication Review* 6 (1985).

Ito, Y., and Y. Oishi. "Cable Television in Japan: Policy and Empirical Findings."

Paper presented at the Advanced Wired Cities: Driving Forces and Social Implications Forum, Washington, D.C., July 12–13, 1984.

Johnson, C. *MITI and the Japanese Miracle: The Growth of Industrial Policy, 1925–1975*. Stanford: Stanford University Press, 1982.

Kahn, H., and A. J. Wiener. *The Year 2000: A Framework for Speculation on the Next Thirty-Three Years*. New York: Macmillan, 1967.

Kato, H. *Communication Policies in Japan*. Paris: UNESCO, 1978.

Kobayashi, K. "Some Critical Remarks on the New Media Research and Development in Japan." *Studies of Broadcasting* 18(1982): 23–49.

Kohyama, K. "Joho Shakai Josetsu" (On information societies). *Bessatsu Chuo Koron Keiei Mondai*, winter issue (1968): 80–105.

Koyama, M. "New Communication Age in Japan." *Keio Communication Review* 6 (1985).

Machlup, F. *The Production and Distribution of Knowledge in the United States*. Princeton: Princeton University Press, 1962.

Masuda, Y. *The Information Society*. Tokyo: Institute for the Information Society, 1980.

Meyer, J. R., et al. *The Economics of Competition in the Telecommunications Industry*. Cambidge, Mass.: Oelgeschlager, Gunn & Hain, 1980.

Ministry of International Trade and Industry. *Sangyo Gorika Hakusho* (Industrial rationalization white paper). Tokyo: Nikkan Kogyo Shimbun-sha, 1957.

———, ed. *Sangyo Kozo no Choki Bijon* (A long-range vision of the industrial structure). Tokyo: Tsusho Sangyo Chosa Kai, 1974.

———, ed. *Yutakanaru Johoka Shakai eno Doh Hyoh* (A milestone to a prosperous information society). Tokyo: Compyuta Eiji-sha, 1982.

———, ed. *Hiyaku suru Johoka* (Leaping informationalization). Tokyo: Compyuta Eiji-sha, 1984.

Ministry of Posts and Telecommunications. *Report on Tama CCIS Experiment Project in Japan*. Tokyo: MPT, 1978.

———. *Report on Present State of Communications in Japan, Fiscal 1982*. Tokyo: MPT, 1983.

Miraigata Komyunikeishon Moderu Toshi Koso Kondankai, ed. *Teletopia Koso: Nyu Media ni Yoru Chiiki Shakai no Hatten wo Mezashite* (Teletopia plan: development of local communities by new media). Tokyo: Kodansha, 1984.

Miura, I. *Tsushin Seisaku no Kadai Tembo* (Problems and perspectives of communications policies). Tokyo: Daiihi Hoki, 1977.

Noll, R. G., and B. M. Owen. *The Political Economy of Deregulation: Interest Groups in the Regulatory Process*. Washington, D.C.: American Enterprise Institute, 1983.

Ozaki, R. S. "Japanese Views on Industrial Organization." *Asian Survey* 10 (October 1970): 872–889.

Pool, I. de Sola. "The Rise of Communication Policy Research." *Journal of Communication* 24, no. 2 (Spring 1974).

———. *The Social Impact of the Telephone*. Cambridge, Mass.: MIT Press, 1977.

Pool, I. de Sola, et al. *Communications Flows*. Tokyo: University of Tokyo Press, 1984.

Research Institute of Telecommunications and Economics (RITE). *Sangyoka Igo no Shakai ni Okeru Joho to Tsushin* (Information and communication in a postindustrial society). Tokyo: RITE, 1968.

———. *Sangyoka Igo no Shakai ni Okeru Denki Tsushin no Yakuwari* (Roles of telecommunications in a postindustrial society). Tokyo: RITE, 1970.

———. *Joho no Nagare kara Mita Chiiki Kaihatsu Koka no Bunseki* (An analysis of the effects of information flow on local development). Tokyo: RITE, 1977(a).

———. *Korekara no Shakai ni Okeru Denkin Tsushin no Yakuwari: "Seikatsu no Shitsu" Kara Mita Chiho Toshi* (Roles of telecommunications in a future society: "quality of life" in local cities). Tokyo: RITE, 1977(b).

Salvaggio, J. L. "An Assessment of Japan as an Information Society in the 1980s." In *Communications and the Future: Prospects, Promises, and Problems,* edited by H. F. Dedsbury, Jr. Bethesda, Md.: World Future Society, 1982.

———. "Social Problems of Information Societies." *Telecommunications Policies*, September 1983, 228–242.

Sho, H. *Hoso Seido Ron no Tameni* (Broadcasting in Japan: systems and issues). Tokyo: Nihon Hoso Shuppan Kyokai, 1963.

Snow, M. S. "Policy Questions in Economic Regulation of Information Societies: Evidence from Japan, the United States, and Other Industrialized Countries." *Keio Communication Review* 6 (1985): 19–38.

Takasaki, N. *Our Concept of "Quality of Life": A Tentative Study of Its Thesis and Practical Application.* Tokyo: Research Institute of Telecommunications and Economics, 1975.

———. *Our Study of "Quality of Life" and Contribution of Telecommunications.* Tokyo: Research Institute of Telecommunications and Economics, 1977.

Tamura, N. *Komyuniti Kyanpein* (Community campaign). Tokyo: Simul, 1977.

Tomita, T. "The Information and Communications Policy in Japan." *Studies of Broadcasting* 14 (1978): 37–61.

Umesao, T. "Joho Sangyo Ron" (On information industries). *Chuokohron*, March 1963.

Ten

Australian Regulatory Policy

Don M. Lamberton

The information intensiveness of the Australian economy and the contrasting information "policies" of recent government administrations bear directly on current regulatory issues. Against this background, it is necessary to outline the nature of the telecommunications industry in historical perspective, taking account of Australia's dependence on imported technology. Examination of current developments such as the acquisition of a domestic satellite system indicates that the Owen-Braeutigam theory of regulation (hereafter O-B theory) is applicable, provided special features of the Australian situation are taken into account, but that the theory needs to be modified to allow for internal organizational aspects. Such modification reflects the contribution of recent thought in information economics and the economics of organization.

AUSTRALIA AS AN INFORMATION SOCIETY

Information occupation data suggest that among the economies for which such data are available, Australia is outranked in terms of information intensiveness by only Canada and the United States. As Table 10.1 indicates, the share of information labor in the economically active population increased from 39.4% in 1971 to 41.5% in 1981.[1] The Canadian percentage was only slightly higher at 39.9% in 1971, but the United States had reached 41.1% as early as 1970. Although Japanese information intensiveness has been rising rapidly, it still lagged behind Australia in the

TABLE 10.1 Information Labor Force (percent of economically active)

Country and Year	Australia		Canada		Japan		United States	
Component	1971	1981	1951	1971	1960	1975	1950	1970
Information production	5.2	6.4	4.4	7.6	2.1	4.5	5.0	7.2
Scientific–technical	0.8	1.6	2.6	5.3	0.6	1.0	1.3	2.1
Consultative services	2.4	3.0			0.5	1.1	1.9	2.7
Information gatherers	0.3	0.2	0.8	1.1	nsc	nsc	0.3	0.3
Market search–coordination	1.7	1.6	1.0	1.2	1.0	2.4	1.5	2.1
Information processors	26.7	27.1	20.1	25.2	12.3	20.6	21.2	26.5
Administrative–managerial	12.4	11.4	10.4	12.3	2.3	4.4	8.6	8.1
Process control–supervisory					nsc	nsc	1.4	2.0
Clerical and related	14.3	15.7	9.7	12.9	10.0	16.2	11.2	16.4
Information distributors	3.4	4.7	2.5	4.7	1.9	2.4	2.3	4.0
Educators	2.9	4.0	2.1	3.9	1.8	2.2	2.1	3.8
Communications workers	0.5	0.7	0.4	0.8	0.1	0.2	0.2	0.2
Information infrastructure	4.1	3.3	2.3	2.4	1.6	2.1	2.2	3.4
Information machine workers	2.3	1.9	0.9	1.3	1.0	1.4	1.0	2.3
Postal–telecommunications	1.8	1.4	1.4	1.1	0.6	0.7	1.2	1.1
Total information	39.4	41.5	29.3	39.9	17.9	29.6	30.7	41.1

Source: OECD. Updating of the data base contained in OECD 1981.

mid-1970s. Disaggregation, as shown in Table 10.1, does not tell very much, but one component deserves mention. The share of information labor represented by "market search and coordination specialists" dropped fractionally in Australia, while it has tended to increase in both Canada and the United States and to increase markedly in Japan. There are, of course, many defects in these statistics; but this fact, together with the comparison in terms of the managerial and administrative components, may link with the need to consider questions of informational and organizational efficiency posed in the final section of this chapter.

Statistics from the same OECD (Organisation for Economic Cooperation and Development) source as those in Table 10.1 indicate that Australia has shared the tendency for routine information activities[2] to grow at a relatively slower rate that the more skill-intensive information-handling tasks. This might be attributable to the impact of new information technologies, although the tendency to assume that the creative activities are comparatively invulnerable to such technologies might well be questioned. Such qualifications aside, the impact of new technologies in the provision of telecommunications services and consequential industrial disputes played a leading role in the creation in 1978 of a Committee of Inquiry into Technological Change in Australia. The terms of reference required the committee "to examine, report and make recommendations on the process of technological change in Australian industry in order to maximise economic, social and other benefits and minimise any possible adverse consequences."

In particular the committee would

(*a*) identify:
   (i) technological change which is occurring or is likely to occur in Australia;
   (ii) new technologies which have the potential for substantial impact in Australia;

   and conduct detailed studies of those areas identified as the most important in order to evaluate the likely effects;

(*b*) examine relevant overseas experience and studies of technological change, and assess mechanisms used to introduce and evaluate new technologies; and

(*c*) review the effectiveness of government policies and programs in facilitating the introduction of new technology (*Myers Report* 1980, 1: 2).

In the context of the telecommunications industry, the committee failed to note the extent to which the new technology was imported. The changes imported were a major source of uncertainty.

It is not possible to effect a direct comparison between Australia and other economies in terms of information occupations by sector of origin. OECD statistics show that for a variety of economies, information intensiveness is not a "service sector" phenomenon (OECD 1981, Table 1.7, p. 33). The information occupations are of considerable importance in the industrial sector, reflecting the growing complexity of activities within that sector with greater need for coordination and planning, together with changing relationships with government, other economies, and international agencies. To this should be added the structural change that has led to an unknown but possibly important shift of "in-house" activities from within industry to the information sector following increased specialization. Despite the lack of comparable statistics in the Australian case, there are qualitative findings indicative of the same trends.[3]

INFORMATION POLICY: CONTRASTING VIEWS

Does the information intensiveness of the Australian economy have any interesting policy implications? The past decade has changed ideas about national information policy.[4] Ten years ago, its mention engendered thoughts of libraries of an old-fashioned kind. The *Jones STISEC Report* of 1973 gave way to the *Jackson Report* on policies for manufacturing industry in 1975; the *Fitzgerald Report* and *Horton Report* of 1976, dealing respectively with poverty and public libraries; the *Coombs Report, Crawford Report, Harries Report,* and *Jessop Report* of 1979, dealing respectively with government administration, structural adjustment, Australia's relations with the Third World, and industrial research and development; the *Myers Report* of 1980 on technological change; the *Kirby Report* of 1981 reviewing productivity and innovation programs; and the current IPAC (Industrial Property Advisory Committee) review of the operation of the patent system.[5] Each was obliged to recognize the increased information intensiveness. The overall result has not been a steady progression from a fragmented view of information policy toward a comprehensive, integrated view. Nevertheless, awareness of the range of problems has increased, even if there has not yet been any great advance in general understanding of the role of information in the economy.[6]

An Australian perspective circa 1978 is provided by a document on the structure of information, computer, and communications policy. This was prepared for the OECD's ICCP (Information Computer Communications Policy) Working Group (now Committee[7]) and was intended:

- (i) to provide an overview of the extent of government involvement in information activities and policy formulation within Australia;
- (ii) to present a picture of the way in which information activities are co-ordinated and relevant problems are managed on a national basis; and
- (iii) to provide a basis for discussion amongst other OECD Member countries preparing national reports on their information, computer and communications policies and structures (OECD, 1978).

It was recognized that all government organizations would be involved in the information process to a greater or lesser extent by virtue of answering queries from other government bodies, parliamentary members, or the general public; by producing submissions, reports, and other publications; and sometimes by funding or offering other forms of assistance to nongovernment organizations that provide information to various sections of the community. The organizations described had a major and specific role in the collection, storage, dissemination, or organization of information over and above those activities that form a normal part of government administrative processes. Most had a role in formulating or implementing government information policy decisions, as well as providing information services to other government agencies, nongovernment organizations, or sections of the community. Those included were national collections and information-disseminating agencies; existing and proposed legislation on information access; computer networks; telecommunications and broadcasting; and scientific and technical information resources and services. The tone of this document was undoubtedly shaped by the ICCP context, itself a reflection of the pioneering OECD effort in information policy matters (see, e.g., OECD 1971). It was noted that the ICCP field was only part of the overall information transfer process: Conferences, seminars, teaching and advisory contacts, and referral centers were also judged important and widely used ways of exchanging and disseminating information.

Moving to the 1980s, Hurst (1981) provides a revision of the ideas contained in the 1978 OECD document, and once again the discussion is restricted by the ICCP context to "a science and technology perspective." He notes the lack of a definitional focus and stresses the difficulties that arise from two awkward characteristics of information activities: pervasiveness and fragmentation of responsibility. He likens this aspect of information policy to science and technology policy: "they overlap significantly and each contains elements of the other." Hurst furnishes elements that define the content of national information policy. The boundary conditions are policy issues (as opposed to technical issues) lying in the primary and secondary information sectors. The two major driving forces giving rise to the issues the policy must address are (1) cost reductions, productivity or quality improvements, and new services and products largely made possible by advances in microelectronics; and (2) the convergence of computer and telecommunications technologies. The specific core issues that form the policy framework are either industrially oriented (e.g., the role of information technologies in stimulating innovation and economic development; structural adjustment to the new industrial forms and infrastructures that are likely to arise) or socially oriented (e.g., questions relating to unemployment, changed working conditions, and manpower requirements).

The final element is the response of government to these identified issues. He concludes: "The question for the information sector has been, and still is, how to arrive at well defined boundaries within the responsibilities and competence of government that will lead to a practical policy framework." His method is to peel away "matters that are purely technical in nature or deal with residual or non-policy information activities" (Hurst 1981, 4–5). These two distinctions are invoked to delimit information policy. The first is illustrated by the details of new information technology or the preparation of an actual impact assessment, as opposed to government response to the impacts. The second distinction is between different kinds of information activity. Hurst resorts to the approach developed in information sector accounting, regarding as relevant for policy purposes information goods and services within the now accepted definitions of the primary and secondary information sectors. The former includes information goods and services sold in markets, and the latter equivalent goods and services provided in-house. The boundary conditions then are policy (as opposed to technical) issues lying in the primary and secondary information sectors.

In view of the existing dispersion and fragmentation of government responsibilities and present institutional structure, it is seen necessary to adopt an issue-by-issue approach. Coordination is needed in some cases but not in others. This approach is a satisfactory option, according to Hurst, as long as the necessary coordinating mechanisms can be provided in time. Here the efforts of the OECD's ICCP Working Group have been of great value. Apart from the collection of a great deal of basic data, it has supposedly identified the major forces causing the rapid expansion of the information sector: the cost of reductions resulting from miniaturization in electronics, and the combination of computers and telecommunications systems. It has also identified relevant policy issues. For example:

Industrial

1. The role of information technologies in stimulating innovation and economic development
2. Structural adjustment
3. Questions related to national equity, independence, and control
4. The role of such measures as tariffs, taxes, and national and international legislation and trade agreements
5. Management of information infrastructures

Social

1. Unemployment effects
2. Changing work conditions and manpower requirements
3. Privacy and access issues
4. Copyright
5. Distribution of benefits and costs
6. National sovereignty, cultural identity, and vulnerability
7. Technology transfer to Third World countries

These industrial and social issues and factors are said by Hurst to form the policy framework, subject to the boundary conditions. "Information policy emerges as a composite of policies dealing with the role of government in assessing and responding to those [core industrial and social] issues and factors" (Hurst 1981, 15). Hurst also focused on the relationship between information policy and S&T policy and the implications for policy mechanisms. Coordination is a more important aspect of policy in these cases than in energy policy because they have common characteristics and difficulties. Both are

(*a*) Diffuse and cross-sectoral
(*b*) Characterized by fragmented government responsibilities
(*c*) Closely identified with innovation and the role of key technologies and supporting infrastructure
(*d*) Typified by the lack of a small group of major issues that might give a common policy focus
(*e*) Associated with far-reaching social consequences

Since science and its applications intrude into the information sector, it was seen as necessary to set aside those cases where primary carriage for policy formulation lies with a non-S&T agency (e.g., protection of privacy with the Attorney General's department). In many cases S&T is the dominant factor (e.g., R&D related to information technologies). In-between cases of shared interests call for multiagency involvement. This illustrates the general approach through coordination that has developed for Australian science and technology. Hurst believes that the mechanisms adopted for S&T policy are also appropriate for information issues. His illustration relates to the role of information technologies in innovation in economic development: "Australia needs a basic and applied research capability in this field. Such a capability, with its associated infrastructure, provides a foundation for our response as a nation to rapidly changing technological demands. It acts as a basis for innovation" (Hurst 1981, 21). What mechanisms can be employed? Several are available:

(*a*) The ARGS supports undirected basic research
(*b*) The CSIRO undertakes broad-ranging R&D
(*c*) NH & MR and National Energy R&D grants support directed research
(*d*) IR&D Incentives Schemes provide support for industrial efforts
(*e*) Individual packages (e.g., the NatSemi package) can be negotiated.[8]

According to Hurst, the range of mechanisms must be seen to depend on the view taken of the role of the market. If the market is the most efficient means of creating and allocating resources, cases in which intervention is justified will generally involve some failure of the market system to act in the national interest (e.g., long-deferred excess of social benefit and costs, defense and other strategic considerations, and international relations).

The 1979 Australian Labor Party National Conference created a National Task Force in New Technology to report to the national executive on the social impact of technological change and to assist in developing national policies. Its report was completed in December 1981, and its suggestions for national information policy were carried almost unchanged into the ALP Science and Technology Platform adopted by the National Conference in Canberra in July 1982. The National Information Policy section of the platform reads as follows:

12.0 *National Information Policy*

Recognising that in an era of rapid technological change access to information is a precondition to national or personal autonomy, the Australian Labor Party adopts the following National Information Policy.

12.1 All Australians are entitled to free access to information and library services of acceptable standard, regardless of where they live, of their social and economic position, language, sex, age, mobility or physical disabilities.

12.2 The effective working of democracy depends on the availability of adequate information and the capacity for its independent evaluation. The right to know, to be informed, is basic to every person. In our society, access to information is a vital resource of government and of the public, and should not be concentrated in the hands of the rich.

12.3 The Australian community is divided between the "information rich" and the "information poor." Information facilities are remote from those who need them most. They do not know what is available and do not know how to remedy their lack of information.

12.4 Growing inequity in "information transfer" threatens the position of individuals relative to governments and corporations. Increasing volume of available information due to new methods of gathering, storing and disseminating may lead to:

(i) increasing tendency towards specialisation and the fragmentation of knowledge;

(ii) a growing sense of "alienation" and "anomie" in many people who feel unable to understand what is going on around them;

(iii) a risk that power will move towards technocrats and away from representative institutions;

(iv) a major threat to privacy from personal data files in private hands.

12.5 Information problems should not continue to be treated in the narrow perspective of science and technology, and left to scientists and experts alone, but should be considered in the broader context of knowledge and social welfare in which information is a fundamental resource.

12.6 Governments must plan for the new technologies and ensure that information systems are not developed in a chaotic fashion for exclusively commercial reasons.

12.7 Legislation should define and codify:

(i) the right of access, where this is in the public interest, of individuals or public or private bodies to relevant non-government information resources;

(ii) the political and social guarantees which individuals and institutions can legitimately expect, including protection of privacy and secrecy;

(iii) the basic rules of reciprocity which should govern relationships between public and private systems and networks;

(iv) a code of ethics for professions and industries concerned in this field.

12.8 The provisions of public library and information services should remain the collective responsibility of the Commonwealth, State, and local levels of Government, funded in part by each.

12.9 Public libraries must become information resource centres, including local data banks, information about access to government services, with greater emphasis on non-book material such as gramophone records, tapes, cassettes, microforms and audiovisual material generally.

12.10 The expansion and extension of all library and information services should be achieved through co-operation and/or contract and the formation of library systems and networks with each service retaining its autonomy within the overall State plan for the development of those services. Already existing information services should be co-ordinated and integrated to avoid duplication and waste of resources.

This ALP platform has increasingly become the basis of the policy of the Labor government that came to power in 1983. There is some sensing that information policy must be paramount; that in contrast to science and technology policy, which has sought coordination of given organizational units, it must seek optimally designed units. However, the Australian experience of national information policy does not reveal much effort to design new organizational units. After long delay, an Australian Libraries and Information Council emerged from the recommendations of the *Horton Report* (1976), but its designated functions and even its initial membership would seem to ensure that it will reflect the thinking of the library community. The ALP National Task Force on New Technology envisaged the establishment of an Australian Information Utility as a statutory corporation. Major users and community groups, along with Telecom, CSIRO, the ABC, and major libraries, were to be represented. The utility would have its own satellites. Although such organizational innovation is to be commended, no details were provided. This was the only national information policy proposal by the task force not incorporated into the science and technology platform.

A basic "science and hardware" emphasis is only slowly being eroded and may well continue to inhibit research into the structural aspects of the information sector and the reflecting of such research by the policy process. One potential change with a shift from the hardware perspective would be lessened confidence in the identity of the driving forces behind the growth of the information sector, with major implications for the telecommunications industry. In addition, the equity aspects have been given inadequate attention in the statements of both government administrations. The present (ALP) government stresses entitlement to free access to information but does not address the consequences of differences in perceptions of the value of information and in capacity to use information. In this and other aspects, the growth of information intensiveness goes beyond national borders. Recent calls for technology policy, particularly the debate about the creation of an Australian microelectronics industry, pose the need for integration of economic, technology, and information policies. So far, there has been little to create an expectation that Australia will be able to emulate Japan's "virtual Manhattan Project," as the fifth-generation computer project has been labeled. The policy environment in which the regulation of telecommunications takes place is, therefore, one characterized by fragmentation and a lack of coordination.

THE AUSTRALIAN TELECOMMUNICATIONS INDUSTRY

Until 1975 the Australian Post Office combined the postal and telecommunications services.[9] The former has been described as "labour-intensive, technically unprogressive" and the latter as "capital-intensive, bursting with technical possibilities" (Butlin et al. 1982, 309). The domestic telecommunications monopoly is vested in Telecom Australia, which has the following statutory obligations under the Telecommunications Act of 1975:

> Plan, establish, maintain, and operate telecommunications services within Australia in such a manner as will best meet the social, industrial, and commercial needs of the Australian people for telecommunications services.
>
> The commission is required to pursue a policy each year directed toward covering all expenditure chargeable to revenue and providing an amount equal to not less than one-half of its capital expenditure.
>
> Rates and charges must be kept as low as practicable, consistent with financial requirements.
>
> The surplus of the commission for a financial year shall be applied in such a manner as the minister determines.
>
> The raising of all loans is subject to the approval of the treasurer and hence the Loan Council.

This monopoly position has the added advantage that it is exempt from the payment of taxes.

Telecom Australia sees its fundamental objectives as follows:

> The availability to Australian customers nationwide of world standard telecommunications services in terms of quality, diversity, price, and accessibility. These telecommunications services are a vital infrastructure in the economy and must reflect social, business, government, and national needs and priorities.
>
> The continued development by Telecom staff of an efficient, responsive national telecommunications service enterprise.
>
> The opportunity for Australian industry to play a part in the production as well as design and development of modern electronic equipment.

Telecom Australia is a statutory corporation subject to government, political, and bureaucratic controls and pressures. It is the nation's largest employer and, in a small economy, a key factor in industrial development and technological capability, as well as a significant instrument in the capital market. Table 10.2 shows recent dimensions of Telecom Australia.

Telecom Australia would argue that it has been successful in business efficiency terms and would support this contention with the following statistics: International comparison of hours of work required in 1982–1983 to pay the annual costs of telephone service for the average residential customer places Australia third after the United States and Canada, the number of hours being 31.7 compared with 21.8 in the United States and 25.6 in Canada. Other countries were reported as Japan, 36.5; West Germany, 39.5; France, 45.1; and the United Kingdom, 49.4. Over the preceding 7 years, Australia had reduced this measure of cost more than had the United States and Canada—Japan had actually increased slightly—but lagged behind West Germany, France, and the United Kingdom. At constant prices, operating cost per service had declined steadily in recent years. Unsatisfied demand had been reduced significantly, while new service connections had risen considerably. More than 80% of new services were now connected within 3 weeks.

TABLE 10.2 Dimensions of Telecom Australia

Assets		$9700m
Staff		88,000
Debit to government		$4566m
Public borrowings		$1735m
Earnings (1982–1983)		$3636m
Capital investment (1982–1983)		$1600m
Profit (1981–1982)		$275m
Self-funding ratio (1982–1983)		77.0%
Return on investment (1981–1982)		
Before interest		9.2%
After interest		3.2%
Growth Rates 1982–1983		
Services		
Telephone services in operation	5,591,700	4.0%
Telex services in operation	39,388	4.0%
Data modems in operation	70,190	25.0%
Major traffic volumes		
Local telephone calls	5,596,000,000	2.6%
Trunk telephone calls	837,000,000	6.5%
International telephone calls	28,000,000	25.0%
Telex calls	46,000,000	5.6%
Telegrams	4,000,000	−9.0%

Source: Telecom Australia. Figures relate to June 1983 unless otherwise indicated.

In terms of telephones in use per 100 population, Australia ranks above the average of OECD countries but below North America (OECD 1983, 22). In terms of telecommunications investment as a percentage of gross domestic product, Australia is highest in the list of OECD countries (OECD 1983, 33). More than 75% of its equipment is purchased from local manufacturers. This reflects official preference for goods manufactured in Australia, with business traditionally divided more or less equally among the firms. Even when (more recently) tenders have been called abroad, it has been made clear that manufacture must take place in Australia, with local firms licensed where necessary (OECD 1983, 39–40). Exports of equipment are minor, and employment in telecommunications equipment equals about one-ninth of the employment in domestic service provision. The policy of encouraging Australian manufacture is rationalized in terms of minimization of inventories, local repair capability, and facilitation of supply under emergency conditions. Table 10.3 shows the analysis of equipment and other purchases in 1981–1982.

Growth rates over the past 7 years have been rapid, as illustrated in Table 10.4. This trend is expected to continue, and growth will include major new developments.

In Telecom's plan to bring automatic telephony to even the most remote parts of the nation, the latest technology will be used. Advanced digital radio systems using solar power will expand the terrestrial network.

TABLE 10.3 Telecom Australia's Equipment Purchases, 1981–1982

	Expenditure ($m)
Major telecommunications items	
Telephone switching equipment	110
Cables	65
Line transmission equipment	24
Radio communications equipment	28
Telephones	29
PABXs	19
Switchboards	5
Other equipment	97
Teleprinters	25
Data terminal equipment	20
ADP equipment	3
Other telecommunications items	145
Other purchases	
Land and buildings, etc.	68
Motor vehicles	22
Miscellaneous plant and equipment	42
Total	702

Source: Telecom Australia.

For mining, pastoral, and tourist ventures requiring special communications packages in a hurry, the Iterra satellite service will use the planned Australian Communications Satellite System (ACSS), which will be introduced by Aussat, a wholly government-owned domestic satellite organization. Viatel, Telecom's national videotex service, was recently introduced to serve business, farmers, and graziers and ultimately the urban householder. The gateway service linking private and public databases to single access points could be a stimulus for the rapidly growing information industry. There will be increased orders for computer and terminal makers, as well as employment opportunities for people to prepare information for videotex presentation. Mobile telephones and paging services will expand. Cellular radio is still in its very early stages of development and is now quite expensive, but plans are in hand to introduce it into the Telecom network when it becomes viable. Meanwhile, paging services are becoming more widespread, with private operators preparing to use the Telecom network in competition with Telecom. Recent adoptions of technological innovations have given Australian business the choice of modern data transmission systems such as the Digital Data Service and the packet-switched Austpac network. For business security, new automatic alarm and telemetry systems were recently introduced when 200 businesses connected to five telephone exchanges in Sydney tested new equipment.

But it is the network itself where most emphasis is being placed on new technology. Optical fiber cables are now in urban use in Brisbane and Melbourne and are planned for Sydney. A trunk system using single-mode optical fibers is being installed between Ballarat and Melton in Victoria. This is a prelude to linking Sydney and Melbourne with a high capacity optical fiber cable within the next few years. New digital microwave radio systems are being installed between capital cities to increase trunk-line capacity by the end of 1985. Smaller systems will be installed on major intrastate routes. These digital transmission systems, coupled with new electronic telephone exchanges, are paving the way for a fully integrated

TABLE 10.4 Australian Telecommunications Growth (percent change, latest 7 years)

Telephone network	+50
Local calls	+65
Trunk calls	+128
STD penetration (up from 75%)	+95
Telex services	+156
Data modems	+834
Manual services in remote areas (reduced from 146,000 to 43,000)	−70
Labor productivity (increased from 8.2 to 12.5% per year)	

Source: Telecom Australia.

digital network to be overlaid on the current national network. This will give Australians a network with advanced customer facilities such as abbreviated dialing, automatic reminder and diversion calls, speed calling, and "call waiting" signaling. These new exchanges will enable Telecom to provide customers with the option of receiving details of their STD calls. This service began in 1984. All this activity is a major undertaking involving a number of manufacturers, and one that is considered necessary to meet anticipated business demand for local-area networks, communicating word processors, and new generation PABXs.

These expectations of new developments were expressed officially by the minister for communications in March 1984. They reflect the continuation of policies that led some historians to describe the Australian experience as "service at any cost" (Butlin et al. 1982, Chap. 11). This can best be understood in terms of the dominance of an engineering rather than an economic approach (Butlin et al. 1982, 295; Young 1980) and Australia's dependence on imported technology.

INTERNATIONAL SERVICES

International services are provided by the Overseas Telecommunications Commission (Australia), or OTC(A). This statutory authority is responsible to the minister for communications but, like Telecom Australia, plays a significant role in policy making. OTC has an obligation to make available international telecommunications services of high quality to all Australians by

Providing reliable, economic overseas telecommunications links for all services at all times

Actively engaging in the research, planning, development, and establishment of new services

Employing advanced technology and management techniques to contain costs and ensure profitable operation at reducing rates of charges

Informing the public of the availability of existing and new services and promoting their use through a comprehensive marketing program

Representing Australia internationally in matters of overseas telecommunications and taking a leading part in promoting improved services to facilitate and encourage social, business, and government communication.

OTC's traffic and revenue growth rates are high, and its profit position is sound. It has always been an active participant in international systems such as INTELSAT and INMARSAT. At a 1982 OECD conference the Australian representative expressed the belief that many of the problems discussed in relation to the Atlantic context also arose in relation to the Pacific, although perhaps less acutely and less urgently (Ergas and Okayama 1984, 171). The Australian government has opposed approval of an Orion-type entity on the Atlantic routes and would presumably favor maintenance of the existing INTELSAT arrangements for the Pacific region.

BROADCASTING SERVICES

The Australian Broadcasting Tribunal is concerned with broadcasting services and, like Telecom Australia and OTC(A), is a statutory authority responsible to the minister for communications. It carried out a public inquiry into cable and subscription services and reported in 1982. The central recommendations were as follows:

Cable television should be introduced.

Separation of ownership of the cable reticulation system and operation of cable television should be permitted.

Private and public sectors should have equal opportunities to own and maintain the cable reticulation system.

Cable television systems should be permitted to carry enhanced services.

A single federal authority should have responsibility for both broadcasting and telecommunications.

These recommendations did not prove palatable to the present government, and action is now bound up with a further review of the regulation of television. In the meantime, the minister for communications has given support to a Broadcasting Tribunal call for review and extension of its powers to make the regulatory scheme for broadcasting operate effectively and in the public interest.

AUSTRALIA'S DEPENDENCE ON IMPORTED TECHNOLOGY

The background to Australia's dependence upon imported technology (see Morris 1983) can be summarized as follows:

Australia is a small, high-income country but slipping in per capita income.

Although it is an "industrialized" economy, three out of four of its workers are in the service sector.

Investment and trading relationships with the rest of the world, more especially the economies of Asia and the Western Pacific region, are changing markedly.

Foreign investment has been a major influence in economic development.

R&D is at a low level by international standards, private investment in R&D being at an extremely low level with government playing the major role.

Australia is a heavy net importer of technology.

Australian patenting is at a low level, comparable to that of Canada.

Industry is not export oriented.

Industries tend to be highly concentrated and of oligopolistic character.

Levels of protection are high and have been long sustained.

The degree of structural change, especially in manufacturing, has been low compared with other OECD countries.

In these circumstances it is no surprise that telecommunications technology has been very largely imported, although earlier in Australian history local initiative in the development of that technology was apparent (Moyal 1983). In general, the adoption of new telecommunications developments from abroad has been rapid. Bishop (1984) has summarized the experience with transmission technology; her results are reproduced in Table 10.5. The engineering approach has combined with the funding system to ensure rapid adaptation of new technology for use in Australia.

THE DOMESTIC SATELLITE DEBATE

Aussat Pty. Ltd. announced the tariffs and conditions applying to the space segment of the domestic satellite system after the first generation of Australian satellites was launched in 1985. Considerable uncertainty attaches to the costs, perhaps two-thirds of the total, related to earth stations and the links to and from earth stations. Initial outlay on the system prior to revenue-producing activities is estimated as approximately $425 million (Hoare 1984, Part 1). The complex process of sorting out the various and conflicting interests is now being delayed by the government's decision to ask the Australian Broadcasting Tribunal to consider how

TABLE 10.5 Diffusion of Telecommunications Transmission Technology to Australia

Technology	Date of World Introduction	Date of Australian Introduction
Telegraph: patent	U.K. 1837	
	U.S. 1838	
Morse line	1844	1854
Telephone: patent	U.S. 1867	1877
exchange	1878	1880
Radio: patent Marconi	1896	
broadcast station	1920	1923
Radar	1935–1939	1939
Coaxial cable	1930s	1936
Television: Baird	1923	
broadcasting	1936	1956
Microwave radio	1945	1959
Satellite: Sputnik	1957	
commercial	1965	1968[a]
		1985[b]
Optical fibers	1970	1982

Source: Bishop 1984.
[a] Use of INTELSAT facilities.
[b] Planned domestic system.

television should be regulated. This step was taken because the present government's information policy favors diversity in the media rather than the increasing concentration, already characteristic of most media activities, that could be expected in the absence of control.

The key issue, however, would appear to be the simple fact that satellite technology has opened up an alternative to Telecom Australia. Recognition of this feature (Hoare 1984, Part 3) by the Australian Telecommunications Employees Association (ATEA) occurred long ago and led to that union's strong opposition to the satellite system. The ATEA is under no illusion that the 25% Telecom shareholding will neutralize the competitive element and realizes that Telecom has already had to take a more competitive stance (e.g., its hastening of the Iterra Network Service). The outcome has been a coalition of the interests of labor and management in defending the Telecom monopoly. Can this be a stable coalition, and can it ward off the competitive threat? Much will depend upon the importance of the combined economies of scale and scope in Telecom and the fact that Aussat is not required to provide a public service and is supposed to operate on a commercial basis and make a profit.[10]

A THEORETICAL PERSPECTIVE

In seeking to draw out the central features of the Australian experience, it is as well to begin by noting that consumers, by and large, have had little direct input to the decision process. There is an Australian Telecommunications User Group (ATUG), but its 170 members are drawn mainly from the business community. Its aim is to improve the level of understanding and knowledge of telecommunications and to lobby government. Given a secure "natural" monopoly, Telecom was free to cross-subsidize, pursue its objective of a telephone in every home, and moderate the impact of new technology from abroad in order to reduce the extent of industrial conflict with the ATEA. While the "natural" monopoly is now threatened, to say the least, there may be some remaining justification in terms of the scale–scope argument.

The definition of regulation based on both function and procedure appears useful for analysis. Noll has argued that this two-dimensional conceptualization of regulation parallels some new theoretical developments about the reasons for the formation of regulatory agencies.[11] The reduction of uncertainty was suggested as a new overriding principle of government. This accords with the O–B theory of regulation and seems not so far removed from the Schumpeterian vision of dynamic benefits.

In the Australian context, the new technologies from abroad constitute the source of greatest uncertainty. In terms of O–B theory, the Australian "natural" monopoly could slow down the process of change. The coalition with labor reinforced the incentive to act in this way.[12] Now that potential competition has become a reality and is seen as a threat by both the monopolist and the labor force, the interest in slowing change is reduced in order to protect both profits and jobs. The outcome of this altered balance between rates of change and current benefits is not subject to much direct consumer response, but there is a check by means of ATUG attitudes. It is possible to envisage another coalition, between ATUG and the domestic telecommunications equipment manufacturers. Time will tell how firmly the manufacturers are under the control of Telecom Australia. In broad terms, the O–B theory seems applicable when allowance is made for the dependence on imported technology and the coalition provoked by the emergence of potential competition.

Other new theoretical developments have relevance. First, Courville et al. (1983, xi) have emphasized the fact that "regulatory bodies are unlikely to have sufficient information on production, cost, and demand conditions, but perhaps must seek much more information on public perceptions and political preferences." These information costs suggest possibilities that organizational design should be seen as variable,[13] in which case the administrative procedures element of the two-dimensional conceptualization of regulation must involve internal organizational aspects.

Second, recent theoretical work in information economics and the economics of organization has suggested some fundamental ways in which the O–B theory's emphasis on stability is reinforced. Full and normal cost-pricing theory has for long stressed the perceived advantages of stable prices (see, e.g., Andrews and Brunner 1975). Now, new theoretical developments are adding to the critique of price flexibility. Casson, for example, is led, in the course of his detailed study of the role of the entrepreneur in the coordination of resources, to consider the firm's preference for stability simply because it has created an organization that has to be managed.[14] It would seem that recognition of this normal state of affairs provides support for the Noll interpretation of the O–B theory—and is also a reminder that effective resource allocation in a market system is not so exclusively related to price signals as one might conventionally assume. This links with the recent trend in economic writings to invoke such concepts as organizational capital, intangibles, information channels, tradition, and even mythology in analyses that have hitherto attempted to rely on traditional concepts of capital and labor. A form of investment is involved—investment that allows analytically for the influence of past events on present decisions (Macdonald, Lamberton, and Mandeville 1983, 2; see also Arrow 1979; Bradburd and Over 1982; McCain 1981; Teubal 1983; and Young 1980).

NOTES

1. These figures are higher than those provided by Lamberton (1977) because the coverage has now been extended to the entire OECD information labor category.

2. This category is the residual of information labor after the exclusion of the "creative" elements of R&D, consultative services, higher management and administration, and education, which are widely regarded as intrinsically labor intensive.

3. See Macdonald et al. (1983) for a regional study of the state of Queensland.

4. For some earlier discussion, see Lamberton (1971, 1974a, 1974b, 1975, and 1976).

5. This committee has not yet reported, but see Mandeville, Lamberton, and Bishop (1982) for some exploration of matters relevant to the committee's terms of reference.

6. Important BIE (Australian Bureau of Industry Economics) reports, too hampered by traditional industrial classifications, could note "the trend towards an information based society" (1981, 245), yet do little to illuminate that trend.

7. With the advent of committee status last year, responsibility for coordination in Australia transferred from the Department of Science and Technology to the Department of Communications—a useful reminder of the fragmentation with which ICCP deliberations must contend.

8. Offsets policy might well be included in this list.

9. The overseas telecommunications component was separated from the domestic with the creation of the Overseas Telecommunications Commission in 1946.

10. Telecom Australia has been given a qualified opportunity to embark on joint ventures with private enterprise, but it is not yet clear if this extends beyond satellites to general telecommunications services. This could prove helpful in the Viatel venture and in the development of EFT. ATEA would appear willing to endorse such expansion (see *Financial Review*, February 28, 1984, 1; February 29, 1984, 1, 8; March 12, 1984, 1, 6).

11. *What Is Regulation*? (Noll 1980). The O–B theory is set forth in Owen and Braeutigam (1978).

12. The technological change agreement between Telecom Australia and its staff organizations is comprehensive and operates currently for a 3-year period to April 30, 1986. See Telecom Australia (1983).

13. See Lamberton (1983, 1984b) for emphasis on the organization as a variable.

14. See also such recent works as Hoenack (1983), Hess (1983), and Lamberton (forthcoming).

REFERENCES

Andrews, P. W. S., and Elizabeth Brunner. *Studies in Pricing*. London: Macmillan, 1975.

Arrow, K. J. "The Economics of Information." In *The Computer Age: A Twenty-Year View*, edited by M. L. Dertouzos and Joel Moses. Cambridge, Mass.: MIT Press, 1979.

Australian Labor Party. *Science and Technology Platform*. Canberra: ALP, 1982.

Bishop, E. J. "The Economic Challenge to the Australian Telecommunications Industry." Draft of a Master's thesis, University of Queensland, 1984.

Bradburd, R. M., and A. Mead Over, Jr. "Organizational Costs, 'Sticky Equilibria,' and Critical Levels of Concentration." *Review of Economics and Statistics* 64 (February 1982): 50–58.

Bureau of Industry Economics. *The Long-run Impact of Technological Changes on the Structure of Australian Industry to 1990-91*. Research Report no. 7. Canberra: AGPS 1981.

Butlin, N. G., A. Barnard, and J. J. Pincus. *Government and Capitalism*. Sydney: Allen & Unwin, 1982.

Coombs Report of the Royal Commission on Australian Government Administration. Canberra: AGPS, 1979.

Courville, L., A. de Fontenay, and R. Dobell, eds. *Economic Analysis of Telecommunications: Theory and Applications*. Amsterdam: North-Holland, 1983.

Crawford Report of Study Group on Structural Adjustment. Vol. 1. Canberra: AGPS, 1979.

Dunn, D. A. "Developing Information Policy." *Telecommunications Policy* 6, no. 1 (March 1982): 21–38.

Ergas, H., and J. Okayama, eds. *Changing Market Structures in Telecommunications.* Amsterdam: North-Holland, 1984.

Fitzgerald Fifth Main Report of the Commission of Inquiry into Poverty. Canberra: AGPS, 1976.

Harries Report of the Committee on Australia's Relations with the Third World. Canberra: AGPS, 1979.

Hess, J. D. *The Economics of Organization.* Amsterdam: North-Holland, 1983.

Hoare, Judith. Part 1, "Domestic Satellites: What You Should Know, but Were Too Confused to Ask." Part 2, "Television and the Satellite: Bluff Poker...and the Game Isn't Finished Yet." Part 3, "How the Satellite Will Expand Business's Communications Options." *Financial Review*, March 26, 27, 28, 1984.

Hoenack, S. A. *Economic Behavior within Organizations.* Cambridge, England: Cambridge University Press, 1983.

Horton Report of the Committee of Inquiry into Public Libraries. Public Libraries in Australia. Canberra: AGPS, 1976.

Hurst, W. N. "Towards a National Information Policy: Some Observations from a Science and Technology Perspective." Paper presented at the National Information Policy Seminar, 1981.

Jackson Report of the Committee to Advise on Policies for Manufacturing Industry. Canberra: AGPS, 1975.

Jessop Report from the Senate Standing Committee on Science and the Environment, Industrial Research and Development in Australia. Canberra: AGPS, 1979.

Jones STISEC Report, Vol. 1, *Scientific and Technological Information Services.* Canberra: National Library of Australia, 1973.

Kirby Report of the Committee to Review Productivity and Innovation Programs. Canberra: AGPS, 1981.

Lamberton, D. M. *The Economics of Information and Knowledge.* Harmondsworth, England: Penguin Books, 1971.

———. "National Information Policy." In *The Information Revolution,* edited by D. M. Lamberton for *The Annals of the American Academy of Political and Social Sciences* 412 (March 1974): 145–151. (a)

———. "The Necessity for a National Information Policy." *Australian Library Journal*, July 1974, 211–216. (b)

———. *Who Owns the Unexpected?* St. Lucia, Australia: University of Queensland Press, 1975.

———."National Policy for Economic Information." *International Social Science Journal* 28, no. 3 (1976): 449–465.

———. "The Structure and Growth of the Communication Industry." In *The Service Sector of the Australian Economy*, edited by K. A. Tucker. London: Croom Helm, 1977.

———. "Information Economics and Technological Change." In *The Trouble with Technology*, edited by J. Macdonald, D. M. Lamberton, and T. D. Mandeville. New York: St. Martin's Press, 1983.

———. "The Economics of Information and Organization." In *Annual Review of Information Science and Technology*, edited by M. Williams. Vol. 19. New York: Knowledge Industry Publications for American Society for Information Science, forthcoming.

———. "The Emergence of Information Economics." In *New Perspectives on Information and Communication*, edited by M. Jussawalla and H. Ebenfield. Amsterdam: North-Holland, 1984.

McCain, R. A. "Tradition and Innovation." In *Economics of Information*, edited by M. Galatin and R. D. Leiter. Boston: Martinus Nijhoff, 1981.

Macdonald, S., D. M. Lamberton, and T. D. Mandeville, eds. *The Trouble with Technology*. New York: St. Martin's Press, 1983.

Macdonald, S., et al. *Technology Employment and the Queensland Information Economy—Report to the Queensland Department of Employment and Labour Relations*. Brisbane, 1983.

Mandeville, T. D., D. M. Lamberton, and E. J. Bishop. *Economic Effects of the Australian Patent System*. Canberra: AGPS, 1982.

Morris, P. J. "Australia's Dependence on Imported Technology—Social Issues for Discussion." *Prometheus* 1, no. 1 (June 1983): 144–159.

Moyal, Ann. "Telecommunications in Australia: An Historical Perspective, 1854–1930." *Prometheus* 1, no. 1 (June 1983): 23–41.

Myers Report of the Committee of Inquiry into Technological Change in Australia. 4 vols. Canberra: AGPS, 1980.

Noll, R. G. *What is Regulation? Notes on the Ontology of Regulatory Policy*. Social Science Working Paper no. 324. Pasadena, Calif.: California Institute of Technology, 1980.

Organisation for Economic Cooperation and Development. *Information for a Changing Society. Some Policy Considerations*. Paris: OECD, 1971.

———. *Government and Information Policy: Australia*. Paris: OECD, Directorate for Science, Technology and Industry, 1978.

———. *Information Activities, Electronics and Telecommunications Technologies Impact on Employment, Growth and Trade*. Vol. 1. Paris: OECD, 1981.

———. *Telecommunications: Pressures and Policies for Change*. Paris: OECD, 1983.

———. *Updating of the Data Base Contained in OECD-ICCP Publication No. 6*, Vol. 1, *Information Activities, Electronics and Telecommunications Technologies*. Paris: OECD, 1984.

Owen, B., and R. Braeutigam. *The Regulation Game: Strategic Use of the Administrative Process*. Cambridge, Mass.: Ballinger, 1978.

Telecom Australia. *Consideration of the Introduction of Technological Change*. Melbourne: Telecom Australia, 1983.

Teubal, M. "The Accumulation of Intangibles by High-Technology Firms." In *The Trouble with Technology*, edited by J. Macdonald, D. M. Lamberton, and T. D. Mandeville. New York: St. Martin's Press, 1983.

Young, D. L. "Telecommunications as an Ecosystem—An Australian Case Study." *Telecommunications Policy* 4, no. 3 (September 1980): 183–207.

PART 3

Retrospect, Conclusions, and Future Research Agenda

Eleven

Telecommunications Policy on Both Sides of the Atlantic: Divergence and Outlook

Eli M. Noam

In 1982, amid much attention and fanfare, the World Center for Computer Science and Human Resourcés (Centre Mondial de l'Informatique et Ressource Humaine) was opened in Paris (Etheridge 1983). French President François Mitterrand personally supported this venture, proclaiming as its goal an understanding of the computerization of society and the development of computer applications for social and economic growth, particularly in the Third World. A noted journalist and politician, Jean-Jacques Servan-Schreiber, was the primary French organizer, and two eminent American computer scientists from the Massachusetts Institute of Technology (MIT), Seymour Papert and Nicholas Negroponte, were chosen to direct research. This project, it was asserted, would fuse American technical know-how with European social concern and humanism in the service of society and the Third World. The Center was generously financed by the French government and was lavishly presented to the public as a major accomplishment.

Yet, within a year the Center was paralyzed, and the American scientists had left. Why had things gone wrong? Among other reasons, the American scientists and the French politicians had different conceptions of the Center. The French wanted to do "something" in the glamorous field of computers and high technology in order to demonstrate France's national commitment to technological leadership. The MIT scientists took the humanist mission of the Center more seriously. They believed that "personal computerization should be democratically available to all people in the world. As a vehicle of change the [Center] should [be] independent of commercial and political interest" (Papert, quoted in Etheridge 1983,

31). They also believed in a collegial process of decision making, "American in style, but alien to [the] French way of doing business" (Negroponte, quoted in Etheridge 1983, 32). Ironically, the American technocrats favored a democratic style of management and goals, which clashed with the style of the leftist French politicians who controlled and subsequently took over the direction of the Center.

Instead of becoming a world center with an international outlook, the Center acquired a parochial outlook; Negroponte said he was "asked to take the interests of French industry increasingly into account," an assertion freely admitted by Servan-Schreiber, who stated that the "French electronics industry . . . is a lot more backward than I realized."

This episode illustrates the dilemma of European countries as they attempt to cope with the revolution in information and telecommunications technologies. European leaders are aware of the importance of this sector, and they realize that the United States and Japan are making impressive gains in it. They want to do "something" in order to attain rapid results, and are willing to commit money and prestige. In the end, however, these efforts cannot transcend fundamental constraints: the self-interests of bureaucracies, the bureaucratic and hierarchical style of decision making, the short-term interests of domestic manufacturers, and scientific nationalism.

By and large, European countries are operating in a mode very similar to the old AT&T regime in the United States; that is, one monopoly (though publicly owned and operated rather than privately owned and publicly regulated) supplies the vast bulk of communications services, both domestic and international, in each country.

Most of the technological advances available in the United States are equally available in Europe. In some instances, the technology in fact originated in European countries. Hence, institutional changes similar to those in the United States could have occurred in Europe, had they been primarily technology-driven. Why have Europeans moved in a different direction from the United States, or, more accurately, why have they essentially maintained intact their institutional arrangements in the telecommunications field, while the U.S. has radically changed its own?

EUROPEAN POLICY OPTIONS IN THE TELECOMMUNICATIONS AND INFORMATION SECTOR: THE POSTAL-INDUSTRIAL COMPLEX

Within the spectrum of European policy responses, one extreme is the United Kingdom, whose government, under Prime Minister Margaret Thatcher, supports a free market economy. Not surprisingly, therefore, British telecommunications policy has been influenced by the American pattern. In several stages, the British government has brought about the separation of the telecommunications monopoly of British Telecom from the postal services and has led it to reorganization as a private corporation subject to some competition. This is documented by Charles Jonscher in Chapter 7.

While Britain is consciously attempting to raise its high-technology standards through market forces, with the government supplying an entrepreneurial environment, French policies have relied on an increase in the governmental role. This is rooted in a statist tradition, and in the economic and social philosophy of the Mitterrand government. The French government has set development of a high-technology electronics industry as a national priority and has chosen to nationalize much of the French electric and telecommunications equipment industry to gain a lever for the achievement of this goal.

The effect is that the French have now created an analog of the old Bell System: a vertically integrated complex of equipment manufacturing coupled with a telecommunications transmission monopoly and an R&D laboratory, all of it government owned. Thus, at the same time that the AT&T telecommunications monopoly in the United States has been divested into several component parts, the French have done the opposite and have assembled, for the first time, the major elements of telecommunications under one ownership.

The telecommunications policy of the Federal Republic of Germany lies somewhere between the liberalization of the United Kingdom and the nationalization of France. The Deutsche Bundespost (DBP) has been loath to relinquish its monopoly power over domestic and international telecommunications, and has primarily striven to protect the status quo. But it has also broadened its definition of the telecommunications sector—in which it is legally privileged—and has created pressures to use the public switched network. One such action has been to reduce customers' ability to lease private lines at a flat rate.

These three positions—liberalization, nationalization, and status quo—are the primary policy choices of European countries, with the latter generally preferred by the key governmental agencies in the telecommunications field, the PTTs (the postal, telephone, and telegraph agencies). In supporting that position, several governmental and private interest groups have joined in a broad and informal coalition that may be termed the "postal-industrial complex."

The key elements in this coalition are the PTTs. With their vast procurement budgets and huge labor forces, PTTs are frequently the largest investors and employers in their countries. They are usually staffed by able and experienced public servants who are effective advocates of their positions and seasoned practitioners of institutional self-preservation.

Apart from their own positions of direct influence, much of the PTTs' power arises from allowing other groups of society to share in the benefits of their monopoly. One such group is the equipment manufacturers, typically very large private companies. In most European countries the market share of the largest four manufacturers in total telecommunications equipment is above 90%. These companies are among the most potent European firms and tend to set the tone for the private sector's telecommunications policy preferences within general industry associations. In the equipment markets, PTTs fill the role of a monopsonist, or primary buyer. The maximum of *joint* profit for both monopsonist (who is a monopolist supplier of the final product) and a group of oligopolists usually lies in some form of cooperative behavior. The PTTs therefore are instrumental in coordinating the industry, an arrangement that can be advantageous to suppliers, who as a result need not compete vigorously against one another.

A variety of barriers are set to protect this cooperation; these include an unwillingness to procure foreign equipment, coordinated development of new technology, and PTT-organized setting of equipment standards.

One consequence of this protective system is that European prices are said to be 60 to 100% higher for switching equipment and 40% higher for transmission equipment than prices in North America (cited in OECD 1983, 44).

The labor unions are in a similar position because PTTs are among the largest national employers, and because employees benefit from salary levels and job security that may not be sustainable under a competitive regime. Furthermore, for unions as well as for the political left, the existing PTT system merits support not only for material but often also for ideological reasons, as a nationalized key industry. The frequently more pronounced political and class divisions in Europe lead to a strong feeling that a critical part of the infrastructure, particularly one with such future importance in the information society, cannot be entrusted to private interests dedicated to the profit motive.

Other members of the postal-industrial coalition are the poor, the elderly, the farmers, and the small towns, all of whom support the PTT system because they fear that a liberalized regime would threaten the subsidy of their service.

The office equipment manufacturers, new computer companies, and data processors have been somewhat outside the postal-industrial complex, at least in the past. In recent years, however, the PTTs have been able to draw them into their orbit, often assuming a key role in domestic industrial policy. This role makes the PTT an important financial backer, valued customer, domestic protector, and international promoter in high-technology markets. They can channel development contracts to domestic industries and undertake tests of such technology. They can also coordinate R&D among manufacturers and provide nontariff protection and export advantages. The PTTs thus assume some of the costs of the early part of the learning curve, and in effect subsidize the development of products that are then offered in the world market. Europeans, of course, assert that defense spending in the United States has filled many of these same functions in the past for American industry and that the encouragement of a high-technology industry is an important governmental function.

Some PTTs, such as the French, have foreign technical assistance organizations that help developing countries plan and operate their telecommunications systems and that are closely linked with national export drives. This makes sense, since the PTTs reap the benefits of future economies of scale and production resulting from foreign countries' orders. If foreign buyers embrace domestic equipment, it tends to reflect favorably on the PTTs' own good judgment in the original selection of the hardware.

EUROPEAN VIEWS ON U.S. DEREGULATION AND THE AT&T DIVESTITURE

Developments in the United States challenge the European status quo in the telecommunications field and threaten the broad postal-industrial coalition that supports and benefits from it.

Informed European interpretation of U.S. developments is usually colored by the prevailing view of telecommunications experts, who are often closely affiliated with the postal-industrial complex. The AT&T divestiture was the largest dismantling and reorganization of any industrial company in history, yet European coverage of the event was superficial. Publications such as *Le Monde, Le Figaro, Der Spiegel*, and *Frankfurter Allgemeine Zeitung* reported the basics of the divestiture agreement of January 1982 but with limited interpretive follow-up. The divestiture itself was generally described as advantageous to AT&T: It was dropping the costly baggage of the regulated operating companies and could now take on IBM. The reportage showed a general lack of understanding of the Federal Communication Commission's (FCC's) *Second Computer Inquiry*, which had already permitted AT&T entry into competitive markets under a fully separated AT&T subsidiary.

European PTTs, in particular, had a great amount of admiration and sympathy for the "old" AT&T. Although the American telephone operating company was privately owned, it had an operating dominance similar to that of European entities. International cooperation in such areas as transatlantic communications had resulted in close links as partners rather than competitors. Indeed, AT&T had even avoided entering the European equipment market, thereby reducing potential friction with European equipment manufacturers and PTTs. The European PTTs were therefore bewildered by the dismantling of AT&T. The decision seemed arbitrary, inefficient, and political. The belief that the efficient and successful AT&T

had been needlessly dismembered by the government is at odds with the view that the divestiture was a great success for AT&T. This inconsistency is not surprising. The notion that the divestiture is advantageous to AT&T is held primarily by those who think in political and strategic terms.

In contrast, the PTTs' view is essentially that of the engineer, with emphasis on orderliness, system continuity, and centrally planned end-to-end service that satisfies economic infrastructure needs as well as social functions of redistribution, and all this in a technically efficient and elegant fashion. This describes, not coincidentally, the PTT's self-image. Hence, the notion of the United States, with its advanced technology and successful telecommunications monopoly, choosing voluntarily to dismember such a system creates deep institutional shock, though this is rarely admitted. In the past, the development and adoption of new technologies provided security to the PTTs; these new technologies now appear to have undermined that security. This perception has resulted in strong defensive reactions, including an interpretation of American developments as rooted in political-ideological values rather than in engineering and technology, and thus as outside scientific rationality.

The PTTs also portray the American circumstances as inherently different from those in European countries and hence not applicable to the situation back home. In doing so, they often misinterpret the present and the past in the United States. In some ways this closely resembles views in the United States, where the AT&T divestiture agreement and its implementation have created an instant nostalgia for the old Bell system, which used to be almost everyone's favorite whipping boy. In this view, AT&T is seen as having been one of America's outstanding organizations, torn apart by economic zealots.

Some Europeans regard U.S. telecommunications liberalization in global strategic terms as an American "war" on Japan. This theme is particularly widespread in France, where the leading newspaper, *Le Monde*, expounded on it in a series of lengthy articles. The main argument was that the United States is engaged in two wars, a military-political one against the Soviet Union and an economic one against Japan.

These observations contain some truth, although the simplistic thesis is misleading. Quite clearly, the U.S. liberalization policy is a response to the widespread desire to induce economic growth and innovation through market forces. The economic conflict with Japan may be used as a domestic argument within the United States, but there is no lack of others.

Some European observers also see the AT&T divestiture as part of a strategic battle of AT&T against IBM. This theme was anticipated in the widely circulated French report on informatization by Nora and Minc (1980). The Nora–Minc report had compared IBM's power and global reach with the universal influence of the Catholic church and the Communist International. These global-strategic views conveniently justify the need for major governmental involvement in stemming the IBM colossus, since economic and technological rivalry has been transformed into international and strategic issues. What is not clear is why the American technological offensive would be advanced by reducing, through divestiture, the power of AT&T. Assuming a global objective, a more plausible American strategy would be to unleash AT&T, with all its resources, instead of reducing them and tying up the giant for years with reorganization. The only logical conclusion is that America expects to advance its global-war strategy against Japan through a domestically competitive regime, in which the regulated monopoly sector is separated and held to a minimum core. The American strategy against Japan is to reduce government involvement; the French strategy in the same war is the opposite.

When Europeans assert, as they frequently do, that the American system is different from the European one, they usually mean that the American system is run for profit, while the European system fulfills social goals as well. There are serious flaws in this simple contrast. On the most basic level, telecommunications policy in the United States has had social goals nearly from the beginning—and continues to have them—including a universal service that assures an affordable access for rural areas and for the poor. The percentage penetration of telephones in the United States has been higher than in any European country, despite the fact that vast areas of America are sparsely populated and that a much larger percentage of the population is poor, or migrant, or outside the main language of communications.

Nor do West European rate structures reflect more social concern than those in the United States, where basic subscriber rates are approximately equal or lower, and long-distance rates are markedly lower. In many European countries, no rate distinction is made between residential and business customers, whereas in the United States business customers pay a substantially higher rate. Rural telephony in the United States is subsidized in a variety of ways, primarily through the rate structure and by low-interest loans from the federal government.

Furthermore, a price comparison needs to take into account the quality differential of services available in the United States, such as convenient operator assistance, itemized telephone billings, the ability to place collect and credit-card calls, and rapid installation. While the size of internal subsidies is likely to decline as the U.S. system moves toward cost-based pricing, it does not imply that subsidies will disappear, though they may be financed differently in the future. The protection of affordable universal service is a high political priority, and U.S. congressional and state regulatory reactions—as in the dispute over the timing of telephone access charges—indicate that America will remain greatly sensitive to the maintenance and protection of universival service, even within a liberalized setting.

It is nevertheless true that the deregulation and divestiture of AT&T have had a distributive effect. To many Europeans, this is seen as part of the economically conservative policies of the Reagan administration, which is regarded as a probusiness restoration. The American political view is that deregulation is not a zero-sum redistributory game and that it is likely to generate overall gains resulting from increased efficiency and dynamism. While European reports of the effects of the AT&T divestiture stress the impact on local rates, one rarely sees any reference to overall cost reductions. For example, the cost of producing a telephone receiver fell from $2.30 to $0.99 within a month (*The Economist*, December 24, 1983, 76). AT&T's goal for 1984 was a 20% reduction in overall manufacturing costs. The company has frozen the salaries of its management and is continuing to reduce its work force, as are the regional companies. In the area of long-distance transmission, a respected financial analyst stated that AT&T's projected operating costs are $0.342 per revenue minute, while those of its rival, MCI, are only $0.179 (*Fortune*, April 16, 1984, 112). This indicates a substantial savings potential in the old AT&T system, which European PTTs considered a paragon of efficiency.

A major argument against liberalization that would open segments of the market to competitors is that of "cream skimming." PTTs argue that they must be allowed high profits in some of their services in order to subsidize others that are less profitable but socially important. It is, however, possible to provide the same subsidies to poor or rural customers through direct taxation and allocation, as is done with most other goods and services. But the political system would not normally permit these massive cross-subsidies if they were transparent. The commitment to a major subsidy of universal service in most European countries would seem to be far from secure once the magnitude of the subsidy became visible.

POLITICAL DYNAMICS AND THE STATUS QUO

It is not clear why a Reaganite pro-big-business policy would be promoted by the dismemberment of the biggest business of them all. Furthermore, the Reagan administration's political priorities are arguably not the driving force in U.S. policy. The pace of technological change dictates some of the options and forces them into the open. Governmental policies in this field respond to a significant extent to the technological realities of low-cost, long-distance satellite and microwave transmission and the computerization of telecommunications. While different political administrations may have approached these questions in a somewhat different fashion, the basic issues—the reduction of the scope of monopoly, the increase in the range of potential competitive service, and the general merging of the telecommunications, computing, and information production industries—have been brought about by historic development rather than by links to any specific presidential administration.

The situation is complex largely because of the multitude of decision points—the FCC, the state regulatory commissions, the Department of Justice, the National Telecommunications and Information Administration, Judge Harold Greene, Congress, and the Department of State. Each of these actors is active in some aspect of telecommunications matters, and most are largely uncoordinated with the others' actions. Hence it is surprising to find any general policy direction at all. It would have been reasonable to expect that these various decision-making bodies would have in effect neutralized each other into paralysis, following the course of U.S. national energy policy. But this has not occurred in telecommunications. The overall direction of U.S. telecommunications policy has been one of fairly steady liberalization, albeit with conflicts between federal and state regulatory and legislative bodies over preserving the cross-subsidy in local rates. This outcome is remarkable to domestic and foreign observers, many of whom see the decision-making process as hopelessly confused.

The U.S. system is certainly different from the orderly process in Europe. In the United States, the system resembles a war with a hundred local battles. But, for all its untidiness, the American policy process has accommodated changes far more rapidly than has the more orderly European governmental decision-making mechanism. This fact may have something to do with the greater pressures for change in the United States, but it also results from the general nature of decentralized decision making. Changes in European telecommunications policy may seem more orderly, better planned, more predictable, and less disruptive. But at some point one realizes that much of the orderliness of the policy debate lies in the fact that there is no real public debate on telephone issues. European telecommunications policy discussions are carried on by government insiders. In addition, there is a general and near-total separation of mass media expertise from telephony expertise. In Germany some discussion was sparked *within* the government by a hard-hitting report of the Monopoly Commission on the DBP, in which the monopoly practices of the Bundespost were criticized severely. This led to an equally hard-hitting rebuttal by the Bundespost. The debate seems not to have been continued, however, and was not joined by nongovernmental groups in the vigorous way that would be typical in the United States.

In contrast, numerous and contending American business and consumer associations, public interest groups, academic critics, churches, and lower levels of government lend their voices to spirited policy debates. This pluralistic interplay is less developed in continental Europe, where there is no involvement of the intellectual community and only limited press coverage. There is no hearings mechanism comparable to FCC or congressional proceedings, and no comparable forums in which dockets can be developed. In most instances there is also no recourse to litigation, which provides an additional way of airing and resolving issues in the United States.

There is in Europe nothing comparable to the creative energy of California's electronics Mecca in Silicon Valley, with its laid-back lifestyle but cutthroat competitive mentality. European governmental efforts at developing a computer industry are usually variations on attempts to re-create something resembling IBM, without taking into account the fact that it is not the large behemoths such as General Electric and Westinghouse, but the fleet-footed upstarts such as Apple, Amdahl, Intel, and Wang that have given IBM the greatest challenge. (To be sure, some of these firms have faced major business reversals.) By backing large establishment ventures, European governments seem to overlook this point. (Not coincidentally, several of these large government-backed manufacturers are also the main telecommunications equipment producers.) This policy has been due partly to a lack of alternatives. Successful engineers in large European countries tend to prefer the security of their employer, and potential entrepreneurs are not as confident of their ability to function as are those in the United States.

But most of all, it is the lack of capital availability that chokes off industrial development fueled by small, innovative firms. There is still only a very limited venture capital market in Western Europe, whereas in the United States it is an abundant source of equity funding for entrepreneurial developers. Western European banks are conservative, tend to do business with well-established companies, and demand greater security than a mere invention. They see their function primarily as that of lenders rather than as underwriters, even though in most European countries the functions of commercial banking and investment banking are not separate, as they are in the United States.

Europeans are self-defeatingly ingenious at finding reasons why the United States and Japan are more innovative in electronics than Europeans are. One frequent argument is that the large size of the domestic American market gives its firms advantages of economies of scale. But the Japanese domestic market is not that much bigger than those of the larger European countries, and is considerably smaller than the combined market of the European Economic Community. Furthermore, the economies-of-scale argument is much overdone, since it overlooks the dynamism of competition as a means to shift the entire cost curve downward rather than merely to move downward along a fixed cost curve. Americans, it is also maintained, are successful in innovation because of their large defense budget. The Japanese, at the same time, are considered to be successful because they do *not* have to spend resources on defense. Japan, it is said, has a high degree of innovation as a result of the destruction of its old industrial capacity in World War II. But the American prominence in high technology is based on its head start as the prosperous victor in World War II. Similarly, Japanese successes are attributed to that country's centralized governmental planning and disciplined work force, whereas for the United States the nonintervention of government and freewheeling firm structures are seen as the keys of success.

The once spectacular European growth rates have already become mediocre or stagnant. Unemployment and social tensions have risen. In many countries, the realization of the emergence of an economy of limits has not yet been integrated into political consciousness. At the same time, the United States, after a long period of stagnation, is in the midst of a technological renaissance.

Of course, European technology has had notable success stories and major achievements. For example, France has been successful in developing digital main exchanges, and the "Smart Card" has a great number of future opportunities. The Prestel videotex system in Britain has been a technological advance. Italian companies have been innovative in assembling robots and in software applications. A German company is a leader in the production of optical fibers. Overall, however, these developments have not been sufficient. The field of communications and electronics is a very fast track, and no one runs it faster than the Americans and Japanese. Although the product markets are varied enough to permit niches, this should not create the illusion of an overall success story.

U.S. TELECOMMUNICATIONS INVOLVEMENT IN EUROPE: EQUIPMENT AND SERVICES

In the equipment field, the primary recent change in American involvement in Europe is the emergence of AT&T as a major entrant in European markets, which is the result of deregulation in general and the AT&T divestiture in particular. For more than half a century, AT&T, despite being the largest telecommunications equipment manufacturer in the world, had no international presence, particularly in Western Europe, because of domestic U.S. restrictions.

The company's new strategy is still to have a low profile in Europe, at the same time aligning itself with European domestic interests. This is a realistic strategy in view of the barriers that any American company faces in European markets. AT&T has first linked itself with Philips, the Dutch electronics giant. Its second major involvement has been through the purchase of shares in Olivetti, the Italian office and small computer manufacturer.

So far, although AT&T's entry into Western Europe has not resulted in actual sales, the implications are threatening to European telecommunications equipment manufacturers. AT&T's technological know-how, its research capability through Bell Labs, as well as its vast economies of scale, can make it into a serious presence in any national market. Hence, its landing on European beaches gives European equipment manufacturers every incentive to push for protective measures. In this rivalry, the role of the government becomes still more central, through its roles as procurer of equipment, setter of standards, promoter of export markets, and facilitator of intra-European protectionism.

The clash of different policy approaches on the two sides of the Atlantic is particularly acute in the field of telecommunications *services*. Historically, U.S. policy in international telecommunications had been to carve up the market into distinct segments, each assigned to different kinds of carriers. The United States, however, has restructured the rules of the game radically within a short period, thus confronting European countries with the necessity of responding unwillingly to a new situation.

The U.S. end of international telecommunications services is made up of several market segments: domestic telephone carriers, domestic record carriers, domestic satellite carriers, international message toll service (MTS) carriers, international record carriers (IRCs), participants in international submarine cable consortia, and the U.S. carrier for international satellite communications (Comsat) in the context of the INTELSAT organization. Though in some instances AT&T participated in several of these market segments, generally speaking the international market was highly compartmentalized, and each submarket was subjected to specific rules. On the European side, things were much less complex. There, the typical arrangement was for the PTT authority to be the sole communications address, both domestically and internationally.

Historically, FCC regulation had not been particularly restrictive with respect to international communications rates. At the same time, the market segmentation just described has led to a lack of competition, as well as to substantial profit margins. This situation was largely unstable, perhaps partially because of the high profitability, and cracks began to appear. The artificial nature of the market segmentation became evident and led to policy responses within a relatively short time.

From the evidence, it seems clear that international transmission is highly profitable, particularly since the advent of communications satellites, which resulted in transmission costs fairly independent of distance. On the rate-setting side, market power was rarely controlled by the FCC, which did not consider it a priority and which did not have the instrumentation of meaningful rate of return regulation at hand. On the contrary, the FCC, through its policy of market segmentation, contributed to the problem by insulating potential competitors from one another.

Eventually the FCC and Congress recognized this and embarked, starting in late 1979, on reversing the course of previous policies and legislation. In a series of rulings in 1979 and 1980 (FCC 79–842; 80–523; 80–585), the FCC largely removed the dichotomy of voice and record carriage, and eliminated the rules prohibiting AT&T and the IRCs from entering one another's markets.

The International Record Carrier Competition Act (Public Law 97–130 of December 29, 1981) amended the Communications Act of 1934 to permit Western Union to engage in IRC service. At the same time, the act permitted the IRCs to provide domestic record service.

With respect to Comsat, the FCC (FCC 82–357) permitted Comsat to go beyond its role as a carriers' carrier and to provide service to customers directly. This was conditional upon a major restructuring of Comsat, which the FCC required. FCC 82–372 separates Comsat's unregulated competitive activities from those that are regulated.

The FCC also determined that it would limit, as far as possible, its role in the allocation of communications circuits between cable and satellites, and would rely instead on competition between those two transmission modes.

If the FCC was well on its way to permitting Comsat direct access to users, it was at the same time considering direct access of other carriers to INTELSAT, bypassing Comsat entirely. In its *Second Computer Inquiry* (77 FCC 2d 384 [1980]), the FCC did this by applying deregulation to international telecommunications as well. That decision allowed enhanced telecommunications services to go beyond "basic" unregulated transmission. In the *Telenet-Tymnet* decision (FCC 82–377), the FCC reaffirmed that the *Second Computer Inquiry* extended to international telecommunications services as well. This meant that enhanced communications services to other countries from the United States would not be subject to regulation of facilities or rate of return.

The next step in the logic of liberalization was for the FCC to reconsider its entire attitude toward INTELSAT by analogy with the U.S. "Open Skies" policy that had allowed domestic satellite competition since 1972. In the international sphere, matters started to come to a head when several private entrepreneurs applied for licenses from the FCC to operate privately owned commercial transatlantic satellite systems. Qualified approval for such competition came in a White House statement in late 1984.

Clearly, INTELSAT and its constituent organizations do not want to see their profits, both as users and shareholders of the INTELSAT consortium, being whittled down by competition. To that end they have enlisted the traditional cross-subsidy argument. In international garb, this argument says that the profits from the high-density transatlantic and North Pacific routes are needed in order to provide a subsidy for low-density traffic to and among Third World countries. But whether subsidies indeed offset monopoly profits so that the total system approximately realizes only normal profits is far from clear.

The question might also be raised as to why European PTTs, if they are mindful of the telecommunications needs of developing countries, cannot assist them by direct contributions in the form of equipment, expertise, or financial subsidies, or through lower communications tariffs for calls to those countries. What is probably of more concern to European PTTs is the threat that competitive transatlantic rates would pose to their own profitable international communications service. It should be noted, however, that services and tariffs recently introduced by INTELSAT address the needs of developing countries for dependable, low-cost communications links.

European countries pursue various defensive strategies against potential American satellite carriers. Two of these may be described as the up-link and down-link strategies. The aim of the up-link strategy is to prevent the FCC from granting a license to applicants from the United States or any other country. This is supported by the argument that under the terms of the INTELSAT treaty, member states have assigned to INTELSAT the monopoly over commercial international satellite telecommunications. The U.S. applicants counter this in two ways. Orion, one of the private U.S. satellite applicants, contends that the INTELSAT treaty covers only public switched communications and does not include private line leasing. The argument of International Satellite Inc. (ISI), a TRT subsidiary, is slightly different. That company plans to offer approximately 15 to 30% of its capacity for common-carrier service rather than exclusively leased lines. It maintains that the terms of the INTELSAT treaty prohibit only those rival systems that would cause "significant economic harm" to INTELSAT, and that its limited operations would not cause such harm, much in the same way that various regional satellite systems have invoked the same treaty clause.

The PTTs' down-link strategy is to prevent the down-link segment of satellite communications by eliminating the ability of satellite carriers to link with European countries. This strategy requires, in effect, a unified front by all European countries against an American beachhead. If that is impossible, the PTTs will attempt to prevent one country's being used as a transfer point to other European countries. As with other cartel-like agreements, they are only as strong as their weakest link. In this instance, it is far from clear whether all European countries would be willing to maintain discipline. The United Kingdom, given its general evolution toward liberalization of telecommunications and its privatization of British Telecom, may not go along over time. London is of such importance as an international telecommunications and service center that a British arrangement with Orion or similar companies would probably be a major blow to any united PTT front. Similarly, as in the case of tax havens, one could expect some European countries, particularly the smaller ones, to find it to their advantage to become international transmission hubs by permitting down-links from non-INTELSAT carriers. This then leaves, as a fallback position, the attempt to prevent the use of such countries as an entry point into the intra-European telecommunications network, a link that in effect would permit some "back door" liberalization.

It is not clear, however, whether limitations against retransmission would be supported by the European antitrust laws. When European countries tried, using CCITT and CEPT rules, to impose similar restrictions on the use of Great Britain as a telex hub by British telex bureaus, the European Commission, in an antitrust proceeding, resoundingly struck down these attempts as a violation of intra-European competitive rules.

INTELSAT also has at its disposal the economic weapon of economies of scale. In other words, it can deter Orion and ISI by offering services at a rate that would preempt the markets sought by potential entrants. This is in fact what appears to be happening. Comsat, whose stake in INTELSAT is considerable, has announced new high-speed data services and rate reductions for other services that can combat the proposed alternative offerings.

U.S. SERVICES DEREGULATION: EUROPEAN REACTIONS AND OPPORTUNITIES

Many complicating factors have now been mentioned that challenge the orderliness of the carefully nurtured international telecommunications regime. Once the distaste for this increased complexity has subsided, however, a situation of potential advantage to the PTTs reveals itself. Being the only address within their countries for AT&T, MCI and others, the PTTs are in a position of a monopsonist that can profitably play off rival American carriers against each other. This ability is known as "whipsawing," and it essentially entails bargaining for operating agreements that are the most advantageous to the PTTs.

In order to prevent this possibility, the FCC has since 1977 enforced a policy requiring that international settlement agreements be uniform for the same routes and that accounting and settlement arrangements be identical. In other words, the FCC officially enforces a cartel among IRCs on settlement agreements.

An instance of potential whipsawing that achieved much attention occurred when Nordtel (the intra-Scandinavian telecommunications body) and the Benelux countries invited all potential suppliers of data communications services to submit bids, and to include the division of accounting as part of their bids. American protectionist reaction was swift—for champions of liberalization—and the Europeans retreated, at least temporarily.

Historically, PTTs have not been particularly hospitable to new U.S. carriers. An extreme example is Japan, which has refused to have any agreement with Western Union, a new entrant in international record traffic. The company, however, has managed to undercut this Japanese policy by routing its traffic to Japan through another country. As a result, the Japanese are losing revenue of more than $1 million per year, according to Western Union (*Business Week,* October 24, 1983, 140–144). This example illustrates how difficult it has become, in an era of instant interlinkage with costs relatively insensitive to distance, to guard the ramparts of protectionism.

Similar and related problems include the use of value-added networks on a leased-line basis. In order to protect their revenues, European PTTs have strenuously opposed resale on leased lines, both domestically and internationally. In the case of value-added services, the problem is that their provision cannot be neatly separated from resale.

Value-added services such as GTE Telenet or Tymnet provide packet switching, for which international private lines are leased. Subscribers to these value-added networks pay for their use. In effect, therefore, some resale or shared use has taken place, since, presumably, the users would otherwise have employed some more conventional form of telecommunications from the PTTs.

With the *Second Computer Inquiry,* enhanced communications services were withdrawn from FCC regulation. For AT&T, such deregulated services were allowed if they were provided by a fully separated subsidiary. Beginning in 1983, enhanced international services were deregulated by the FCC. The commission did not determine the treatment of international resale services, however.

The European PTTs view all this as anathema. In retaliation, they have threatened to employ methods such as the following: disallowing leased lines altogether; disallowing all those that are connected to some form of switch at the opposite end; or, most likely, changing the tariff structure from a flat rate to a usage-sensitive rate, with the possibility of setting rates so as to make the usage of leased lines unattractive.

Interestingly enough, however, the large-scale deregulation of enhanced communications services in the United States would present yet another opportunity to European entities and PTTs by allowing them to enter the American market freely, through U.S. subsidiaries, using existing Comsat and INTELSAT links. This could be done without additional international negotiations or agreements. The asymmetry of this possibility, when compared to the difficulties put in the way of the American carriers trying to enter in the opposite direction, is striking. Such an imbalance would surely evoke protectionist measures in the United States of the same kind to which the United States objects in Europe.

MISCELLANEOUS U.S.–EUROPEAN CONFLICT AREAS

One important concern in international telecommunications is the way in which European PTTs utilize American long-distance carriers for communication originating in Europe. It is one thing for an American customer to designate MCI, GTE, Sprint, or AT&T as the carrier of choice, ultimately routing the call to its European destination. When a European customer wishes to call an American city, however, the choice as to which U.S. long-distance carrier will transmit the call and realize the subsequent revenue is in the hands of the PTT. Until now, all voice traffic has been routed over AT&T. But how should the PTTs react to a competitive offering? For the PTTs, the monitoring and accounting for dealings with multiple American correspondents is a headache they would prefer not to incur, although it may become easily bearable if it provides a chance to drive a better bargain in the United States.

One possibility, of course, would be to permit the European users to indicate in some fashion which American long-distance carrier they would prefer. An example would be the use of several country codes, rather than one, for the United States, with a different code assigned to each U.S. international carrier. There are a number of technical objections to this proposal, none of them particularly convincing in view of the current sophistication of communications technology. Another objection is that multiple codes would impose an extra cost on the PTTs. This extra cost, however, could be compensated by the American carriers, who would thus gain access. The primary problem, one suspects, is that the introduction of such a choice of communications services, together with the possibility of advertising campaigns by various American carriers directed at European customers, would drive home the fact that network competition is possible today. For these reasons, it is unlikely that this kind of consumer choice will be granted to European users in the foreseeable future. Instead, present negotiations center on the ways in which the PTTs might allocate their U.S.–bound traffic by choosing among AT&T and its competitors. One way would be to negotiate market shares in advance; another would be to have a fixed share-allocation formula. The most logical approach might well be to allocate American-bound traffic to American carriers in the same proportion as those carriers supply traffic to Europe.

Another potentially destabilizing development would be for AT&T, newly awakened in its international involvement generally, to bypass Comsat or INTELSAT. The reverberations would be of such magnitude that these organizations would seek to protect themselves politically and economically. Despite pressure to contain the system as it is, it is clear that a potential disequilibrium situation exists. Thus it will be difficult to maintain intact the narrow funnel through Comsat and INTELSAT, particularly since the alternative of a transatlantic cable is available to AT&T.

In addition to challenges posed by multiple U.S. carriers for Europe–U.S. traffic, and by potential satellite bypass incentives for AT&T internationally, there is a third problem area—that of information itself, and its processing. Briefly stated, on-line data information systems have emerged in the United States in response to new market opportunities. Once these systems are established, it is relatively inexpensive to service additional customers in European countries. American on-line data bases have thus achieved a very strong presence in European markets. This situation is opposed by the European suppliers of similar services and by their governments, who fear information and processing dependence on the United States.

These information-flow problems involve, in the first instance, the nature of protection of national sovereignty. For example, the French government has expressed its concern with the use of American econometric forecasting and planning models that could be used to forecast French economic trends, since this could presumably give Americans access to, and some control over, confidential French economic data. Most of the concern, however, lies in the area of privacy protection. Various European countries have enacted data privacy rules ensuring the privacy of data collected on an individual and stored electronically. The internationalization of data flows, however, makes it possible for data to be transported across national boundaries, providing a loophole in the national protection of data privacy.

From the beginning, however, there was a trade protectionist element to regulation and legislation ostensibly aimed at preservation of national sovereignty and individual privacy. Domestic computer manufacturers and data enterprises could benefit greatly from requirements that would restrict the flow of data in ways that would make domestic processing necessary.

A fourth motive for transborder data flow (TBDF) restrictions, in addition to sovereignty, privacy, and trade protectionism, involves the desire of PTTs to shore up their monopolistic positions by strengthening their new alliance—one that could otherwise not have been expected—with the emerging electronic data processing industries. It is clear that TBDF can be effectively maintained and monitored only if there is a firm control by the state over the conduits, namely through the PTTs.

EQUIPMENT SALES OPPORTUNITIES FOR EUROPE PRESENTED BY U.S. DEREGULATION

The liberalization of the American telecommunications industry and the divestiture of AT&T have provided Europe with opportunities in the American telecommunications equipment market. The AT&T divestiture frees the Bell operating companies (BOCs) to buy equipment from other suppliers. Previously, the BOCs had been largely dependent on Western Electric, an AT&T subsidiary, for equipment procurement.

American technical standards are somewhat different from those in

Europe, and thus European equipment cannot simply be shipped to the United States. After appropriate modifications, however, the vast American market could be opened to European manufacturers, if quality and price were found acceptable by American companies and consumers.

Most European manufacturers have been slow to examine their export opportunities to the United States, reflecting the cautious way in which those firms do business. One cannot expect them to permanently shy away from the huge American market, however. The potential opening of the American market is some of the best news that European manufacturers must have had in a long time. After all, the other European countries' markets are largely closed to them. In the developing world, deliveries to oil-exporting countries have declined after the initial large orders were placed. This reflects the decline in infrastructural investment in OPEC countries generally, following the drop in the world price of oil. In other Third World markets, funds available for telecommunications are more meager, and the technology ordered need not incorporate the state of the art. Indeed, the traditional electromechanical switches are probably more advantageous for these countries, since they can be serviced domestically. Moreover, in the more advanced of the developing countries, domestic equipment manufacturers have been established, and their governments have provided them with the same protection from foreign competition that is enjoyed by European manufacturers. Thus, the free international telecommunications market for sophisticated equipment is quite limited. In fact, the largest such market is now in the United States. Hence, ironically, many of the strongest advocates of protectionist policy in telecommunications procurement will now seek their fortunes in the newly liberalized U.S. environment.

As in the case of services, however, this asymmetry entails a contradiction that may be at the root of the uneasiness with which European firms consider entry into the U.S. market. It takes no great imagination to expect strong American pressure of reciprocity on European countries. Hence, the invitation to enter the American market is in fact a two-edged sword. It bears with it the obligation of entrants to reduce or eliminate restrictions on entry into their own protected markets.

CONCLUSION

American and European policies have diverged in recent years. Technological change has reduced the extent of a core natural monopoly, and this has led in the United States to entrepreneurial initiatives, a restructuring of the industry, and a reduction of government involvement. In Europe (except for the United Kingdom), similar underlying technical developments have led to a stiffening of the protective coalition of the PTT system.

Telecommunications policy is increasingly being presented as industrial policy, that is, as a central component in developing an advanced electronics industry. This strategy, however, has yielded impressive results neither in technology nor in telecommunications services. Given the rapidity of developments, the orderly pace of centralized government decision making has been constraining. The insiders' tendency to rely on established firms has been similarly conservative. In the United States, the communications and information sector has opened rapidly to new players. But in most European countries the defensive posture of the inside coalition has been strong and effective. Given the breadth of its support, it is likely to prevail for some time, even if it is tempered on occasion. In such an environment, more government-sponsored initiatives are likely to share the fate of the Paris Center for Computer Science and Human Resources described at the beginning of this chapter: an ambitious substitution of symbolism for a fundamental economic framework that can accommodate change and technological dynamism. And while this divergence of telecommunications policies runs its course, the United States and Western Europe, partners at the two ends of the transatlantic communications pipeline, will find it increasingly more difficult and yet unavoidable to translate the technical ease of communications into institutional coordination.

At this time, the liberalization of U.S. telecommunications, though partly a threat to the European status quo, is also an opportunity for the export of hardware and services, and for a monopsonistic bargaining position. Yet these opportunities also undermine the status quo through their demonstration effect and their asymmetry to the possibilities U.S. firms have of operating in Europe. More than economic theories or political pressure, the dynamics of business opportunities for Europeans may set off a partial liberalization to entry of U.S. telecommunications firms, and a softening of the divergence in telecommunications on the two sides of the Atlantic.

REFERENCES

"And a Prosperous New Year." *The Economist,* December 24, 1983, 76.

"Can AT&T Compete in Long Distance?" *Fortune,* April 16, 1984, 112–116.

Etheridge, James. "Center of Controversy." *Datamation* 240 (June 1983): 31–34.

Financial Times. World Telecommunications Supplement. October 24, 1983.

"La Guerre Mondiale de la Communication." *Le Monde*, January 11–14, 1984.

Nora, Simon, and Alain Minc. *The Computerization of Society*. Cambridge, Mass.: MIT Press, 1980.

Organisation for Economic Cooperation and Development. *Telecommunications: Pressures and Policies for Change.* Paris: OECD, 1983.

U.S. General Accounting Office. "FCC Needs to Monitor a Changing International Telecommunications Market." *GAO/RECD,* March 14, 1983, 86–92.

Twelve

Regulating Telecommunications, Information, and the Media: An Agenda for Future Comparative Research

Marcellus S. Snow

Compiling an agenda for future research was a major aspect of the National Science Foundation grant underlying this book, as well as a specific mandate to the participants in the workshop it funded. This final chapter has as its goal to distill from the written contributions of the authors, as well as from their 3 days of lively and often provocative verbal interchange at the Washington, D.C., workshop, those topics and questions that emerged as the most vital to a clearer understanding of telecommunications regulation in the industrialized countries.

Some of the agenda items to be listed and discussed have been treated extensively in one or more of the chapters of this book. An example is the interaction of the political, legislative, and philosophical outlook and institutions of a country with its regulatory apparatus, a topic touched on by Youichi Ito, Charles Jonscher, Gordon Kaiser, and Jean-Paul Voge and discussed at length by Roger Noll. Other issues cropped up in only one or two chapters, often quite casually, and subsequently engaged the interest of the other writers. Examples here are Charles Jonscher's distinction between service and facilities competition, and Don Lamberton's discussion of organizational obsolescence and inertia in telecommunications. A third category of items entered the agenda for future research only after verbal discussions at the workshop, not having surfaced in any of the chapters of this book. These topics include the amenability of "technical" solutions (of a legal, economic, or engineering variety) to the political process; costs and benefits of regulation; and reflections on the difficulty of organizing and financing transnational, collaborative, comparative research in telecommunications and information policy.

Whatever their source, topics and questions deemed important for future research constitute the balance of this chapter. The next section presents a synoptic classification of regulatory trends in all seven countries as a basis for formulating the research program. The section that follows contains the individual agenda items. After this, there is a section that summarizes and expands slightly on the research agenda. The rough division of labor between Chapter 1 and the present chapter is this: the conclusions reached in the sections of Chapter 1 that deal with telecommunications regulation and cross-country comparisons are my own, intended as a backdrop for the body of the text. Those presented in this chapter flow from the ideas of the contributors and from the outcome of their verbal interchange.

A TAXONOMY OF REGULATORY APPROACHES: BACKGROUND FOR A RESEARCH AGENDA

Deregulation of the telecommunications sector in the United States and Canada, as the chapters by Alan Baughcum and Gordon Kaiser have shown, has been broad, swift, and dramatic during the past 15 years. Developments in the United States, culminating in the divestiture of AT&T in 1984, have usually been followed by analogous actions in Canada with a lag of several years. Virtually no technological lag, however, has been apparent.

The remaining five countries examined in this book can be analyzed into three additional classifications with respect to their reaction to deregulatory trends in North America.

1. *Privatization and demonopolization* (Japan, United Kingdom). In both Great Britain and Japan, as the papers of Charles Jonscher and Youichi Ito indicate, the major domestic carrier has been privatized, either partially or entirely; it has been subjected to some measure of competition as well. The changes in Japan have been more dramatic than those in Great Britain, both absolutely—full versus partial privatization, and much more complete competition, including some from overseas—and relatively, given the traditionally slower pace of administrative evolution and reform in Japan. Both countries see their new telecommunications regulatory legislation in part as a means of channeling the efficiency gains from competition into building the infrastructure for further informatization of their economies. The sources of these developments are different in each country, as we have seen. In Great Britain, the dynamic of adoption came from the government's political–ideological belief in economic competition and in reducing the size and influence of the public sector. The Japanese

legislation, by contrast, emerged in the context of an interministerial conflict between the Ministry of International Trade and Industry and the Ministry of Posts and Telecommunications. MITI, the views of which prevailed, favored a microeconomic, industry-based approach, while MPT had broader macroeconomic and sociocultural goals in mind.

2. *State activism to foster cooperation and decentralization* (France). France appears very much as a case *sui generis,* with its continuing stress on the role of the state in telecommunications. There is, to be sure, an analogy with Australia, which, like France, had a recent shift to the left in its national government and does not appear particularly favorable toward greater market forces in the telecommunications sector. For its part, as Jean-Paul Voge has shown, the French government has interpreted its 1981 electoral mandate as a charge to decentralize French telecommunications and broadcasting; in addition, it seeks, where possible, to promote cooperative rather than competitive solutions to problems in those sectors. Many smaller European countries seem to be following the French lead in maintaining the role of state activism in telecommunications. This approach has been described by Voge as a "socioeconomic equilibrium between competition and cooperation, and between uniformity and diversity." The coming of age of ISDN networks, for example, is seen as promoting less rather than more diversity, and a greater rather than a smaller role for PTTs. Regional initiatives, however, are being promoted by new broadcasting legislation, again in the unique context of the historically overcentralized French state.

3. *Extensive study with little change of the PTT's role* (Australia, West Germany). As the chapters by Don Lamberton and Karl-Heinz Neumann indicate, both Australia and West Germany have undertaken extensive, detailed studies of regulatory options in their telecommunications, information, and media sectors. These have generally urged more competition with the dominant carriers, but have not gone so far as to suggest their privatization. In addition, new services important to business users, such as resale of circuits, have been proposed. Nevertheless, due partly to recent changes of government in those countries, such proposals have not been translated into political consciousness or entered the legislative process. Furthermore, the advent of the domestic satellite system in Australia and of country-wide cabling in West Germany have become politically controversial and have thereby decelerated the pace of change in telecommunications regulation in those countries.

Having categorized each of the seven countries in terms of the pace and direction of its regulatory policy, we turn now to a summary of individual trends deemed worthy of continuing attention in those countries.

AN AGENDA FOR FUTURE RESEARCH: PARTICULARS

Services versus Facilities Competition; Horizontal versus Vertical Competition

Charles Jonscher, in Chapter 7, distinguishes between what he calls horizontal competition—pitting different firms in a given information industry against each other—and vertical competition, which occurs among firms in different industries, typically telecommunications and data processing. He asks as a matter of policy whether the "key axis of competition" is (in an American context) between AT&T and its telecommunications rival MCI, or between AT&T and its data processing rival IBM. Thus, government policy regarding competition becomes at once industrial policy (given horizontal competition) and technology policy (given vertical competition).

A related notion is that of competition in services as opposed to competition in facilities. The current debate regarding competition with INTELSAT by private carriers on the North Atlantic satellite routes (see Snow 1984a, 1985) offers an example. INTELSAT has announced its opposition to facilities competition, arguing that it would result in wasteful duplication. It is prepared, however, to lease its own transponders to potential service competitors for resale to end users. Facilities competition, in Jonscher's terminology, would be horizontal—between two firms offering the same components of an integrated service package. Service competition, in contrast, would be vertical—firms offering different parts of a given end-to-end service package. Carl Christian von Weizsäcker defines as "rate arbitrage" a particular kind of service competition involving value-added activity.

The arresting simplicity and logic of this classification lead naturally to the question whether it might be of further use analytically and conceptually. Little work to date has done justice to, or even taken account of, this promising distinction, and it is an obvious candidate for consideration in future research.

Decentralization versus Deregulation; Cooperation versus Competition

In Chapter 5, Jean-Paul Voge asked whether decentralization of a telecommunications administration could accomplish some of the objectives usually reserved for deregulation or privatization. In doing so he drew on his own contributions to the considerable literature on economic and information aspects of organizational complexity. He also stressed what is perhaps the strongest argument against competition, namely the presence of unexhausted economies of scale and scope, given the smaller range of demand and output in European countries than in the United States. Indeed, the typical size of the seven postdivestiture regional Bell companies in the United States is on a par with the market size of the larger European countries.[1] To what extent can decentralizing a monopoly carrier, while maintaining its monopoly, accomplish what deregulation and demonopolization are supposed to do? Some of these tasks are (1) to increase the variety of services and responsiveness of civil servants vis-à-vis the user community; (2) to reduce costs and align them with prices; (3) to promote technological progress; and (4) to ease the transition of an advanced industrial economy from a base of manufacturing to one of information.

The issue of cooperation as an alternative to competition is related. An important question is the kind of cooperation (or decentralization) being proposed. A number of conceptual frameworks suggest themselves. One could take the idea of a cooperative in its technical, economic sense, as INTELSAT does, by forming a cooperative of owners and users in which ownership quotas are periodically updated to reflect each member's share of recent past usage.[2] Another outlook that might be appropriate is the "social economy" approach that draws on the early English cooperative literature. The German variant of this school, *Gemeinwirtschaft,* offers various arguments in favor of retaining state ownership, operation, and entrepreneurship of public utilities (see Thiemeyer 1983). Some of those arguments are surprisingly similar to the neoclassical justification for maintaining a natural but unsustainable monopoly free from competition, since such competition would demonstrably increase the overall cost of production to consumers (see Snow 1984b). Finally, Jean-Paul Voge's discussion of star versus tree models in organizational structures makes explicit how cooperative modes of behavior might be introduced within telecommunications enterprises, if not necessarily among them.

Causal Relationships between Regulatory Form and Technology

Endogenizing the institutional form of regulation, that is, making it a variable in a complex model instead of taking it as externally given, was seen as a major task of future research. Thus, although it is clear that technology affects the choice of regulatory form, as Don Lamberton has asserted (with an emphasis on information technology in Australia that is by and large imported), it is also true that the choice of regulatory form often affects the development of a technology. Roger Noll's example of how cable television regulation affects cable technology in the American setting has already been cited. It has also been argued that the regulatory arrangements now governing INTELSAT—by establishing a global system and globally averaged pricing rather than a network of regional systems with disaggregated pricing—led to a technology that is less attuned to the needs of individual regions and of the developing countries in general.

From a theoretical point of view, there is no difficulty involved in this kind of bidirectional causality; indeed, it contributes to the richness of the analytical model chosen and is one of the main justifications for a system of simultaneous econometric equations. The challenge comes in specifying the equations so as to capture the underlying causal mechanisms most effectively.

Technical and Political Qualifications of Neoclassical Welfare Analysis

Research such as that of Neumann, Schweizer, and von Weizsäcker (1983), using neoclassical welfare theory, demonstrates the considerable superiority of "optimal" pricing regimes—such as Ramsey pricing—to the politically determined tariff structures imposed by most PTT monopolies. Yet several qualifications to this kind of approach were noted by the authors of the book, and their discussion at the workshop was sufficient to suggest that more research needs to be conducted on the validity of the assumptions, methodology, and conclusions of cost–benefit approaches to telecommunications pricing.

The first variety of objections might be termed technical. At least three different variants of these technical objections emerged. First, there is hesitation about the dependability of the underlying cost and production data and the consequent accuracy of the cost and production functions that can be derived from such data. Communications carriers usually have strategic incentives to distort or conceal costs from the regulatory authorities; and even with the best of intentions, modern cost accounting technology is still struggling with conceptual and practical difficulties in the measurement and particularly the allocation of telecommunications costs. Second, externalities—economic relationships not captured in the pricing mechanism—qualify any conclusions of welfare analysis (see Leff 1984). An example of an externality in telecommunications is the so-called network effect: Each new subscriber to a network increases the value of network access to existing subscribers, but this is seldom reflected in the price mechanism. A third source of technical reservations derives from social and perhaps psychological considerations. These emerged in Don Lamberton's chapter on Australia: Many Australians apparently prefer the security and predictability of the price structure under ministerial monopoly to the lower but generally more unpredictable and rapidly changing prices that tend to result from competition.

Political qualifications of neoclassical welfare analysis, as opposed to the technical qualifications listed above, touch on concerns raised by Roger Noll in Chapter 3. These involve the ability of tightly organized groups of potential "losers" to frustrate any political transition to a regulatory and pricing regime that would increase aggregate individual welfare. "Gainers" are by contrast often poorly organized and have a more diffuse or marginal interest in change. Eli Noam, in Chapter 11, has characterized many of these well-organized "losers" as members of the "postal–industrial complex" that helps the European PTTs to support the status quo. Carl Christian von Weizsäcker refers in Chapter 2 to "well-known compensation principles in economics" by which "it is possible to compensate the losses out of the gains of the winners and thereby to make everybody better off." Such qualifications to conventional cost–benefit analysis are an intriguing but certainly difficult challenge to be investigated as an exercise in applied political economy; they will arise in connection with other research agenda items as well.

Effects of U.S. Deregulation on PTTs in Other Countries

Eli Noam's analysis of this topic helped the authors identify it as an important item for future research. For example, the asymmetry of structure and policies on the two sides of the Atlantic has caused conflicts, such as opposition by European PTTs to U.S. resale of leased lines in order to protect their revenues. Despite these potential difficulties, however, the deregulated American environment allows new opportunities for entry by subsidiaries of European PTTs in both service and equipment markets. Jean-Paul Voge's chapter has outlined the breadth and activities of the French PTT's many subsidiaries, for example. Yet there is a danger that in the long run, the U.S. Congress will insist on the reciprocity of such access. Youichi Ito's account of recent Japanese legislation indicates the depth of the American resolve to be allowed access to the newly deregulated Japanese telecommunications environment. It seems reasonable to predict similar American efforts to obtain access to European telecommunications markets as they are opened to domestic and perhaps European competition.

Innovation versus Adaptation; "Service at any Cost"

Don Lamberton touched on these two related topics in the unique setting of Australia and in the very broad context of the information sector of the economy, of which telecommunications, broadcasting, and the newer electronic media are proper subsets. The novelty and insight of his observations induced the authors to list this complex of issues among those on the agenda for future research.

"Service at any cost" basically reflects the predominance of engineering over economic considerations. Innovation, in the context of a developed country like Australia that is nonetheless underpopulated and heavily dependent on imported technology, is tantamount to extensive and generally costly reliance on foreign sources. The alternative to innovation from abroad is adaptation at home, and Lamberton sees the latter as a cost-effective alternative approach to providing the technology appropriate to the Australian case.

The priority of engineering over economic considerations, as well as the preference for innovation rather than adaptation, seem to be departures from the neoclassical norm of cost minimization. In the Australian context, these preferences are similar to the already noted appeal of higher but stable prices (and costs) under regulation as opposed to lower but unpredictable prices (and costs) under deregulation.

The persistence of such departures from cost-minimizing technologies and regulatory arrangements intrigued the authors of this book and prompted them to put this topic on the agenda for future research. It is clear that this is a difficult research problem that will embrace many of the social sciences, for it involves the investigation of preferences arising from social and psychological as well as economic needs.

Causes of Organizational Obsolescence and Inertia in Telecommunications

Once more, Don Lamberton's description of the Australian case provided material from a unique setting that was seen to have quite broad significance and implications—the reasons for obsolescence and inertia in bureaucratic organizations dealing with telecommunications. A more direct way to pose the question is to ask why PTTs generally tend to oppose change, particularly deregulation of various kinds. One possible reply is that the civil servants in a PTT ministry perceive their own perquisites and careers as threatened by any change, especially a change to a more competitive environment in which market forces rather than bureaucratic fiat determine the pace and direction of innovation.

Bits and pieces of this theme emerge in other chapters of this book as well. Jean-Paul Voge, for example, mentioned the economic and information aspects of increasing organizational complexity; and diseconomies of large organizations are a phenomenon familiar in both theory and application within the neoclassical framework. In addition, Charles Jonscher notes the galvanizing effect that the threat of competition from the Mercury consortium has had on civil servants in the British Post Office; apparently they have become more efficient and responsive to users' needs. Finally, we have noted Eli Noam's analysis of the power of PTT organizations in Western Europe, whether by design or otherwise, to orchestrate segments of society fearing that they have more to lose than to gain from telecommunications deregulation. These combine to form a transnational "postal–industrial complex" to preserve the status quo. As he noted, this constellation of political, economic, and social forces—embracing the trade unions, intellectuals, the elderly, large contractors, the poor, the political left, and those in rural areas—has been by and large successful in doing so.

If we view organizational obsolescence and inertia as a form of economic inefficiency—in other words, as a failure to minimize costs—then a number of promising avenues of approach suggest themselves. The recent literature on contestability of market structure (see Baumol, Panzar, and Willig 1982), for example, stresses the ability of the mere threat of competitive market entry, as opposed to its reality, to induce efficiency or optimizing behavior on the part of the incumbent firm, given certain assumptions such as costless entry into and exit from the market in question. In addition, earlier seminal insights by Averch and Johnson (1962) indicate how rate-of-return regulation can distort a monopolist's investment incentives toward inappropriately capital-intensive behavior. Accordingly, as entry into telecommunications becomes liberalized, it might well be expected—and already seems to have been confirmed in the British case, at least by casual observation—that obsolescence and inertia on the part of PTTs and their employees will decrease, and greater cost-minimizing (optimizing) behavior will be induced. Whether this outcome can be predicted by a model specified with sufficient scientific rigor and verisimilitude, and whether it has indeed occurred as a matter of empirical fact, are questions well suited to a future research agenda.

The Interaction of Legislative and Regulatory Structures and Philosophies with the Outcome of the Regulatory Process

This research item on various interactions arose directly from the chapter by Roger Noll and its subsequent discussion at the research workshop. To illustrate the relationship between economic and institutional considerations, it will be recalled that he posited a diagram with "institutional ease of entry" (ranging from "none" to "no control") on the vertical axis and "organizational structure" (reflecting degree of oligopoly as well as degree of attenuation of public control, and ranging from "competitive private industry" to "public ministerial monopoly") on the horizontal axis. Most of the world, he stated, was still near a point far to the right on the horizontal axis (i.e., near public ministerial monopoly with no entry allowed). Recent events, such as the AT&T divestiture in the United States and the telecommunications legislation in Great Britain and Japan, had moved certain telecommunications entities in a northeasterly direction on the diagram, toward less entry control and less organizational rigidity.

Four different theoretical perspectives were proposed in Roger Noll's chapter, and it will be instructive to review and comment on them now. The first, normative welfare economics, has been cited and occasionally found wanting in the research agenda items already discussed in this chapter. Efficiency, either that of the engineer or of the economist, is the major consideration here, although tradeoffs with subjective notions of equity are often explicitly recognized. Each country can be assumed to have its own preferred point along such a tradeoff, although tradeoffs are not cardinally comparable across countries. Thus the linkage with subjective ideas of equity offers the possibility of some interaction with the political system, although the nature or structure of this interaction is not specified.

The second perspective is statist theories, based on such diverse authorities as Karl Marx, Max Weber, and Talcott Parsons. Once more there is no explicit linkage from the economy to the state. The objective of the state is taken to be the channeling of growth so as not to be internally disruptive, and the enhancement of its power in the international arena. In telecommunications, a statist question might be the extent to which industries benefiting from network expansion help or hurt the power structure of the state. The statist perspective is dominant among European social scientists.

In the third approach, pluralist theory, the influence of the Chicago school predominates. In this view, policy evolution is seen as the outcome of interaction among persons and groups; the stakes of different groups, as well as the political pressures that they exert, must be measured to determine the outcome. According to Roger Noll's perspective, the pluralist paradigm essentially sees government as a black box mediating between the forces acting on it and the policy outcome it produces. He views pluralist theory as a model of policy determination rather than of regulation per se; it is the dominant mode of thought in the United States and to a lesser extent in West Germany.

In terms of a framework for future comparative research on telecommunications policy, the contributors to this book agree, by and large, with Noll's view that institutional theory, the fourth approach, is the most promising. In this framework, "political institutions matter" and "can be regarded as exogenous for short-term policy" (see Noll 1983; Noll and Owen 1983). Furthermore, the details of the political system and its functioning are not conveniently isolated in a conceptual black box. Figure 3.2, for example, illustrates the diagrammatic relationship between the degree of legislative power on the vertical axis (ranging from very little, as in a parliamentary system, to autonomy of legislation, as in the U.S. Congress) and method of election of parliamentarians on the horizontal axis (ranging from nationwide proportional representation, as in the Netherlands and Israel, to single-member districts elected by a plurality, as in the United Kingdom).

The authors generally agree that data of this nature are important in that they indicate the pressure points at which issues are brought to bear:

The institutional approach makes explicit the structures by which policy guidelines become policy outcomes. In some countries, for example, there is essentially no "intermediation" in this process, whether in the United Kingdom (with its direct connection between parliamentarians and civil servants) or in the "corporatism" of smaller European countries and Japan, where the government itself structures the incentives necessary to bring the private partners to an understanding. West Germany exhibits a modest amount of intermediation in its broadcasting legislation and environmental courts. More structured intermediation is to be found in the proceduralism of health and safety regulation in the United States. As in the case previously cited regarding the two-way causality between regulatory form and technology, the contributors agree that the kind of intermediation examined in an institutional framework should be considered endogenous rather than as exogenously given.

Two final examples illustrate the wealth of detail available to a model that endogenizes and describes the political process and does not confine it to a conceptual black box. The first is the allocation of resources for staff, budget, and infrastructure to regulatory bodies. Such bodies might be vested with broad powers but at the same time be unable to exercise them effectively because of lack of staff, particularly when confronted by the generally much larger and more expert staffs of the entities they regulate. Second, the recruitment, professional conditions, and socialization of policy makers vary considerably and importantly from country to country and should be investigated in greater depth. The presence or absence of a "best and brightest" public-service tradition, with or without elite training schools for top civil servants, is a significant aspect of that variation.

Political Viability and Amenability to Implementation of "Technically" Optimal Regulatory Regimes

While optimization within a framework of technical constraints is most often associated with the analytical mode of neoclassical welfare economics, reasonable facsimiles of such "technical" welfare analysis are also possible within the paradigms of other disciplines, such as engineering, law, and communications theory. Using as examples the chapters of this book, it might be said that the country treatments of Alan Baughcum, Don Lamberton, and Karl-Heinz Neumann use an economic mode of exposition; those of Youichi Ito and Jean-Paul Voge draw on communication and information theory; Charles Jonscher's employs an engineering framework; and that of Gordon Kaiser has a legal orientation. Each contributor examines the extent to which both the present and any possible future regulatory regime could maximize some conception of overall social welfare.

Upon reflection and discussion, however, the contributors became aware that they had neglected important questions about the nature of the political forces affecting any transition from a situation of lower social welfare to one of higher social welfare, whatever the technical measure or disciplinary outlook used to determine those welfare levels. The concern that emerged, and that is to be posed to future researchers, might be phrased as follows: Could such "technical" solutions (e.g., "optimal" pricing, network optimization, maximization of information flow, design of regulatory statutes), even if implemented by a benevolent and omniscient philosoper-king, (1) function as well as theory predicts; and (2) be accommodated by a plausible transition path into the political process, even if those solutions did operate at a technically acceptable level? This question impinges in turn on the nature and organization of the political forces favoring and opposing a change from the status quo. Let us assume for the sake of exposition that overall social welfare is in fact increased by such a change.

This book is not wholly without discussion of the political nuances of the transition path mentioned above. Eli Noam, for example, notes the heterogeneous but powerful nexus of forces opposed to regulatory change in Western European countries. Carl Christian von Weizsäcker suggests in Chapter 2 that introducing competition with the PTT could be made more politically feasible by requiring competitors to pay an access fee for connection to the PTT's network. The fee would be set at a level that would limit the market share of competing firms to a predetermined percentage. Roger Noll investigates several dimensions of political organization and activity that impinge on the regulatory process by which such transitions occur. Youichi Ito examines the subtleties of the jurisdictional battle between two ministries of the Japanese government. Jean-Paul Voge calls attention to unique political and historical factors in contemporary France that have nurtured a consensus for decentralization rather than deregulation of telecommunications in that country. Yet, by and large, there was a feeling that this important complex of issues had not been addressed sufficiently.

Existing political theory offers a framework for analysis (see, for example, Olson 1982). It posits that any potential change with concentrated costs and diffuse benefits will lose to the status quo. An example is the issue of telephone access charges in the United States, the implementation of which was first frustrated and then delayed, presumably on behalf of the minority of lower-income individuals for whom the costs of higher telephone access charges would outweigh the benefits of lower long-distance rates. Those benefiting, by contrast, from higher access charges—as part of the overall realignment of costs with prices in telecommunications services—had a more diffuse distribution of benefits and were not as willing or able to represent themselves politically.

Changes with concentrated benefits and diffuse costs, by contrast, can often be implemented; examples include the case of airline deregulation in the United States, a broadly bipartisan effort that began in the mid-1970s and was one of the first major victories of neoclassical welfare analysis in the political arena.

What is the nature of the costs and benefits associated with telecommunications deregulation in industrialized countries? Which are diffuse and which are concentrated, and how are potential gainers and losers organized? Do total benefits of change outweigh total costs, and how are such costs to be measured and discounted? What is the distributional pattern of benefits and costs? Can taxes or subsidies from gainers partly offset the burdens of losers, and if so, how efficiently? Many of these questions have been posed in the broader context of cost–benefit analysis but have yet to be addressed with sufficient focus and rigor in the telecommunications sector.

Social and Macroeconomic Aspects of Telecommunications Regulation

The economist's approach to telecommunications has generally been from the microeconomic standpoint of industrial organization and regulatory theory. As a consequence, the interaction of this important sector with the economy as a whole has received little attention. Youichi Ito's analysis, for example, highlights this bias in the case of Japan. MITI, with its microeconomic "industrial policy" approach favored by economists, was able to prevail against MPT, which had a broader view of the telecommunications sector, whether as part of the economy as a whole or more generally in its interaction with society at large.

Two recent exceptions to this general trend point the way for future research into the macroeconomic implications of the telecommunications sector. First, initial work has been done on the effect of business cycles on telecommunications activity, and vice versa. The second example has already been mentioned: that of the broader information sector in the economy at large. The extraordinary attention focused on telecommunications, far out of proportion to its purely quantitative significance in the gross national product of industrial countries, derives to a considerable extent from its crucial role in maintaining an infrastructure for the larger information sector of which it is a part. Information, in turn, is now known to be replacing manufacturing as the principal activity of the late-twentieth-century world economy, at least in the advanced industrial democracies discussed in this volume. We have already noted Porat's (1977) pioneering work in identifying this sector and its influence. In addition, Youichi Ito in Chapter 9 discusses the establishment by Japanese scholars of the "information society" school, which attempts an even broader synthesis of telecommunications and information with the society as a whole. Finally, Don Lamberton's discussion of Australia is perhaps the most explicitly focused on the links of the information sector with the macroeconomy.

Nonetheless, the contributors recognized the need for more examination of macroeconomic aspects of telecommunications and information. They realized the need to extend and supplement the industrial organization and regulatory paradigm in order to provide a suitably broad conceptual framework.

Challenges in Organizing and Financing Comparative Research in Telecommunications and Information Policy

A good deal of sociocultural reflection took place among the contributors to this book about obstacles to organizing and financing transnational, collaborative, comparative research in telecommunications and information policy. Strictly speaking, this is not part of the research agenda, but concerns instead the conditions under which it would be necessary for any such research to be carried out. Because the authors expressed views on this topic that were quite uniform and strongly held, however, it seems appropriate to include them at the end of the agenda for future research questions that has been presented in this concluding chapter.

Four particular concerns are mentioned here, reflecting those raised most often by the authors. This is certainly not an exhaustive list; it will serve its purpose if it succeeds in attracting the attention of future researchers. Unlike the other agenda items arrived at in this chapter, these matters reflect the personal experiences of the researchers and their reactions to those experiences.

1. *Preference of funding agencies for their own nationals.* In general, it seems logical and unobjectionable that national research funding agencies—such as the National Science Foundation in the United States and the Conseil National de la Recherche Scientifique in France—favor their own nationals in dispensing research grants. Such agencies are, ultimately, funded by taxpayers and are subject to overall political oversight and regulation on a national level. Yet this arrangement works against assembling the large, multinational teams that are necessary to conduct successful collaborative research that is both transnational and comparative.

One might argue that international or regional organizations, such as the World Bank, UNESCO, or the OECD, should be in a better position than national agencies to fund transnational, collaborative, comparative research in telecommunications regulation. Yet there is a sense in which even these organizations are no more than the sum of their parts, namely the national governments that fund them. Two obstacles, both perhaps ultimately surmountable, would appear to exist in approaching such international agencies for funding. First, the conviction that telecommunications and its regulation are sufficiently important areas to merit large-scale transnational collaborative research efforts, while well documented in this volume and elsewhere, is not universal among economists or other social scientists. Second, there is an undeniably normative-prescriptive content in much of the approach that might be too politically sensitive for organizations drawing their finances from a heterogeneous group of member states. The few international or regional organizations devoted entirely to telecommunications (excluding operating agencies like INTELSAT)—such as the International Telecommunication Union and the Pacific Telecommunications Council—are potentially promising funding sources but have a strong interest in Third World telecommunications. Regulatory questions of the kind discussed in this volume are more relevant to industrialized countries.

2. *Support of research versus support of research workshops.* It appeared ironic and counterproductive to the workshop participants that their airfare and other expenses could be covered by a grant, whereas their actual research could not. A similar bias was found to exist in the funding habits and regulations of most national research agencies. This seemed like a case of the tail wagging the dog. If a choice were to be made, would it not be better to fund the research and let the dissemination take care of itself, perhaps through existing scholarly journals? To be sure, there was no objection to scientific workshops, seminars, or colloquia per se; on the contrary, the present one was considered so successful that there was considerable sentiment for scheduling another to follow up on progress in attacking the research agenda proposed in this chapter. But with little money to fund international collaborative research as such, workshops devoted to the dissemination of such research have a doubtful long-term viability.

3. *Asymmetries in the institutional origin of telecommunications experts.* Although the composition of the contributors to this book does not necessarily bear it out, many of them remarked that American and non-American approaches to organizing relevant research efforts were sufficiently different to make the process a difficult one. In general, it often happens that American academics end up talking to opposite numbers, not in European and Japanese universities, but in PTTs, other ministries, government research institutes, and international organizations. The extent to which this asymmetry might present difficulties to either side depends on a number of factors, such as the ability and inclination of nonacademics to engage in theoretical or politically sensitive research and to make long-term research time dependably available.

4. *Asymmetries in interests and focus of U.S. and non–U.S. scholars.* Paralleling the asymmetry of institutional affiliation was one of focus and

interest, which derives in turn from the regulatory framework and perhaps even the philosophical outlook in different industrialized countries. To be more specific, the contributors to this book noted a relative lack of scholars in Europe and elsewhere with interests in telecommunications when compared to the United States. The United States, however, seemed to have relatively (though not absolutely) fewer broadcasting and mass communications scholars when compared to other industrialized countries.

This has led, in turn, to an imbalance of research focus and output. While many American scholars have written—a number of them critically, such as Eli Noam in this volume—about telecommunications regulatory policy, fewer non-American researchers seem to have interested themselves in regulatory policy.[3] In contrast, there is a plethora of mostly critical assessments of broadcasting policy in the United States and elsewhere by non-American experts (see, for example, Hoffmann-Riem 1981), but less attention to this topic by American scholars. As a result, Americans and non-Americans often tend to talk past each other at international conferences and workshops where it is assumed that the same aspect of "telecommunications" is being addressed.

One can account for this second asymmetry in part by observing that each group of scholars addresses and reacts to domestic policy priorities, perhaps projecting them abroad. Telecommunications deregulation is a burning topical issue in the United States, but less so elsewhere, although this book should certainly convince its readers that the trend in other countries is changing rapidly. Similarly, the formulation and conduct of broadcasting policy in Europe and other non-U.S. countries is a continuing public policy issue of high priority because of the large government role in broadcasting there, one usually encompassing ownership, operation, and oversight of radio and TV stations. Radio and television are seen as arbiters of mass culture and political opinion in Europe and elsewhere, but by and large as vehicles of entertainment in the United States.

THE RESEARCH AGENDA: SUMMARY AND EXAMPLE

The contributors to this volume, particularly those approaching their subject matter from an economic point of view, were somewhat surprised at the strongly interdisciplinary nature of the proposals they arrived at for future research. Many had prepared their material in the expectation of stimulating debate and new insights within the well-established paradigm of neoclassical welfare economics, perhaps in the economic subdisciplines of industrial organization or regulatory theory. Instead, the agenda compiled in this chapter reveals concerns extending well beyond that paradigm.

Lest the views of the contributors be interpreted as being more iconoclastic than they in fact are, it seems appropriate to complete this chapter by exercising the editor's prerogative in two ways. First, it should be stressed that the neoclassical welfare (cost–benefit, normative) approach has not been found defective or wrong. It appears instead to have been found incomplete or unduly restrictive in its assumptions. This conclusion is by no means unprecedented, but it gains new urgency as a result of the scrutiny and care with which the contributors to this volume have arrived at it. A careful rereading of this chapter will indicate that most of the agenda items involve the need for extensions or generalizations of the welfare-maximizing paradigm rather than its replacement.

Second, to dispel the impression that no research items were uncovered that need attention *within* the established framework of neoclassical economics, one such topic is outlined here that has surfaced periodically throughout this book and in the research workshop as well. This is the question of sustainability of natural monopoly.

The relevant literature on sustainability[4] turns first on a definition of natural monopoly, a technical condition known as subadditivity of the cost function. This means that a given market basket of goods can be produced more cheaply by one firm than by two or more. For decades, however, policy analysis of natural monopoly in public utilities was based on the unlikely assumption of a single output. Sustainability theory made the conceptual jump of allowing for two or more outputs by a given firm or group of firms. Let us assume two outputs at respective levels x and y, where $C(x,y)$ measures the cost. Production can be engaged in either by a single firm or by two separate firms; in the latter case the levels of output are x_1 and y_1, and x_2 and y_2, respectively, where $x = x_1 + x_2$ and $y = y_1 + y_2$. In this multiproduct setting, the property of natural monopoly (cost subadditivity) requires the condition

$$C(x, y) < C(x_1, y_1) + C(x_2, y_2)$$

This allows natural monopoly to occur under two quite separate conditions. First, the two smaller firms can produce the same mix of products, but on a smaller scale, for example, $x_1 = x_2 = x/2$ and $y_1 = y_2 = y/2$. In this case, subadditivity would require

$$C(x, y) < 2C(x/2, y/2)$$

which is a multiproduct version of economies of scale. The second possibility, which has no single-product analog, is that each of two smaller firms could completely specialize in one of the two outputs, for example, $x_1 = x$, $x_2 = 0$, $y_1 = 0$, and $y_2 = y$. Then subadditivity yields

$$C(x, y) < C(x, 0) + C(0, y)$$

In this case, the cost function is said to exhibit economies of scope, meaning that a monopolist can produce both outputs more cheaply than can two firms each specializing in one of the outputs.[5]

Economies of scope are related to the more established concepts of joint and common costs, reflecting complementarities in the production process. They are vital in considering the nature of the cost function and its implications for regulatory policy in the face of claims regarding the alleged presence of a natural monopoly. We consider now the related concept of sustainability of a natural monopoly and then proceed to a policy illustration.

When there is only one output, a firm with a natural monopoly need not worry about market entry by competitors. In the multiproduct case, however, an incumbent firm enjoying a natural monopoly—and thus generally economies of both scale and scope—might still fail to prevent profitable entry by rivals if competition is allowed. Such competitors would usually choose to produce a proper subset of what is offered by the monopolist, for example by specializing in one or more individual product lines. To put this differently: Although a single firm—by virtue of cost subadditivity—is always able to offer a given market basket of output at least cost, there exist cases in which rival firms still have financial incentives to enter the market and compete away part of the incumbent's business. When this happens, the incumbent must cut back production, and the overall cost of the same total output rises because of cost subadditivity. This is what is called an unsustainable natural monopoly. If no such incentives for profitable entry exist, the monopoly is said to be sustainable (see Baumol, Panzar, and Willig 1982, 192–198; Sharkey 1982, 84–110).

The presence or absence of an unsustainable multiproduct natural monopoly is a vital public policy question for regulatory authorities. Stated simply, overall public welfare would be served by allowing competition with a sustainable monopoly but forbidding it with an unsustainable monopoly. This issue is particularly relevant in the telecommunications sector, which is inherently multiproduct in nature and typically involves natural monopoly, or at least claims of natural monopoly, as well. Analysis of this issue to date includes a discussion of the effect of possible economies of scope between network and terminal equipment operation enjoyed by the Deutsche Bundespost (see Knieps, Müller, and von Weizsäcker 1981) and estimation of multiproduct cost functions and determination of the extent and sustainability of natural monopoly in the predivestiture AT&T system (see Evans and Heckman 1983, 253–282). Sustainability considerations, generally stated in a static framework, abstract from dynamic benefits of competition such as technological innovation and greater product diversity.

As an issue for future research, the crucial consideration involves obtaining accurate and reliable cost data from communications carriers so that cost functions can be specified and estimated. These cost functions can then be examined for properties such as natural monopoly, economies of scale and scope, and sustainability.

Finally, properties other than sustainability of monopoly are relevant to the question of allowing competition, and a number of these countervailing considerations are listed elsewhere (see Snow 1984a). Nevertheless, this issue stands out as a crucial research task still to be carried out within the neoclassical paradigm.

NOTES

1. For a discussion of economies of scale and scope in the context of sustainability of natural monopoly, see the final section of this chapter.
2. See Snow (1976, 147–149) for a financial model of INTELSAT.
3. For counterexamples, see Müller and Vogelsang (1979) and Wieland (1984).
4. See Chapter 1, Note 2, for relevant literature.
5. Generalization to any number of outputs and firms adds no essentially different conclusions. Intermediate cases of partial specialization and partial diversification, capturing economies of both scale and scope, are of course more probable than the polar examples shown.

REFERENCES

Averch, Harvey, and Leland Johnson. "Behavior of the Firm under Regulatory Constraint," *American Economic Review* 52 (1962): 1052–1069.

Baumol, William J, John C. Panzar, and Robert D. Willig. *Contestable Markets and the Theory of Industry Structure*. New York: Harcourt Brace Jovanovich, 1982.

Evans, David S., and James J. Heckman. "Multiproduct Cost Function Estimates and Natural Monopoly Tests for the Bell System." In *Breaking Up Bell: Essays on Industrial Organization and Regulation*, edited by David S. Evans. New York: North-Holland, 1983, 253–282.

Hoffman-Riem, Wolfgang. *Kommerzielles Fernsehen: Rundfunkfreiheit zwischen ökonomischer Nutzung und staatlicher Regelungsverantwortung: das Beispiel USA*. Baden-Baden: Nomos Verlagsgesellschaft, 1981.

Knieps, Günter, Jürgen Müller, and Carl Christian von Weizsäcker. *Die Rolle des Wettbewerbs im Fernmeldebereich*. Baden-Baden: Nomos Verlagsgesellschaft, 1981.

Leff, Nathaniel H. "Externalities, Information Costs, and Social Benefit-Cost Analysis for Economic Development: An Example from Telecommunications." *Economic Development and Cultural Change* 32 (1984): 255–276.

Müller, Jürgen, and Ingo Vogelsang. *Staatliche Regulierung*. Baden–Baden: Nomos Verlagsgesellschaft. 1979.

Neumann, Karl-Heinz, Urs Schweizer, and Carl Christian von Weizsäcker. "Welfare Analysis of Telecommunication Tariffs in Germany." In *Public Sector Economics,* edited by Jörg Finsinger. New York: St. Martin's Press, 1983.

Noll, Roger G. "The Political Foundations of Regulatory Policy." *Zeitschrift für die gesamte Staatswissenschaft* 139 (1983): 377–404.

Noll, Roger G., and Bruce M. Owen. *The Political Economy of Deregulation.* Washington, D.C.: American Enterprise Institute, 1983.

Olson, Mancur. *The Rise and Decline of Nations: Economic Growth, Stagflation, and Social Rigidities.* New Haven: Yale University Press, 1982.

Porat, Marc U. *The Information Society.* 9 vols. Washington, D.C.: U.S. Department of Commerce, Office of Telecommunications, 1977.

Sharkey, William M. *The Theory of Natural Monopoly.* New York: Cambridge University Press, 1982.

Snow, Marcellus S. *International Commercial Satellite Communications: Economic and Political Issues of the First Decade of INTELSAT.* New York: Praeger, 1976.

———. "Competition by Private Carriers in International Commercial Satellite Traffic: Conceptual and Historical Background." Paper presented at Tracing New Orbits Conference, Research Program in Telecommunications and Information Policy, Graduate School of Business, Columbia University, November 30, 1984. (a)

———. "The State as Stopgap: Social Economy and Sustainability of Monopoly in the Telecommunications Sector." Honolulu, Hawaii: University of Hawaii at Manoa. 1984, Mimeograph. (b)

———. "Arguments For and Against Competition in International Satellite Facilities and Services: A U.S. Perspective." *Journal of Communication* 35, No. 3 (1985).

Thiemeyer, Theo. "Deregulation in the Perspective of the German *Gemeinwirtschaftslehre.*" *Zeitschrift für die gesamte Staatswissenschaft* 139 (1983): 405–418.

Wieland, Bernhard. *Die AT&T-Entflechtung und ihre wirtschaftstheoretischen Leitbilder.* Bad Honnef, West Germany: Deutsche Bundespost, 1984.

Index